D0209125

THIRD EDITION

Costing Human Resources

The Financial Impact of Behavior in Organizations

WAYNE F. CASCIO
University of Colorado at Denver

456-0401

Kent Series in

HUMAN RESOURCE MANAGEMENT

Series Consulting Editor: Richard W. Beatty
Institute of Management and Labor Relations at Rutgers University

PWS-KENT Publishing Company
BOSTON

PWS-KENT
Publishing Company
20 Park Plaza
Boston, Massachusetts 02116

Editor: Rolf A. Janke
Assistant Editor: Kathleen M. Tibbetts
Production Editor: Susan L. Krikorian
Interior/Cover Designer: Julie Gecha
Interior Illustrator: George Nichols
Compositor: Graphic Composition, Inc.
Manufacturing Coordinator: Peter D. Leatherwood
Text Printer/Binder: Courier/Stoughton

©1991 by PWS-KENT Publishing Company. All rights reserved. No part of this book may be reproduced, stored in a retrieval system, or transcribed, in any form or by any means, electronic, mechanical, photocopying, recording, or otherwise, without the prior written permission of the publisher, PWS-KENT Publishing Company.

PWS-KENT Publishing Company is a division of Wadsworth, Inc.

Printed in the United States of America.

3 4 5 6 7 8 9 – 99 98 97

Library of Congress Cataloging-in-Publication Data
Cascio, Wayne F.
Costing human resources: the financial impact of behavior in organizations / Wayne F. Cascio—3rd ed.
p. cm.—(Kent human resource management series)
Includes bibliographical references and index.
ISBN 0-534-91938-3
1. Labor costs—Accounting. I. Title. II. Series.
HF5681.L2C37 1991 90-14219
658.15′53—dc20 CIP

to Dorothy and Joey,
my most valued assets

Series Preface

It is with considerable pride that we offer an expanded Kent Series in Human Resource Management from PWS-KENT Publishing Company. The original four books on federal regulation, human resource costing, compensation, and performance appraisal were a great success, as evidenced by both academic and trade sales. We thank you for your support of this series.

The first revision of the series offered significant updating and expansion of the four original texts. We also added two new books to the series, in benefits and human resource information systems. We are currently developing new series entries in recruitment and human resource planning, and we plan to add titles in areas such as executive development, human resource strategy, and collective bargaining.

As organizations face the new competition created by global markets, deregulation, and advancing technology, they are beginning to "resize," and they are looking at human resources as a source of competitive advantage. Preparing to gain, sustain, or regain competitive advantage raises concerns about the fact that human resources are indeed an organization's most expensive and least well-managed resource. Certainly, organizations have designed and engineered systems that include specific planning and control methods and tools for material resources, financial resources, information systems, and time management. The new competition, however, recognizes the need for better utilization of human resources. Ultimately, this series is designed to have an impact on the practice of human resources in the contemporary economic environment. Implementing these approaches to solving human resource problems will be the ultimate proof of its success.

Many people have helped in the development of this important series. I would like to thank Keith O. Nave for the original idea and Wayne Barcomb for his faith to expand it; and Rolf Janke and Kathleen Tibbetts for their enthusiastic support of the continued revision.

Richard W. Beatty

Preface

Over the past thirty years or so, a large amount of literature on the general subject of costing human resources has accumulated. Much of this literature has developed in three fields—accounting, economics, and psychology—and much of it is unknown to academics and practicing managers alike.

For some time now, I have had the uneasy feeling that a lot of what we do in the human resource management field is largely misunderstood and underestimated by the organizations we serve. In part, we in the field are responsible for this state of affairs because much of what we do is evaluated only in statistical or behavioral terms. Like it or not, *the language of business is dollars, not correlation coefficients.*

Consider a familiar example. An organization hires a consultant to develop a new selection program because its current program is affecting protected groups adversely, and the organization fears a lawsuit. The consultant develops a more valid selection procedure that eliminates the problem. The organization is now happy because it can stay out of court. However, it would be even happier if it knew that the more valid procedure would save it $100,000 per year in bad personnel decisions.

Methods are now available for estimating the dollar value of human resource programs, and *Costing Human Resources* examines available methods in a number of key areas. No attempt is made to be comprehensive, but some of the methods in this book are versatile enough to be applied in areas that the book does not address specifically.

I have thoroughly enjoyed writing this book—in no small part because the more I researched applicable methods for costing human resources, the more comfortable I felt about the ability of members of the field to assign accurate dollar amounts to their activities. Indeed, I am now fully confident that human resource management can stand right alongside the other functional areas of business when it comes to vying for resources based on results achieved, results that are measured in dollars.

The third edition of *Costing Human Resources* includes several major changes, including the addition of two new chapters. Chapter 5 uses many examples from actual company studies to assess the costs and benefits of the effects of employee assistance and wellness programs at the level of the individual firm. Chapter 12 focuses on tying together the previous 11 chapters, integrating measures of outcomes whose objective is to reduce costs (for example, turnover or absenteeism) with those whose objective is to increase productivity (for example, utility analysis of selection or training programs). The assumption underlying the development of this chapter is that human resource professionals need to adopt strategic perspectives so that they can align their activities with the competitive strategies of the broader organizations that they serve. Actual company examples show how this can and has been done.

Most of the features of the previous editions have been retained but updated to reflect newer research findings. Some of these include: (1) a new summary and critique of human resource accounting; (2) new company examples of the causes, costs, and methods for dealing with employee turnover and absenteeism; (3) revised treatment of the costs and consequences of smoking at work, as well as the legality of imposing smoking bans; (4) expanded treatment of the role of the computer and spreadsheet programs in the analysis of the costs of labor contracts; (5) improved treatment of the theory of utility analysis; (6) updated comparative research results and break-even results for alternative SD_y procedures; and (7) improved treatment of costing procedures for off-site meetings, analysis of training costs, and practical illustrations of the use of utility analysis in examining the economic impact of training.

As in the previous edition of this book, an instructor's manual will accompany the third edition of *Costing Human Resources*. The instructor's manual includes complete solutions to all end-of-chapter problems in the text. The text can be used in university-level courses in human resource management, either as a supplement to or in conjunction with other textbooks in the Kent Series in Human Resource Management. Practicing human resource managers will also find this book to be valuable.

Finally, I would like to acknowledge the valuable contribution of Dr.

Karen Lyness, Vice President of Corporate Human Resources at Citibank, in helping me to maintain a strong emphasis on strategic human resource management in Chapter 12, the capstone of the book.

Wayne F. Cascio
Denver, November 1990

Contents

1 *The Costs—and Benefits—of Human Resources* **1**

Human Resource Accounting **2**
Costing Employee Behaviors **7**
Plan of the Book **13**
Exercises **14**
References **15**

PART I Costing Employee Turnover, Absenteeism, and Smoking 17

2 *The High Cost of Employee Turnover* **19**

Identifying and Measuring Turnover Costs **23**
Monitoring and Managing Turnover **41**
Dealing with Employee Turnover **43**
Exercises **52**
Worksheet **54**
References **56**

3 *The Hidden Costs of Absenteeism and Sick Leave* **58**

Estimating the Cost of Absenteeism **60**
Interpreting Absenteeism Costs **69**
Managing Absenteeism and Sick-Leave Abuse **71**
Exercises **77**

Worksheet **78**
References **79**

4 *Costing the Effects of Smoking at the Work Place* 81

The Consequences of Smoking **81**
Absenteeism **84**
Medical Care, Morbidity, and Premature Mortality **85**
Other Insurance Costs **88**
On-the-Job Time Lost **88**
Property Damage, Depreciation, and Maintenance **90**
Involuntary Smoking and Employee Morale **91**
Aggregate Costs of Smoking at the Work Place **93**
Is a Smoking Ban Legal? **94**
Exercises **96**
References **97**

PART II Costing EAPs and Wellness Programs, Attitudes, and Collectively Bargained Agreements 101

5 *Costing the Effects of Employee Assistance and Wellness Programs* 103

EAPs—Prevalence, Attributes, Costs, and General Benefits **104**
Difficulties in Evaluating EAPs **106**
Costing the Effects of Employee Wellness Programs **113**
Why It Is Difficult to Evaluate Wellness Programs **118**
Data Needed to Evaluate a Wellness Program **121**
Company-Level Evaluations of Wellness Programs **122**
The Future of Employee Assistance and Wellness Programs **125**
Exercises **126**
References **127**

6 *The Financial Impact of Employee Attitudes* 130

Measuring the Costs of Development Programs **133**
Early Attempts to Estimate the Financial Impact of Attitudes **134**
The Behavior Costing Approach **136**

A Final Word **143**
Exercises **146**
References **146**

7 *Labor Contract Costing* 149

Average Compensation for the Bargaining Unit **151**
Role of the Computer in Collective Bargaining **166**
Exercises **170**
References **173**

PART III Personnel Programs: A Return-on-Investment Perspective 175

8 *Utility: The Concept and Its Measurement* 177

Overview **178**
Utility Models **179**
Appropriate Applications of Each Model **194**
Exercises **199**
References **200**

9 *Estimating the Economic Value of Job Performance* 202

Cost-Accounting Approach **203**
Global Estimation of the Dollar Value of Job Performance **209**
The Cascio-Ramos Estimate of Performance in Dollars (CREPID) **213**
System Effectiveness Technique **221**
Superior Equivalents Technique **222**
Comparative Research **224**
Exercises **225**
References **226**

10 *Valid Selection Procedures Can Pay Off* 229

The Utility of a Selection Test for Radial Drill Operators **230**
The Utility of a Selection Test for Computer Programmers **233**
The Utility of an Assessment Center as a Selection Device **245**

Conclusion **250**
Exercises **254**
References **255**

11 *Estimating the Costs and Benefits of Human Resource Development Programs* 257

Example 1: Determining Off-Site Meeting Costs **258**
Example 2: The Value of Structured Versus Unstructured Training in Basic Skills **262**
Example 3: Estimating the Costs and Benefits of Proposed or Ongoing HRD Programs **271**
Exercises **278**
References **279**

12 *Integrating Alternative Measures of Behavioral and Performance Outcomes* 281

Linking Effective Human Resource Management to Profits **282**
Strategic Human Resource Management **284**
Alternative Competitive Strategies **288**
Conclusion **292**
Exercises **293**
References **293**

***Appendix A: The Taylor-Russell Tables* 295**

***Appendix B: The Naylor-Shine Table for Determining the Increase in Mean Criterion Score Obtained by Using a Selection Device* 303**

***Index* 314**

1

The Costs— and Benefits— of Human Resources

Human resource management activities—those associated with the attraction, selection, retention, development, and utilization of people in organizations—commonly are evaluated in behavioral or statistical terms. Behavioral measures include measures of the reactions of various groups (top management, personnel specialists, applicants, or trainees), what individuals have learned, or how their behavior has changed on the job. Statistical measures include various ratios (for example, accident frequency or severity); percentages (for example, labor turnover); measures of central tendency and variability (for example, mean and standard deviation of cash register shortages and surpluses); and measures of correlation (for example, validity coefficients for selection programs). More and more, however, the need to evaluate human resource management activities in *economic* terms is becoming apparent. In the current climate of rising costs for labor and benefits and rising costs for energy and raw materials, operating executives justifiably demand estimates of expected costs and benefits of personnel programs. Methods for estimating these costs and benefits have been available for years (Brogden, 1949; Cronbach and Gleser, 1965), but not until the mid 1970s did behavioral scientists begin to concentrate on describing and measuring employee behavior in economic terms. Such measurement requires an interdisciplinary approach, a collaboration between accounting and behavioral science, that should be encouraged. Personnel specialists have been accused of not contributing to their organizations, of being so isolated and parochial that they really do not understand how business works, and of being incapable of reading a financial statement (Foulkes and Morgan, 1977). Consider a comment by Fitz-Enz (1980):

> Few human resource managers—even the most energetic—take the time to analyze the return on the corporation's personnel dollar. We feel we aren't valued in our own organizations, that we can't get the resources we need. We complain that management won't buy our proposals and wonder why our advice is so often ignored until the crisis stage. But the human resources manager seldom stands back to look at the total business and ask: Why am I at the bottom looking up? The answer is painfully apparent. We don't act like business managers—like entrepreneurs whose business happens to be people. (p. 41)

For many human resource (HR) managers caught up in the wave of mergers, acquisitions, and restructurings that characterized the 1980s, there simply was no other option *except* to change this perspective. Many did. Consider this appraisal by *Business Week* of the strategic importance of human resource management (HRM): "It is the most dramatic change in a managerial function since financial executives rose to power in the 1960s conglomerate era" (1985, p. 58).

Today more and more HR executives sit on top executive councils. By understanding how markets work in general and how their own organizations function in particular, they make meaningful contributions to strategic business decisions. They have embraced successfully the challenges to think and to act like businesspeople, and they are being treated as full partners along with other members of top management (Dyer and Holder, 1988; Wagel, 1990).

Carefully designed, valid personnel programs do contribute to bottom-line success. The personnel manager will benefit by taking advantage of methods now available for demonstrating this contribution. This chapter outlines some of the key areas to consider in demonstrating the costs and benefits of personnel programs, but first let us distinguish the current approach to costing human resources from its predecessor, human resource accounting.

HUMAN RESOURCE ACCOUNTING

There are no generally accepted accounting procedures for employee valuation. The first major attempt at employee valuation was made by the R. G. Barry Corporation of Columbus, Ohio. Barry's 1967 annual report described the inauguration of human resource accounting (HRA) procedures as a first step in the development of sophisticated measurement and accounting procedures that would enable the company to report accurate estimates of the worth of the organization's human assets. Barry accumulated costs in individual subsidiary accounts for each manager under five categories: recruiting, acquisition; formal training and familiarization; informal training, informal familiarization; experience; and development. A full description of the nature of expenses analyzed is given by Woodruff (1970). Costs were amortized over the expected working lives of individuals (or sometimes shorter periods), and unamortized costs (for example, when an individual left the company) were written off.

This is the *historical cost* (i.e., expenses actually incurred) approach to employee valuation. It is an *asset model* of accounting; that is, it measures the organization's investment in employees. For the purpose of external reporting (to inform interested parties of the financial position and of the results of operations of a company, with emphasis on performance measurement), it is widely viewed as most appropriate (Tsay, 1977). The historical cost approach is relatively objective; it facilitates comparisons of levels of human resource investment on a basis consistent with accounting treatment of other assets, and it seems a fair matching of benefits exhaustion with expense in particular time periods (Brummet, Flamholtz, and Pyle, 1968).

The method is not without its disadvantages, however, as Baker (1974) has noted. First, historical cost valuation is based on the false assumption that the dollar is stable. Second, the detection and write-off of abortive expenditures involve a great deal of subjectivity. Third, since the assets valued are not salable, there is no independent check of valuation. Finally, this approach only measures costs to the organization; it ignores completely any measure of the value of the employee to the organization. Hence, the soundness of the investment in human resources is not directly indicated.

In view of the shortcomings of the historical cost approach, it seems prudent to examine other bases of valuation that might provide supplemental information. These fall broadly into three categories: replacement cost, present value of future earnings, and present value to the organization (that is, profit contribution).

Replacement Cost

One alternative to measuring the historical cost of an employee is to measure the cost of replacing that employee. According to Flamholtz (1985), replacement costs include recruitment, selection, compensation, and training costs (including the income foregone during the training period). A recent example of the replacement cost approach was presented by Flamholtz, Searfoss, and Coff (1988). Flamholtz (1971) pointed out that it is easier in practice to estimate replacement cost than market value, and the former might therefore be adopted as a surrogate measure of the latter.

On the other hand, it might be argued just as plausibly that the substitution of replacement for historical cost does little more than update the valuation, at the expense of importing considerably more subjectivity into the measure (Baker, 1974; Scarpello and Theeke, 1989). Also, replacement cost valuation may lead to upwardly biased estimates because an inefficient firm may incur greater costs (Steffy and Maurer, 1988). Finally, one might question the usefulness of such a measure. The principal actions in which these data would be relevant would be in dismissing and replacing staff. Most organizations make such decisions too infrequently to make it worthwhile to build into the accounting system the regular production of replacement cost data on all employees.

Present Value of Future Earnings

Lev and Schwartz (1971) proposed an economic valuation of employees based on the present value of future earnings, adjusted for the probability of employees' deaths. That is, the organization determines what an employee's future contribution is worth to it today. That contribution can be measured by its cost or the salary wages the organization will pay the employee. The measure is an objective one because it uses widely based statistics such as census income returns and mortality tables. However, the measure is severely limited because it assigns a value to the *average* rather than to any specific group or individual. Therefore, the organization does not benefit by monitoring the efficiency of its investment in employee development, since the investment would have little or no impact on the present valuation of future earnings.

Baker pointed out three other faulty assumptions underlying this method. If the present value of future earnings is regarded as a fair appraisal of the individual's economic worth to an organization, then (1) subject to any profit expectancy built into the discount rate applied, because worth is equal to future cost, the employing organization is indifferent to whether it pays the cost to obtain the value or not (that is, whether the employee is retained or not); in either case it comes out even. (2) Insofar as earnings exclude fringe costs, the organization is indeed better off without this resource. (3) Consequently, the value of past recruitment and development of the employee is zero in (1) or negative assuming (2).

Value to the Organization

The value of a professional athlete's services is often determined by how much money a particular team, acting in an open competitive market (the free agent draft), is willing to pay him or her. An analogous approach might also be taken in other types of organizations. Hekimian and Jones (1967) proposed that where an organization had several divisions seeking the same employee, the employee should be allocated to the highest bidder and the bid price incorporated into that division's investment base. On the surface this approach has merit, but in practice the opportunities to use it are relatively rare. If the objective is to evaluate opportunity costs (that is, the potential profit lost by failing to take the optimal course of action in a given situation), then the appropriate inclusion in the investment base is the highest unsuccessful bid. Moreover, the soundness of the valuation depends wholly on the information, judgment, and impartiality of the bidding divisions.

An alternative aggregate valuation approach has been proposed by Hermanson (1964). It involves establishing the net present value of expected wage payments (discounted at the economy rate of return on owned assets for the latest year) and applying to this a weighted efficiency ratio (the rate of income on owned assets for all firms in the economy). As noted earlier, use of such broadly based statistics appears to diminish the precision of the calculations in general. It also incorporates unrelated risk factors into the efficiency ratio calculation. Moreover, human resources so valued would apparently subsume all other intangible assets of a goodwill nature.

Advocates of human resource accounting make a strong and compelling case for the need for this kind of measurement, but they tend to ignore the fact that dollar values cannot always be attached to the information that is collected. Thus, HRA may be of much more limited application than is commonly supposed (Baker, 1974). Perhaps the major limitation of these early approaches to HRA is that they reflect only inputs and not effectiveness. They are *human asset accounting* models that focus exclusively on investments in people (inputs); they ignore completely information about the output those resources produce.

In view of the conceptual and methodological limitations of human asset models, Pyle (1970) suggested that HRA be extended to compute returns on assets and returns on investments. This approach properly compares input and output measures but still fails to distinguish between individual and group effects that produce variability in output. The search continues for a single, limited criterion measure for HRA, but to expect that such a measure will be developed is unrealistic (Tsay, 1977). Consider the following summary comments from three reviewers of the HRA literature regarding the value and feasibility of HRA data. Mirvis and Lawler (1983), following the implementation of two "action research projects" involving the creation of new information systems in organizations, noted:

> Most organizations do not want to make a public accounting of how well they manage people and, more to the point, . . . they do not want to be held accountable for it. (p. 175)

Ferguson and Berger (1985), following a review of the HRA literature, wrote:

> As tempting as it is to try to establish a balance sheet value for a firm's human assets, such attempts are probably doomed; at this point it is not possible to calculate a figure that is both objective and meaningful. (p. 29)

After reviewing over 140 articles and several books on human resource accounting, Scarpello and Theeke (1989) concluded:

> At the theoretical level, HRA is an interesting concept. If human resource value could be measured, the knowledge of that value could be used for internal management and external investor decision making. However, until HRA advocates demonstrate a valid and generalizable means for measuring human resource value in monetary terms, we are compelled to recommend that researchers abandon further consideration of possible benefits from HRA. (p. 275)

A new approach focuses on attaching dollar estimates to the behavioral outcomes produced by working in an organization. Criteria such as absenteeism, turnover, and job performance are measured using traditional organizational tools, and then costs are estimated for each criterion. For example, in costing labor turnover, dollar figures must be attached to separation costs, replacement costs, and training costs. This method, which measures not the value of the individual but the economic consequences of his or her behavior, measures behavior in terms that are taken seriously by most decision makers—those of dollars. This approach is termed an *expense* model of HRA (Mirvis and Macy, 1976). It is the approach taken in this book to costing human resources, and we shall develop it further in the next section.

In summary, an organization uses human resource accounting *asset models* to reflect its investment in employees. Asset models assess the value of employees, treating them as capitalized resources (i.e., the economic concept of human capital). In contrast, an organization uses human resource accounting *expense models* to measure the economic effects of employees' behavior.

COSTING EMPLOYEE BEHAVIORS

The general idea of costing human resources is not a new one. A classic article by Brogden and Taylor (1950) addressed the potential for developing on-the-job performance criteria expressed in dollars. They noted:

> The criterion should measure the contribution of the individual to the overall efficiency of the organization. It centers on the quantity, quality, and cost of the finished product. Such factors as skill are latent—their effect is realized in the end product. (p. 90)

The contribution each employee makes is not related to the size of a firm's investment in an employee, but is directly related to how each person works and what is produced.

What is different in the general costing approach is the quantification in financial terms of a set of common behavioral and performance outcomes. Standard cost-accounting procedures are applied to employee behavior. To do this, the cost elements associated with each behavior must be identified and their separate and independent dollar values computed. Costs can be conceptualized in two ways. One reflects *outlay costs* (for example, materials used in training new employees) versus *time costs* (for example, supervisors' time spent orienting the new employees). A second distinguishes between *fixed, variable,* and *opportunity costs.* Fixed costs are costs that are independent of production rate; variable costs are costs that rise as the production rate rises. Opportunity costs reflect what the organization might have earned had it put the resources in question to another use. An example of a variable cost would be the overtime cost incurred because of absenteeism; a fixed cost would be the salary and fringe benefits for personnel who replace the absentees; and an opportunity cost would be the profit lost during the replacement process. These distinctions are important because only variable costs are related directly to behavior. Fixed costs are incurred regardless of behavioral occurrences, and opportunity costs are realized only if some employees put their free time to productive use while others do not (Macy and Mirvis, 1976).

Each behavior has associated with it distinct costs to an organization, but in most organizations these costs are unknown. Consider the following four reasons why this is so (Fitz-Enz, 1984):

1. *Personnel people do not know how to measure the costs of behavior.* Many practitioners have little or no background in statistics or psychometrics (the application of mathematics and statistics to mental measurement). Few publicly offered personnel workshops focus on quantitative techniques, and some masters degree programs in the behavioral sciences do not even require courses on statistics. Finally, organizations in the past generally did not train their personnel managers to measure their results. Given these quantitative gaps, the lack of emphasis on measurement of human resource activities is not surprising.

2. *Top management has accepted the myth that personnel activities cannot be evaluated in quantitative terms.* Since most personnel or human resource departments do not measure the results of their efforts in quantitative terms, management remains unaware that it can be done and therefore doesn't request it.

3. *Some personnel managers do not want to be measured.* Clearly this type of manager is a dying breed, yet we still encounter some who truly do not want to have their departments assessed by quantitative measures—and almost without exception, their position in the organization is not one of importance.

4. *A number of human resource managers would like to apply some measures to their function, but they haven't been able to do so.* Those individuals should rest assured of four things: it can be done; it does not take a great deal of extra work; a valid business reason exists for doing it; and they can expect to be recognized and rewarded for their efforts.

Contrary to common belief, *all* aspects of human resource management (including morale) can be measured and quantified in the same manner as any operational function. However, while such a statement is technically true, qualitative assessment of critical features of the HRM system, such as the degree to which any proposed HRM program fits with the strategic direction of a business, is no less important. Consider briefly just six important functions where carefully conceived, enlightened personnel policies can pay off:

- compensation policies and procedures
- benefits programs and insurance premiums

- personnel taxes
- recruiting, training, and management development
- affirmative action
- turnover and outplacement

These are some of the major areas where cost savings are easily demonstrated, productivity most rapidly increased, and turnover reductions effected most quickly. For maximum efficiency, all of the areas must work in conjunction with each other, but for purposes of illustration we will discuss each one separately.

Compensation Policies and Procedures

Organizations that do not fully understand what a position is worth often either overpay or underpay their employees. The result is that incompetent, overpaid employees do not leave and competent, underpaid employees do not stay. Of course, the key to avoiding this situation is a properly structured compensation plan that provides ranges accurately reflecting market worth in that geographic area. The compensation structure need not be complicated or costly. A billion-dollar electrical wholesale distributor operating in over 150 locations in forty-nine states retained a major consulting firm to develop a compensation structure; the consulting fees were $490,000. Later a personnel manager, with the help of three college students, developed a program one summer whose midpoints were within one dollar per week of the consultants' ranges for nonexempt personnel and within ten dollars per month for exempt personnel (Driessnack, 1979).

Benefits Administration

Human resource managers usually strive to obtain the most benefits for the dollar, but they do not always monitor the administration of benefits programs to ensure that dividends, refunds, or increased benefits are obtained when the premiums exceed the benefit payout. When benefits exceed premiums, insurance carriers are quick to notify an organization of the need for increased premiums the following year. They usually will *not* inform an organization when a dividend will be available for overpayment; the organization must ask for it.

The benefits chosen must be competitive with other organizations in the same industry and geographic area. Many organizations offer competitive benefits, but often they do not enforce their own policies, to their disadvantage. For example, sometimes employees are absent more than the sick-leave policy allows but still receive payment for excessive absences. Or worse, sometimes an organization imposes no limit on paid sick days, yet no one is criticized in performance appraisals for excessive absence. Attendance and punctuality are measurable costs and are an integral part of performance (see Chapter 3).

Personnel Tax Management

Some personnel taxes are controllable to the same degree as insurance costs. For example, federal and state unemployment taxes are usually based on work force turnover. In other words, an organization builds up an account in these funds and its account is charged when one of its employees collects unemployment insurance. The federal government requires each employer to pay a federal unemployment tax (FUTA) of 6.2 percent on the first $7,000 earned by each employee. The first 0.8 percent ($56) is paid directly to the federal government, and the remaining 5.4 percent is paid to the state. The 5.4 percent may be adjusted up or down by the state depending on its past experience with unemployment insurance claims from a particular employer. The personnel director is responsible for ensuring that the organization is not paying a higher rate than necessary. As turnover is controlled, these rates can often be reduced. For example, for all employers in the United States, the average cost of unemployment insurance per worker was $279 in 1984, $231 in 1987, and $224 in 1988 ("Labor Letter," 1989). The same is true for social security taxes—7.65 percent (paid by the employer and matched by the employee) of the first $51,300 in earnings in 1990. Turnover again plays an important role in this area, since two people filling a $100,000-per-year position during the course of a year could cost a company almost twice the normal social security tax deduction for one employee in that position (see Chapter 2).

Recruiting, Training, and Management Development

No single area provides a greater opportunity to waste (or save) organizational financial resources than recruiting, training, and management development. No area requires greater expertise, yet recruiting is often one of the first functions assigned to a personnel trainee.

An effective recruiter thoroughly understands the compensation structure of the organization, job requirements, political conditions in the various departments for which he or she is recruiting, and the temperament of the managers who will be interviewing and selecting the new candidates. All too often recruiters lack such thorough understanding. To make matters worse, unrealistically high job specifications lead to hiring overqualified personnel. The Equal Employment Opportunity Commission (EEOC), in evaluating positions in government and industry, found that more than 65 percent of the positions that required a college degree could easily be handled by a high school graduate (Driessnack, 1979). The result is that a higher starting salary must be paid for the high-potential recruit. Lack of a challenging work environment for overqualified workers leads to low morale, increased absenteeism, and high turnover. A department responsible for this situation would be forced to provide a detailed explanation for an unwise $100 purchase, yet when spending an excess of $5,000 or more in salary for an overqualified employee, the department is not questioned.

Poor selection and training methods are even more insidious. Consider as an example the selection and training of a police officer. The complete process (recruitment, physical and mental testing, interviewing, background check, twelve to eighteen weeks at a police academy, and trainer and trainee salaries) may cost as much as $50,000 or more per officer. At a regional police training academy in the southeastern United States, 300 recruits per year were trained at an annual cost of $15,000,000 (300 × $50,000). Of the 300 recruits, an average of 45, or 15 percent per year, dropped out. At an average cost of $30,000 per dropout, the academy was losing $1,350,000 per year. When a more extensive test battery to select trainees was implemented, the validity of the selection process (i.e., the correlation between test scores and academy performance) improved from 0.20 to 0.30 (a gain of 50 percent). This cut the number of academy dropouts from an average of forty-five to thirty-six, for an annual savings of $270,000. The potential savings from carefully developed selection and training programs can even be greater in some situations (see Chapters 10 and 11).

Affirmative Action Control

Most organizations recognize that the provision of equal employment opportunity for women, minorities, and older workers makes good business sense. However, human resource management executives have the financial responsibility to see that affirmative action does not result in declining productivity or become an expensive social exercise. A company should not have to lower bona fide occupational qualifications in order to select minorities or women when a little more effort and a wider search could result in recruiting qualified minorities and women. Training older, competent, experienced minorities and women for challenging positions also makes good sense. Instead, many companies recruit young, inexperienced minority and female MBAs and place them in positions that require a far higher level of managerial competence than usually expected from a recent graduate. When these employees don't measure up, the companies are stuck with token minorities or women whom they are afraid to fire, and so they downgrade the positions and bear the financial loss. This is an unnecessary expense for any company, it retards the minorities' and women's future growth, and it has undesirable side effects on other employees.

Perhaps personnel mismanagement's most damaging and costly effect on industry and society is in the area of age discrimination. With society's emphasis on youth, often the older manager is fired in a corporate reorganization. Sometimes this is a thinly disguised subterfuge to avoid paying pensions. The odds are 5 to 1 that a recent college graduate will leave within the first three years of employment. Among public accounting firms, the odds are 7 in 10 that a new hire will leave within five years (Ameiss and Williams, 1981). The odds of a fifty-year-old recruit staying with an organization for fifteen productive years are far greater (Driessnack, 1979). A comparative turnover analysis (accompanied by turnover cost data) between new college graduates and older workers may well stimulate decision makers to question the wisdom of hiring only young applicants.

Turnover and Outplacement

The control of turnover costs is the joint responsibility of the HR executive and the line manager. Chapter 2 will show how to compute these costs. When turnover costs become excessive, the cause of the turnover can usually be identified by division, department, manager, and even individual supervisor. Then the organization must take corrective action (for example, retraining, work redesign, or changes in the compensation structure), for the cost savings can be large.

One of the more unpleasant aspects of human resource management is layoffs, yet even here an organization can save money through sensible outplacement policies (Sweet, 1989). Internal personnel staff can handle nonexempt workers, but a consulting firm that specializes in outplacement may be a wise investment for handling executives. Consulting firms teach terminated executives how to develop and market their assets: how to construct a resume, write letters, interview, and negotiate salary. They show them how to develop the "hidden market," the estimated 80 percent of management jobs that are never advertised. As a result of outplacement counseling, the executive may well find a new position quickly and at a higher salary. More important, he or she maintains a good rapport with the old company, and often becomes a supplier or a customer. Finally, bridging pay rather than severance pay allows the executive to seek new employment while maintaining the image and status essential to him or her. When the employee finds new employment, the bridging pay stops. Often the difference between the bridging pay and large severance allowances saves more than the fees charged by the consultant.

This is just a brief look into the potential contributions to the bottom lines that can be made by effective human resource management practices in six areas. Although we have examined each one separately, our ultimate objective should be to develop a uniform financial reporting system for the HRM function as a whole. As time and resources permit, the design should phase in several aspects of each personnel function, including employment, compensation, employee relations, and training. As each new area is added to the measurement system, a synergistic effect takes place. Previously unrecognized relationships between functions become visible. The staff begins to recognize how its work is interconnected, and in time, the systems approach to financial measurement of the total human resource management function can be a very powerful tool indeed.

PLAN OF THE BOOK

The intent of this book is to examine some important areas in which costs can be attached to personnel activities, to identify important cost elements, and to show how they may be combined to yield valid cost estimates. A great deal has been written on these topics, and integrating this information is essential to developing practical costing procedures. The payoff from doing so may be enormous.

In Part I, we consider procedures for costing personnel decisions to quit, to be absent, and to smoke. The high costs of turnover and absenteeism have been recognized for some time, but few managers are aware that the cost of smoking at the workplace is over $2,800 per smoker per year (see Chapter 4).

In Part II, we examine the costs and benefits of employee assistance programs (EAPs) and wellness programs, as well as the financial impact of employee attitudes and collectively bargained agreements. Although EAPs and wellness programs have been popular for some time now, the economic benefits accruing from them are not determined easily. In Chapter 5, therefore, we will consider the methods used to determine the relative costs and benefits associated with these programs, and the outcomes resulting from them. Employee attitudes may affect job behaviors, but the financial impact of attitudes on job behaviors also can be measured and dollar estimates assigned to targeted improvements in job attitudes. Such figures can lend strong support to arguments for the adoption of a training or development program.

Labor contract costing is an extremely important area, since failure to estimate accurately the real cost of improvements in wages, hours, or conditions of employment can be disastrous. Chapter 7 will show how these costs can be estimated properly.

In Part III, we direct considerable attention to the concept of utility or overall worth, so that managers of human resources can adopt a return on investment perspective with respect to personnel selection, job performance measurement, and training and development efforts. Finally, in Chapter 12, we consider evaluation of the entire HR function using qualitative as well as quantitative measures. Wise decisions about personnel programs demand a knowledge of their costs and benefits. Admittedly, such a view encompasses issues of program design, implementation, and evaluation in both tangible (dollar) and intangible terms, but such a view is essential. Comprehensive assessment requires that the HR system be viewed as a network of interacting components.

EXERCISES

1. Discuss the advantages and disadvantages of the historical cost, replacement cost, and present value of future earnings approaches to employee valuation.

2. How are human resource accounting expense models different from human resource accounting asset models?

3. Explain how effective human resource management activities can yield financial benefits in the following areas: compensation; benefits; personnel taxes; recruitment, selection, and training; affirmative action; and turnover and outplacement.

REFERENCES

AMEISS, R. P., and WILLIAMS, D. E., JR. (1981, August). Human resource accounting in industry. *CA Magazine, 114,* 113–118.

BAKER, G. M. N. (1974). The feasibility and utility of human resource accounting. *California Management Review, 16*(4), 17–23.

BROGDEN, H. E. (1949). When testing pays off. *Personnel Psychology, 2,* 171–183.

BROGDEN, H. E., and TAYLOR, E. (1950). The dollar criterion—Applying the cost accounting concept to criterion construction. *Personnel Psychology, 3,* 133–154.

BRUMMET, R. L., FLAMHOLTZ, E., and PYLE, W. (1968). Human resource accounting—A challenge for accountants. *Accounting Review, 43,* 217–224.

CRONBACH, L. J., and GLESER, G. C. (1965). *Psychological tests and personnel decisions* (2nd ed.). Urbana, IL: University of Illinois Press.

DRIESSNACK, C. H. (1979). Financial impact of effective human resources management. *Personnel Administrator, 23,* 62–66.

DYER, L., and HOLDER, G. W. (1988). A strategic perspective of human resource management. In L. Dyer (Ed.), *Human resource management: Evolving roles and responsibilities.* Washington, D.C.: Bureau of National Affairs, pp. 1-1–1-46.

FERGUSON, D. H., and BERGER, F. (1985). Employees as assets: A fresh approach to human-resources accounting. *The Cornell H.R.A. Quarterly, 25* (4), 24–29.

FITZ-ENZ, J. (1984). *How to measure human resources management.* New York: McGraw-Hill.

FITZ-ENZ, J. (1980). Quantifying the human resources function. *Personnel, 57* (3), 41–52.

FLAMHOLTZ, E. G. (1971). A model for human resource valuation: A stochastic process with service rewards. *Accounting Review, 46,* 235–267.

FLAMHOLTZ, E. G. (1985). *Human resource accounting.* San Francisco: Jossey-Bass.

FLAMHOLTZ, E. G., SEARFOSS, D. G., and COFF, R. (1988). Developing human resource accounting as a decision support system. *Accounting Horizons, 2,* 1–9.

FOULKES, F. K., and MORGAN, H. M. (1977, May–June). Organizing and staffing the personnel function. *Harvard Business Review, 55,* 142–154.

HEKIMIAN, J. S., and JONES, C. H. (1967, January–February). Put people on your balance sheet. *Harvard Business Review, 45,* 107–113.

HERMANSON, R. H. (1964). *Accounting for human assets.* East Lansing, MI: Bureau of Business and Economic Research.

Human resources managers aren't corporate nobodies anymore. (1985, December 2). *Business Week*, pp. 58, 59.

Labor letter. (1989, March 21). *Wall Street Journal*, p. 1.

LEV, B., and SCHWARTZ, A. (1971). On the use of the economic concept of human capital in financial statements. *Accounting Review, 46*, 103–112.

LIKERT, R. (1967). *The human organization, its management and value*. New York: McGraw-Hill.

MACY, B. A., and MIRVIS, P. H. (1976). A methodology for assessment of quality of work life and organizational effectiveness in behavioral-economic terms. *Administrative Service Quaterly, 21*, 212–226.

MIRVIS, P. H., and LAWLER, E. E., III. (1983). Systems are not solutions: Issues in creating information systems that account for the human organization. *Accounting, Organizations, and Society, 8*, 175–190.

MIRVIS, P. H., and MACY, B. A. (1976). Human resource accounting: A measurement perspective. *Academy of Management Review, 1*, 74–83.

PYLE, W. C. (1970, September). Human resource accounting. *Financial Analysts Journal, 10*, 68–78.

SCARPELLO, V., and THEEKE, H. A. (1989). Human resource accounting: A measured critique. *Journal of Accounting Literature, 8*, 265–280.

STEFFY, B. D., and MAURER, S. D. (1988). Conceptualizing and measuring the economic effectiveness of human resource activities. *Academy of Management Review, 13*, 271–286.

SWEET, D. H. (1989). Outplacement. In W. F. Cascio (Ed.), *Human resource planning, employment, and placement*. Washington, D.C.: Bureau of National Affairs, pp. 2-236–2-261.

TSAY, J. J. (1977). Human resource accounting: A need for relevance. *Management Accounting, 58*, 33–36.

WAGEL, W. H. (1990). On the horizon: HR in the 1990s. *Personnel, 67* (1), 11–16.

WOODRUFF, R. C., JR. (1970). Human resources accounting. *Canadian Chartered Accountant, 97*, 156–161.

PART I

Costing Employee Turnover, Absenteeism, and Smoking

2

The High Cost of Employee Turnover

Turnover rates and costs for many organizations are unacceptably high. Turnover rates are widely available and easily calculated. For example, a monthly turnover rate may be computed by the formula

$$\frac{\Sigma \text{ turnover incidents}}{\text{average work force size}} \times 100$$

where Σ means "sum of." Typical monthly turnover rates, as reported by the Bureau of National Affairs, are shown in Exhibit 2.1. As the table indicates, the average monthly rates by year are approximately one percent. This represents an average annual turnover rate of almost 12 percent of the work force for all companies. Turnover can represent a substantial cost of doing business. As examples, consider the results Corning Glass Works found when it tallied *only* its out-of-pocket expenses for employee turnover, such as interview costs and hiring bonuses. That number, $16–$18 million annually, led to investigations into the causes of the turnover, and in turn to new policies on flexible scheduling and career development. Merck & Company, the pharmaceutical giant, found that, depending on the job, turnover costs 1.5 to 2.5 times the annual salary paid for it (Solomon, 1988). The cost of turnover (separation, replacement, and training) in the retail automobile industry averages over $18,000 per salesperson (Ashbach, 1989). Finally, in 1986, the U.S. Navy estimated that it would lose 550 fighter pilots due to attrition. At a cost of $1,000,000 to train one new fighter pilot, that adds up to an annual training cost alone of over half a billion dollars ("Navy Worried," 1986)!

Unfortunately many organizations are unaware of the actual cost of

EXHIBIT 2.1 Typical monthly turnover rates

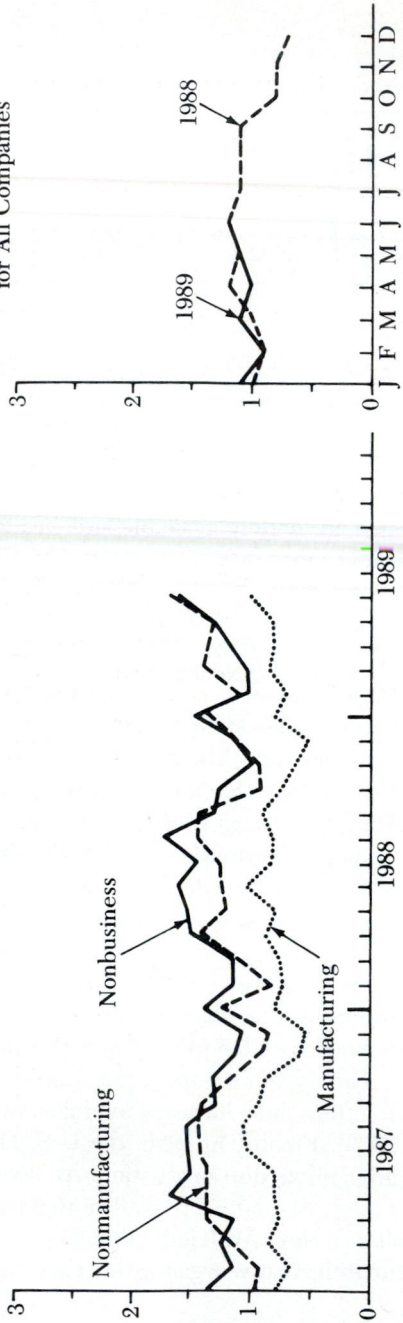

EXHIBIT 2.1 Continued

Average Median Turnover: January–June (percent of work force)

All Companies	1.1
Number of Employees	
Up to 250	1.2
250–499	1.5
500–999	1.0
1,000–2,499	0.9
2,500 and more	0.8
Industry	
Manufacturing	0.8
Nonmanufacturing	1.4
Finance	1.6
Nonbusiness	1.3
Health Care	1.6
Region	
Northeast	1.4
South	1.1
North Central	0.9
West	1.3

Source: BNA's job absence and turnover report—2nd quarter 1989. Reprinted by permission from *Bulletin to Management*, copyright 1989 by the Bureau of National Affairs, Inc., Washington, D.C.

turnover. And unless this cost is known, management may be unaware of the need for action to prevent controllable turnover and may not develop a basis for choosing among alternative programs designed to reduce turnover. Organizations need a practical procedure for measuring and analyzing the costs of personnel turnover, especially since the costs of hiring, training, and developing personnel are now viewed as investments that must be evaluated just like other corporate resources. The objective in costing human resources is not only to *measure* the relevant costs, but also to develop methods and programs to *reduce* the costs of human resources by managing the more controllable aspects of these costs.

Turnover is defined as any departure beyond organizational boundaries (Macy and Mirvis, 1976). Turnover may be voluntary on the part of the employee (for example, resignation) or involuntary (for example, requested resignation, permanent layoff, retirement, death). Some reasons for leaving, such as "another job that offers more responsibility," "returning to school full time," or "improved salary and benefits," are more controllable than other reasons, such as employee death, chronic illness, or spouse transfer. Once the costs of employee turnover are known, therefore, an organization must determine which of these costs are reasonably controllable and focus attention on reducing them.

Remember, however, that all turnover is not bad, and expecting any one program to eliminate turnover completely is unrealistic. Some mistakes in selection are unavoidable, and employee turnover, to the extent that it is concentrated on erroneous acceptances into the organization, can have a cleansing effect, for it makes room for new employees whose abilities and temperaments better fit the organization's needs. Other employees may have burned out, reached a plateau of substandard performance, or developed such negative attitudes toward the organization that their continued presence is likely to have harmful effects on the motivation and productivity of their co-workers. Here again, turnover can be beneficial. In contrast to these passive noncontributors, a few active noncontributors may willfully violate organizational rules concerning, for example, drug or alcohol abuse at work, fighting, or stealing company property. Turnover among these individuals is also likely to have a salutary effect on organizational health and productivity.

Thus, the organization must determine what kinds of turnover are harmful and then attempt to reduce these. This reduction may be accomplished by redesigning jobs to enhance opportunities for responsibility and decision making, providing better working conditions, improving salaries and benefits, or by clarifying and opening up promotional opportunities. We will have more to say on these issues later, but first we need to develop procedures for identifying and measuring turnover costs.

IDENTIFYING AND MEASURING TURNOVER COSTS

The general procedure for identifying and measuring turnover costs is founded on the premise that in measuring turnover, the organization must consider three major, separate cost categories: separation costs, replacement costs, and training costs (Smith and Watkins, 1978). In addition, it also must consider the difference in dollar-valued performance between leavers and their replacements. For each of these categories, we shall first present the relevant cost elements and formulas, and then provide numerical examples to illustrate how the formulas are used. The "pay rates" referred to in each category of costs refer to "fully loaded" compensation costs; that is, direct pay plus the cost of benefits.

Separation Costs

Exhibit 2.2 presents the key cost elements, together with appropriate formulas for each, that apply to separation costs. These include exit interviews (S_1); administrative functions related to termination, such as deletion of the employee from payroll, personnel, and benefits files (S_2); separation pay, if any (S_3); and unemployment tax, if applicable (S_4). Thus:

$$\text{total separation costs } (S_T) = S_1 + S_2 + S_3 + S_4$$

The cost of exit interviews is composed of two factors, the cost of the interviewer's time (preparation plus actual interview time) and the cost of the terminating employee's time (time required for the interview × weighted average pay rate for all terminated employees). This latter figure may be calculated as follows:

$$\text{weighted average pay rate per terminated employee} = \frac{\Sigma\,(\text{pay rate}_i \times \text{number of employees terminated at pay rate}_i)}{\text{number of employees terminated during the period}}$$

Times for exit interviews may be estimated in one of two ways (since these data are not recorded routinely): (1) time a random sample of exit

EXHIBIT 2.2 Measuring separation costs

Cost Element	*Formula*				
Exit interview (S_1)	= cost of interviewer's time	= (time required prior to interview	+ time required for interview)	× interviewer's pay rate during period	× number of turnovers during period
	cost of terminating employee's time	= time required for the interview	× weighted average pay rate for terminated employees	× number of turnovers during period	
Administrative functions related to termination (S_2)	= time required by personnel department for administrative functions related to termination	× average personnel department employee's pay rate	× number of turnovers during period		

Separation pay (S_3)	= amount of separation pay per employee terminated	× number of turnovers during period				
Unemployment tax (S_4)	= (unemployment tax rate − base rate)	× [($7,000 × number of employees earning at least $7,000) + (weighted average earnings if less than $7,000) × (number of employees earning less than $7,000)]	+ unemployment tax rate	× ($7,000 or weighted average earnings if less than $7,000	× number of turnovers during period)	

Source: Cascio, W. F. (1989). *Managing human resources: Productivity, quality of work life, profits* (2nd ed.). New York: McGraw-Hill.

interviews over the course of some period, say three months, or (2) interview a representative sample of managers who conduct exit interviews regularly and develop an average or weighted average of their estimated times.

Each organization should specify exactly what administrative functions relate to terminations and the time required for them. Each of those activities costs money, and the costs should be documented and included when measuring separation costs.

Separation pay, for those organizations that offer this benefit (it is not legally required under the Fair Labor Standards Act), can usually be determined from the existing accounting information system. Executives earning $50,000 to $150,000 per year can expect an average of eight months' severance pay if forced to leave their jobs. Chief executive officers, on the other hand, can expect, on average, just over ten months' pay ("Labor Letter," 1988).

In all states, employers' unemployment tax rates (applied to the first $7,000 of each employee's earnings) are based upon each employer's history of claims. Organizations with fewer claims for unemployment benefits are subject to a lower unemployment tax than organizations with more unemployment claims. This increase in unemployment tax due to higher claims is an element of separation costs.

In practice, high turnover rates that lead to high claims for unemployment compensation by former employees increase the cost of unemployment tax in two ways. First, the state increases the employer's tax rate (called the "penalty" in this instance). Second, the employer must pay additional regular unemployment tax due to the turnovers. For example, consider a 100-employee firm with a 20 percent annual turnover rate (i.e., 20 people). The total increase in unemployment tax is computed as follows:

The Penalty:

$$(\text{new tax rate minus base rate}) \times [\$7{,}000 \times (100 + 20)]$$
$$= (5.4\% - 5.0\%) \times [\$840{,}000] = \$3{,}360$$

Additional Unemployment Tax Due to Turnover:

$$(\text{new tax rate}) \times (\$7{,}000 \times \text{number of turnovers during period})$$
$$= (5.4\%) \times (\$7{,}000 \times 20) = \$7{,}560$$

Total Additional Unemployment Tax Due to Turnover:

$$\$3{,}360 + \$7{,}560 = \$10{,}920$$

What about the incremental costs associated with social security taxes? These costs should be included only if the earnings of those who leave exceed the taxable wage base for the year. Thus, in 1990, the taxable wage base was $51,300 and the tax rate was 7.65 percent. If an employee, for example, earning $30,000 per year leaves after six months, the employer pays tax only on $15,000. If it takes one month to replace the employee, the replacement earns five months' wages or $12,500. Thus the employer incurs no additional social security tax because the total paid for the position for the year is less than $51,300. However, if the employee who left after six months was a senior manager earning $125,000 per year, the employer would already have paid the maximum tax due for the year for that employee. If a replacement works five months (earning $52,083) the employer then incurs additional maximum social security tax for the replacement.

A final element of separation costs that should be included, if possible, is the cost of decreased productivity due to employee terminations. This may include the decline in the productivity of an employee prior to termination or the decrease in productivity of a work group of which the terminating employee was a member. Unfortunately in many situations, unless an ongoing productivity assessment program is functioning, the computation of this cost is simply too difficult and expensive to justify expending resources for its measurement.

Let us now illustrate the computation of separation costs over one year for Wee Care Children's Hospital, a 200-bed facility that employs 1,200 people. Let's assume that Wee Care's monthly turnover rate is 2 percent. This represents 24 percent of the 1,200 person work force per year or about 288 employees. From Exhibit 2.2 we apply the following formulas (all costs are hypothetical):

Exit Interview (S_1)

interviewer's time = (15 min. preparation + 45 min. interview) × $15/hour interviewer's pay rate × 288 turnovers during the year
= $4,320

terminating employee's time = 45 min. interview time × $11.80/hour weighted average pay rate[1] × 288 turnovers during the year
= $2,548.80

---

[1]weighted average pay rate per terminated employee

$$= \sum_{i=1}^{m} \text{pay rate}_i \times \text{no. employees terminated at pay rate}$$

$$= \frac{(9.65 \times 75) + (10.55 \times 87) + (11.50 \times 65) + (14.16 \times 37) + (18.75 \times 14) + (22.35 \times 10)}{288}$$

$$= 11.80/\text{hour}$$

$$\text{total cost of exit interviews} = \$4{,}320 + \$2{,}548.80 = \$6{,}868.80$$

Administrative Functions (S_2)

$$\begin{aligned} S_2 &= \text{time to delete each employee} \times \text{personnel specialist's pay/hour} \\ &\quad \times \text{number of turnovers during the year} \\ &= 1 \text{ hour} \times \$12.02 \times 288 \\ &= \$3{,}461.76 \end{aligned}$$

Separation Pay (S_3)

Suppose Wee Care Children's Hospital has a policy of paying one week's separation pay to each terminating employee. Using the weighted average pay rate of the 288 terminating employees as an example, \$11.80/hour × 40 hours/week = \$472 average amount of separation pay per employee terminated.

$$\text{total separation pay} = \$472 \times 288 = \$135{,}936.00$$

Unemployment Tax (S_4)

Let us assume that because of Wee Care's poor experience factor with respect to terminated employees' subsequent claims for unemployment benefits, the state unemployment tax rate is 5.4 percent, as compared with a base rate of 5.0 percent. Let us further assume that turnovers occur, on the average, after four and a half months (18 weeks). If the weighted average pay rate of terminating employees is \$11.80 per hour, then the weighted average earnings per terminating employee exceed \$7,000.

The dollar increase in unemployment tax incurred because of Wee Care's poor experience factor is therefore:

$$\begin{aligned} &(5.4\% - 5.0\%) \times [\$7{,}000 \times (1{,}200 + 288)] \\ &= (0.004) \times [\$7{,}000 \times 1{,}488] \\ &= \$41{,}664 \text{ \{Penalty\}} + (5.4\%) \times (\$7{,}000 \times 288) \\ &= \$108{,}864 \text{ \{Additional Tax\}} \\ \textit{Total increase} &= \$41{,}664 + \$108{,}864 \\ &= \$150{,}528 \end{aligned}$$

Now that we have computed all four cost elements in the separation cost category, total separation costs (ΣS_1, S_2, S_3, S_4) can be estimated. This figure is:

$$
\begin{aligned}
S_T &= S_1 + S_2 + S_3 + S_4 \\
&= \$6{,}868.80 + \$3{,}461.76 + \$135{,}936 + \\
&\quad + \$150{,}528 \\
&= \$296{,}794.56
\end{aligned}
$$

Replacement Costs

Costs incurred by an organization in replacing a terminated employee are defined as replacement costs. Exhibit 2.3 shows the cost elements and the formulas for estimating them. As the exhibit indicates, there are eight categories of replacement costs:

1. communication of job availability
2. preemployment administrative functions
3. entrance interviews
4. testing
5. staff meetings
6. travel/moving expenses
7. postemployment acquisition and dissemination of information
8. employment medical exams

The costs of communicating job availability will vary by type of job and targeted labor market. Depending on the methods used in recruitment, these costs may range from the cost of a classified advertisement in a local newspaper to employment agency fees borne by the employer (see Cascio, 1991, Chapter 9). Typically these costs can be obtained from existing accounting records. However, to the extent that this communication process requires considerable time from personnel department employees, the cost of their time should also be included in replacement costs.

Administratively, several tasks are frequently undertaken in selecting and placing each new employee—for example, accepting applications, screening candidates, and checking references. These procedures can be expensive. For example, background investigations can cost an average of $500 per candidate (Jacobs, 1985). Unfortunately, the time required to perform these activities is not documented routinely by organizational information systems. However, the methods described earlier for estimating exit interview time requirements may be applied in determining the time necessary for preemployment administrative functions.

Virtually all organizations use entrance interviews to describe jobs, to communicate employee responsibilities and benefits, and to make some general assessments of candidates. The costs incurred when completing

EXHIBIT 2.3 Measuring replacement costs

Cost Element	*Formula*			
Communicating job availability (R_1)	= [advertising and employment agency fees per termination	+ (time required for communicating job availability	× personnel department employee's pay rate)]	× number of turnovers replaced during period
Preemployment administrative functions (R_2)	= time required by personnel department for preemployment administrative functions	× average personnel department employee's pay rate	× number of applicants during period	
Entrance interview (R_3)	= time required for interview	× interviewer's rate	× number of interviews during period	
Testing (R_4)	= (cost of materials per person	+ cost of scoring per person)	× number of tests given during period	

Staff meeting (R_5)	= time required for meeting	× (personnel department employee's pay rate	+ department representatives' pay rate)	× number of meetings during period
Travel/moving expenses (R_6)	= (average travel cost per applicant	× number of applicants)	+ average moving cost per new hire	× number of new hires
Postemployment acquisition and dissemination of information (R_7)	= time required for acquiring and disseminating information	× average personnel department employee's pay rate	× number of turnovers replaced during period	
In-house medical examinations (R_8)	= [(time required for examination	× examiner's pay rate)	+ cost of supplies used]	× number of turnovers replaced during period
OR				
Contracted medical examinations (R_9)	= rate per examination	× number of turnovers replaced during period		

Source: Cascio, W. F. (1989). *Managing human resources: Productivity, quality of work life, profits* (2nd ed.). New York: McGraw-Hill.

entrance interviews are a function of the length of the interview, pay rates of interviewers involved, and the number of interviews conducted. Clearly links exist between valid selection procedures and reduced turnover. If decision makers are to be able to make sound cost/benefit decisions regarding elements of the selection process, these costs (and benefits) must be documented. This chapter focuses on costs; Chapter 9 will detail the benefits to be derived from valid selection procedures.

Many firms use preemployment testing of one sort or another—for example, aptitude, achievement, drug, and honesty testing. To account properly for the costs of these activities, consider the costs of materials and supplies as well as the cost of scoring the tests. The costs of materials and scoring for aptitude, achievement, and honesty tests are often less than $15 per candidate. Drug testing costs between $17 and $25 for a simple screening test, and confirming a positive test with more accurate equipment—a step recommended by most specialists—costs an additional $50 to $75 (Wessel, 1989).

For some classes of employees, especially top level managers or other professionals, a meeting may be held between the personnel department and the department holding the vacant position. The estimated time required for this meeting multiplied by the sum of the pay rates for all employees involved provides a measure of this element of replacement costs. Travel and moving expenses can be extremely costly to organizations that pay these costs. Travel costs for candidates from a local labor market are minimal (carfare, parking, tolls), but travel costs for candidates who must fly in and stay in a hotel can average over $1,000. Moving expenses can cover a range of cost elements from mortgage differentials, lease-breaking expenses, company purchase of the old house, costs of moving personal effects from the old to the new location, closing costs, hook-up fees for utilities, and more. "Fully loaded" moving costs averaged $36,000 in 1989 ("Relocation Challenge," 1990).

The seventh category of replacement costs is postemployment acquisition and dissemination of information. Pertinent information for each new employee must be gathered, recorded, and entered into various subsystems of a human resource information system (for example, personnel records, payroll files, employee benefits records). If flexible, cafeteria-style benefits are offered by an organization, than a personnel specialist could spend considerable time in counseling each new employee. Managers must estimate the time required for this overall process for each replaced employee, and then multiply it by the wage rates of HR department employees involved. Once this cost is multiplied by the number of turnovers, an estimate of the total cost of acquiring and disseminating information to new employees has been computed.

Preemployment medical examinations are the final element of replacement costs. The extent and thoroughness, and therefore the cost, of such examinations varies greatly. Some organizations do not require them at all, some contract with private physicians or clinics to provide this service, while others use in-house medical personnel. If medical examinations are contracted out, the cost can be determined from existing accounting data. If the exams are done in-house, their cost can be determined based upon the supplies used (for example, x-ray film, laboratory supplies) and the staff's time required to perform each examination. If the new employee is paid while receiving the medical examination, then his or her rate of pay should be added to the examiner's pay rate in determining total cost. The following text estimates replacement costs for a one-year period based on Exhibit 2.3 for Wee Care Children's Hospital.

Job Availability (R_1)

Assume that fees and advertisements average $250 per turnover, that three more hours are required to communicate job availability, that the personnel specialist's pay rate is $12.02 per hour, and that 288 turnovers are replaced during the period. Therefore:

$$R_1 = [\$250 + (3 \times \$12.02)] \times 288 = \$82{,}385.28$$

Preemployment Administrative Functions (R_2)

Assume that preemployment administrative functions to fill the job of each employee who left comprise five hours. Therefore:

$$R_2 = 5 \times \$12.02 \times 288 = \$17{,}308.80$$

Entrance Interview (R_3)

Assume that, on the average, three candidates are interviewed for every one hired. Thus, over the one-year period of this study, 864 (288 × 3) interviews were conducted. Therefore:

$$R_3 = 1 \times \$12.02 \times 864 = \$10{,}385.28$$

Testing (R_4)

Assume that aptitude tests cost $5 per applicant for materials, another $5 per applicant to score, and that as a matter of personnel policy Wee Care uses drug tests ($30 per applicant) as part of the preemployment process. The cost of testing is therefore:

$$R_4 = (\$10 + \$30) \times (288 \times 3) = \$34{,}560$$

Staff Meeting (R_5)

Assume that each staff meeting lasts one hour, that the average pay rate of the new employee's department representative is $22, and that for administrative convenience such meetings are held, on average, only once for each three new hires (288 ÷ 3 = 96). Therefore:

$$R_5 = (\$12.02 + \$22) \times 96 = \$3{,}265.92$$

Travel/Moving Expenses (R_6)

Assume that Wee Care pays an average of $50 per applicant in travel expenses, and that moving expenses of $36,000 are incurred, on average, for only one of every eight new hires. Therefore:

$$\begin{aligned} R_6 &= [\$50 \times (288 \times 3)] + (\$36{,}000 \times 36) \\ &= \$43{,}200 + \$1{,}296{,}000 \\ &= \$1{,}339{,}200 \end{aligned}$$

Postemployment Acquisition and Dissemination of Information (R_7)

Assume that two hours are spent on these activities for each new employee. Therefore:

$$R_7 = 2 \times \$12.02 \times 288 = \$6{,}923.52$$

Preemployment Medical Examination (R_8 and R_9)

Assume that if the medical examinations are done at the hospital (in-house) each exam will take one hour, the examiner is paid $30 per hour, x-rays, laboratory analyses, and supplies cost $60, and 288 exams are conducted. Therefore:

$$R_8 = [(1 \times \$30) + \$60] \times 288 = \$25{,}920$$

If the exams are contracted out, let us assume that Wee Care will pay a flat rate of $100 per examination. Therefore:

$$R_9 = \$100 \times 288 = \$28{,}800$$

Wee Care therefore decides to provide in-house medical examinations for all new employees.

Total replacement costs (R_T) can now be computed as the sum of R_1 through R_8:

$$R_T = \$82{,}385.28 + \$17{,}308.80 + \$10{,}385.28 + \$34{,}560 + \$3{,}265.92 + \$1{,}339{,}200 + \$6{,}923.52 + \$25{,}920$$
$$R_T = \$1{,}519{,}948.80$$

Training Costs

In virtually all instances, replacement personnel must be oriented and trained to a standard level of competence before assuming their regular duties. As we shall see in Chapter 11, this often involves considerable expense to an organization. For the present, however, assume that replacement employees are either placed in a formal training program or assigned to an experienced employee for some period of on-the-job training, or both. The cost elements and computational formulas for this category of turnover costs are shown in Exhibit 2.4. The three major elements of training costs are: (1) informational literature, (2) instruction in a formal training program, and (3) instruction by employee assignment.

The cost of any informational literature provided to replacement employees must be considered a part of orientation and training costs. Unit costs for those items may be obtained from existing accounting records. Multiplying the unit costs by the number of replacement employees hired during the period yields the first cost factor in determining training costs.

New employees may also be involved in a formal training program. The overall cost of the training program depends on the cost of two major components: costs associated with trainers and costs associated with trainees. While an organization incurs 100 percent of the costs associated with training replacements for employees who leave, the cost associated with trainers depends on the extent to which formal training is attributable to turnover. Since it is unlikely that the *total* cost of a training program can be attributable solely to turnover, managers must determine the proportion of training costs that is due to turnover, and that which is due to other factors, such as planned expansion of the work force. For the sake of simplicity, the costs of facilities, food, and other overhead expenses have not been included in these calculations.

Instead of, or in addition to, instruction in a formal training program, new employees may also be assigned to work with more experienced employees for a period of time or until they reach a standard level of competence. The overall cost of this on-the-job training must be determined for all replacement employees hired during the period, for it is an important element of training costs.

Notice that in Exhibit 2.4 the cost of reduced productivity of new employees while they are learning is not included as an element of overall

EXHIBIT 2.4 Measuring training costs

Cost Element	*Formula*
Informational literature (T_1)	= cost of informational package × number of replacements during period
Instruction in a formal training program (T_2)	= [length of training program × average pay rate of trainer(s) × number of programs conducted × proportion of training costs attributed to replacements] + [average pay rate per trainee × total number of replacements trained during period × length of training program]
Instruction by employee assignment (T_3)	= number of hours required for instruction × [(average pay rate of experienced employee × proportional reduction in productivity due to training × number of experienced employees assigned to on-the-job training) + (new employee's pay rate × number of instructions during period)]

Source: Cascio, W. F. (1989). *Managing human resources: Productivity, quality of work life, profits* (2nd ed.). New York: McGraw-Hill.

training costs. This is not because such a cost is unimportant. On the contrary, even if an organization staffs more employees to provide for a specified level of productivity while new employees are training, the cost of a decrease in the quantity and quality of goods or services produced is still very real. Less experienced employees may also cause an increase in operating expenses due to inefficient use of supplies and equipment. All of these costs are important, and when they can be measured reliably and accurately they should be included as an additional element of training costs. The same is true for potential productivity gains associated with new employees. Such *gains* serve to offset the *costs* of training. However, in many organizations, especially those providing services (for example, credit counseling, customer services, patient care in hospitals), the measurement of these costs or gains is simply too complex for practical application.

The following text estimates the total cost of training employee replacements at Wee Care. Using the formulas shown in Exhibit 2.4, Wee Care estimates the following costs over a one-year period.

Informational Literature (T_1)

If the unit cost of informational literature is $10, and 288 employees are replaced, the total cost of informational literature is:

$$T_1 = \$10 \times 288 = \$2{,}880$$

Instruction in a Formal Training Program (T_2)

New employee training at Wee Care is conducted ten times per year, and each training program lasts 40 hours (one full week). The average pay for instructors is $25 per hour, the average pay rate for trainees is $11.50 per hour, and of the 576 employees trained on the average each year, half are replacements for employees who left voluntarily or involuntarily. The total cost of formal training attributed to employee turnover is therefore:

$$\begin{aligned} T_2 &= (40 \times \$25 \times 10 \times 0.50) + (\$11.50 \times 288 \times 40) \\ &= \$5{,}000 + \$132{,}480 \\ &= \$137{,}480 \end{aligned}$$

Instruction by Employee Assignment (T_3)

To ensure positive transfer between training program content and job content, Wee Care requires each new employee to be assigned to a more experienced employee for an additional week (40 hours). Experienced employees average $17 per hour, and their own productivity is cut by 50 percent while they are training others. Each experienced employee supervises two trainees. The total cost of such on-the-job training for replacement employees is therefore:

$$\begin{aligned} T_3 &= 40 \times [(\$17 \times 0.50 \times 144) + (\$11.50 \times 288)] \\ &= 40 \times (\$1{,}224 + \$3{,}312) \\ &= 40 \times \$4{,}536 \\ &= \$181{,}440 \end{aligned}$$

Total training costs can now be computed as the sum of T_1, T_2, and T_3:

$$T_T = \$2{,}880 + \$137{,}480 + \$181{,}440 = \$321{,}800$$

Performance Differences Between Leavers and Their Replacements

A final factor to consider in the tally of net turnover costs is the uncompensated performance differential between employees who leave and their replacements. We will call this Difference in Performance (*DP*). *DP* needs to be included in determining the net cost of turnover because replacements whose performance exceeds that of leavers reduce turnover costs, and replacements whose performance is worse than that of leavers add to turnover costs.

To begin measuring *DP* in conservative, practical terms, compute the difference by position in the salary range between each leaver and his or her replacement. Assume that performance differentials are reflected in deviations from the midpoint of the pay grade of the job class in question. Each employee's position in the salary range is computed as a "compa-ratio"; that is, salary is expressed as a percentage of the midpoint of that employee's pay grade. If, for example, the midpoint of a pay grade is $20,000 (annual pay), an employee earning $16,000 is at 80 percent of the midpoint. Therefore his or her compa-ratio is 0.80. An employee paid $20,000 has a compa-ratio of 1.0 (100 percent of the midpoint rate of pay), and an employee paid $24,000 has a compa-ratio of 1.2 because he or she is paid 120 percent of the midpoint rate of pay. Compa-ratios generally vary from 0.80 to 1.20 in most pay systems (Henderson, 1989).

To compute *DP*, use the following formula:

$$DP = \sum_{i=1}^{n} (CR_l - CR_r)MP_i$$

where DP is difference in performance between leaver and replacement, $\Sigma_{i=1}^{n}$ is summation over all leavers and their replacements; CR_l is compa-ratio of leaver; CR_r is compa-ratio of replacement; and MP_i is annual rate of pay at the midpoint of the pay grade in question. Consider the following example:

$$
\begin{aligned}
CR_l &= 0.80 \quad CR_r = 1.0 \quad MP_i = \$20{,}000 \\
DP &= (0.80 - 1.0) \times \$20{,}000 \\
DP &= (-0.20) \times \$20{,}000 \\
DP &= -\$4{,}000
\end{aligned}
$$

DP is therefore *subtracted* from total turnover costs because the firm is gaining an employee whose performance is superior to that of the employee who was replaced.

If the compa-ratio of the leaver was 1.0, that of the replacement was 0.80, and the pay-grade midpoint was $20,000, then $DP = \$4{,}000$. These costs are *added* to total turnover costs because the leaver was replaced by a lesser performer.

Why are differences in performance assumed to covary with differences in pay? Actually, this assumption is true only in a perfect labor market (Pappas and Hirschey, 1989). In a perfectly competitive labor market, every worker earns the marginal revenue product accrued to the firm from his or her labor. Since workers are assumed to be interchangeable because they are all equally qualified, the firm is indifferent to workers whose compa-ratios are 0.80, 1.0, or 1.20. Each worker is paid exactly what he or she is "worth."

Perfectly competitive labor markets exist for many entry-level jobs (e.g., management analysts), but labor markets are often imperfect above the entry level because workers develop what economists call "firm-specific human capital" (Becker, 1964). Workers who have specific job knowledge that is valued by their firms (e.g., in banking, automobiles, computers) or who promote synergy by contributing to the overall effectiveness of their work groups are especially valuable to their firms. Their value is reflected only partly in their higher wages. Wages reflect what economists call "opportunity costs," or the value of a worker's second best employment opportunity. Competitors are only able to offer a wage that reflects the economic value of a worker to *them*. Therefore, opportunity costs and the wage rates paid to valued employees tend to reflect only the portion of a worker's economic value that is easily transferable from one employer to another (i.e., "generic"). The portion of an employee's value that is not easily transferable, the firm-specific component, typically is reflected only partially in employee wages, if at all. Thus the economic value of workers with firm-specific human capital is above their wage (opportunity cost) level, but can be assumed to be proportionate to these wages. If an employee with substantial amounts of firm-specific human capital leaves the firm and is replaced by a worker who lacks such firm-specific human capital, the replacement will receive a lesser wage. However, if a poor performer leaves and is replaced by a worker with more human capital, albeit non–firm-specific, then the replacement will receive a higher wage than the leaver. The difference between rates of pay for leavers and their replacements thus represents an indicator, although an imperfect one, of the "uncompensated performance differential" due to firm-specific human capital, and it must be considered when determining the net costs of turnover.

The assumption that excess value to the firm is a function of wages paid and that excess value and wages covary in a linear (straight-line) fashion is conservative. In practice the relationship can be curvilinear (positive or negative), but for our purposes the conservative assumption of a linear relationship between excess value and wages is appropriate.

For Wee Care, assume that the net $DP = +\$100{,}000$. On average, therefore, the firm hired slightly poorer performers than it lost. The following equation, which uses the four major components of employee turnover, represents the total cost of employee turnover:

$$\text{Total Cost of Turnover} = S_T + R_T + T_T + DP$$

where S_T is total separation costs; R_T is total replacement costs; T_T is total training costs; and DP is net differential performance between leavers and their replacements. For Wee Care the total cost of 288 employee turnovers during a one-year period was:

$$\$296{,}794.56 + \$1{,}519{,}948.80 + \$321{,}800 + \$100{,}000 = \$2{,}238{,}543.40$$

This represents a cost of $7,772.72 for each employee who left the hospital.

The purpose of measuring turnover costs is to improve managerial decision making. That is, once turnover figures are known, managers have a more realistic basis for choosing between current turnover costs and instituting some type of turnover reduction program, such as increased compensation and nonwage benefits, job enrichment, realistic job previews, and expanded recruitment and selection programs. The final section of this chapter examines this issue in greater detail.

MONITORING AND MANAGING TURNOVER

In managing turnover, the firm's goal should be to retain employees who are valuable to the organization in terms of overall performance and replaceability (Dalton, Todor, and Krackardt, 1982). Taken together, performance and replaceability have an important bearing on the consequences of turnover for an organization, as shown in the performance-replaceability strategy matrix in Exhibit 2.5.

Although turnover may be voluntary or involuntary, we will focus on voluntary turnover, much of which is controllable. Turnover may be functional for the organization (loss of unproductive employees) or dysfunctional (loss of valued employees). Fortunately, cumulative evidence of the relationship between performance and turnover across 24 studies and 7,717 employees indicates that good performers are significantly less likely to leave an organization than poor performers (McEvoy and Cascio, 1987). The loss of employees in cells A, B, or C in Exhibit 2.5 represents dysfunctional turnover. The organization highly values those in cell A because they are high performers who are difficult to replace. Two types of employees tend to be particularly difficult to replace: (1) those whose specific knowledge about some aspect of the organization or its environment is difficult to acquire and crucial to effective performance and (2) those whose skills are in relatively short supply. An example of a valuable type of cell-A employee would be an effective line manager of a U.S. firm operating in a foreign country—someone familiar with local customs, language, and traditions, as well as the industry and the organization.

Employees in cell D are average performers who can be replaced easily. Whether turnover among the members of this group is functional or dysfunctional depends on the net costs of turnover. If the costs of replacement and training are low (e.g., for data-entry clerks) and the leaver is replaced by a better performer (*DP* is negative), then turnover is functional for the organization. If the opposite conditions are found (e.g., in the case of a geologist for an oil company), then the turnover is dysfunctional for the organization. Over the long run, it is functional to replace low performers in any organization, whether or not they are easy to replace. Cells E and F of Exhibit 2.5 show individuals in this category.

What are the implications of the model in Exhibit 2.5, and how can it be used to improve the strategic management of turnover? The model suggests that simple tabulation of turnover rates could mask serious underlying problems. Perhaps few employees leave, but the majority of those who do leave fall in cell A. Merely inspecting the rates of turnover could lead the organization's analysts to conclude—falsely—that they

Exhibit 2.5 The performance-replaceability strategy matrix

Performance	Replaceability: Difficult	Replaceability: Easy
High	A Highly dysfunctional turnover (Retain/develop employee; prepare backup)	B Dysfunctional turnover (Retain/develop employee)
Average	C Dysfunctional turnover (Retain; prepare backup)	D Functionality depends on costs (Retain)
Low	E Short-run dysfunctional/ Long-run functional (Prepare backup; increase performance or terminate)	F Functional turnover Increase performance or terminate)

Source: Martin, D. C., and Bartol, L. M. Managing turnover strategically. Reprinted from the November 1985 issue of *Personnel Administrator*, copyright 1985, the American Society for Personnel Administration, 606 N. Washington Street, Alexandria, VA 22314.

don't have a turnover problem. The crucial issue in analyzing turnover, therefore, is not how many employees are leaving, but the performance and replaceability of those who are leaving versus those who are staying (Martin and Bartol, 1985).

The first step in implementing the model in Exhibit 2.5 is to classify each position in the organization according to ease of replaceability. This straightforward exercise should be done jointly by human resource managers and line managers from various units of the organization. The next step is to complete the performance-replaceability strategy matrix by using the performance appraisals of position incumbents, which can be collected from personnel records. The result is an assessment of the performance and replaceability of each employee in the organization. Having done that, the organization is in an excellent position to monitor and manage turnover relative to its overall strategic plan (Martin and Bartol, 1985). It could use this information to monitor turnover in terms of who is leaving which positions and to obtain unit and overall organizational patterns. Using the model also facilitates the planning of appropriate human resource programs (e.g., career development, training, succession planning, and recruiting).

Each of the cells in Exhibit 2.5 calls for a different strategy, although the strategies are related and can be part of an overall human resource management approach. The basic strategies are shown in parentheses within each category. The arrows indicate the generally desirable movements of employees across cells.

The performance-replaceability strategy matrix is only as useful as it is current, and in most organizations things don't stay current for very long. The replaceability ratings of various positions might change as a result of new directions in strategic plans. At the same time, individual performance levels might improve as a result of feedback and constructive management of performance problems. In short, an organization must periodically reevaluate the performance-replaceability strategy matrix in order to remain responsive to organizational needs. The most practical approach for most organizations is to review replaceability and performance in conjunction with the annual performance appraisal cycle. To be meaningful, such a review must consider shifts in strategic plans and related implications for staffing. The reevaluation process then becomes the mechanism through which turnover patterns continually are monitored and human resource programs are modified to meet the emerging needs of an organization's strategic plan (Martin and Bartol, 1985).

DEALING WITH EMPLOYEE TURNOVER

Now that we know how to cost turnover, and assuming management decides the costs are intolerable, how can we best deal with the problem? Although a complete treatment of solutions is beyond the scope of this chapter, we can distinguish voluntary turnover among newcomers from voluntary turnover among employees who have been with the organization for some time (at least a year).

One reason newcomers leave is that their inflated expectations about a job or organization often are not met after they begin working. Much of this turnover is unnecessary and therefore controllable. Over the last fifteen years a number of studies have shown that when the expectations of job applicants are lowered to match organizational reality, job acceptance rates may be lower, but job satisfaction and job survival are higher for those who receive a realistic job preview (RJP). Wanous (1980) suggests three reasons why RJPs work so well. The first is a vaccination effect: job candidates are given a small dose of organizational reality during the recruitment stage to protect against the negative aspects of real organizational life. The second is a self-selection, matching effect: since people strive to be satisfied, they tend to choose organizations that they believe will lead to personal satisfaction. The better the information that the job candidates possess, the more effective their choices can be. A final reason for the success of RJPs is a personal commitment effect: when individuals believe that they made a decision without coercion or strong inducements from others, they tend to be much more committed to the decision.

Nevertheless, RJPs are not appropriate recruitment strategies for all types of jobs. They are most appropriate (1) when few applicants are actually hired, (2) when they are used with entry-level positions (since those coming from outside to inside an organization are more likely to have inflated expectations than those who make changes internally), and (3) when unemployment is low (since job candidates are more likely to have other options).

As an example, consider a realistic recruitment program developed for telephone operators at Southern New England Telephone Company (SNET). The company-wide turnover rate at SNET was 30 to 40 percent per year, but for operators in the first six months it was 100 percent or higher. Even a modest reduction in the operator turnover rate would pay handsome dividends. Following the analysis of a telephone operator's job, an outline was prepared of the major positive and negative job characteristics, as reported by the operators and their supervisors. This outline served as a script for a fifteen-minute film to be used as an alternative to the traditional recruiting film that the organization was then using. Interviews with six experienced operators were videotaped for later editing. Exhibit 2.6 shows areas that were covered by both films, as well as those aspects unique to each one.

EXHIBIT 2.6 Job characteristics emphasized by each job preview film

Overlap Between Films

1. Customers can be quite unfriendly at times.
2. Work is fast paced.
3. Some operators receive satisfaction from helping out customers.
4. Action sequences of operators at work:
   a. emergency call
   b. "wise guy" calling operator
   c. credit card call
   d. overseas call
   e. directory assistance operators at work
   f. "nasty" customer calling operator
5. Dealing with others (customers, co-workers) is a large part of the job.

Nonoverlap Characteristics

Realistic Film	*Traditional Film*
1. Lack of variety.	1. Everyone seems happy at work.
2. Job is routine; may become boring.	2. Exciting work.
3. Close supervision; little freedom.	3. Important work.
4. Limited opportunity to make friends.	4. Challenging work.
5. Receive criticism for bad performance, but no praise when deserved.	
6. Challenging initially, but once learned is easy and not challenging.	

Source: Wanous, J. P. (1975, July–August). Tell it like it is at realistic job previews. *Personnel, 52,* 57. Copyright © 1975 by AMACOM, a division of American Management Associations. All rights reserved.

After viewing the realistic film, the applicant was given a pamphlet to reinforce the major points of the film (see Exhibit 2.7). Applicants were shown the film after they had been offered a job but before they had accepted it.

EXHIBIT 2.7 Pamphlet used in conjunction with realistic job preview films

You have seen the film preview of the operator's job for two reasons:

1. We want you to know about the job before you decide if you want to be an operator.
2. If you become an operator, you will have a better idea of what to realistically expect on the job.

You are now given this folder which summarizes many important characteristics of the operator's job.

If you are a telephone operator, you can realistically expect:

- varied schedules—work on weekends, holidays, and at odd hours
- that regular attendance is required
- to help people complete calls or look up numbers for them
- that work will be closely supervised
- steady employment; full pay during training; good benefits and retirement
- routine work requiring strict attention to standard procedures
- that wage increases will be determined by job performance
- that accuracy and speed in work are required

Source: Wanous, J. P. (1980). *Organizational entry* (p. 53). Reading, MA: Addison-Wesley.

The RJP program paid off. After the experiment 50 percent of the traditional-film group survived at least six months, while 62 percent of the realistic-film group survived, and with higher job satisfaction scores.

A quantitative cumulation of research results from fifteen experiments that used RJPs (total sample size = 5,250) indicated that RJPs improve retention rates, on average, by approximately 9 percent (McEvoy and Cascio, 1985). Such improvement can result in substantial savings to an organization. Suppose, for example, that turnover costs an average of $7,000 per employee. For every 100 employees that an organization has in a job category, therefore, it can expect to save over $60,000 through the application of RJPs prior to hire.

Psychological and Performance Tests

One way to reduce turnover is to screen out potential leavers during the selection process. Psychological tests, although far from perfectly accurate, are capable of identifying future employees who will leave their jobs.

In one study of public safety officers, for example, optimally weighted test scores identified the greatest number of officers who were terminated within five years after hire (68 to 75 percent), but also resulted in false predictions of termination for 28 to 36 percent of the hired officers (Inwald, 1988). Clearly the relative social and economic costs of erroneous acceptances and erroneous rejections should be considered by decision makers prior to implementing any such testing program.

Job performance or work sample tests have been used to instill realistic attitudes in prospective employees. Performance tests usually refer to standardized measures of behavior used to assess the ability to do rather than the ability to know. Performance tests may be classified either as *motor*, involving physical manipulation of things (for example, tests for jobs like carpenter, mechanic, mason), or as *verbal*, involving problems that are primarily language-oriented or people-oriented (for example, tests for jobs like maintenance supervisor, programmer/analyst, library assistant) (Asher and Sciarrino, 1974).

To demonstrate the impact of performance testing on turnover, Cascio and Phillips (1979) examined the results of a broad spectrum of performance tests (eleven motor and ten verbal) used by a city government over two years. The tests were matched as closely as possible (in tasks, tools, equipment, work setting, and proportion of time spent on various activities) to actual job requirements. For example, in the test for sewer pumping station operator (a promotional exam for laborers that requires no previous experience), all testing, proctoring, and rating was done underground at the sewer pumping station. During an initial one-hour instruction period a sewer mechanic explained and demonstrated, as if he were the applicants' supervisor, procedures for the general maintenance of sewer pipes and equipment—how to clean filters, grease fittings, read a pressure chart, and so on. Several applicants left immediately after the demonstration. During a second hour each applicant was required to repeat the demonstration (applicants were also free to ask questions) as if he or she were on the job. Applicants were then rated on the degree to which they (1) understood instructions, (2) followed the prescribed procedures, (3) asked questions when they were unsure of something, and (4) followed safety practices (used protective masks and other equipment). Follow-up interviews revealed that those who qualified for and accepted the job had a good idea of what they were getting into and felt that for them the job represented a step up the career ladder.

To examine the impact of performance testing on turnover, data on turnover were gathered for one year prior to the introduction of performance testing and for a period (from nine to twenty-six months) after performance tests were introduced. Turnover rates for the twenty-one jobs during the year prior to performance testing varied from 0 to 300 percent, with an overall average of 40 percent. The turnover rate for these same jobs after performance tests was less than 3 percent. Using the formulas presented earlier for calculating actual turnover costs (separation, replacement, and training costs) the 37 percent reduction in turnover translated into savings of $336,199 for the city ($638,206 in 1990 dollars) during the nine to twenty-six month period after the introduction of performance tests.

Prehire Payback Agreements

Concerned about rising costs and job hopping, a variety of companies now require that new employees promise to repay costs associated with replacement, training, or education if they leave within a certain period. Prehire payback agreements most often apply to occupations short of qualified workers, where companies that must spend heavily on training worry about the pirating of employees by competitors.

Concerns like these prompted American Airlines to institute such an agreement for prospective pilots. The agreement forbids those who quit voluntarily within a year of the start of initial training from working for most U.S. airlines for the remainder of the one-year period. It also requires that a pilot who leaves within a year of the completion of initial training must repay a prorated part of his or her $10,000 training cost.

Government contractors have an additional reason for requiring payback agreements. Because the government pays a share of each employee's relocation expenses, a 1981 regulation requires the employee to reimburse the government if he or she resigns within a year (Ward, 1985).

Payback agreements have prompted complaints from the AFL-CIO, which likens them to indentured servitude. Companies respond that they are just trying to protect themselves from being exploited. When Lockheed Corporation adopted a payment assistance plan for employees seeking college degrees in their spare time, for example, it didn't want workers to "get a degree and then use it as an excuse to run off and get another job" (Ward, 1985, p. 27). So Lockheed requires that employees reimburse the company for the educational assistance unless they stay on at least a year after completing a degree.

What has been the experience of companies that have used payback agreements? Electronic Data Systems Corp. reports that of the approximately 7,000 systems engineering payback agreements signed since it started a program in 1981, less than one percent have gone into litigation.

When litigation is unavoidable, however, the company usually wins. In one case, for example, when an employee refused to pay back $9,000 in training costs, a Texas court ordered the employee to repay the company $9,000 plus interest and attorney's fees—a total of $10,407.

Despite criticism of these plans by many unions, at least one, the Sheet Metal Worker's Union, has instituted its own training payback plan. The union's scholarship loan agreement requires that those who complete the union's training program must repay the cost in cash or by working for union companies for ten years. Workers who leave a union shop and either work for a nonunion competitor or set up a competing nonunion business owe a prorated training cost to the union. Says a union spokesperson: "It doesn't mean that a person can't do whatever he wants to do; just don't use our money to do it" (Ward, 1985, p. 27).

Changes in Compensation

Two other strategies for reducing turnover are increased salary and nonwage benefits, and job enrichment. In fact, among human resource executives, raising salaries is the top-rated strategy for decreasing turnover (Zippo, 1982). In some circumstances noncompetitive compensation policies are a major cause of high turnover, especially if the attraction and expected utility of alternative jobs is high. Thus a large chain of convenience stores in the southeastern United States was experiencing a turnover rate among store clerks of over 100 percent a year before conducting an in-depth study of the causes of the turnover. Most of those who quit worked in hazardous areas during the evening or midnight shifts. Exit interviews and an attitude survey of present employees soon disclosed why. The parent company paid the legally required minimum wage to entry-level clerks at all stores regardless of work shift or store location. Further, security was lax and the stores were robbed regularly. To remedy this situation the company retained a security consultant to implement tighter security measures at all outlets, and management instituted a shift differential of 150 percent for the midnight shift and 75 percent for the evening shift. On top of this a flat premium of $50 a week ($2,600 a year) was offered to those working in areas defined as hazardous. Within a year after these changes were instituted, turnover declined to 40 percent, still high but reduced by over 60 percent from the earlier situation. Unfortunately, since the company made other changes (security procedures) along with the changes in compensation, the direct impact of the changes in compensation on turnover is unknown. However, the turnover problem was unlikely to improve by itself unless some changes were made.

Job Enrichment

A final strategy for reducing turnover is job enrichment. While the theory and implementation of job enrichment are beyond the scope of this chapter (see Cunningham and Eberle, 1990; Hackman and Oldham, 1980), let us describe an enrichment strategy applied by Hackman, Oldham, Janson, and Purdy (1975) to a keypunching job at the Travelers Insurance Company. The theory and technology underlying their approach is shown in Exhibit 2.8. According to the theory, positive personal and work outcomes (high internal work motivation, high work performance, high work satisfaction, and low absenteeism and turnover) result when an employee experiences three critical psychological states (experienced meaningfulness of the work, experienced responsibility for work outcomes, and knowledge of results of work activities). The employee must possess all three of the psychological states for the positive outcomes to be realized.

The theory asserts that these critical psychological states are created by five core dimensions:

- *skill variety*: the opportunity to perform a wide range of operations or use a wide variety of equipment and procedures
- *task identity*: the opportunity to do an entire piece of work such that employees can identify the result of their efforts
- *task significance*: the degree to which the job has a substantial impact on the lives or work of other people
- *autonomy*: the extent to which employees have a major say in scheduling their work, selecting the equipment they will use, and deciding on procedures to be followed
- *feedback*: the extent to which an employee receives useful, believable information regarding his or her job performance

This approach includes a set of *implementing concepts* that provide guides for action to be taken. The five implementing concepts are

1. forming natural work units—identifying basic work items and grouping them into natural categories
2. combining tasks—if possible, combining existing and fractionalized tasks to form larger modules of work
3. establishing client relationships by identifying clients of the work, establishing the most direct contact possible, and setting up criteria by which the client can judge the quality of the product or service he or she receives

EXHIBIT 2.8 A theoretical model of the job design process

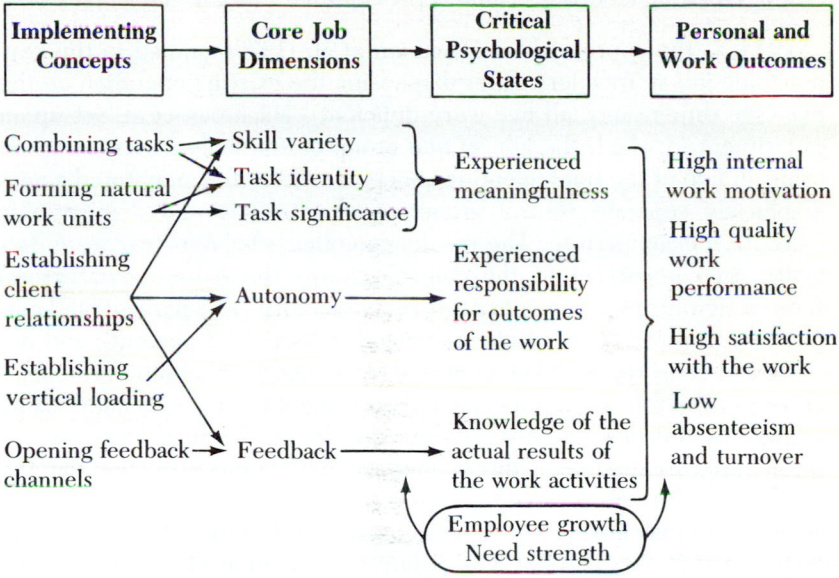

Source: Hackman, J. R., Oldham, G., Janson, R., and Purdy, K. (1975). A new strategy for job enrichment. *California Management Review, 17* (4), 62. © 1975 by the Regents of the University of California. Reprinted by permission of the Regents.

4. establishing vertical loading—closing the gap between planning, doing, and controlling the work; for example, by granting additional authority or discretion to the worker in setting schedules, quality control, and methods used
5. opening feedback channels by establishing client relationships, placing quality control close to the worker, providing summaries of performance to the worker

As shown in Exhibit 2.8, the implementing concepts are tied directly to the core job dimensions in the following ways:

1. Forming natural work units enhances task identity and task significance.
2. Combining tasks affects skill variety and task identity.
3. Establishing client relationships relates directly to skill variety, autonomy, and feedback.

4. Vertical loading fosters autonomy.
5. Opening feedback channels provides feedback to the worker.

This is the approach that Hackman et al. (1975) applied to the keypunching job at Travelers. After diagnosing the existing operation on the five core dimensions (all five were deficient), Hackman et al. set up an experiment in which the jobs of one group of employees were enriched using all five of the implementing concepts, while they monitored a geographically separate control group, similar in size and demographic makeup, for comparison. The results compiled after one year were dramatic. In comparison to the control group, the experimental group showed significant improvements in work quantity (39.8 percent) and employee attitudes (job satisfaction scores increased 16.5 percent), and decreases in error rate (1.53 percent to 0.99 percent) and absenteeism (24.1 percent). The role of the supervisor also changed from closely supervising employees and dealing with crises to developing feedback systems and setting up work modules—that is, managing. Travelers estimated that the job-enrichment efforts would save the company $91,937 annually. At an assumed annual inflation rate of 6 percent, those annual savings have grown to $220,332 in 1990. Quantitative cumulation of research results from five job enrichment experiments (total sample size = 1,242) found that implementation of job enrichment can improve retention rates an average of roughly 17 percent (McEvoy and Cascio, 1985). Again this represents a substantial potential savings to organizations. If turnover costs an average of $7,000 per departing employee, an organization can expect to save almost $120,000 in reduced turnover costs for every 100 employees in a particular job category.

Clearly a number of alternative strategies for reducing turnover in organizations exist, but the first step, as noted earlier, is to calculate the *cost* of turnover. Only then can managers make rational decisions based on the expected costs and benefits of each of the options available.

EXERCISES

1. Ups and Downs, Inc., a 4,000-employee organization, has a serious turnover problem, and management has decided to estimate its annual cost to the company. Following the formulas presented in Exhibits 2.2, 2.3, and 2.4, a personnel specialist collected the following information. Exit interviews take about 45 minutes (plus 15 minutes preparation); the interviewer, a personnel specialist, is paid an average of $13 per hour; and over the last year Ups and Downs, Inc., experi-

enced a 27 percent turnover rate. Three groups of employees were primarily responsible for this: blue collar workers (40 percent), who make an average of $14.60 per hour; clerical employees (36 percent), who make an average of $10.50 per hour; and managers and professionals (24 percent), who make an average of $23.30 per hour. The HR department takes about 90 minutes per terminating employee to perform the administrative functions related to terminations, and on top of that, each terminating employee gets two weeks' severance pay. All of this turnover also contributes to increased unemployment tax (old rate = 5.0 percent; new rate = 5.4 percent), and since the average taxable wage per employee is $14.90 this is likely to be a considerable (avoidable) penalty for having a high turnover problem.

It also costs money to replace those terminating. All preemployment physicals are done by Biometrics, Inc., an outside organization that charges $100 per physical. Advertising and employment agency fees run an additional $250, on the average, per termination, and personnel specialists spend an average of four more hours communicating job availability every time another employee quits. Preemployment administrative functions take another two and a half hours per terminating employee, and this excludes preemployment interview time (one hour, on average). Over the past year Ups and Downs, Inc.'s records also show that for every candidate hired, three others had to be interviewed. Testing costs per applicant are $8 for materials and another $8 for scoring. Travel expenses average $50 per applicant, and one in every ten new hires is reimbursed an average of $36,000 in moving expenses. For those management jobs being filled, a 90-minute staff meeting was also required, with a department representative (average pay of $22.75 per hour) present. In the last year seventeen meetings were held. Finally, postemployment acquisition and dissemination of information took 75 minutes, on the average, for each new employee.

And of course all these replacements had to be trained. Informational literature alone cost $11 per package, the formal training program (run twelve times last year) takes four 8-hour days, and trainers make an average of $24 per hour. New employees made an average of $11.50 per hour, and about 65 percent of all training costs can be attributed to replacements for those who left. Finally, on-the-job training lasted three 8-hour days per new employee, with two new employees assigned to each experienced employee (average pay = $17.25 per hour). During training each experienced employee's productivity dropped by 50 percent. Net DP was +$100,000. What did employee turnover cost Ups and Downs, Inc., last year? How much per employee who left? (Use the worksheet provided for all computations.)

2. Management has decided that the cost of employee turnover at Ups and Downs, Inc., is intolerable. As an outside consultant, you have been retained to do two things. First, prepare a presentation to management that will help the managers better understand why employees leave. Second, recommend two *detailed* programs for reducing the turnover problems at Ups and Downs, Inc. (To do this, make whatever assumptions seem reasonable.)

WORKSHEET

Separation Costs

Exit interview cost of interviewer's time =

cost of terminating employees' time =

Administrative functions related to terminations =

Separation pay =

Unemployment tax =

Total separation costs =

Replacement Costs

Communicating job availability =

Preemployment administrative functions =

Testing =

WORKSHEET (continued)

Staff meeting =

Travel/moving expenses =

Postemployment acquisition and dissemination of information =

Contracted medical examinations =

Total replacement costs =

Training Costs

Informational literature =

Instruction in a formal training program =

Instruction by employee assignment =

Total training costs =

WORKSHEET (continued)

Net differential in performance =

Total turnover costs =

Total cost per terminating employee =

REFERENCES

ASHBACH, N. W. (1989, April). *The cost of turnover in the retail automobile industry*. Unpublished manuscript, Executive MBA Program, University of Colorado.

ASHER, J. J., and SCIARRINO, J. A. (1974). Realistic work sample tests: A review. *Personnel Psychology*, *27*, 519–533.

BECKER, G. S. (1964). *Human capital*. New York: National Bureau of Economic Research.

CASCIO, W. F. (1991). *Applied psychology in personnel management* (4th ed.). Englewood Cliffs, NJ: Prentice-Hall.

CASCIO, W. F., and PHILLIPS, N. F. (1979). Performance testing: A rose among thorns? *Personnel Psychology*, *32*, 751–766.

CUNNINGHAM, J. B., and EBERLE, T. (1990). A guide to job enrichment and redesign. *Personnel*, *67* (2), 56–61.

DALTON, D. R., TODOR, W. D., and KRACKARDT, D. M. (1982). Turnover overstated: The functional taxonomy. *Academy of Management Review*, *7*, 117–123.

HACKMAN, J. R., and OLDHAM, G. R. (1980). *Work redesign*. Reading, MA: Addison-Wesley.

HACKMAN, J. R., OLDHAM, G. R., JANSON, R., and PURDY, K. (1975). A new strategy for job enrichment. *California Management Review*, *17*, 57–71.

HENDERSON, R. I. (1989). *Compensation management* (5th ed.). Englewood Cliffs, NJ: Prentice-Hall.

INWALD, R. E. (1988). Five-year follow-up study of departmental terminations as predicted by 16 preemployment psychological indicators. *Journal of Applied Psychology*, *73*, 703–710.

JACOBS, S. L. (1985, March 11). Owners who ignore security make worker dishonesty easy. *Wall Street Journal*, p. 25.

Labor letter. (1988, November 8). *Wall Street Journal*, p. A1.

MACY, B. A., and MIRVIS, P. H. (1976). Measuring the quality of work and organizational effectiveness in behavioral-economic terms. *Administrative Science Quarterly, 21*, 212–226.

MARTIN, D. C., and BARTOL, K. M. (1985). Managing turnover strategically. *Personnel Administrator, 30*, (11), 63–73.

MCEVOY, G. M., and CASCIO, W. F. (1985). Strategies for reducing employee turnover: A meta-analysis. *Journal of Applied Psychology, 70*, 342–353.

MCEVOY, G. M., and CASCIO, W. F. (1987). Do good or poor performers leave? A meta-analysis of the relationship between performance and turnover. *Academy of Management Journal, 30*, 744–762.

Navy worried about growing jet losses. (1986, March 23). *Honolulu Star Bulletin & Advertiser*, pp. A-1, A-4.

PAPPAS, J. L., and HIRSCHEY, M. (1989). *Fundamentals of Managerial Economics* (3rd ed.). Hinsdale, IL: Dryden.

Relocation challenge. (1990, February). *Mt. States Employers Council Bulletin*, p. 5.

SMITH, H. L., and WATKINS, W. E. (1978). Managing manpower turnover costs. *Personnel Administrator, 23*, (4), 46–50.

SOLOMON, J. (1988, December 29). Companies try measuring cost savings from new types of corporate benefits. *Wall Street Journal*, p. B1.

WANOUS, J. P. (1980). *Organizational entry: Recruitment, selection, and socialization of newcomers*. Reading, MA: Addison-Wesley.

WARD, J. L. (1985, July 16). Firms forcing employees to repay some costs if they quit too soon. *Wall Street Journal*, p. 27.

WESSEL, D. (1989, September 7). Evidence is skimpy that drug testing works, but employers embrace practice. *Wall Street Journal*, p. B1.

ZIPPO, M. (1982). Dealing with absenteeism and turnover: Some current problems. *Personnel, 59*, 43–45.

3

The Hidden Costs of Absenteeism and Sick Leave

On a national level, employee absenteeism is estimated to cost the U.S. economy over $40 billion per year in reduced productivity ("Labor Letter," 1986). This is an enormous loss of productivity, a substantial debit in the national economic ledger. Unfortunately a national, or macro, perspective, while important, masks the costs borne by individual organizations in the economy. The costs of employee absenteeism can also be estimated at the level of the individual organization (at the micro level), although not quite as easily as regularly computed expenditures such as rent, direct labor, building depreciation, or utilities. As one observer noted:

> Traditional accounting and personnel information systems simply don't generate data which reflect the estimated dollars-and-cents costs of absenteeism. While many organizations regularly compute *time* lost to absenteeism (hours, days, etc.) by employee and department, few organizations translate the collective act of staying away from work into *economic* terms. (Kuzmits, 1979, p. 29)

Despite these difficulties, the costs of absenteeism are very real even if they are buried in an assortment of production, personnel, and accounting records. Until the magnitude of these costs is known, management will find it difficult to determine the extent of the problem, to estimate its effect on overall productivity or profits, or to formulate strategies for dealing with it. General Motors, for example, estimates that absenteeism costs the company $1 billion *each year*. Figures like these shocked policy makers into taking action. The company recognized that a large part of absenteeism costs could be attributed to alcohol and drug abuse. Since 1972, over 50,000 workers voluntarily have used the substance-abuse prevention program that the company established, and absenteeism has been reduced as a result ("People," 1984). At Union Bank, executives approved spending $430,000 for a day-care center only after seeing savings projections. Two years later the bank found that users of the day-care center were absent 1.7 fewer days than individuals in a control group, and that their maternity leaves were 1.2 weeks shorter than those for other employees. Annual savings from these two items alone were $35,000 (Solomon, 1988).

Absenteeism is any failure to report for or remain at work as scheduled, regardless of reason. The use of the words "as scheduled" is significant, for this automatically excludes vacation, personal leave, jury duty leave, and the like. A great deal of confusion can be avoided simply by recognizing that if an employee is not on the job as scheduled he or she is absent, regardless of cause. The employee is not available to perform his or her job, and that job is probably being done less efficiently by another employee or is not being done at all.

> Another point of primary importance is the fact that absenteeism is to be judged on the record, and the record only. While this may seem elementary, it is essential. There is a tendency to view some absences as "excusable" and others as "inexcusable." Judgments concerning the nature of illness causing the absence also tend to make some absences seem "better" or "worse" than others, and the length of service of the employee makes certain absences seem excusable. Actually, the only absence which is really inexcusable is the absence due to malingering, but, unfortunately, it is difficult or nearly impossible to provide evidence to substantiate malingering, and mere suspicions can be erroneous. Regardless, excused time is by no means a right. Absence is absence regardless of reason—even for medically verified illness. Failure to recognize this simple fact will result in an attempt to make judgments that simply cannot be made. (*City and County Government*, October 1980, 14:3)

At the outset, let us be clear about what this chapter does and does not include. It does not examine the causes of absenteeism, such as emotional–physical fatigue (cf. Hackett, Bycio, and Guion, 1989). Nor does it focus on the noneconomic consequences of absenteeism, such as higher likelihoods of accidents of replacement workers (cf. Goodman and Garber, 1989). Rather, the primary focus in this chapter is on the economic consequences of absenteeism, and on methods for managing absenteeism and sick-leave abuse.

ESTIMATING THE COST OF ABSENTEEISM

The following procedure will estimate the cost of absenteeism for a one-year period, although the procedure can be used just as easily to estimate these costs over shorter or longer periods as necessary.[1] Much of the information required should not be too time-consuming to gather if an organization regularly computes labor cost data and traditional absence statistics (for example, absenteeism rate = Σ [absence days ÷ average work force size] × working days or Σ [hours missed ÷ average work force size] × working hours). Although some estimates will involve discussions with both staff and management representatives, the time spent should be well worth the effort. The overall approach is shown in Exhibit 3.1.

To illustrate this approach, examples will accompany each step. The examples use the hypothetical firm Presto Electric, a medium-sized manufacturer of electrical components employing 3,000 people; they are as realistic as possible in order to illustrate the problems and costs related to employee absenteeism.

Step 1

Determine the organization's total employee-hours lost to absenteeism for the period for all employees—blue collar, clerical, and management and professional. Include both whole-day and part-day absences, and time lost for all reasons except organizationally sanctioned time off such as vacations, holidays, or official "bad weather" days. For example, absences for the following reasons should be included: illness, accidents, funerals, emergencies, or doctor's appointments (whether excused or unexcused).

As a basis for comparisons, Exhibit 3.2 illustrates monthly job absence rates as reported by the Bureau of National Affairs. While the time series data shown in Exhibit 3.2 clearly reflect a seasonal component (highest rates in January and February, lowest rates in June, July, and August), average monthly rates by year do not indicate a long-term trend, at least for the years shown.

In our example, assume that Presto Electric's personnel records show

[1]The method that follows is based upon that described by F. E. Kuzmits in "How Much Is Absenteeism Costing *Your* Organization?" *Personnel Administrator*, June 1979, *24*:29–33.

EXHIBIT 3.1 Total estimated cost of employee absenteeism

1. Compute total employee hours lost to absenteeism for the period.
2. Compute weighted average wage or salary/hour/absent employee.
3. Compute cost of employee benefits/hour/employee.

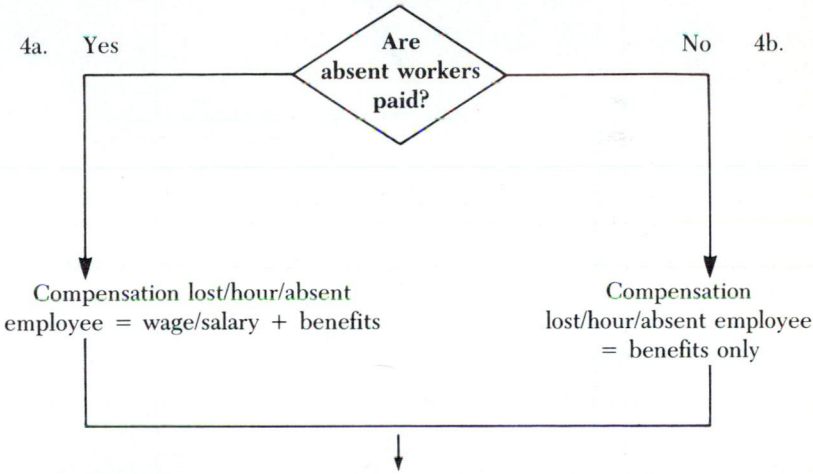

5. Compute total compensation lost to absent employees (1. × 4a. or 4b. as applicable).
6. Estimate total supervisory hours lost to employee absenteeism.
7. Compute average hourly supervisory salary + benefits.
8. Estimate total supervisory salaries lost to managing absenteeism problems (6. × 7.).
9. Estimate all other costs incidental to absenteeism.
10. Estimate total cost of absenteeism (Σ 5., 8., 9.).
11. Estimate total cost of absenteeism/employee (10. ÷ total no. of employees).

EXHIBIT 3.2 Typical monthly job absence rates

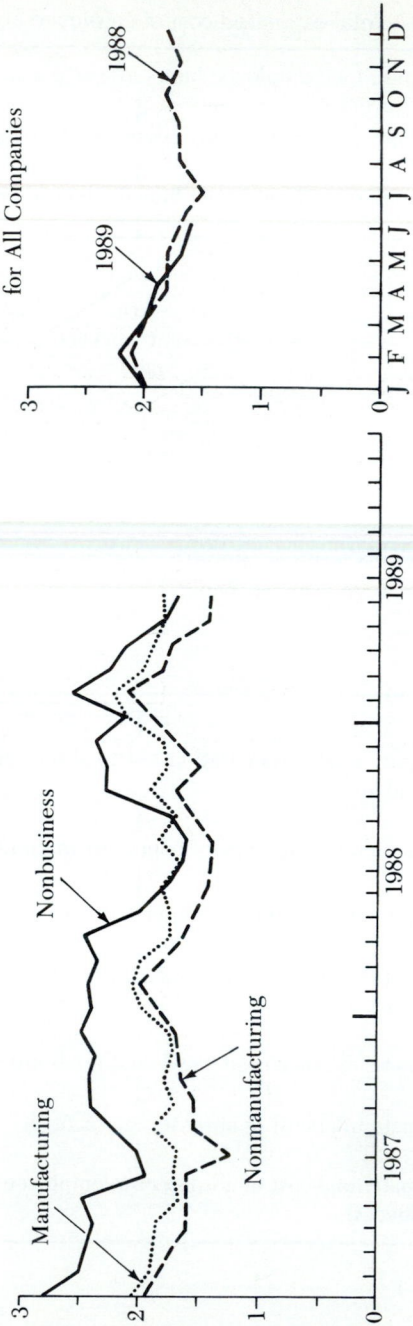

EXHIBIT 3.2 Continued

Average Median Absence: January–June (percent of scheduled workdays)

All Companies	1.9
Number of Employees	
Up to 250	1.7
250–499	1.8
500–999	1.9
1,000–2,499	2.1
2,500 and more	2.6
Industry	
Manufacturing	2.0
Nonmanufacturing	1.7
Finance	1.8
Nonbusiness	2.1
Health Care	1.8
Region	
Northeast	2.1
South	2.0
North Central	1.8
West	1.9

Source: BNA's job absence and turnover report—2nd quarter 1989. Reprinted by permission from *Bulletin to Management*, copyright 1989 by the Bureau of National Affairs, Inc., Washington, D.C.

117,600 total employee-hours lost to absenteeism for all reasons except vacations and holidays during the last year. This figure represents an absence rate of 2 percent of scheduled work time, about average for manufacturing firms (see Exhibit 3.2). Begin by distinguishing hours scheduled from hours paid. Most firms *pay* for 2,080 hours per year per employee (40 hours per week × 52 weeks). However, employees generally receive paid vacations and holidays as well, time for which they are not scheduled to be at work. If we assume two weeks vacation time per employee (40 hours × 2), plus 5 holidays (40 hours), annual hours of *scheduled* work time per employee are 2,080 − 80 − 40 = 1,960.

Total scheduled work time for Presto Electric's 3,000 employees is therefore 3,000 × 1,960 = 5,880,000. Given a 2 percent rate of annual absenteeism, total scheduled work hours lost to employee absenteeism are 117,600.

Step 2

Compute the weighted average hourly wage/salary level for the various occupational groups that claimed absenteeism during the period. If absent workers are not paid, skip this step and go directly to step 3.

For Presto Electric, assume that about 75 percent of all absentees are blue collar, 20 percent clerical, and 5 percent management and professional. For purposes of illustration we also will assume that all employees are paid for sick days taken under the organization's employee benefits program. The average hourly wage rate per absentee is estimated by applying the appropriate percentages to the average hourly wage rate for each major occupational group. Thus:

Occupational Group	*Approximate Percent of Total Absenteeism*	*Average Hourly Wage*	*Weighted Average Hourly Wage*
Blue collar	0.75	$13.85	$10.39
Clerical	0.20	11.20	2.24
Management and professional	0.05	23.40	1.17
			$13.80 total

Step 3

Estimate the cost of employee benefits per hour per employee. The cost of employee benefits (profit sharing, pensions, health and life insurance, paid vacations and holidays, and so on) is about 30 to 40 percent of total payroll, and 40 to 45 percent in the case of capital-intensive establishments such as steel mills and oil companies ("Employers Told," 1985). One procedure for computing the cost of employee benefits per hour per employee is to divide the total cost of benefits per employee per week by the number of hours worked per week.

First, compute Presto's weekly cost of benefits per employee. Assume that the average annual salary per employee is $13.80 per hour (which happens to correspond to the result we observed in step 2, though this need not be the case) × 2,080 (hours paid for per year), or about $28,704. Let us further assume:

average annual salary × 35 percent	=	average cost of benefits per employee per year
$28,704 × 0.35	=	$10,046.40
average cost of benefits per employee per year ÷ 52 weeks/year	=	average weekly cost of benefits per employee
$10,046.40 ÷ 52	=	$193.20
average weekly cost of benefits per employee ÷ hours worked per week	=	cost of benefits per hour per employee
$193.20 ÷ 40	=	$4.83

Step 4

Compute the total compensation lost per hour per absent employee. This figure is determined simply by adding the weighted average hourly wage/salary per employee (item 2 in Exhibit 3.1) to the cost of employee benefits per hour per employee (item 3 in Exhibit 3.1). Thus:

$$\$13.80 + \$4.83 = \$18.63$$

Of course if absent workers are not paid, then item 4 in Exhibit 3.1 is the same as item 3.

Step 5

Compute the total compensation lost to absent employees. Total compensation lost, aggregated over all employee-hours lost, is determined simply by multiplying item 1 by item 4.a or 4.b, whichever is applicable. In our example:

by multiplying item 1 by item 4.a or 4.b, whichever is applicable. In our example:

$$117{,}600 \times \$18.63 = \$2{,}190{,}888$$

Step 6

Estimate the total number of supervisory hours lost to employee absenteeism for the period. Unfortunately, since existing records seldom provide the information necessary to compute this figure, it will be more difficult to estimate than wage and benefits estimates. As a first step, estimate the average number of supervisory hours spent per day dealing with all the problems stemming from employee absenteeism, problems such as

1. production problems
2. instructing replacement employees
3. checking on the performance of replacements
4. counseling and disciplining absentees

Such an estimate can be accurate only if the staff member making it talks to the first-line supervisors and higher level managers who deal directly with employee absence problems. A representative sample of supervisors should be interviewed with a semistructured interview format to help them refine their estimates. Areas to probe, in addition to those in the preceding list, include the effects of typically high-absence days (Mondays, Fridays, days before and after holidays, days after payday). No published data, no industry-wide averages, are available to determine whether or not these estimates are reasonable. However, it is true of estimates in general that the more experience companies accumulate in making the estimates, the more accurate the estimates become (Wikstrom, 1971).

After you have estimated the average number of supervisory hours spent per day dealing with employee absenteeism problems, compute the total number of supervisory hours lost to the organization by multiplying three figures:

1. the estimated average number of hours lost per supervisor per day
2. the total number of supervisors who deal with problems of absenteeism

3. the number of working days for the period (including all shifts and weekend work)

In our example, assume that Presto Electric's data in these three areas are:

1. estimated number of supervisory hours lost per day: 0.5 hours
2. total number of supervisors who deal with absence problems: 100
3. total number of working days for the year: 245

The total number of supervisory hours lost to employee absenteeism is therefore:

$$0.5 \times 100 \times 245 = 12{,}250$$

Step 7

Compute the average hourly wage rate for supervisors, including benefits. Be sure to include only the salaries of supervisors who normally deal with problems of employee absenteeism. Typically, first-line supervisors in the production and clerical areas bear the brunt of absenteeism problems. Estimate Presto Electric's cost for this figure as follows:

average hourly supervisory salary:	\$16.30
cost of benefits per hour (35% of hourly salary):	+5.705
total compensation per hour per supervisor:	\$22.005

Step 8

Compute total supervisory salaries lost to problems of managing absenteeism. This figure is derived simply by multiplying total supervisory hours lost on employee absenteeism (step 6) times average hourly supervisory wage (step 7). Thus:

$$12{,}250 \times 22.005 = \$269{,}561.25$$

Step 9

Estimate all other costs incidental to absenteeism that were not included in the previous steps. This last item is a catchall of costs, unique to each organization, that clearly relate to absenteeism but that fall outside the boundaries of all the other costs we have considered so far. Such costs might include the following items:

- temporary help
- labor pools for absent workers
- overtime premiums
- machine downtime
- quality problems
- production losses
- inefficient materials usage

As in step 6, these estimates will be difficult because many of the components are not reported routinely in accounting or human resource information systems. Initially therefore, determination of the cost elements to be included in this category, plus estimates of their magnitude, should be based on discussions with a number of supervisory and management personnel. Over time, as the organization accumulates experience in costing absenteeism, it can make a more precise identification and computation of the costs to be included in this miscellaneous category.

At Presto Electric, assume that overtime premiums, production losses, and inefficient materials usage as a result of absenteeism caused an estimated financial loss of $250,000 for the year.

Step 10

Compute the total estimated cost of employee absenteeism. Having computed or estimated all the necessary cost items, we now can determine the total annual cost of employee absenteeism to Presto Electric. Simply add the individual costs pertaining to wages and salaries, benefits, supervisory salaries, and other costs incidental to absenteeism (Σ items 5, 8, and 9). As Exhibit 3.3 demonstrates, this cost is over $2.7 million per year.

Step 11

Compute the total estimated cost of absenteeism per employee per year. In some cases this figure (derived by dividing the total estimated cost by the total number of employees) may be more meaningful than the total cost estimate because it is easier to grasp. In the case of our hypothetical firm, Presto Electric, this figure was $903.48 per year for each of the 3,000 employees on the payroll.

EXHIBIT 3.3 Total estimated cost of employee absenteeism

Item		*Presto Electric*
1.	Total employee-hours lost to absenteeism for the period	117,600
2.	Weighted average wage/salary per hour per absent employee	$13.80
3.	Cost of employee benefits per hour per absent employee	$4.83
4.	Total compensation lost per hour per absent employee	
	a. if absent workers are paid (wage/salary plus benefits)	$18.63
	b. if absent workers are not paid (benefits only)	
5.	Total compensation lost to absent employees (total employee-hours lost × 4.a or 4.b, whichever applies)	$2,190,888.00
6.	Total supervisory hours lost on employee absenteeism	12,250
7.	Average hourly supervisory wage, including benefits	$22.005
8.	Total supervisory salaries lost to managing problems of absenteeism (hours lost × average hourly supervisory wage—item 6 × item 7)	$269,561.25
9.	All other costs incidental to absenteeism not included in the above items	$250,000.00
10.	Total estimated cost of absenteeism (Σ items 5, 8, and 9)	$2,710,449.00
11.	Total estimated cost of absenteeism per employee (total estimated costs ÷ total number of employees)	$903.48

INTERPRETING ABSENTEEISM COSTS

In order for these absenteeism costs to be interpreted meaningfully, they should be evaluated against some predetermined cost standard or financial measure of performance, such as an industrywide average. This is basically the same rationale organizations use when conducting pay surveys to determine if their salaries and benefits are competitive. Unfortunately, absenteeism cost data are not published regularly, as are pay surveys. Very little data are available to help determine whether the level of dollars and cents lost to employee absenteeism is a significant problem.

The costs of absenteeism to individual organizations occasionally do appear in the literature, but these estimates are typically case studies of individual firms rather than survey data from specific industries.

Is the effort to analyze the absenteeism costs of the individual organization worthwhile? The answer is yes for at least two compelling reasons (Kuzmits, 1979). First, such an analysis calls management's attention to the severity of the problem. Translating behavior into economic terms enables managers to grasp the burdens employee absenteeism imposes, particularly in organizations suffering from severe absence problems. A five-, six-, or even seven-figure cost is often the spark needed for management to make a concerted effort to combat the problem. Second, an analysis of the problem creates a baseline for evaluating the effectiveness of absence control programs. Comparing the quarterly, semiannual, and annual costs of absenteeism across various departments and supervisory work units provides a measure of the success—or lack of success—of attempts to reduce the problem. Organizations with computerized absence reporting systems should find this additional information relatively easy and inexpensive to generate.

A common question at this point is "Are these dollars real?" Since supervisors are drawing their salaries anyway, what difference does it make if they have to manage absenteeism problems? The last question may be valid, but what is the best possible return to the organization for that pay?

We'll compare Firms A and B, identical in regard to all resources and costs—all supervisors earn the same salary, work the same hours, manage the same-size staff, and produce the same kind of product. But absenteeism in Firm A is very low, and in Firm B it is very high. The salary officers' records show the same pay to supervisors, but the accountants show higher profits in Firm A than in Firm B. Why? Because the supervisors in Firm A spend less time managing absenteeism problems. They are more productive because they devote their energies to planning, scheduling, and troubleshooting. Instead of working a ten- to twelve-hour day (which the supervisors in Firm B consider "normal"), they wrap things up after only eight hours. In short, reducing the hours that supervisors must spend managing absenteeism problems has two advantages: (1) it allows supervisors to maximize their productivity and (2) it reduces the stress associated with repeated ten- to twelve-hour days, which in turn enhances the quality of the supervisors' work lives.

The material thus far describes the idea of *opportunity costs*—the difference between the maximum return that could be earned (Firm A) and that which actually was earned (Firm B). Supervisors in Firm B did put in their time to earn their pay, but those in Firm A made better use of their time while on the job. So the answer to the question "Are these dollars real?" is yes, but in all probability they are *underestimates*, because they reflect only the payroll costs of supervisors' time, not the productive dollar value of that time.

MANAGING ABSENTEEISM AND SICK-LEAVE ABUSE

No Work, No Pay at Honda USA

Over a two-year period, Honda's absenteeism rate averaged just 2 percent in an industry that has been plagued by chronic absenteeism problems. For example, General Motors reported that absenteeism had run as high as 40 percent at one of its West Coast plants, and that it had to hire additional employees to keep production lines moving. How did Honda do it? According to the company, the low rate of employee absenteeism is due to the "Honda System." At the heart of the system is a simple dictum: no work, no pay. Absences shorter than seven days are not compensated, but absences longer than seven days are reimbursable through insurance.

On the other hand, if employees do report on time, and do not punch out early, they earn progressively larger and larger bonuses. The minimum bonus is $24 for four weeks of perfect attendance, but it graduates upward based on seniority. A worker with a year of perfect attendance moves into another category, and the bonus continues to build. Absenteeism control is only one part of Honda's broader management system, but one indicator of the program's success is the inability of the United Auto Workers to organize Honda employees, despite repeated attempts to do so (Allan, 1983).

Discipline Without Punishment

Sunnen Products Company of St. Louis, like Honda, relies on a combination of discipline and reward to control employee absenteeism. But that's where the similarity between the companies ends. Unlike Honda, Sunnen uses "discipline without punishment." After a series of warnings following a certain number of unexplained absences, a worker must take a day off *with* pay to decide whether to stay or to leave the job. The day off represents discipline, but the full day's pay does not represent punishment. According to the company, 25 percent stay and shape up ("Labor Letter," 1985).

Controlling Absenteeism Through Positive Incentives

The preceding absenteeism control methods focus either on punishment or on a combination of reward and punishment. The next approach focuses exclusively on rewards; it provides incentives for employees to come to work, rather than punishments for not coming to work. This "positive incentive absence control program" was evaluated over a five-year period: one year before and one year after a three-year incentive program (Schlotzhauer and Rosse, 1985).

A 3,000-employee nonprofit hospital provided the setting for the study. The experimental group contained 164 employees who received the positive-incentive program, and the control group contained 136 employees who did not receive the program. According to the terms of the hospital's sick-leave program, employees could take up to ninety-six hours—twelve days per year—with pay. Under the positive-incentive program, employees could convert up to twenty-four hours of unused sick leave into additional pay or vacation. To determine the amount of incentive, the number of hours absent was subtracted from 24. For example, 24 minus 8 hours absent equals 16 hours of additional pay or vacation. The hospital informed eligible employees both verbally and in writing.

During the year prior to the installation of the positive-incentive program, absence levels for the experimental and control groups did not differ significantly. During the three years in which the program was operative, the experimental group consistently was absent less frequently, and this difference persisted during the year following the termination of the incentives. The following variables were *not* related to absence: age, marital status, education, job grade, tenure, or number of hours absent two or three years previously. Two variables *were* related to absence, although not as strongly as the incentive program itself: gender (women were absent more than men) and number of hours absent during the previous year.

Had the incentive program been expanded to include all 3,000 hospital employees, net savings were estimated to have been $42,000 per year. This is an *underestimate,* however, since indirect costs were not included. Indirect costs include such things as

- overtime pay
- increased supervisory time for managing absenteeism problems

- costs of temporary labor
- intentional overstaffing to compensate for anticipated absences

Cautions: A positive-incentive program may have no effect on employees who view sick leave as an earned "right" that should be used whether one is sick or not. Moreover, encouraging attendance when a person has a legitimate reason for being absent—for example, hospital employees with contagious illnesses—may be dysfunctional.

In and of itself, absence may simply represent one of many possible symptoms of job dissatisfaction. Attendance incentives may result in "symptom substitution," whereby declining absence is accompanied by increased tardiness and idling, decreased productivity, and even turnover. If this is the case, an organization needs to consider more comprehensive interventions that are based, for example, on the results of an attitude survey.

Despite the potential limitations, the study warranted the following conclusions:

- Absenteeism declined an average of 11.5 hours per employee (32 percent) during the incentive period
- Net dollar values to the organization (direct costs only) are based upon wage costs of $11.67 per hour (comprised of $8.98 in direct wages plus 30 percent more in benefits)
- Savings were $22,010 per year (11.5 hours × average hourly wage [$11.67] × 164 employees)
- Direct costs to the hospital included 2,194 bonus hours at an average hourly wage of $8.98 per hour = $19,702
- Net savings were therefore $2,308 per year, for an 11.7 percent return on investment ($2,308 ÷ $19,702)

No-Fault Absenteeism

An alternative approach to controlling employee absenteeism relies on the concept of "no-fault" (Kuzmits, 1984). The no-fault absenteeism system eliminates fault as a basis for determining whether absenteeism or tardiness is to be excused. Under the no-fault policy, an employee is either at work or is absent, and each type of absence carries a predetermined penalty, with the exception of a few clearly defined, nonchargeable offenses.

The no-fault system defines absences in terms of *occurrences*. An occurrence is an absence of any length—a one-day absence and a three-day absence are treated as two occurrences. Management's costliest and most troublesome absenteeism problem is the chronic offender: the employee who incurs many single-day absences. Under the no-fault approach, the chronic offender quickly accumulates multiple occurrences and is subject to disciplinary action. On the other hand, an employee who is absent three or four consecutive days is probably ill. Thus the no-fault approach places heavy penalties on the chronic absentee and light penalties on the employee who is, in all likelihood, absent because of sickness.

All absences, regardless of reason, are chargeable for purposes of disciplinary action. Hence an employee either is at work or is not, and the burden of responsibility for good attendance is placed squarely on the shoulders of each employee. Exhibit 3.4 outlines the specific provisions of one such no-fault policy. Note the reward system that is built into this policy. Employees can remove one occurrence through each calendar month of perfect attendance. The policy thus includes positive inducements for good attendance, as well as negative sanctions for abusing sick leave. It was written primarily to alter the behavioral patterns of chronic absentees and to provide a fair, concise disciplinary procedure for frequently absent employees who are unable or unwilling to change their behavior.

Does no-fault absenteeism work? A comparison of one year's experience under a traditional sick-leave policy that included provisions both for excused and unexcused absences with one year's experience under a no-fault policy provided some interesting evidence. The study was conducted with 289 blue collar unionized employees of a cabinet manufacturer in Louisville, Kentucky. Results indicated significant improvements under the no-fault policy in all forms of attendance (absence occurrences, tardiness, partial absences, and no-calls). In addition, disciplinary decisions were simplified considerably, and employees knew at all times where they stood within the system. Finally, absence-related union grievances dropped from fifteen in the year prior to the no-fault system to four during the first year with the no-fault system (Kuzmits, 1984).

A no-fault policy clearly has several advantages:

- It applies to all employees regardless of circumstances.
- Supervisors cannot judge the legitimacy of absences, so that bias does not determine whether an absence should be excused or unexcused.
- Disciplinary decisions are clear, since they are directly related to the number of occurrences, or points, that an employee accumulates.

As a result of excessive absenteeism and/or tardiness, disciplinary action may be required and will be based on frequency of occurrences in accordance with the following:

1. Absenteeism is defined as being absent from work on any scheduled work day, even though the employee has reported.
2. Each period of consecutive absence will be recorded as "one occurrence" regardless of the number of days' duration.
3. Tardiness will be considered to be reporting to work within ten minutes of the scheduled starting time. One occasion of tardiness will be charged as one-quarter of an absence occurrence.
4. Employees who report to work late, as provided for in the reporting regulations, or who leave before the end of the shift (with management's permission) will be charged with one-half of an absence occurrence for either of these occurrences.
5. Employees who are absent without call-in will be charged with two occurrences of absence for that occasion.
6. Absence due to funeral leave, military obligation, jury duty or union business (each as defined by the labor contract) and further including hospital confinement and work-incurred injury, will not be recorded as an occurrence of absence for purposes of disciplinary action.
7. For each calendar month of perfect attendance, an employee with an absentee record will have one occurrence deducted from the absentee record.
8. Absence records will be maintained for a consecutive twelve-month period, starting with the employee's first occurrence of absence. All absence records and warning slips which are one year old or older shall not be considered for purposes of disciplinary action under this policy.

Corrective discipline will be administered according to the following:

- Three occurrences, or points, within a twelve-month period: Verbal warning.
- Five occurrences, or points, within a twelve-month period: Written warning.
- Seven occurrences, or points, within a twelve-month period: Second written warning.
- Twelve occurrences, or points, within a twelve-month period: Discharge.

The above policy is in addition to action that may be taken when cumulative time lost from work for any reason substantially reduces the employee's services to the company.

Source: Kuzmits, F. E. Is your organization ready for no-fault absenteeism? Reprinted from the December 1984 issue of *Personnel Administrator*, copyright 1984, the American Society for Personnel Administration.

Arbitrators support the no-fault system because of its objective standards, uniform administration, progressive disciplinary procedures, automatic exceptions, and opportunities to "cleanse" the record through perfect attendance.

On the other hand, a no-fault policy is not without its disadvantages, and these must be considered carefully:

- Because the system leaves no room for supervisory discretion, individual circumstances cannot be considered when charging an employee with an absence or an occurrence or when making a disciplinary decision.
- An occurrence is defined as an absence of *any length*. Some employees may therefore "game" the system by recognizing, for example, that a three-day absence entails the same penalty as a one-day absence.
- Employees may continue to "game" the system by rationalizing, "I've got twelve occurrences a year; I'm going to use them." These employees feel that sick leave is a right ("Use it or lose it") rather than a privilege.
- Unions may resist a no-fault policy if they perceive it as part of a "give-back" bargaining strategy.[2]
- Short-term illnesses, even if medically verified, result in chargeable absences. Although arbitrators generally have upheld this aspect of the no-fault policy, unionized employees that traditionally have enjoyed such paid leave will probably oppose it.

Like any other human resource management program, a no-fault absenteeism policy should be considered in light of the particular problems faced by management. No-fault seems to work best in controlling high incidences of one-day absences, partial absences, and tardiness; in distinguishing excused from unexcused absences; and in clarifying the disciplinary system and the organization's absenteeism policy. Finally, it virtually eliminates employee perceptions of supervisory inequity in the interpretation of absenteeism policy and the imposition of discipline for excessive absenteeism.

---

[2]Such a collective bargaining strategy by unions involves concessions of gains previously won on wages and benefits. It was a fairly common practice in the 1980s as unions worked with managements to help their companies survive in the face of adverse business conditions. Subsequently, unions have found that such "give-backs" are hard to win back for their members.

Consolidated Annual Leave

The consolidated annual leave approach to controlling absenteeism and the abuse of sick leave allows employees to manage their own sick and vacation time and to take a day off without having to offer an explanation. Sick days, vacation time, and holidays are consolidated into one "bank" to be drawn out at the employee's discretion. If the employee uses up all of this time before the end of the year and needs a day off, that time is unpaid. On the other hand, employees can convert unused time to vacation or can accrue time and be paid for a portion of it.

Employers (primarily banks and hospitals) that have instituted this kind of policy feel that it is a "win–win" situation for employees and managers. It eliminates the need for lying by employees (that is, abuse of sick leave), and it takes managers out of the role of enforcers. Employees typically view sick leave days as a right—that is, "use them or lose them." Consolidated annual leave policies provide an incentive to employees not to take unnecessary time off because excessive absence is still cause for dismissal. As one HR director noted: "Under the traditional policy, people with good attendance records were being penalized. This policy rewards people for properly managing their time off" (Eicher, 1988).

EXERCISES

1. Consolidated Industries, an 1,800-employee firm, is faced with a serious, and growing, absenteeism problem. Last year total employee-hours lost to absenteeism came to 119,808. Of the total employees absent, 65 percent were blue collar (average wage of $14.10 per hour), 25 percent were clerical (average wage of $11.60 per hour), and the remainder were management and professional (average salary $21.07 per hour). On the average, the firm spends 38 percent more of each employees' salary on benefits, and as company policy, pays workers even if they are absent.

The 45 supervisors (average salary of $16.21 per hour) involved in employee absenteeism problems estimate they lose 25 minutes per day for each of the 245 days per work year just dealing with the extra problems imposed by those who fail to show up for work. Finally, the company estimates it loses $129,500 in additional overtime premiums, in extra help that must be hired, and in lost productivity from the more highly skilled absentees. As HR director for Consolidated Industries your job is to estimate the cost of employee absenteeism so that management can better understand the dimensions of the problem. (Use the worksheet provided to record your answers.)

2. Inter-Capital Limited is a 500-employee firm faced with a 3.7 percent annual

absenteeism rate over the 1,960 hours that each employee is scheduled to work. About 15 percent of absentees are blue collar (average wage $13.90 per hour), 55 percent are clerical employees (average wage $11.20 per hour), and the remainder are management and professional workers (average salary $21.50 per hour). About 40 percent more of each employee's salary is spent on benefits, but employees are not paid if they are absent from work. In the last six months, supervisors (average salary of $15.95 per hour) estimate that managing absenteeism problems costs them about an hour a day for each of the 245 days per work year. It's a serious problem that must be dealt with, since about 20 supervisors are directly involved with absenteeism. On top of that, the firm spends approximately $96,000 more on costs incidental to absenteeism. Temporary help and lost productivity can really cut into profits. Just how much is absenteeism costing Inter-Capital Limited per year per employee? (Use the worksheet provided to record your answers.)

3. As a management consultant, you have been retained to develop two alternative programs for reducing employee absenteeism at Consolidated Industries (question 1). Write a proposal that addresses the issue in specific terms. Exactly what should the firm do? (To do this make whatever assumptions seem reasonable.)

WORKSHEET: TOTAL ESTIMATED COST OF EMPLOYEE ABSENTEEISM

Item	*Consolidated Industries*	*Inter-Capital Limited*
1. Total employee-hours lost to absenteeism for the period	_____	_____
2. Weighted average wage/salary per hour per absent employee	_____	_____
3. Cost of employee benefits per hour per employee	_____	_____
4. Total compensation lost per hour per absent employee		
a. if absent workers are paid (wage/salary plus benefits)	_____	_____
b. if absent workers are not paid (benefits only)	_____	_____
5. Total compensation lost to absent employees (total employee-hours lost × 4a or 4b, whichever applies)	_____	_____
6. Total supervisory hours lost on employee absenteeism	_____	_____

WORKSHEET (continued)

Item	Consolidated Industries	Inter-Capital Limited
7. Average hourly supervisory wage, including benefits	_____	_____
8. Total supervisory salaries lost to managing problems of absenteeism (hours lost × average hourly supervisory wage—item 6 × item 7)	_____	_____
9. All other costs incidental to absenteeism not included in the above items	_____	_____
10. Total estimated cost of absenteeism—summation of items 5, 8, and 9	_____	_____
11. Total estimated cost of absenteeism per employee (total estimated costs ÷ total number of employees)	_____	_____

REFERENCES

ALLAN, W. (1983, May 7). No work, no pay slices Honda absenteeism. *Rocky Mountain News*, p. 2A.

EICHER, D. (1988, December 14). Bosses favoring mental health days. *Denver Post*, pp. 1D, 4D.

Employers told to publicize cost of fringe benefits. (1985, July 8). *Hartford Courant*, p. C8.

GOODMAN, P. S., and GARBER, S. (1989). Absenteeism and accidents in a dangerous environment: Empirical analysis of underground coal mines. *Journal of Applied Psychology, 73*, 81–86.

HACKETT, R. D., BYCIO, P., and GUION, R. M. (1989). Absenteeism among hospital nurses: An ideographic–longitudinal analysis. *Academy of Management Journal, 32*, 424–453.

KUZMITS, F. E. (1979). How much is absenteeism costing your organization? *Personnel Administrator, 24*, (6), 29–33.

KUZMITS, F. E. (1984). Is your organization ready for no-fault absenteeism? *Personnel Administrator, 29*, (12), 119–127.

Labor letter. (1985, April 23). *Wall Street Journal*, p. 1.

Labor letter. (1986, July 29). *Wall Street Journal*, p. 1.

People. (1984, April 14). *Rocky Mountain News*, p. 2.

SCHLOTZHAUER, D. L., and ROSSE, J. G. (1985). A five-year study of a positive incentive absence control program. *Personnel Psychology, 38*, 575–585.

SOLOMON, J. (1988, December 29). Companies try measuring cost savings from new types of corporate benefits. *Wall Street Journal*, p. B1.

WIKSTROM, W. S. (1971). *Manpower planning: Evolving systems*. New York: The Conference Board, Report No. 521.

4

Costing the Effects of Smoking at the Work Place

More than 25 percent of the U.S. population does it every day. Generally it declines as educational levels increase. About 30 percent of all men and about a fourth of all women do it, according to the 1989 surgeon general's report ("Crusade," 1990). What is it? *Smoking.*

THE CONSEQUENCES OF SMOKING

Health Risks

More than 50,000 scientific studies have documented the health hazards of smoking. According to the surgeon general's report entitled, "The Health Consequences of Smoking: Nicotine Addiction," more than twenty years of research by over fifty scientists suggests that cigarette smoking is addictive—and should be treated with the same caution as illegal street narcotics (Gorman, 1988). The surgeon general has called it "the chief preventable cause of death in our society and the most important public health issue of our time"; and further, "tobacco is responsible for 1 out of every 6 deaths in the U.S." (Gorman, 1988, p. 54).

Somber statistics on the health hazards of smoking abound. Tobacco use prematurely kills 390,000 Americans annually, or about 1,070 a day—roughly the equivalent of two or three jumbo jets crashing every day, with no survivors (Toufexis, 1989). Cigarette smokers experience a 70 percent greater death rate from coronary heart disease than do nonsmokers. For heavy smokers—those who smoke two or more packs per day—the overall coronary death rate is two to three times greater. Further, women who use birth-control pills and smoke run a risk of heart disease ten times greater than do women who neither use oral contraceptives nor smoke (Herzlinger and Calkins, 1986). Even women who smoke as few as one to four cigarettes a day double or triple their risk of having a heart attack. Large-scale research has shown clearly that there is no safe level of smoking (Leary, 1987). Worse yet, women who inhale passive smoke for three or more hours a day are not only more likely to develop cancer of the cervix (which kills about 6,000 women every year in the United States) than women who do not inhale passive smoke, but such "involuntary smokers" are as much at risk as are active smokers ("Yet Another Deadly Link," 1989).

Among heart patients who quit smoking, mortality is one-third less ("New AMA Journal," 1986). For a typical ex-smoker, the risk of heart attack after one year approaches that of a person who has never smoked, and the risk of lung cancer after five to ten years approximates that of a person who has never smoked (Herzlinger and Calkins, 1986).

Economic Consequences of Smoking

Cigarette manufacturing is among the world's most profitable businesses. In the United States alone, it generated over $55 billion in retail sales in 1988. On average, the profit margin on cigarettes is 35 percent, while in other manufacturing businesses, profit margins of more than 10 percent are considered good (McGill, 1988). Unfortunately, the economic impact of the adverse health consequences of smoking is dwarfed by the economic gains to the tobacco industry.

In the United States, as well as in Australia, Canada, Switzerland, and the United Kingdom, between 3 and 9 percent of total health care costs ($12 to $35 billion per year) are incurred to treat smoking-related ills. In the United States, lost income due to death and lost work due to illness costs another $27 to $61 billion per year. Together, the health care costs and economic losses therefore cost the United States between $38 and $95 billion annually, or about $1.25 to $3.15 over and above the cost of every pack of cigarettes sold (Chandler, 1986). A person under the age of fifty-four who smokes one or two packs a day will incur, on average, up to $34,000 in extra medical bills and lost earnings during his or her lifetime as a direct result of smoking-related heart and lung disease and cancer (Findlay, 1984).

Legal Actions by State and Local Governments

Forty-four states and numerous localities now have ordinances against smoking on public transportation and in other public places, including schools, hospitals, auditoriums, theaters, and government buildings. Moreover, 70 to 80 percent of U.S. corporations—acting under new laws or in response to complaints from workers—have adopted or plan to adopt policies that restrict smoking in offices and other indoor work sites (McFadden, 1989).

The industry-funded Tobacco Institute continues to challenge the validity of findings that report the adverse health consequences of smoking and the legality of smoking bans by companies. Given the magnitude of the economic consequences at stake, such a position is not surprising.

The health consequences of smoking are well understood, but the cost consequences for businesses that allow smoking at work are not, although executives are growing more aware of the cost elements involved. The research outlined in this chapter indicates that the absenteeism rate among smokers averages 50 percent higher than the rate for nonsmokers. Smokers' early disability rates and early mortality rates may be almost 300 percent higher than those for nonsmokers. When these and other secondary consequences of smoking are translated into dollars, the incremental cost to business of hiring smokers is greater than $2,800 per year per employee. This chapter outlines eight sources of these costs and develops dollar estimates based on current research. The eight areas we shall consider are:

- absenteeism
- medical care
- morbidity and premature mortality
- insurance
- on-the-job time lost
- property damage and depreciation
- maintenance
- involuntary smoking

The purpose of this chapter is not to advocate the imposition of no-smoking hiring and working policies. Rather, the purpose is to present current research on the effects of smoking at the work place, to discuss the cost implications for human resource management, and to let each reader decide whether smoking bans are warranted. Top managers of organizations may or may not choose to impose smoking bans, but whatever their decision, it should be based on a rational consideration of the costs and consequences of the issues involved. One final word of caution: the cost estimates described here are just that—estimates. Smoking behavior, employee mix, physical plant, type of production function, and other factors vary widely across business settings. In some circumstances the figures may be gross over- or underestimates, but the factors involved and the methods for estimating their costs are likely to apply across settings. Many of the ideas in this chapter are drawn from the work of William Weiss, who has been responsible for much of the research done in this area. To begin, the easiest consequence of smoking to quantify is employee absenteeism.

ABSENTEEISM

These incremental absenteeism rates illustrate the impact of smoking on employee absenteeism in the United States (Mihalik, 1986; U.S. Department of Health and Human Services, 1979; and U.S. Public Health Service, 1981): male smokers, 56.8 percent; female smokers, 45.1 percent.

Incremental absenteeism is the incidence of smokers' absenteeism over and above that of nonsmoking peers. Combining the cross-sectional averages for all ages and all dosages, 56.8 percent (males) and 45.1 percent (females) yields an absenteeism rate approximately 50 percent greater for smokers in general than for nonsmokers. This differential rate declines sharply after age forty-four, as many absence-prone smokers leave the work force altogether due to death or disability (U.S. Department of Health and Human Services, 1979). Altogether, businesses lose 80 million work days each year to smoking-related illnesses (Mihalik, 1986).

Smoker and nonsmoker absenteeism rates may vary to some extent depending on each organization's mix of ages and education level (highly educated persons have much lower rates of smoking), but on the average each smoker on the payroll will be absent over three days per year more than nonsmokers. This figure is determined as follows:

- Assume an overall company average absenteeism rate of approximately 2.5 percent of scheduled work time.
- Incremental absenteeism for smokers is 50 percent; $0.025 \times 1.5 = 0.0375$, or 3.75 percent of scheduled work time.
- Annual scheduled work time is 2,000 hours (40 hours/week $\times$ 50 weeks).

- Hours absent for nonsmokers: 2,000 × 0.025 = 50 per year.
- Hours absent for smokers: 2,000 × 0.0375 = 75 per year.
- Days absent for nonsmokers: 6.25 per year.
- Days absent for smokers: 9.37 per year.
- Additional days absent for smokers: 3.12 per year.

A detailed analysis of costing employee absenteeism, which was presented in Chapter 3, will not be repeated here. As an example though, adopt the all-company average estimated cost of absenteeism per year per employee ($903) we computed for Presto Electric. Let us assume that 30 percent of Presto's work force smokes; 3,000 × 0.30 = 900 employees. On the average, therefore, the annual cost of absenteeism for each nonsmoker is $903 − 25% = $677.25 and for each of the 900 smokers on the payroll $903 + 25% = $1,128.75.[1] The total additional cost per year per smoker is therefore $451.50.

Virtually every one of these cost estimates has been challenged by pro-smoking forces. Many of their arguments are reasonable, and should be examined critically. With respect to absenteeism, for example, Solomon (1983) argues that in order to make any sense of the incremental cost of absenteeism, we must know *why* workers are absent. Factors such as age, gender, substance abuse, personal problems, general health, job satisfaction, and commuting time—in addition to smoking—have been linked to employee absenteeism. Any particular organization, therefore, must compare the demographic and occupational characteristics of smokers and nonsmokers, and then compare the work-loss rates for equivalent demographic and occupational groups.

MEDICAL CARE, MORBIDITY, AND PREMATURE MORTALITY

Differences between smokers and nonsmokers in the relative incidence of disease (morbidity), need for medical care, and premature mortality affect several factors that ultimately are paid for by the employer. Some of these factors are contributions to health, disability, and life insurance plans; taxes for state and federal unemployment compensation; and taxes

[1]Assuming absenteeism rates and costs are linearly related, a 50 percent differential in absenteeism rates for smokers and nonsmokers yields a savings, on the average, of 25 percent of the estimated all-company average absenteeism cost for nonsmokers, and an incremental cost, on the average, of 25 percent for smokers.

for federal social security and medicare programs. The overall mortality rate for a cross section of adult age groups is 70 percent greater for smokers than nonsmokers (Herzlinger and Calkins, 1986), but this figure underestimates the differential for those in their prime working-age years. It also underestimates the differential for those who smoke excessively. Thus men between the ages of thirty-five and forty-four, for example, who smoke more than forty cigarettes per day suffer a mortality rate 272 percent higher than nonsmoking men in the same age bracket (U.S. Department of Health and Human Services, 1979). Heavy smokers also use the nation's health care system at least 50 percent more than nonsmokers do (Kristein, 1977).

Disability rates are also much higher among smokers. The Alexandria, Virginia, fire department observed that 73 percent of those taking early disability retirement over a five-year period were smokers. This is well above the 33 percent smoking rate in the adult population. The department estimated that early retirements due to disability cost the fire district an additional $300,000 over normal retirements. Another way of stating the problem is that 33 percent of the employees were contributing 73 percent of the early retirements. This represents a disability rate for smokers that is five and a half times greater than that for nonsmokers. To illustrate: suppose 33 percent of a 4,000-person work force smokes (1,332 people). Suppose further that in any given year about 100 employees take early retirement. If, on the average, 73 of the early retirees are smokers, then:

- 1,332/73 or 1 of every 18.2 smokers takes early disability retirement, as compared with
- 2,668/27 or 1 of every 98.8 nonsmoking employees
- 98.8/18.2 = 5.43 times as many smokers as nonsmokers who take early disability retirement

Does not violate ADA?

On the basis of these figures, Fire Chief Charles Rule decided to hire only nonsmokers—a decision that will ultimately save the taxpayers of Alexandria millions of dollars (*Wall Street Journal*, November 7, 1978). By 1989, about thirty fire departments nationwide prohibited new firefighters from smoking on or off the job (Geyelin, 1989).

A mutual agreement between labor and management in Holden, Massachusetts, led to a nonsmokers-only hiring policy for police officers to be written into a union contract (Wald, 1985). The town noted that the last three police officers to retire did so on disability pensions from high blood pressure or heart disease. Under Massachusetts law, both disorders are presumed to be job-related. Two of the three men smoked. Their pensions are set at 72 percent of the officers' regular salary for life—an aggregate cost of $36,000 a year, plus increases to make up for inflation, for as long as they live. One man is in his early forties, and the others are in their early fifties. Finally, $36,000 represents 9 percent of the police department's annual personnel budget. Is it any surprise that the town took action to limit its future liabilities?

For purposes of estimating the costs of increased medical care, morbidity, and premature mortality for smokers over nonsmokers, assume that 50 percent of all savings flow directly to the employer. Luce and Schweitzer (1978) reported in the *New England Journal of Medicine* that, on the average, smokers require an additional $358 per person per year for medical care alone, and an additional $1,186 per year for discounted lost earnings due to morbidity and premature mortality.[2] Reductions in the extra costs of medical care required by smokers—contributions to health, disability, and life insurance plans; taxes for state and federal unemployment compensation; and taxes for federal social security and medicare programs—certainly represent tangible savings to employers. (To some extent, these costs have been included previously in the costs of incremental absenteeism for smokers.) For example, one company estimated that its smoking control program reduced payments for health insurance by $73 *per employee* (not just per smoker) per year (Herzlinger and Calkins, 1986). In reference to the discounted lost earnings argument, Solomon (1983) has observed that if workers fail to earn wages because they are ill or because they die, the "lost" earnings are a private cost to them, not a cost to their employers. True enough, but the employer suffers an opportunity cost associated with the lost productivity of the ill or deceased worker. For purposes of establishing savings to the firm, 50 percent of the costs associated with extra medical care and discounted lost earnings is a reasonable compromise. It may be a while before the entire $772 [($358 + $1,186) × 0.50] per employee is realized by the organization, but the saving does represent a realistic objective in long-range policy projections.

Industries that invest substantial resources in training personnel should consider carefully the early disability and mortality differentials between smokers and nonsmokers at various age intervals. Consider an example presented by Weiss (1981c):

[2]Estimates are in 1990 dollars. Lost earnings are assumed to approximate the value lost to the employer from premature retirement or death, reflecting both the costs of investments in human resource development (amortized over a shorter time span than for nonsmokers) and the lost return for early termination of the employee's services.

> Large public accounting firms defend their "youth only" hiring practices because of the 10 to 15 years needed to develop the skills and judgment required of partners. Wanting to enjoy at least 20 years of a partner's peak productivity makes it mandatory to begin the training process at an early age, preferably early twenties. If firms spent more time studying the disability and mortality rates during this period of peak productivity (ages 35–55), they might discover that age is not the only agent causing accountants to decay. The chance of living to take that mandatory retirement, for a 22-year-old smoker, is only one third of that for a 22-year-old nonsmoker. Is it worth the substantial investment to train young smokers to be good accountants (in the hereafter)? (p. 6)

OTHER INSURANCE COSTS

Other opportunity costs besides lost earnings are associated with higher rates of mortality and disability among smokers. Major insurance companies now offer substantial discounts to nonsmokers. For example, on life insurance premiums the State Mutual Life Assurance Company of America is offering policies to nonsmokers at a cost 30 percent less than comparable coverage for smokers. The reduced rates are the result of an extensive study by the company that shows that death rates in all age categories were more than twice as high for smokers than for nonsmokers. Firms that have rigid no-smoking policies can negotiate fire insurance premium reductions of 25 percent and more (Weiss, 1981a).

Economist Marvin Kristein of the American Health Foundation estimates that smokers cost an extra $140 (in 1990 dollars) per year in other insurance costs (Kristein, 1980). Accidental injury and related workers' compensation costs constitute half of this cost per year per smoker, and the remaining half is due to higher insurance premiums for fire, life, and wage continuation policies. These totals were based on studies showing that smokers have twice the accident rate of nonsmokers due to carelessness caused by attention loss, eye irritation, coughing, and hand interference.

ON-THE-JOB TIME LOST

Estimates of the amount of on-the-job time lost to the smoking ritual—lighting, puffing, informal breaks—vary among sources from a low of 8 minutes per day (Kristein, 1980) to a high of 15 to 30 minutes per hour

(Weiss, 1980). The latter estimate was reported by a general contractor in Seattle who stopped taking bids from smokers after firing a dry-wall craftsman who lost 30 minutes of every hour to his smoking habit. As a basis for our cost estimate, let us use a conservative compromise of 30 minutes per day for cigarette smokers and 55 minutes per day for pipe smokers, as reported by the *Wall Street Journal* ("Labor Letter," May 8, 1979).

If 30 minutes of every 8-hour work day are lost to the smoking ritual, then in a 250-day work year, 30 × 250 or 7,500 minutes are lost. Over a 120,000-minute work year this represents a 6.25 percent productivity loss. Pipe smokers lose approximately 11.25 percent of the work year. Thus, assuming all other factors remain constant (that is, assuming all nonsmokers do not have a similar time-consuming habit, like drinking coffee), eight nonsmokers can do the work of nine pipe smokers. To carry this example further, if we assume that one of every five smokers puffs a pipe, then a weighted average of

$$\begin{aligned} 0.80 \times 30 &= 24 \\ 0.20 \times 55 &= \underline{11} \\ & \quad 35 \text{ minutes per day is lost to smoking.} \end{aligned}$$

In a 480-minute (8-hour) day, then 35/480 or 0.072916 of each day is lost to the smoking ritual. This represents 18.2 days per year in lost productivity:

$$\begin{aligned} &120{,}000 \text{ minutes per work year} \\ &\qquad \times 0.072916 = 8{,}749 \text{ minutes per year loss} \\ &\quad 8{,}749 \text{ minutes per year} \\ &\div 480 \text{ minutes per work day} = 18.2 \text{ days/year} \end{aligned}$$

Assuming an overall company average annual cost of absenteeism per employee of $903 (see Chapter 3) and an average of 6.25 days absent per year per employee, each day's absence costs the firm about $145. Therefore, 18.2 days costs employers an additional $2,639 per year per smoker. For jobs in construction and the trades where tools go down when smokers light up, the cost may be considerably higher (Weiss and Miller, 1985).

Is this figure of $2,639 realistic? Probably not, for it assumes that nonsmokers do not take an equivalent 18.2 days per year for other forms of leisure (Solomon, 1983). Hence, while organizations do not get eight full hours of productivity from workers, and computing the associated dollar cost to employers of the productivity loss can be enlightening, such lost time cannot reasonably be ascribed *solely* to smoking. Moreover, consider the results of a productivity analysis of fifty-three credit managers at the Farm Credit Services bank. The study was designed to assess relationships between health and productivity. As expected, factors such as regular exercise, sleeping between six and seven hours per night, and refraining from between-meal snacks were associated with increased productivity. The study also found—unexpectedly—that smokers are 2.5 percent *more effective* at making the best use of their time ("Study," 1984). In view of these findings, we will not consider the dollar costs in productivity associated with on-the-job time lost due to smoking in our overall estimate of the cost of smoking at work.

PROPERTY DAMAGE, DEPRECIATION, AND MAINTENANCE

The estimates to be described in this category are based upon interviews reported by Weiss (1981a) with business owners and executives of organizations that have implemented no-smoking policies. In some cases the estimates admittedly are rough, but as more firms begin to track costs in this category from before to after implementing smoking bans, the accuracy of the data will improve.

Property damage and depreciation are roughly equivalent phenomena for estimating incremental costs for most businesses.[3] Furniture, carpeting, and draperies are generally replaced when damaged, and the damage often results from cigarette burns. Estimates of the useful lives of commercial furnishings are based primarily on the employer's tolerance for burn spots and on the expected frequency of the appearance of burns. Since no-smoking policies eliminate a primary cause of depreciation, commercial furnishings should have longer useful lives.

The costs of removing tobacco odors should be considered. Tobacco odors are caused primarily by pyridine, a strong irritant that is produced when nicotine burns. Consider the effects on the operation of an air conditioner, for example. Controlled studies have shown that when someone lights a cigarette, cigar, or pipe in an air-conditioned environment, the air conditioning demands can jump as much as six times above the normal requirement in order to control odor (American Lung Association, 1977). This means that a smoke-free building can be constructed at a cost 30 percent less than one that is built to accommodate smokers ("No Smoking," 1983).

[3]Depreciation, as used in estimating out-of-pocket costs, refers to *actual* deterioration of an asset's usefulness, as opposed to its usage in accounting terminology.

At Radar Electric Company in Seattle, for example, intervals between furniture and fixture replacements are expected to at least triple as a result of the company's no-smoking policy. Firms that employ costly precision machinery have long recognized the damage that can be caused by smoke merely circulating in the surrounding air. Interview results indicate that employers expect to save at least $500 per smoker per year from the longer intervals between replacement of furnishings and equipment. This excludes occasional patch-up work on carpeting, which can run as high as $100 per repair.

Maintenance is another area of savings for smoke-free businesses. For example, Merle Norman Cosmetics trimmed general housekeeping maintenance costs by 10 percent per year since implementing its smoking ban in 1976 (*Wall Street Journal*, November 7, 1978). Routine cleaning may be reduced by as much as 60 percent, due in part (according to interviews with owners of smoke-free businesses) to a more cleanliness-conscious work force when smoking is banned (Weiss and Miller, 1985). Some organizations are able to limit the washing of interior glass surfaces (windows, showcases) to an annual, instead of monthly, routine. Repainting of interior surfaces is also required less often.

Estimates of savings resulting from reduced maintenance are again rough, but $500 per smoker was seen as reasonable by interviewees. One employer who had forty smokers on his payroll before implementing a strict no-smoking policy was able to reduce his cleaning force by one person and reduce his average painting and window-washing work by two-thirds, thereby saving $30,000 per year from maintenance alone—$750 per smoker. Another study reported that the combined costs of extra insurance and maintenance were $650 per smoker ("An Economic Case," 1986). A $500 per smoker per year figure for savings in maintenance costs alone seems to be a reasonably conservative estimate.

INVOLUNTARY SMOKING AND EMPLOYEE MORALE

Despite compelling evidence, a number of employers still are oblivious to the health hazard imposed on nonsmokers who live and work around smokers. A study published in the *New England Journal of Medicine* concluded that "the deleterious effects of passive smoking may occur in proportion to the exposure of nonsmokers to smokers in the home, the work place, and the community . . . with exposure to a two-pack-a-day smoker equivalent to smoking three cigarettes a day" (Russell, 1984). This damage to nonsmokers is approximately one-fifth of that to normal smokers (Wynder and Stellman, 1977). Another study, published in the scientific journal *Environment International*, estimated that 46,000 nonsmoking Americans die each year from diseases induced by environmental tobacco smoke. Roughly 32,000 of those deaths are from heart disease, 3,000 are from lung cancers, and another 11,000 are blamed on tobacco-induced cancers other than lung cancer (Graf, 1989).

Evidence like this is profoundly affecting Americans' attitudes about passive smoking. According to the American Lung Association, 87 percent of Americans—smokers and nonsmokers—believe that all companies either should prohibit smoking or restrict it to designated areas ("Will Smoking," 1987).

To gauge the impact of involuntary smoking on business costs, let us apply the one-fifth figure (Wynder and Stellman, 1977) to our estimate of incremental costs from excess medical care, discounted lost earnings from morbidity and premature mortality, and incremental absenteeism.

medical care ($358 × 0.50)	$179
morbidity and premature mortality (discounted lost earnings) ($1,186 × 0.50)	593
absenteeism	451
total incremental cost	$1,223

total incremental cost ($1,223) × ⅕ = $245

Thus, on the average, each smoker is increasing the per worker expenses of nonsmokers by $245 per year. Furthermore, since two of every three workers are nonsmokers, the incremental cost due to their health impairment is $490 per smoker per year.

Although the incremental costs associated with smoking at the work place may appear substantial thus far, employers who have imposed no-smoking policies insist that the major savings, by far, stem from higher employee morale. They argue that smoke-free environments are clean, healthy, and conducive to good working relationships (Weiss, 1981b), but no cost data associated with higher morale are offered. This is understandable, since the benefits of higher morale are difficult to quantify (see Chapter 5). The important point for the human resource manager is that the total cost presented in Exhibit 4.1 is probably a conservative estimate, for it does not include what most employers regard as the most substantial savings of a no-smoking policy.

EXHIBIT 4.1 Additional annual cost of employing smokers and allowing smoking at the work place

Absenteeism	$451[a]
Medical care	179[b]
Morbidity and premature mortality (discounted lost earnings)	593[b]
Insurance (excluding health)	140[c]
On-the-job time lost ($2,639)	0[a]
Property damage and depreciation	500[d]
Maintenance	500[d]
Involuntary smoking	490[e]
Total cost per smoker per year	$2,853

[a]Assumes that overall company average cost of absenteeism is $903 per year per employee and that smokers are absent 50 percent more often.

[b]Based on Luce and Schweitzer (1978) adjusted for 1990 dollars.

[c]Based on Kristein (1980) adjusted for 1990 dollars.

[d]Based on interviews by Weiss (1981a).

[e]Based on Wynder and Stellman (1977) and Luce and Schweitzer (1978).

Source: Adapted from Weiss, W. L. (1981, May). Can you afford to hire smokers? The May 1981 issue of *Personnel Administrator*, copyright 1981, the American Society for Personnel Administration.

AGGREGATE COSTS OF SMOKING AT THE WORK PLACE

The additional yearly costs associated with each smoker on the payroll are summarized in Exhibit 4.1. Another way of viewing the entries in the exhibit is the cost savings that employers might expect from a policy that prohibits smoking on company premises and restricts all future hiring to nonsmokers.

As noted earlier, nonsmokers now constitute two-thirds of the adult population in the United States.

As Exhibit 4.1 indicates, the estimated total additional annual cost per smoker is $2,853. An interval of estimates may be more representative. Published studies estimate that the incremental costs associated with hiring smokers range from $624 to $4,500 per year (Nichter, 1989). The Boeing Company estimates it will save $10 million per year by implementing a smoking ban among its 85,000 employees. Further, an in-house survey for Goodyear estimated that the 2,960 employees who smoke at its Akron headquarters cost the company about $2 million a year in smoking-related problems. Indeed, these costs might be much higher in industries in which smoking may aggravate occupational diseases, such as the asbestos and textile industries (Margolick, 1985).

IS A SMOKING BAN LEGAL?

As noted earlier, some firms have banned altogether smoking by customers, clients, or employees on company premises. Indeed, a growing number of firms are refusing to hire smokers (1 percent in 1987, 6 percent in 1989; Geyelin, 1989)—but are such bans legal? Given the power of the tobacco industry, a Supreme Court test is almost inevitable, although no such case has yet been decided. A key legal question is whether a ban on hiring smokers is an invasion of privacy. Legal specialists say that any such challenge will have a better chance against a public employer than a private one, because private companies are covered by legislation, not by constitutional prohibitions against intrusive or discriminatory government behavior.

In special circumstances, however, the policy of even a public agency to hire only nonsmokers may be upheld. Thus, an Oklahoma City firefighter trainee was fired for smoking on an off-duty lunch break, in violation of the fire department's ban on all smoking activity on or off the job. The trainee fought his dismissal all the way to a federal appeals court in Denver, claiming that his rights to liberty and privacy were infringed. The appeals court rejected that argument, reasoning that the fire department's policy was reasonably intended to promote the health of its new recruits—a consideration that the court said outweighed the trainee's right to smoke (Geyelin, 1989).

Unions have been more accommodating. According to the AFL-CIO, no-smoking rules raise contradictory issues for union members. "The trade union principle is [that] what the officers do off duty is none of the employer's business. . . . The higher trade union principle is that we're for whatever a group of members agrees to" (Wald, 1985, p. 33L).

On the other side, nonsmokers and employers raise two countervailing arguments: the rights of nonsmokers, whose health is impaired by sidestream and mainstream inhalation,[4] and the incremental costs to em-

[4] Sidestream smoke goes directly into the air from the burning end of a cigarette, cigar, or pipe. Mainstream smoke is that which the smoker puffs through the mouthpiece when he or she inhales or puffs—and then exhales.

ployers. In the last decade, for example, nonsmokers successfully have sued companies that failed to protect them from the fumes created by smokers. In most of the suits, nonsmokers argued that the sidestream smoke from their co-workers' cigarettes had either created or worsened a physical disability. By failing to segregate smokers, the nonsmokers claimed, employers violated their duty to provide a safe and healthy work environment. They asked the court to order the employer to provide a smoke-free environment—and won (Feaver, 1988). Some firms have found the cost of juggling desks too high and have banned smoking entirely. Pacific Northwest Bell, with headquarters in Seattle, outlawed smoking when it learned that its remodeling costs would be $60,000.

At least three important lessons can be learned from firms that have imposed restrictions on smoking. (1) Involve both smokers and nonsmokers in drafting company regulations. (2) Be firm, but allow ample time for workers to become accustomed to new limits, perhaps by gradually introducing steps. This is exactly the approach taken by Ford Motor Company as it introduced restrictions covering over 160,000 workers (Levin, 1989). (3) Employers should simultaneously offer and promote stop-smoking programs. Studies have also shown that while peer pressure is an important element in enforcing "clean air" programs, peer support for smokers who are struggling to quit is helpful too. In many instances, some sympathy, understanding, and encouragement can often go farther than open confrontation (Malcolm, 1987).

Yet the overwhelming majority of organizations in the United States and abroad permit smoking. In some of these firms, smoking policies are the result of a rational weighing of the evidence. In one survey, for example, 24 percent of the responding companies said that they had considered and rejected a smoking policy for the work place. They did so for the following reasons: Employees wouldn't accept it (59%); Employees can handle problems on their own (58%); It's too difficult to implement (39%); They haven't received any complaints about smoking (29%); and It would decrease morale (20%) ("Smoking Policies," 1985). No one can guarantee that a smoking ban will immediately improve annual profits by $2,853 per reformed, or displaced, smoker. On the other hand, the accumulated evidence among firms that have imposed such bans indicates the following trends:

- Personnel costs decline (absenteeism, incidence of disease, and accidents).
- Maintenance costs decline.

- Actual physical depreciation on furniture and equipment slows substantially.
- Insurance rates can be decreased through renegotiation for new fire, health, accident, and disability coverage.
- Employee morale improves.
- Customers and clients adjust without adverse repercussions.

Smoking is a matter of individual choice in most organizations, and certainly there are other ways to increase productivity and profits without imposing a smoking ban. On the other hand, policy makers owe it to their organizations, to their employees, and to their stockholders to evaluate all of the available evidence bearing on this issue before adopting policies for or against smoking.

EXERCISES

1. You are the president and chief executive officer of a forty-person management consulting firm. Company headquarters consist of a six-room suite of offices in a downtown professional building. Most of your people are out in the field on business trips on any given day. Your work force is composed of the following:

Males	*Females*
10 aged 24–44	11 aged 24–44
14 aged 45–65	5 aged 45–65

Approximately one-third of each group (male-female) smokes. Write a one- to two-page memorandum to your employees explaining your reasoning for *not* imposing a smoking ban.

2. The Meyers Company employs 2,800 workers in the manufacture of precision components for medical and surgical equipment. About half the workers are male, most in their twenties and thirties. Two workers staff each work station, and work stations are spaced every six feet. Last month the company imposed a smoking ban, and the workers' union immediately filed a grievance on behalf of the 40 percent of the work force that smokes. As a personnel specialist assigned to the labor relations section, write a short paper summarizing management's arguments for the smoking ban.

3. As a staff member of the General Accounting Office of the federal government, your assignment is to review the evidence for and against smoking at the work place and prepare a report for use in upcoming congressional hearings on the subject. A smoking ban, if adopted, will affect over one million federal workers.

You are a member of one four-to-six person team working at a federal agency in Washington, D.C. Divide up the work any way you'd like, but be sure that your final report represents a balanced view of both sides of the issue.

REFERENCES

American Lung Association. (1977). *Second-hand smoke*. New York: American Lung Association.

An economic case for banning smoking? (1986, January 18). *Science News, 129* (1), 40.

CHANDLER, W.U. (1986, July). The devastating costs of tobacco addiction. *USA Today Magazine*, Vol. 115, No. 2494, pp. 80–81.

Crusade: Smoke-free USA. (1990, February 21). *USA Today*, pp. 1a, 6a.

FEAVER, T. (1988, May). *Smoking in the workplace*. Unpublished manuscript, Executive MBA Program, University of Colorado.

FINDLAY, S. (1984, March 27). Two packs a day can cost you $34,000. *USA Today*, p. 3.

GEYELIN, M. (1989, April 21). The job is yours—unless you smoke. *Wall Street Journal*, p. B1.

GORMAN, C. (1988, May 30). Why it's so hard to quit smoking. *Time*, p. 56.

GRAF, T. (1989, January 29). Indoor smoke ranks among top health dangers. *Denver Post*, pp. 1H–2H.

HERZLINGER, R. E., and CALKINS, D. (1986). How companies tackle health care costs: Part III. *Harvard Business Review, 64* (1), 70–80.

KRISTEIN, M. M. (1977). Economic issues in prevention. *Preventive Medicine, 6*, 252–264.

KRISTEIN, M. M. (1980, November 13). *How much can business expect to earn from smoking cessation*? Paper presented at the Connecticut Lung Association Conference, "Smoking in the Workplace," New Haven, Connecticut.

Labor letter. (1979, May 8). *Wall Street Journal*, p. 1.

LEARY, W. E. (1987, November 19). Study details risk to women smokers. *New York Times*, p. A21.

LEVIN, D. P. (1989, April 22). Ford to ban smoking in offices by Jan. 1. *New York Times*, p. 27.

LUCE, B. R., and SCHWEITZER, S. O. (1978, March 9). Smoking and alcohol abuse: A comparison of their economic consequences. *The New England Journal of Medicine*, 569–571.

MALCOLM, A. H. (1987, February 20). Mounting drive on smoking stirs tensions in workplace. *New York Times*, pp. A1, A16.

MARGOLICK, D. (1985, March 27). Antismoking climate is encouraging suits against the tobacco industry. *New York Times*, pp. 1C–3C.

MCFADDEN, R. D. (1989, September 15). Smoking restrictions increased dramatically in recent years. *New York Times*, p. A20.

MCGILL, D. C. (1988, December 24). Cigarette industry financing wide war on smoking bans. *New York Times*, pp. 1, 37.

MIHALIK, M. (1986). Clearing the air at work. *Prevention Magazine*, *38* (4), 61–63.

New AMA journal deals entirely with risks of smoking. (1986, March 5). *Denver Post*, p. 15A.

NICHTER, R. (1989). *Guide to a smoke-free workplace*. Boulder, CO: GASP of Colorado.

No smoking signals from the workplace. (1983, September). *Saturday Evening Post*, *255* (No. 6), pp. 36–40.

RUSSELL, C. (1984, September 27). Exposure to smoke affects health. *Washington Post*, p. A2.

Smoking policies. (1985, September 3). *Wall Street Journal*, p. 23.

SOLOMON, L. (1983). The other side of the smoking worker controversy. *Personnel Administrator*, *28*, 72, 73, 101.

Study indicates smoking and age speed up workers. (1984, October 24). *Denver Post*, p. 21A.

TOUFEXIS, A. (1989, January 23). A not-so-happy anniversary. *Time*, p. 54.

U.S. Department of Health and Human Services. (1979). *Smoking and health: A report of the surgeon general*. Washington, D.C.: Government Printing Office.

U.S. Public Health Service. (1981). *The health consequences of smoking for women*. Washington, D.C.: U.S. Government Printing Office.

WALD, M. L. (1985, November 16). Pact with police bars smoking on or off job. *New York Times*, p. 33L.

Wall Street Journal. (1978, November 7). p. 1.

WEISS, W. L. (1981). Can you afford to hire smokers? *Personnel Administrator*, *26* (5), 71–78. (a)

WEISS, W. L. (1981, March). Profits up in smoke. *Personnel Journal*, 60. (b)

WEISS, W. L. (1981, February). *Warning: Smoking is hazardous to your business*. Unpublished manuscript, Albers Graduate School of Business, Seattle University, Seattle. (c)

WEISS, W. L. and MILLER, B. W. (1985). *The smoke-free workplace*. Buffalo, NY: Prometheus.

Will smoking hinder you in a job search? (1987, December). *Glamour*, p. 110.

WYNDER, E. L., and STELLMAN, S. D. (1977, December). Comparative epidemiology of tobacco-related cancers. *Cancer Research*, 37, 4608–4622.

Yet another deadly link. (1989, March 27). *Time*, p. 82.

PART II

Costing EAPs and Wellness Programs, Attitudes, and Collectively Bargained Agreements

5

Costing the Effects of Employee Assistance and Wellness Programs

"The corporate culture has historically told employees to leave their personal problems at home. But for most employees, that's no longer possible, because nobody is at home to solve those problems" (*Wall Street Journal*, January 9, 1990, p. B1.). Consider these sobering facts:

1. Substance abuse and mental illness cost U.S. companies over $100 billion per year, or at least $3,000 per employee.

2. More than 100 million work hours are lost in any given week because of these problems according to the Bureau of Labor Statistics ("Employee," 1989).

3. As a consequence of employee alcohol and drug abuse, U.S. businesses are estimated to suffer annual productivity losses of $30.1 billion (Farkas, 1989).

4. In the aggregate, personal problems are estimated to affect 18 percent of the workforce, resulting in a productivity loss of 25 percent (Masi, 1984).

5. Among substance abusers, absenteeism is sixteen times greater and the accident rate is 400 percent greater than that of the nonabusing population of employees (Quayle, 1983). Further, the problem drinker uses eight times more medical care (Cherskov, 1987).

6. Substance abuse among General Motors' 472,000 workers and their dependents cost the automotive company $600 million in 1988 ("Substance," 1988).

7. More than one woman in ten is assaulted by her companion each year, and one-third of this group, 1.8 million women, is severely attacked. The abuse exists at every level of society, and the effects spill over into the workplace. In a study of 50 battered women in New York, lost work time was common. Half the women said they missed an average of at least three days of work per month because of abuse at home; 64 percent said they were late to work because of violence; 75 percent said they phoned friends, counselors, physicians, and lawyers on company time, because they could not do so at home (Freudenheim, 1988).

Statistics like these lead to one inescapable conclusion: the personal problems of troubled employees have a devastating economic impact on employers. To deal with these problems, more and more employers have adopted programs that focus either on rehabilitation (employee assistance programs, or EAPs) or on prevention (wellness programs). In this chapter, our objective is not to describe the structure, content, or operational features of such programs, but rather to present methods for estimating their economic impact at the level of the individual firm. In the first part of the chapter, we will focus on EAPs, and in the second part of the chapter, we will focus on wellness programs.

EAPs—PREVALENCE, ATTRIBUTES, COSTS, AND GENERAL BENEFITS

An EAP is a system that provides confidential, professional care to employees whose job performance is or may become adversely affected by a variety of personal problems. Supervisors are taught to look for symptoms of declining work performance such as the following, and then to refer employees to the EAP for professional help: predictable absenteeism patterns (for example, Mondays, Fridays, or days before or after holidays), unexcused or frequent absences, tardiness and early departures, arguments with fellow employees, causing injuries to other employees through negligence, poor judgments and bad decisions, unusual on-the-job accidents, increased spoilage or breaking of equipment through negligence, involvements with the law, or deteriorating personal appearance (Filipowicz, 1987).

Two major forces, legal and economic, have combined to fuel the development of EAPs. In the legal arena, civil rights legislation, federal rehabilitation laws, and erosion of the at-will doctrine severely constrain an employer's ability to fire employees (Farkas, 1989). Employers are becoming more economically aware of the considerable "sunk" costs invested in employees in the form of recruitment, selection, and training. They are also well aware of the substantial costs of replacing employees who leave (see Chapter 2). For these reasons, employers are finding that rehabilitation of troubled employees is more cost effective than simply firing them. As of 1989, there were 14,000 to 17,000 EAPs in the United States, and many other such programs in Canada as well (Sperling, 1989).

Critical Attributes for a Successful EAP

One review found ten critical attributes for a successful EAP (Dickman and Emener, 1982): top management backing, labor support, confidentiality of EAP data, easy access, supervisor training, union steward training (if employees are so represented), insurance involvement, breadth of service components (to handle a wide variety of problems), professional leadership of the EAP, and follow-up/evaluation to measure the effectiveness of the program.

Costs and General Benefits

A cost evaluation of an EAP offered by an outside agency (Professional Employee Advisement Program) revealed an annual charge of $30 to $40 per employee (Leib, 1986). For this fee, each employee is entitled to receive:

- three sessions of assessment and referral per year with a licensed clinician
- twenty-four hour, seven-day-a-week telephone hot line with a guaranteed two-hour response time
- emergency consultation
- mailings to each employee's home four times per year outlining the provisions of the EAP
- "check stuffers"—promotional inserts about the EAP in weekly pay envelopes
- three workshops per year for employees about their EAP; three for supervisors on how to identify troubled employees
- guaranteed confidentiality

The program managers also found that employees use the EAP for the following reasons: drug and alcohol problems (38 percent), domestic problems (20 percent), problems with one's children (24 percent), and job stress (18 percent). It is important to emphasize that program costs, as well as reasons for using an EAP, are both likely to vary across situations. The figures above are merely illustrative.

Returns on investment in EAPs have fluctuated wildly from $2 to $20 returned for every $1 invested. Savings purportedly derive from improved attendance, reduced use of the health plan, and greater productivity (Klarreich et al., 1987a).

DIFFICULTIES IN EVALUATING EAPs

Actual results may not be quite as rosy as have been reported in the literature or in the media. Evaluation may be ex-ante (estimates computed before implementation of an EAP) or ex-post (measurement of the costs and benefits of actual program operations and impacts after the fact). Evaluation may be expressed in qualitative terms or in quantitative terms.

If evaluation is expressed in quantitative terms—as many operating executives demand—there are two major problems. One is how to establish all program costs and benefits. To establish its costs, an EAP must incorporate an information system that can track factors such as insurance use, absenteeism, performance analysis, accidents, and attendance data. A second problem is how to express and translate the costs and benefits into monetary values. Benefits derived from an EAP may be very difficult to translate into economic terms. In addition, unless proper experimental controls are exercised, cause–effect relations between EAP involvement and one or more dependent variables may be difficult or impossible to identify. These ideas are summarized in Exhibit 5.1.

In the following nine sections, therefore, we will present detailed methods for expressing the returns of EAPs in economic terms for the following dependent variables: productivity, turnover, unemployment costs, outpatient versus inpatient treatment for substance abuse, absenteeism, savings in supervisors' time, accidents, savings in training and replacement costs, and the use of insurance benefits.

Productivity

The productivity losses associated with troubled employees can be staggering. One method for determining the productivity cost (ex-ante) attributable to employees who abuse alcohol was developed by Parker et al.

EXHIBIT 5.1 Three difficulties in evaluating EAPs

1. Identification of *all* program costs and benefits
2. Expression of costs and benefits in economic terms
3. Demonstration that implementation of the EAP has caused changes in outcomes of interest

(1987). They recommend that the following formula be computed separately for each age–gender cohort. Costs for all age–gender cohorts should then be summed.

Equation 1

No. of workers in age–gender cohort in workforce
× Proportion of workers in age–gender cohort with alcohol abuse problems
× Annual earnings
× Productivity decrease attributable to alcohol
= Cost of alcohol-related reduced productivity

Two key inputs to this formula that might be difficult to acquire are (1) the proportion of workers in each age–gender cohort with alcohol abuse problems, and (2) the productivity decrease attributable to alcohol. Over all cohorts, however, national figures suggest that 5 to 10 percent of a typical work force suffers from alcohol abuse ("Substance Abuse," 1988) and that the figure may be as high as 10 to 15 percent among construction workers ("Labor Letter," 1988). In well-controlled studies, productivity losses attributable to alcohol abuse have ranged from 14 to 21 percent (Parker et al., 1988). However, Masi (1984) suggested that personal problems, *in toto*, affect 18 percent of the work force resulting in an estimated productivity loss of 25 percent. It is important to note that the latter figure is an *estimate*, not a precise number derived on the basis of controlled research. It is used in the calculations shown below simply for illustrative purposes. Keep this in mind in analyzing the example, and in applying the formula to actual work situations.

For one age–gender cohort in any given workforce, inputs to Equation 1 might be:

100 workers in age–gender cohort in work force
× 10% with alcohol abuse problems
× Annual earnings of $25,000 per worker in cohort
× 20% Productivity decrease attributable to alcohol
= Cost of alcohol-related reduced productivity of $50,000

At a more general level, the City of Phoenix, through its Project Concern, developed the following formula to determine the costs due to troubled employees, as well as (ex-ante) the amount of money that could be saved in terms of improved productivity through an EAP (Wagner, 1987):

Equation 2

1. To determine average annual wage of employees, divide average total number of employees into annual payroll for employees.
2. To obtain the payroll for troubled employees, multiply average annual wage by 18 percent of the total number of employees (average percentage of troubled employees identified by Masi, 1984).
3. To determine present loss due to troubled employees, multiply result of step 2 by 25 percent (average productivity loss estimated by Masi, 1984).
4. To identify potential amount saved per year by an EAP, multiply the result of step 3 by 50 percent (actual success rate reported by Project Concern).

To illustrate, let us assume that a firm employs 100 workers, at an annual payroll cost of $2.5 million, or $25,000 per worker (step 1). To calculate the payroll for troubled employees, let us assume that 18 percent or 18 workers are troubled × $25,000 annual earnings/worker = $450,000 (step 2). To determine the present cost of reduced productivity for these troubled workers, multiply $450,000 × 25 percent = $112,500. Finally, to determine the potential amount of money that could be saved per year through an EAP, multiply $112,500 × 50 percent = $56,250.

Note that potential savings reflect only the cost of labor, and labor is only one component of productivity. Such savings are therefore conservative, for they do not reflect the contribution of improved use of capital and equipment that can be realized by a fully productive employee.

Turnover

Turnover savings realized through the implementation of an EAP may be termed "opportunity savings" because they reflect costs that were not actually incurred. An example of such ex-post evaluation was provided by St. Benedict's Hospital in Ogden, Utah (Featherston and Bednarek, 1987). Over the two-year period of the study, the hospital's turnover rate averaged 31 percent. Using this rate, out of sixty-seven employees who were involved with the EAP, 67 × 31 percent = about 21 who should have quit. Since only six actually did quit, the fifteen expected turnovers were avoided through EAP counseling. Replacement costs for nursing and nonnursing employees averaged $1,900. Hence, $1,900 × 15 = $28,500 (excluding the cost of the EAP program itself).

Unemployment Compensation

The St. Benedict's Hospital study reported that employees who quit drew unemployment compensation for an average of six weeks. Using the hospital's average hourly wage rate at the time of the study, $6.50 × 15 people × 40 hours/week × 6 weeks = $23,400. Obviously, this figure could be considerably larger if either the hourly rate, the number of employees saved, or the duration of the unemployment compensation were to increase.

Outpatient Versus Inpatient Treatment for Substance Abuse

There is a large difference in costs between outpatient and inpatient treatment for substance abuse. For example, outpatient costs range from $5 to $100 per counseling session, and generally last from six weeks to one and one-half years. The cost of a typical month-long residential program ranges from $7,000 to $12,000 or more (Sperling, 1989).

Given that the costs of treatment for psychiatric and substance abuse are rising at about twice the rate of medical inflation (Pearson, 1989), which is rising at two to three times the rate of inflation in general, employers must investigate less costly alternatives. For example, preferred provider organizations can save about 35 percent of the total costs of inpatient care (Pearson, 1989). United Technologies did even better (Bensinger and Pilkington, 1985). After examining literature for the two types of treatment showing that the relative levels of effectiveness are no different, the firm chose to adopt an outpatient treatment program. Over a one-year period, this program resulted in 50 percent less time off the job for treatment, 50 percent fewer days of sick pay (relative to what would have been incurred with an inpatient program), and no out-of-pocket expenses for treated employees.

United Technologies treats approximately 225 employees for substance abuse each year, at a cost differential of between $2,300 and $8,800 per treated employee per year, relative to the cost of an inpatient residential program. These savings therefore total between $500,000 and $2 million in direct treatment costs each year.

Absenteeism

Klarreich et al. (1987b) studied the impact of a form of psychotherapy known as rational–emotive therapy (RET) applied in the context of an in-house EAP. Their three-year (ex-post) study investigated the impact of RET in a large oil company. The population served by the EAP consisted of about 2,500 white collar, nonunion personnel in a major metropolitan area. During the three-year study, the program serviced 600 employees, 96 percent of whom had problems other than alcohol or drugs. The problems were personal–emotional (54 percent), job-related behavior (22 percent), marital or family (20 percent), and alcohol or drugs (4 percent). The average number of sessions per client over the three-year period was 4.1.

Absenteeism data were available for two of the three years of the study. During this time, 431 employees used the EAP, and 364 completed RET counseling. Absenteeism data were complete and available for 295 of these emloyees. Attrition was due to the fact that data had to be available for one year prior to involvement with the EAP and one year after it.

One year prior to their involvement with the EAP, these 295 employees were absent a total of 3,033 days. One year after their involvement, the same 295 employees were absent only a total of 878 days, a reduction of 74 percent. According to the company's accounting department, one day of absence costs an average of $144.50. When this value is multiplied by the number of days of absenteeism saved (2,155), the result is $311,398 for the days saved. This estimate is conservative because complete data were not available for the 364 employees who completed treatment. However, the figure is overstated to the extent that the costs of the therapy sessions themselves were not taken into account.

Savings in Supervisors' Time

In the same study, Klarreich et al. (1987b) reasoned that if the EAP were not available, supervisors would be forced to deal with employee problems. The minimum time in hours that supervisors did not have to deal with problems is equal to the total number of hours spent in counseling sessions for the employees in the study (1,880 hours). Thus, the supervisors had at least 1,880 hours to carry out their duties more effectively. The average cost of one hour of supervisory time was $23.80. Therefore, $23.80 × 1,880 = $44,744, which the authors reported as "the net benefit in dollars." The term "net" implies that the cost of the program itself was subtracted from the total benefits. Since this cost was not reported, we really do not know what the savings (if any) in supervisory time might have been.

Accidents

One might expect that troubled employees would be involved in more on-the-job accidents than employees who are not troubled. An EAP might be able to save a company money if the number of accidents could be reduced. In fact, statistics bear this out, as illustrated in a three-and-one-half year study by AT&T of the effects of its EAP.

This ex-post study followed each of 110 employees for twenty-two months before and twenty-two months after their involvement with the company's EAP program (Gaeta et al., 1982). To be conservative, estimates were not used. In areas where savings formulas could be developed, cost figures for actual company expenditures were used. However, in estimating benefits, the study did not include the cost of creating the EAP or of training supervisors and other staff personnel.

To be considered in the study, accidents must have involved lost work time. The cost per accident (in 1990 dollars) of $5,130 is the actual company cost for expenses, including administrative costs, medical expenses, replacement costs, and disability expenses under law. Costs associated with lost productivity and lost time were not included in this figure. As the following data show, the reduction in the cost of accidents for EAP clients during the twenty-two months following their involvement in the program was $107,730.

	No. of Accidents	*Cost per Accident*	*Total Cost*	*Difference*
Before EAP	26	$5,130	$133,380	
After EAP	5	5,130	25,650	$107,730

Savings in Training and Replacement Costs

Motorola's EAP in Austin, Texas has developed some methodologies that have served as measures of costs and benefits (Starr and Byram, 1985). Net savings in training and replacement costs are shown below. Actual numbers of employees are not shown since Motorola treats this information as confidential.

Let us assume that 10 percent of 2,500 employees (250) can be expected to quit each year. Potential turnover costs may be stated as follows:

	No. of People	*Individual Cost*	*Total Cost*
Production	150	$ 750	$ 112,500
Office/technical	50	1,500	75,000
Exempt	50	25,000	1,250,000
Total potential cost			$1,437,500

Actual number of employees who terminate or quit after EAP involvement:

	No. of People	*Individual Cost*	*Total Cost*
Production	24	$ 750	$18,000
Office/technical	4	1,500	6,000
Exempt	3	25,000	75,000
Total actual cost			$99,000

To obtain the total actual cost:

Annual budget	$175,000
Terminations/quit	99,000
Hospitalization	95,000
Total actual cost	$369,000

To total the return on investment (ROI):

Potential cost	$1,437,500
Actual cost	369,000
Total	$1,068,500
ROI	$1,068,500/$369,000
	= 2.90, or approx. 3 : 1

Compiling these data year after year is particularly useful because the data can be compared and trends can be identified.

Use of Insurance Benefits

Another measure that is frequently used to evaluate EAPs is use of insurance benefits. This type of measure may be most informative when computed on an ex-post basis, that is, after an EAP has been in operation for a number of years. The use of insurance as a measure of EAP involvement may actually increase at first because of referrals for counseling. However, referrals are likely to stabilize over time. The method described here for computing benefit/cost ratios was developed originally by Foote et al. (1978). It can be used in an organization that uses an information system (in conjunction with its EAP) capable of tracking such data. Costs shown refer to average annual health insurance costs incurred by a single EAP client. To be useful, therefore, such costs must be aggregated over all EAP users.

Medical Costs

A. Before intervention	$3,000
B. After intervention (C + D)	700
C. Costs incurred due to intervention	500
D. Other medical costs	200
Cost savings (A − B)	$2,300

Then we obtain the benefit/cost ratio:

Benefit/Cost Ratio

Cost savings	2,300
Costs of the intervention	500
ROI	2,300/500 = 4.6, or $4.60 saved for every $1 spent on the program

The nine categories of EAP outcomes that we have presented are summarized in Exhibit 5.2. However, there is no one model of EAP evaluation that is universally appropriate, and, as we have seen, firms have tended to emphasize one or more of the outcomes shown in Exhibit 5.2. What can we conclude? Judicious choice of the outcomes of interest, careful measurement of costs and benefits in economic terms, and the use of one or more control groups will permit stronger inferences regarding the practical impact of EAPs.

COSTING THE EFFECTS OF EMPLOYEE WELLNESS PROGRAMS

The *theory* of employee wellness programs is simple: it is cheaper to keep an employee healthy and on the job than it is to pay the costs of ill health, rehabilitation, and replacement. Convinced that if employees were healthier they would take sick days less often, two out of every three companies in the United States with fifty or more workers have some type of wellness program designed to prevent illness ("Labor Letter," 1989).

Wellness has been defined as the state of health in which an individual is physically and mentally capable of maintaining the highest quality

EXHIBIT 5.2 Some possible outcomes that EAPs may affect

- Productivity
- Turnover
- Unemployment Costs
- Inpatient or Outpatient Treatment for Substance Abuse
- Absenteeism
- Use of Supervisors' Time
- Accidents
- Training and Replacement Costs
- Insurance Benefits

of life through self-responsibility and self-management ("Get," 1986). Wellness programs refer to combinations of activities or interventions designed to promote healthy life-styles. Such emphasis seems well placed, since life-styles are responsible for 51 percent of all reported health problems (Fritz, 1984), and health problems are expensive.

Why Establish a Wellness Program?

Health care costs represent more than 11 percent of our gross national product, and are galloping along at an annual inflation rate of about 15 percent. In fact, in manufacturing industries health related costs are now the third largest cost element—behind raw materials and straight pay. General Motors now spends more for health care than it does for steel. Chrysler estimates that the cost of health care adds an average of $700 to the purchase price of its cars (Andrews, 1989). Facts like these provide a strong incentive for companies to look for short- and long-term ways to reduce these costs. Wellness programs hold the promise of reducing health care costs over the long term.

As Terborg (1988) has noted, however, companies that adopt wellness programs do not do so based solely on the anticipated financial return on their investments. They do so because their employees want them, because they believe it is a worthwhile benefit to offer their employees, and because they think it will reduce health care costs and improve morale and productivity. Costs and benefits are important in the context of these other criteria. Across a large sample of firms that have established such programs, many companies report consistently that improving the health of their employees is the most important consideration, employee morale is second, and economic gains (such as lower health care costs, absenteeism, and turnover; and increased productivity) are third (Warner, 1987).

While companies adopt wellness programs for a variety of reasons, Howard (1987) has noted that, in a free-enterprise economy, the bottom line is the great persuader. For American business, health care costs threaten to reduce profits just as surely as competitors from Europe and the Far East. In the opinion of many, wellness programs may be the best weapon to hold the line.

Levels and Types of Wellness Programs

Most authorities in the field of wellness stress the importance of defining a strategy when such a program is introduced. Generally such a strategy includes the following features (Howard, 1987):

- Identify individual risk factors among employees, using screening and assessment tools.
- Educate employees about risk factors and the relationship to disease.
- Motivate employees to reduce the risk factors.
- Encourage employees to make a personal commitment to risk reduction.
- Offer specific programs to control major risk factors such as smoking, substance abuse, excess weight, and high blood pressure.
- Follow up and support employees in their efforts to change.

Wellness programs can be implemented at three functional levels (Gebhardt and Crump, 1990). Level I programs attempt to make employees aware of the consequences of unhealthful habits. Such programs may include health fairs, screening sessions, newsletters, or educational classes.

Level II programs involve lifestyle modification by providing specific programs. For example, the wellness program offered by the Adolph Coors Company offers traditional classes in exercise, weight loss, smoking cessation, stress management, and diet and nutrition. It also includes such nontraditional offerings as specially designed aerobics classes for older employees; pre- and postnatal exercise, dietary, and nutritional programs; classes in anger management and parenting skills; screening in breast cancer and skin cancer for employees and spouses; dental education; and rehabilitation for employees with cardiac and orthopedic problems (Andrews, 1989). The goal of Level II programs is to provide employees with a knowledge base to help alter negative health habits.

Level III programs attempt to create an environment at work that will assist employees in sustaining their healthy life-styles and behaviors. Some common changes include eliminating cigarette machines; providing healthy food and beverages in vending machines, the company cafeteria, and at meetings; labeling foods with nutritional information; building covered areas for storage of employee bicycles to encourage bicycling to work instead of driving; and prohibiting staff expense reimbursements for alcoholic beverages (Sciacca, 1987; Terborg, 1988).

Problem: Participation by Employees "At Risk"

Before any company jumps on the wellness bandwagon, it should be aware of a major problem: employee participation. While there are many wellness programs available, evidence indicates that only a small percentage of employees participates in them. In their review of the literature, Gebhardt and Crump (1990) found that participation in worksite fitness programs usually ranges from 15 to 30 percent for white collar workers, with an occasional high participation rate of 50 percent. However, the same white collar workers, prior to their participation, weighed less and were less likely to smoke than were nonparticipants. This suggests that a high percentage of "at risk" employees are not participating in the programs. Participation among blue collar workers in workplace fitness programs (3 to 5 percent) is even less.

However, fitness is not the same thing as wellness. Fitness programs help participants develop and maintain bodily shape, tone muscles, become trim, and lose or control weight. Wellness, on the other hand, is the absence of illness, years of life gained, reduction of disease symptoms, and decrease of risk factors (Andrews, 1989). In a survey of 141 employers nationwide by the Health Research Institute, blue collar workers had the highest level of participation at 42.3 percent (Kittrell, 1988). The key to attracting workers is emphasis on facts such as: (1) wellness can help reduce lost time from work due to accidents, (2) participation will not affect employment status, and (3) participation will not be considered a substitute for worksite safety initiatives (Metcalfe, 1987).

The challenge, therefore, is to recruit and retain high-risk individuals—those who are most likely to get sick and to cost the most in medical claims. The trick is to get enough high-risk employees into the wellness program to generate a "critical mass," a point at which cost savings begin to accrue. Unfortunately, no one knows yet what number the critical mass needs to be (Aberth, 1986).

Incentives for Participation

To boost low participation rates in employee wellness programs, many firms (more than seven out of ten in one survey, Kittrell, 1988) offer inducements to employees. For example, Berol Corporation, a Connecticut manufacturer of pens, offers employees a return of $500 if they have no health care claims over a one-year period (Howard, 1987). Other types of incentives include awards for physical fitness and health; cash bonuses for miles run, swum, or cycled; pay for perfect attendance; discounts or rebates for health club memberships; reimbursement for health care copayments; or time off during work for participation (Gettings and Maddox, 1988; Kittrell, 1988). Now that we know how wellness programs work, it seems reasonable to ask, "What do they cost?"

The Cost of Wellness Programs

The cost of offering a wellness program includes direct costs, such as fees paid to vendors, and indirect costs, such as lost employee time during participation. Direct costs vary considerably depending on the method of delivery. Programs that enlist the services of organizations such as the American Heart Association, the American Cancer Society, or the Red Cross, may be much less expensive than those delivered by a private, for-profit company.

Other direct costs include the construction or modification of facilities, promotional materials, and, perhaps, incentive payments to employees for their participation. However, costs will be lower if employees must pay a fee to participate, or if they must participate in wellness activities on their own time (Fletcher, 1987).

Terborg (1988) reported that the annual cost to a company for each participant in a comprehensive health promotion program ranges from about $100 to over $1,000, with costs typically in the range of $400 to $500. Costs vary considerably, however, depending on the size of an organization and the extent of the facilities and programs offered. For example, a small company with fewer than 100 employees should be able to start a program with an investment of a few thousand dollars and annual expenditures of only $5,000 to $10,000 (Howard, 1987), a cost of about $100 per employee.

In the Health Research Institute survey described earlier (Kittrell, 1988), responding companies employed a total of 3.66 million people in the United States. They reported an average cost per start-up of a wellness program as $99.10 per eligible employee for internal costs, plus $18.37 per eligible employee for outside costs.

Kimberly-Clark's Neenah, Wisconsin, plant falls toward the high end in wellness expenditures. It incorporates Levels I, II, and III of wellness activities. For example, it has a $2.5 million fitness facility, offers a variety of wellness-related and first aid classes, and it also offers occupational health nursing services. The program is open to spouses and retirees, and costs about $400 per year for each of the 5,500 eligible employees, or about $2 million annually (Fletcher, 1987).

This magnitude of expenditures leads naturally to our next question, "What are firms getting in return?" Before we can answer that question, however, we need to consider some of the difficult problems associated with the evaluation of wellness programs.

WHY IT IS DIFFICULT TO EVALUATE WELLNESS PROGRAMS

The savings that accrue from participation in a wellness program are variable. The basic difficulty in estimating these savings lies in choosing which health-related costs are actually reduced. To deal with this problem, some firms have established wellness programs with specific objectives. Sunbeam Corporation's wellness program focuses specifically on reducing the rising costs associated with premature births. Pennzoil targets early cancer detection and treatment. The American Cancer Society estimates that the costs associated with treating just one individual's late-detected cancer can be $60,000 or more. To date, Pennzoil has invested more than $100,000 in the program, has detected precancerous conditions in 150 employees, and malignancies in fourteen. However, Pennzoil recovered more than its initial investment cost by detecting just two cancerous conditions in the early stage (Andrews, 1989). These programs with specific objectives make evaluation more straightforward. This is not true, however, for the great majority of firms that have implemented wellness programs.

While companies that market their wellness programs provide statistics to support their claims of savings in health care costs, calculating how much any given employer can expect to save is difficult because program sponsors use different methods to measure and report cost–benefit data. As the director of the Health Research Institute noted, "The offerings of programs are light years ahead of the measurement of the programs" (Hembree, in Fletcher, 1987, p. 26).

When a program's effects are measured, and *for how long* they are measured are crucial considerations. For example, DuPont found that the greatest drop in absenteeism due to illness occurred in the first two or three years, then it leveled off. Other effects, which might not appear for three years or longer, are so-called *lagged effects*. The greatest savings should accrue over time because of the chronic nature of many illnesses that wellness programs seek to prevent. However, employers should actually expect to see an *increase* in health care claims after initial health assessments are done, as employees remedy newly identified problems (Fletcher, 1987).

A major problem is that many companies have no control groups when evaluating their programs. Without a control group of nonparticipating employees, there is no way to tell how much of the improved health is due to the wellness program and how much is due to the general fitness craze (Aberth, 1986).

Another limiting factor is the availability of data. Often firms commit to health promotion without any corresponding commitment to data collection (Smith, 1987). Without data, evaluation is impossible. Typically, however, the evaluation of a wellness program relies on some form of cost–effectiveness or cost–benefit analysis.

Cost–Effectiveness Analysis

Cost–effectiveness (C/E) analysis identifies the cost of producing a unit of effect within a given program. To illustrate, let us see an example presented by Smith et al. (1986). Suppose a worksite hypertension control program incurs an annual cost of $20,000 for a 100-employee population. The average reduction in diastolic blood pressure per treated individual is 8 millimeters of mercury (mm/Hg). The C/E ratio is:

$$\$20{,}000/100 \div 8 \text{ mm/Hg} = \$25 \text{ per mm/Hg reduction}$$

C/E analysis permits comparisons of alternative interventions designed to achieve the same goal. For example, the $25 cost per mm/Hg reduction achieved by the above program could be compared to alternative programs not offered at the worksite. Unfortunately, C/E analysis fails to address the issue, from a financial perspective, of whether the program should have been offered in the first place. Further, the benefits are not expressed in monetary terms. Cost–benefit analysis overcomes the latter problem.

Cost–Benefit Analysis

Cost–benefit (C/B) analysis is similar to C/E analysis in that both focus on goals, costs, and benefits. The difference is that C/B analysis expresses benefits in monetary terms. One of the most popular forms of C/B analysis is return on investment (ROI) analysis. Although traditionally associated with investments in hard assets, ROI analysis also can be used to evaluate returns on investments in wellness activities (Smith et al., 1986) by relating program profits to invested capital. It does so in terms of a ratio in which the numerator expresses some measure of profit related to the project, and the denominator represents the firm's investment in the program (Smith et al., 1986).

Suppose a wellness program costs a firm $250,000 during its first year of operation. The measured saving from reduced absenteeism is $13,000; from reduced employer health care payments (assuming a self-funded plan) is $25,000; and from reduced employee turnover is $12,000. The ROI before interest and taxes would be calculated as follows:

Benefit Type	*Benefit Amount*
Reduced absenteeism	$13,000
Reduced health care payments	$25,000
Reduced employee turnover	$12,000
Total expected benefits	$50,000

ROI = Total expected benefit/program investment
ROI = $50,000/$250,000 = 20%

The advantage of ROI is that it blends in one number all the major ingredients of profitability, and the ROI statistic can be compared with other investment opportunities inside or outside of a company. It is also simple and widely accepted.

However, as Terborg (1988) has noted, while the logic and techniques of C/E and C/B analysis (including ROI) appear straightforward, there are several unresolved issues. There is much subjectivity in the choice of variables to include in these models, in estimating the dollar value of indirect costs and indirect benefits, in estimating the timing and duration of program effects, and in discounting the dollar value of costs and benefits that occur in future time periods. Because of this subjectivity, it is important to conduct sensitivity analyses (to examine the impact of variations in as-

EXHIBIT 5.3 Difficulties in evaluating wellness programs

1. Identification of the health-related costs that actually decreased
2. Program sponsors use different methods to measure and report costs and benefits
3. Program effects may vary depending on *when* they are measured (immediate versus lagged effects)
4. Program effects may vary depending on *how long* they are measured
5. Few studies use control groups
6. Data on effectiveness are limited, in the
   - Choice of variables
   - Estimation of the economic value of indirect costs and benefits
   - Estimation of the timing and duration of program effects
   - Estimation of the present values of future benefits

sumptions on C/E and C/B ratios) and break-even analysis (see Chapter 10) to identify the minimum levels of dependent variables (such as early cancer detections or savings in absenteeism) that will allow recovery of investments in the wellness program.

A summary of the wellness program evaluation issues discussed thus far is presented in Exhibit 5.3.

DATA NEEDED TO EVALUATE A WELLNESS PROGRAM

A sound experimental design is one that allows cause-and-effect relationships to emerge. Gebhardt and Crump (1990) have outlined an ideal evaluation strategy that includes an initial determination of the demographics of an organization (age, gender, race, ethnicity), expected participation rates, and start-up and maintenance costs required to reach an organization's goals (such as reducing the incidence and costs of undetected cancerous conditions).

The next step is to develop a testing and tracking system that will quantify the outcomes of the wellness program for both participants and nonparticipants. Pre- and postcomparisons can be made for both groups in terms of behavioral changes, health care costs, fitness level, absenteeism, turnover, injury rate and severity, productivity, and job satisfaction. Quantifiable variables (such as health care costs, absenteeism) should be

EXHIBIT 5.4 How to evaluate a wellness program

1. Classify employees according to demographic characteristics.
2. Determine expected participation rates.
3. Estimate program start-up and maintenance costs.
4. Develop a testing and tracking system to quantify outcomes for participants and nonparticipants.
5. Measure pre- and post-program changes on outcomes of interest.
6. Analyze quantitative variables separately by demographic group and by participation or nonparticipation in the program.
7. Conduct cost–benefit analyses of present and future benefits; determine the present values of all such benefits.

analyzed separately by demographic or socioeconomic cohort, and for both participants and nonparticipants.

Finally, C/B analyses should include present and future benefits, expressed in current dollar values. While all of the features described are rarely included in actual evaluations of wellness programs, they represent an ideal to aim for. A summary of these ideas is presented in Exhibit 5.4. Now let us examine published results from several firms that have attempted to assess the outcomes of their wellness programs.

COMPANY-LEVEL EVALUATIONS OF WELLNESS PROGRAMS

The benefits of wellness programs may be expressed in terms of a number of possible outcomes. We shall examine three of them: health care costs, absenteeism, and turnover.

Health Care Costs

A study by the Pacific Mutual Life Insurance Company found that illness due to poor nutrition costs employers $30 million annually. Individuals with cardiovascular disease related to high blood pressure cost industry 27 million work days and $4 to $5 billion per year. Back problems cause a loss of 91 million work days per year and more than $9 billion in lost productivity, disability payments, and lawsuits (Renner, 1987). Another study found that nonexercising employees use 60 percent more sick-time hours than their counterparts who jog, swim, bike, or engage in other forms of regular exercise each week (Gettings and Maddox, 1988).

Demonstration of a cause-and-effect relationship between wellness program expenditures and health care costs avoided is far from an exact science. Nevertheless, longitudinal research now shows that employees' unhealthy behaviors lead to significantly higher health care costs over time. Thus, a four-year study of 15,000 workers at Control Data Corporation revealed that employees with the worst life-style habits had the highest medical bills. For example, people whose weekly exercise was equivalent to climbing fewer than five flights of stairs or walking less than one-half mile spent 114 percent more on health care claims than those who climbed at least fifteen flights of stairs or walked one and one-half miles a week. Less surprisingly, people who smoked an average of one or more packs of cigarettes a day had 118 percent higher medical expenses than nonsmokers. Health care costs for obese people were 11 percent higher than those for thin ones. And workers who routinely failed to use seat belts spent 54 percent more days in the hospital than those who usually buckled up (James, 1987).

As we noted earlier, some companies have established very specific objectives for their wellness programs. As an example, consider the mammography screening program used by Coors. By calculating exactly how many examinations showed breast cancer in the early stages, Coors can accurately calculate the costs avoided, assuming that without mammography the problem would have gone undetected and the cancer would have matured. Coors spent $232,500 to perform 2,500 screenings, and avoided $828,000 in health care costs. This yielded the company a savings of $595,500, or an ROI of greater than 3.5 : 1 (Johnson, 1988).

Descriptions of three other studies are drawn from the excellent literature review provided by Gebhardt and Crump (1990). Johnson & Johnson conducted a health care cost analysis of its Level II and Level III fitness and wellness programs using 11,000 employees who were employed continuously from 1979 to 1983. Employees were divided into three groups, depending on how long the programs had been in effect in their companies: thirty months, eighteen to thirty months, or no program. Since medical costs and health care use were affected by age, gender, and job class (hourly versus salaried employees), statistical procedures were used to take into account differences in these variables as well as differences in other variables such as baseline differences in fitness level, health parameters, and location. All costs were adjusted to 1979 dollars, and weighted by the individual cost indexes of the state in which each company resided.

These analyses showed that employees with either the thirty-month or the eighteen- to thirty-month programs had significantly lower health care costs than employees in companies without wellness programs. By the fifth year, both program groups demonstrated lower inpatient admissions and hospital days per 1,000 employees than the nonprogram companies. Companies with programs realized average savings (in 1979 dollars) of $245,079 per year. However, since the authors of the original study did not provide program costs, it is not possible to determine the ROI.

Prudential Insurance Company instituted a voluntary fitness program for sedentary, white collar workers engaged in clerical, underwriting, claims, and management jobs. The study, conducted over a five-year period, included individuals employed for at least one year prior to entry into the program, and one year after entry into the program. Results showed that the average sick days for the exercisers dropped 20.1 percent when compared to their previous year's sick days (each person was compared to his or her own baseline) prior to entry into the program. This represented a 31.7 percent savings in salary costs and a 45.7 percent savings in major medical costs for each participant in the exercise program. The savings in major medical costs occurred during a year when health costs for the nation rose 13.9 percent. The program cost $120.60 (in 1980 dollars) per participant, and saved $353.88 per participant, for a net savings of $233.28, or a savings in company health care costs of $1.93 for every $1 used to operate the program.

Blue Cross and Blue Shield of Indiana studied the impact of its onsite health promotion program (Level I and Level II) for 667 participants and 1,744 nonparticipants from 1978 to 1982. Analysis of these two groups six months prior to initiation of the program indicated that health care payments were similar for both groups. After the first six months, costs for participants actually increased, as participants sought medical care for newly discovered health conditions. However, the benefit payments (hospital inpatient and outpatient, major medical, and medical-surgical) across the 4.75 years of the study were 24 percent lower for participants. In 1978 dollars, the health care cost savings per employee ($143.60) exceeded the total program cost per employee ($98.86) by a ratio of 1.45 : 1. When the start-up costs were amortized over the 4.75-year period, the ROI increased to 2.51 : 1 ($143.60/$57.23).

Absenteeism and Turnover

Cost savings from wellness programs can also be derived from the reduction of costly behaviors such as absenteeism and turnover. Absenteeism has been shown to drop 20 percent to 55 percent for programs ranging in length from one to five years (Gebhardt and Crump, 1990).

For example, Cox et al. (1981) studied white collar employees at two similar insurance companies. In Company A, 435 employees enrolled voluntarily in a 30-minute exercise program that met three times per week at an onsite facility. Absenteeism for this group was compared to that of the 846 employees in the same company who did not participate, and to the 577 employees in Company B, which served as the control group. Prior to the implementation of the fitness program, members of all three groups had similar absenteeism rates. One year later, absenteeism dropped by 22 percent among the exercisers in Company A. This represented an average reduction of 1.3 days per employee. If the same result could be observed for all 1,281 employees in Company A, Cox et al. (1981) estimated a net savings to the company (in 1981 dollars) of $83,265 per year.

Cox et al. (1981) also investigated relative rates of turnover among exercisers and nonexercisers in Company A for one year prior to the initiation of the program and ten months after initiation of the program. Turnover rates in the two groups were not significantly different prior to the inception of the program. Although the program period of ten months was short, the exercisers had significantly less turnover (1.5 percent) than the nonexercisers (15 percent). Because tenure with the company was similar for the members of both groups (roughly eight to eleven years), turnover was not attributed to differences in past employment history. (However, it may be that better performers were in the exercising group, and better performers are less likely to leave, McEvoy and Cascio, 1987). The savings, calculated using training costs of $6,250, difference in turnover rate (13.5%), and program participation rate (20%) prorated over ten months, were $203 per company employee per year, resulting in an annual company savings of $260,043 (in 1981 dollars).

THE FUTURE OF EMPLOYEE ASSISTANCE AND WELLNESS PROGRAMS

Based on the research reviewed in this chapter, it is clear that EAPs and wellness programs can yield significant payoffs to organizations that adopt them. However, it also is clear that the programs do not work under all circumstances and that the problems associated with assessing relative costs and benefits may be complex. At the very least, we need more well-controlled, longitudinal studies to investigate program costs and benefits, and the extent to which behavior changes are maintained over time. Second, as Gebhardt and Crump (1990) have noted, the type and structure of programs should be evaluated for their success and impact on different populations of workers (older–younger, male–female, blue collar–white collar, racial or ethnic group), especially in light of the changes in the work force that are expected by the year 2000. We need to understand the factors that affect employee participation or nonparticipation, as well as the factors that promote long-term changes in behavior. If we then build these factors into EAP and wellness programs, and if we are successful in attracting troubled or at-risk employees into the programs, then the programs will flourish, even in an era of limited resources in organizations.

EXERCISES

1. What is the difference between ex-ante and ex-post evaluation? Describe the major problems associated with the evaluation of EAPs.

2. Sobriety, Inc., a marketer of substance abuse programs, is concerned about the cost of alcohol abuse among its own employees. Based on the following data, what is the productivity cost associated with employees who abuse alcohol? Among all cohorts, the productivity decrease attributable to alcohol abuse is 20 percent.

Age–Gender Cohort	*No.*	*Percentage with Alcohol Abuse Problems*	*Average Annual Earnings of Cohort*
Males, 25 and under	43	7%	$18,000
Males, 26–44	59	10%	29,000
Males, 45 and over	38	5%	37,000
Females, 25 and under	41	5%	19,000
Females, 26–44	64	10%	30,000
Females, 45 and over	34	7%	35,000

3. The following data show terminations, replacement, and training costs for the 4,000 employees of Hulakon, Inc., for one year. In any given year, 12 percent of the employees can be expected to quit.

Employee Group	*No. of Employees*	*Individual cost of Replacement and Training*
Production	250	$ 1,500
Clerical	175	2,000
Management	55	14,000

As a result of involvement in the company's EAP, the following numbers of employees actually quit:

Employee Group	No. of Employees
Production	75
Clerical	40
Management	12

Hospitalization costs comprised $126,000 or 56 percent of the total amount annually budgeted for the EAP. What is Hulakon's ROI for its employee assistance program for this one year?

4. Your firm is considering establishing an EAP, but it is unsure of which provider to select. Top management has asked you to assess the strengths and weaknesses of possible providers. Make a list of questions to ask each one.

5. Top management has asked you to summarize results from available studies regarding the relationship between employee lifestyle behaviors and health care costs. Present your results in a report.

6. Use Johnson & Johnson's program as an example to illustrate the difficulties associated with evaluating worksite wellness programs. Cost–effectiveness and cost–benefit analyses are often used in such evaluations. What are the relative advantages and disadvantages of these methods?

REFERENCES

ABERTH, J. (1986, October). Worksite wellness programs: An evaluation. *Management Review*, pp. 51–53.

ANDREWS, C. (1989). *The Coors wellness program.* Unpublished manuscript, Executive MBA Program, University of Colorado.

BENSINGER, A., and PILKINGTON, C. F. (1985). Treating chemically dependent employees in a non-hospital setting. *Personnel Administrator*, *30*, 45–52.

CHERSKOV, M. (1987, June 20). Substance abuse in the workplace. *Hospitals*, pp. 68–73.

COX, M. H., SHEPHARD, R. J., and COREY, P. (1981). Influence of an employee fitness programme upon fitness, productivity, and absenteeism. *Ergonomics*, *24*, 795–806.

DICKMAN, F., and EMENER, W. G. (1987). *Employee assistance programs: Basic concepts, attributes, and an evaluation.* Alexandria, VA: Personnel Administrator Reprint Collection Series, Employee Assistance Programs, pp. 39–44.

Employee assistance programs: EAPs of the next decade could be broader. (1989, December). *Employee Benefit News*, pp. 115–116.

FARKAS, G. M. (1989). The impact of federal rehabilitation laws on the expanding role of employee assistance programs in business and industry. *American Psychologist*, *44*, 1482–1490.

FEATHERSTON, H. J., and BEDNAREK, R. J. (1987). *A positive demonstration of concern for employees*. Alexandria, VA: Personnel Administrator Reprint Collection Series, Employee Assistance Programs, pp. 36–38.

FILIPOWICZ, C. (1987). *The troubled employee: Whose responsibility?* Alexandria, VA: Personnel Administrator Reprint Collection Series, Employee Assistance Programs, pp. 5–10.

FLETCHER, M. (1987, February 16). Wellness plan savings are difficult to measure. *Business Insurance*, pp. 26, 28.

FOOTE, A., ERFURT, J., STRAUCHY, P., and GAZZARDO, T. (1978). *Cost-effectiveness of occupational employee assistance programs: Test of an evaluation method*. Ann Arbor, MI: Institute of Labor and Industrial Relations.

FREUDENHEIM, M. (1988, August 23). Employers act to stop family violence. *New York Times*, pp. A1, D5.

FRITZ, W. S. (1984). Maintaining wellness: Yours and theirs. *Nursing Clinics of North America*, pp. 263–269.

GAETA, E., LYNN, R., and GREY, L. (1982, May–June). AT&T looks at program evaluation. *EAP Digest*, pp. 22–31.

GEBHARDT, D. L., and CRUMP, C. E. (1990). Employee fitness and wellness programs in the workplace. *American Psychologist*, 45, 262–272.

"Get the Glow." (1986). *Wellness process*. Golden, CO: Adolph Coors Company.

GETTINGS, L., and MADDOX, E. N. (1988, April). When health means wealth. *Training and Development Journal*, pp. 81–85.

HOWARD, J. S. (1987, May–June). Employee wellness: It's good business. *D&B Reports*, pp. 34–37.

JAMES, F. B. (1987, April 14). Study lays groundwork for tying health costs to workers' behavior. *Wall Street Journal*, p. 37.

JOHNSON, S. (1988, June). Breast screening's bottom line—lives saved. *Administrative Radiology*, p. 4.

KITTRELL, A. (1988, March 28). Wellness plans can save money: Survey. *Business Insurance*, pp. 9–11.

KLARREICH, S. H., DIGIUSEPPE, R., and DIMATTIA, D. J. (1987). Cost effectiveness of an employee assistance program with rational-emotive therapy. *Professional Psychology: Research and Practice, 18*, 140–144. (a)

KLARREICH, S. H. DIGIUSEPPE, R., and DIMATTIA, D. J. (1987). EAPs: Mind over myth. *Personnel Administrator, 32* (2), 119–121. (b)

Labor letter. (1988, December 6). *Wall Street Journal*, p. A1.

Labor letter. (1989, January 17). *Wall Street Journal*, p. A1.

LEIB, J. (1986, September 1). Companies wrestle with substance abuse. *Denver Post*, pp. 1E, 6E.

MCEVOY, G. M., and CASCIO, W. F. (1987). Do good or poor performers leave? A meta-analysis of the relationship between performance and turnover. *Academy of Management Journal, 30*, 744–762.

MASI, D. (1984). *Designing employee assistance programs.* New York: American Management Association.

METCALFE, L. L. (1987). The plant worker—singing the health and fitness blues. *Fitness in Business, 1* (6), 230, 233–234.

PARKER, D. L., SHULTZ, J. M., GERTZ, L., BERKELMAN, R., and REMINGTON, P. L. (1987). The social and economic costs of alcohol abuse in Minnesota, 1983. *American Journal of Public Health, 77*, 982–986.

PEARSON, J. M. (1989). Controlling treatment costs of substance abuse and psychiatric problems. *Personnel, 66* (10), 12–17.

POWELL, K. E., THOMPSON, P. D., CASPERSEN, C. J., and KENDRICH, J. S. (1987). Physical activity and incidence of coronary heart disease. *Annual Review of Public Health, 8*, 253–287.

QUAYLE, D. (1983). American productivity: The devastating effect of alcoholism and drug abuse. *American Psychologist, 38*, 454–458.

RENNER, J. F. (1987, March–April). Wellness programs: An investment in cost containment. *EAP Digest*, pp. 49–53.

SCIACCA, J. P. (1987, November). The worksite is the best place for health promotion. *Personnel Journal*, pp. 42–49.

SMITH, K. J. (1987, December). A framework for appraising corporate wellness investments. *Internal Auditor*, pp. 28–33.

SMITH, K. J., HAIGHT, G. T., and EVERLY, G. S., JR. (1986, February). Evaluating corporate wellness investments. *Internal Auditor*, pp. 28–34.

SPERLING, D. (1989, March 9). More employers help foot the detox bill. *USA Today*, p. 5D.

STARR, A., and BYRAM, G. (1985). Cost/benefit analysis for employee assistance programs. *Personnel Administrator, 30* (8), 55–60.

Substance abuse cost at work: $100 billion. (1988, December 12). *Denver Post*, p. 1A.

TERBORG, J. R. (1988). The organization as a context for health promotion. In S. Oskamp and S. Spacapan (Eds.), *The social psychology of health.* Newbury Park, CA: Sage, pp. 129–174.

WAGNER, W. G. (1987). *Assisting employees with personal problems.* Alexandria, VA: Personnel Administrator Reprint Collection Series, Employee Assistance Programs, pp. 45–49.

WARNER, K. E. (1987, Spring). Selling health promotion to corporate America: Uses and abuses of the economic argument. *Health Education Quarterly*, 39–55.

6

The Financial Impact of Employee Attitudes

A number of studies in behavioral science have examined the relationship between job attitudes and absenteeism, turnover, tardiness, job performance, strikes, grievances, and voting behavior in union elections (see Goodman et al., 1988; Mobley, 1982; Zalesny, 1985; and Zimbardo et al., 1990 for reviews). Attitudes are internal states that are focused on particular aspects of or objects in the environment. They include three elements: *cognition*, the knowledge an individual has about the focal object of the attitude; the *emotion* an individual feels toward the focal object; and an *action* tendency, a readiness to respond in a predetermined manner to the focal object.

Job satisfaction may be viewed as a multidimensional attitude; it is made up of attitudes toward pay, promotions, co-workers, supervision, the work itself, and so on. Management is interested in employees' job satisfaction principally because of the relationship between attitudes and behavior. Other things being equal, it is assumed that employees who are dissatisfied with their jobs (hold negative attitudes about various aspects of the work environment) will tend to be absent or late for work, or to quit more often than those whose attitudes are positive. Work force productivity therefore suffers. To explain the connection between attitudes and behavior, we must look at the precursors of attitudes: each individual's beliefs (Ajzen and Fishbein, 1980). Attitudes are a function of beliefs.

Generally speaking, a person who believes that a particular behavior will lead mostly to positive outcomes will hold a favorable attitude toward that behavior. A person who believes that the behavior will lead mostly to negative outcomes will hold an unfavorable attitude. According to this approach, any behavior can be predicted from a person's attitude toward it, provided that the measure of attitude corresponds to that measure of behavior (that is, they are evaluated in similar terms). A review of the attitude-behavior literature generally supports this position, and even more so supports a revision to the original theory that takes into account "perceived control"—situational or behavioral obstacles to performance (Chaiken and Stangor, 1987). Similar support has been found in studies that investigated smoking behavior (Loken, 1982) and the use of seat belts (Jonah, 1984). Experimental evidence in organizational behavior literature also indicates that improved job satisfaction can reduce absenteeism, turnover, tardiness, and grievances (Campbell and Campbell, 1988).

From a costing perspective, the important questions are: what is the financial impact of the behavioral outcomes associated with job attitudes, and can we measure the costs associated with different levels of job satisfaction and motivation? Behavioral scientists need to be able to speak in dollars-and-cents terms when they argue the merits of human resource development programs designed to change attitudes or improve job satisfaction. As discussed in Chapters 2 and 3, methods for attaching costs to absenteeism and turnover are fairly well developed. Measures of employee attitudes are even more finely developed (Feldman and Lynch, 1988). This chapter will show how the two types of measures, financial and attitudinal, can be synthesized to produce an estimate in dollars of the costs and benefits of human resource development programs designed to improve employee attitudes.

Exhibit 6.1 presents a model of financial assessment that was developed by Mirvis and Macy (1976). The exhibit depicts several different development programs (x_1 to x_5). Three distinct accounting activities are necessary for evaluating these programs. The first is a *cost model* needed for identifying the firm's direct costs and losses in productive time attributable to the development effort. The second is an *effectiveness model* used for measuring and validating the effects of a project on the work environment and employees' attitudes, behaviors, and performance, and expressing these effects in financial terms. The third is a *synthesizing model* to compare the costs and benefits of a program. Both social and financial goals can then be contrasted with project costs in order to identify the most cost-beneficial development program (see Chapter 11). That is, programs are judged successful if expenditures are outweighed by the present value of future benefits.

EXHIBIT 6.1 Cost–benefit model for human resource development programs

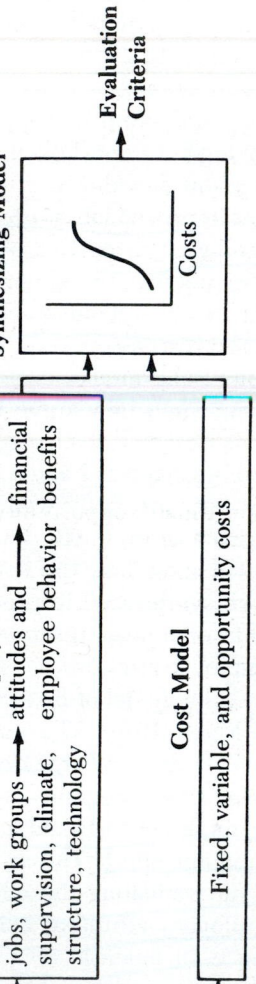

Source: Mirvis, P. H., and Macy, B. A. (1976). Accounting for the costs and benefits of human resource development programs: An interdisciplinary approach. *Accounting, Organizations, and Society, 1,* 181.

MEASURING THE COSTS OF DEVELOPMENT PROGRAMS

Although this issue is considered in much greater detail in Chapter 11, for the present we'll distinguish three broad classes of costs: fixed, variable, and opportunity costs (see page 7). Fixed costs include salaries, wages, and benefits associated with employees' lost time and the resulting unabsorbed overhead costs (see Chapters 2 and 3). Variable costs include, for example, consultants' fees and expenses associated with their activities. These costs vary depending on the type of program and the intensity and duration of the development activities. They should be reported in deflated dollar terms. To do this, simply divide the costs for any year by the Consumer Price Index (CPI)/100 for that year. For example, assume that the 1986 CPI is 100; the 1990 CPI is 118; 1986 costs are $10,000; and 1990 costs are $13,000. The *apparent* increase in costs is $3,000 or 30 percent. However, the *real* increase in costs is $13,000/1.18 = $11,016.95, which is only 10.17 percent ($1,016.95/$10,000).

The worksite also incurs variable costs in the form of lost worker productivity and overtime. Finally, opportunity costs reflect the profit contribution of the employees' lost time. We can also conceive of an additional opportunity cost, the "opportunities foregone" (Rothenberg, 1975) that might have been realized had the resources allocated to the program been directed toward other organizational ends.

On the other side of the ledger we can distinguish fixed, variable, and opportunity savings resulting from successful development programs. Fixed savings might be realized if some of the service demands placed on the personnel, industrial relations, safety, and quality control departments were reduced. Variable savings might include improved marginal productivity through increased product quality and quantity, limited overtime, reduced consumption of supplies and materials, and less unscheduled maintenance. Wages and other expenses due to absenteeism, accidents, and grievances (including the expense of maintaining a replacement work force) might also decrease. Finally, opportunity savings might be realized if the work time that supervisors spent in replacing absent employees or turnovers could be put to more productive use (Mirvis and Macy, 1976). Behavioral-economic measurement provides the methods for documenting these cost savings. Conceptually, the synthesis of costs and effectiveness measures seems straightforward. Indeed, two studies have proposed methods for undertaking such calculations. We'll examine the limitations of each method in order to illustrate the complexity of the problem, and then present a third approach that circumvents many of the shortcomings of the first two methods.

EARLY ATTEMPTS TO ESTIMATE THE FINANCIAL IMPACT OF ATTITUDES

Human Asset Valuation

Myers and Flowers (1974) present a simple framework for measuring human assets. Job performance is viewed as the end product of a five-part flow process: knowledge, skills, health, availability, and attitudes add up to job performance. The individual's knowledge enables him or her to direct skills, and the individual's health enables him or her to apply them. The individual must be available when needed and must have the desire to apply his or her talents and energy toward productive effort. The five dimensions are not additive, so that if any one of them is lacking, the others are rendered ineffective. Before deciding to improve one dimension, therefore, consideration must be given to the level of the others. Thus it may not be cost effective to improve the job knowledge of an employee who has a poor attitude. The first priority may well be to improve attitudes before attempting to improve job knowledge.

According to Myers and Flowers, job attitudes are a symptom of the other four human assets as these are interpreted by each individual's personal value system. Therefore a quantitative, reliable measure of attitudes is probably the best single measure of how well an individual uses all five assets. However, attitude survey results should not be lumped together indiscriminately. Each attitude score should be weighted by the individual's job grade level and company tenure. The higher the job grade level and the longer the tenure with the firm, the higher the weight attached to that individual's score. Myers and Flowers attempt to quantify attitudes by multiplying salary dollars times weighted attitude scores to measure the potential dollar value increases that would be associated with improved employee attitudes (see Exhibit 6.2).

This approach is a traditional approach to human asset valuation; it assigns a value to individuals rather than to their behavior. Employees' salaries are equated with their value to the organization, and it is assumed that attitudinal improvements make employees more valuable to the organization. As Mirvis and Lawler (1977) have noted, this approach suffers from three shortcomings. First, it doesn't state the effects of improved attitudes on job behavior. We don't know whether attitudinal improvement implies higher employee productivity, lower absenteeism, reduced

EXHIBIT 6.2 Human asset valuation approach to dollarizing attitudes

Unit: *Digital Assembly*

Individual	*Annual Salary*	*Job Grade*	*Tenure*	*Attitude Weight*	*Attitude Score*	*Weighted Attitude Score*
1. Tom Hill	$30,000	18	15	6	1.05	6.30
2. Cindy Fleming	$19,000	12	6	3	1.12	3.36
3. Ben Williams	$43,000	23	22	9	1.25	11.25
4. Judy Francis	$21,000	12	6	3	1.26	3.78
5. Amy Fox	$34,000	19	15	7	1.16	8.12
	$147,000			28		32.81

$$\text{attitude index} = \frac{(\Sigma \text{ weighted attitude score})}{(\Sigma \text{ attitude weights})} = \frac{32.81}{28} = 1.17$$

$$\text{dollarized attitudes} = \text{attitude index} \times \text{annual payroll} = 1.17 \times \$147{,}000 = \$171{,}990$$

$$\text{gain} = \$171{,}990 - \$147{,}000 = \$24{,}990$$

$$\text{gain per person} = \$4{,}998$$

turnover, or some combination of these. Second, this approach ignores whether the actual savings associated with any behavioral changes will equal their estimated value improvement (that is, validation of predicted savings). Finally, Myers and Flowers present no data on the relationship between the attitudes they measure and the behaviors of employees. At best, this framework provides a way for organizations to judge the impact of organizational investment on employee morale. It provides no clues to the direct financial impact of job satisfaction and motivation.

The Unit Cost Approach

The unit cost approach to assigning dollar values to attitudes was developed by Likert (1973) and Likert and Bowers (1973). Rather than trying to assign a value to the overall worth of an employee to an organization, this method attempts to determine the short-term costs of employee behavior by correlating standardized attitude scores with unit cost. It then predicts changes in unit cost from anticipated changes in attitudes and argues that the cost change represents the economic impact of the attitudes.

This approach also has problems, as Mirvis and Lawler have noted. The first problem stems from the choice of unit cost as a performance criterion. Cost per unit includes fixed costs (those incurred regardless of the number of units or level of service produced) and variable costs (those directly related to the level of activity). *Only variable costs can be affected immediately by such employee behaviors as increased productivity and reduced absenteeism and turnover.* Furthermore, both cost components are influenced by inflationary trends. The inclusion of fixed costs and inflationary trends in the criterion measure builds in a significant amount of variance that has nothing to do with changes in attitudes.

A second problem with this approach is that it ignores the processes that intervene between changes in attitude and changes in unit cost. That is, previous research suggests that improvements in job satisfaction should reduce levels of absenteeism and turnover, which in turn should result in lower unit cost. Simply relating attitudes to unit costs and bypassing the intervening processes ignores this sequential effect. The resulting relationship and financial consequences might well be over- or understated.

A third problem with the unit cost approach is its assumption of a constant attitude-behavior relationship over time. In fact, improvement in attitude scores could be accompanied by stronger or weaker predictive relationships to behavior. Predicted savings based on a constant relationship would understate the resulting benefits if the relationship was stronger than had been assumed, and it would overstate the benefits if the relationship was weaker than had been assumed. A final problem with this approach is that it relies on analysis at the work-group level, but much of the behavior change would occur at the individual level. Unless organizations are extremely large, relationships derived at the group level may be unreliable indicators of individual-level change.

In view of the shortcomings of the human asset valuation and unit cost approaches, we do not recommend that they be used. An awareness of their shortcomings is instructive, however, especially as a yardstick for measuring progress in methods proposed subsequently. One of these approaches, behavior costing, was developed by Mirvis and Lawler (1977).

THE BEHAVIOR COSTING APPROACH

Behavior costing is based on the assumption that attitudinal measures are indicators of subsequent employee behaviors. These behaviors can be assessed using cost accounting procedures, and they have economic implications for organizations. Only short-term direct costs associated with the behaviors are used. This approach clearly builds on the unit cost approach of Likert and Bowers.

The conceptual framework underlying behavior costing stems from expectancy theory, which emphasizes that employees' behavior at work is the result of choices about whether to appear at the work place ("participation-membership" [March and Simon 1958]) and of choices about how to behave at work ("work strategies" [Lawler, 1973]). This framework assumes that employees will be more likely to come to work than be absent or quit if they obtain satisfaction from their jobs. And they are likely to give more effort and choose more effective job performance strategies if they expect to be rewarded either intrinsically or extrinsically for their efforts (Vroom, 1964).

These ideas suggest that attitudinal indexes of employee satisfaction and job involvement should be the best predictors of participation-membership since they reflect perceptions of the rewards associated with being at work (Lawler, 1973). Employee intrinsic motivation should be the best predictor of job performance, since it reflects some of the performance outcomes contingent on doing a good job: competence, achievement, and self-realization.

A Test of the Theory

These theoretical ideas were tested empirically on a sample of 160 tellers from twenty branches of a midwestern banking organization. The tellers (average age, thirty) were predominantly female (94 percent). They served as cashiers, handling customer deposits, withdrawals, and other transactions.

Attitude measures were taken from the Michigan Assessment of Organizations (Survey Research Center, 1975), and reflected intrinsic satisfaction (six items), organizational involvement (two items), and intrinsic motivation (three items). For example:

- *intrinsic satisfaction*: please indicate how satisfied you are with the following aspects of your job: (1) the chances you have to do the things you do best; (2) the chances you have to learn new things; (3) the opportunity to develop your skills and abilities.
- *organizational involvement*: is what happens in this branch really important to you?
- *intrinsic motivation*: when you do your job well, do you feel you've done something worthwhile? Do you get a feeling of personal satisfaction from doing your job well?

Measures of participation-membership behavior and work performance were collected monthly after administration of the attitude questionnaire. Using standardized definitions and measures of behavioral outcomes (Macy and Mirvis, 1976), the following data were collected:

- *short-term absence or illness*: unauthorized absences of less than three consecutive days, including short-term illness and absence for personal reasons.
- *voluntary turnover*: voluntary employee departure from the bank, excluding terminations, maternity leaves or turnovers, and transfers.
- *teller balancing shortages*: the number of shortages in tellers' balances (overpayments to customers).

Results of the Teller Study

Over a three-month period there was no statistical measure of relationship (correlation, r) between absenteeism and turnover, and there were few significant correlations between absenteeism and shortages (median $r = -0.06$) or turnover and shortages (median $r = 0.15$). The absenteeism measure reflected some stability across months 1, 2, and 3 ($r_{12} = 0.61$, $r_{23} = 0.71$, $r_{13} = 0.52$). However, no one who was absent the first month was absent the next two months. In contrast, the number of teller balancing shortages was more stable ($r_{12} = 0.82$, $r_{23} = 0.71$, $r_{13} = 0.59$).

Each behavior has a cost to the organization. The major cost elements associated with turnover and absenteeism were outlined earlier in Chapters 2 and 3. With respect to teller shortages, the direct cost was estimated to be $17.55 per shortage.[1] This figure includes the cash outlay minus recoveries, and is reported in constant dollar terms. Each incident of absenteeism was estimated to cost $141.73 of which $49.14 (salary) was a variable cost (since the supervisor must either find a suitable replacement or extend the existing staff). The total cost of each turnover incident was estimated at $5,379.31, of which $626.97 (direct hiring costs) was variable.

The distinction between variable and total costs is important, for a reduction in absenteeism and turnover will result in variable-cost savings only. A reduction in fixed costs or realization of opportunity savings depends on subsequent reallocation of fixed costs or staff workloads. Thus

[1]All costs are expressed in terms of 1990 dollars, assuming an average annual inflation rate of 6 percent between 1977 and 1990.

fixed costs and opportunity savings were not included in the financial estimates.

Exhibit 6.3 shows the relationship between teller attitudes and absenteeism, turnover, and balancing shortages three months later. Correlations between attitudes and turnover are low, negative, and significant (that is, statistical relationships of that magnitude would occur, on the average, fewer than five times out of a hundred by chance alone). This is consistent with results found in other research (Mobley, 1982). Notice also the significant negative correlation between tellers' intrinsic motivation and shortages three months later. Finally, the high negative correlation between satisfaction and absenteeism is probably an artifact. July is a primary vacation month for the tellers and some took additional, unauthorized days off. The findings suggest that the most dissatisfied employees took this extra time off. Further, individual absences varied over time, and the correlations between attitude measures and absenteeism fluctuated over the three-month reporting period. Thus the cost savings attributable to reduced absenteeism may be particular to the measurement period.

We are now in a position to relate the attitudinal measures to financial results and to estimate the potential benefits resulting from improvements in employee attitudes. The statistical approach for doing this was developed by Likert (1973). As an example, we'll relate tellers' intrinsic motivation scores ($M = 6.11$, $SD = 0.96$) and the average number of balancing shortages per month ($M = 3.07$, $SD = 1.74$).[2] To estimate the potential savings from a 0.5 standard deviation improvement in motivation, the steps are as follows:

1. present cost level = average number of balancing shortages × cost per incident
   = 3.07 × \$17.55
   = \$53.88 per employee per month
2. planned attitudinal improvement = 0.5 *SD*
3. estimated behavioral improvement = (planned attitudinal improvement in *SD* units) × (*SD* of balancing shortages) × ($r_{mot., shortages}$)
   = 0.5 × 1.74 × −0.23
   = −0.20

[2] M = mean; SD = standard deviation, a measure of the variability or dispersion of scores about their mean.

EXHIBIT 6.3 Relationship between attitudes and behavior (lagged three months)

Attitudes (measured in April)	Behaviors (measured in July)		
	Absenteeism	Turnover	Shortages
Intrinsic satisfaction	−0.81[a]	−0.20[b]	0.10
Job involvement	0.08	−0.29[a]	−0.12
Intrinsic motivation	−0.26[a]	−0.16[b]	−0.23[a]

[a]$p < 0.01$

[b]$p < 0.05$

Source: Mirvis, P. H., and Lawler, E. E., III. (1977). Measuring the financial impact of employee attitudes. *Journal of Applied Psychology*, *62*, 4.

4. new behavioral rate = present average number of shortages + estimated behavioral improvement
   = 3.07 + −0.20
   = 2.87 per employee per month
5. new cost level = new behavioral rate × cost per incident
   = 2.87 × $17.55
   = $50.37 per employee per month

A similar procedure was used to estimate the cost levels associated with the other attitudes that were measured (see Exhibit 6.4). For most measures, more positive attitudes are associated with lower costs. The cost figures are conservative for they reflect only the variable costs per teller for one month. For the bank tellers as a whole ($N = 160$) over a one-year period, an improvement in teller satisfaction of 0.5 standard deviations was estimated to result in direct savings of $37,676. Potential total savings were estimated to be $266,957.

Advantages of the Behavior Costing Approach

Behavior costing has three important advantages. First, it is a practical method for relating attitudes to costs that can be used in a wide variety of organizations. Moreover, it has the potential to increase significantly the impact and usefulness of attitudinal data. By focusing attention on employee satisfaction and motivation, results of the behavior costing approach could stimulate changes designed specifically to improve satisfaction and motivation.

A second advantage of this approach is that it relates attitudes to fu-

EXHIBIT 6.4 Costs per month per teller

		Cost (in dollars)			
Attitude	*Change*	*Absenteeism*	*Turnover*	*Shortage*	*Total*
Intrinsic satisfaction	+0.5*SD*	5.11	21.69	55.41	82.21
	0	11.60	36.35	53.90	101.85
	−0.5*SD*	18.09	51.04	52.37	121.50
Job involvement	+0.5*SD*	12.25	15.10	50.37	77.72
	0	11.60	36.35	53.90	101.85
	−0.5*SD*	10.96	57.61	57.39	125.96
Intrinsic motivation	+0.5*SD*	9.49	24.63	50.37	84.49
	0	11.60	36.35	53.90	101.85
	−0.5*SD*	13.71	48.08	55.74	117.53

Note: All costs are expressed in terms of 1990 dollars.

Source: Adapted from Mirvis, P. H., and Lawler, E. E., II. (1977). Measuring the financial impact of employee attitudes. *Journal of Applied Psychology, 62*, 6.

ture costs. Thus, organizations could use it as a way of diagnosing future costs, and as a basis for initiating programs designed to reduce those costs. This makes it possible for managers to estimate the cost savings and potential benefits associated with improved morale and group functioning.

Conceptually, behavioral cost measures should be most sensitive (in comparison to other indicators) to changes in employee satisfaction and motivation (Lawler and Rhode, 1976). A third advantage of the behavior costing approach (the attitude–costs model presented in this chapter), therefore, is that it provides a method for an empirical test of that hypothesis. It yields the financial measure most related to employee attitudes. Traditionally, human resource accounting has valued employee service at gross book value (the original investment expense), net book value (the original investment minus depreciation), and economic value (the anticipated financial return of the investment). In contrast, behavior costing shifts the emphasis from assigning a value to employees to assessing the economic consequences of their behavior (Mirvis and Lawler, 1977).

Problems with the Behavior Costing Approach

Despite its advantages, the behavior costing approach also creates a number of difficulties. One important issue concerns validation of the predicted cost savings. This only can be done by observing what happens when attitude changes actually occur. To test the validity of the cost figures presented earlier, Mirvis and Lawler collected data one year later from the same tellers. At that time the tellers' personal motivation had increased to 6.25 or 0.145 standard deviations. Actual shortages had decreased to $46.31 (in 1990 dollars) per month, somewhat below the anticipated level, but in the predicted direction. This kind of evidence suggests that the changes in attitude caused the changes in behavior, but since behavior costing is based upon correlational analyses, other causal explanations are possible.

Two additional problems in predicting behavioral rate changes and costs from attitudinal data stem from the nature of the attitude-behavior relationship. The first problem has to do with the appropriateness of the time lag. Mirvis and Lawler used a three-month lag, but they also examined one- and two-month lags. They found relationships between attitudes and behavior in all cases, but the relationships were stronger in the three-month lag. The superiority of the three-month lag is consistent with findings in the economic literature (Katona, 1975), but findings in the organizational literature suggest that a variety of time lags produce significant effects (Meyer and Raich, 1983; Taylor and Bowers, 1972). At this time, therefore, the safest course is probably to collect time-series data on attitudes and behavior at multiple measurement points, and then choose the interval that yields the most stable and representative relationships.

A related problem concerning the stability of attitude-behavior relationships is that the size and form of the relationship between these variables can change over time. In the Mirvis and Lawler study, for example, secondary analyses revealed that monthly time-series relationships between a single item measure of intrinsic satisfaction and teller shortages ranged from −0.67 to −0.06 over a four-month period. Unless this relationship is stable, predicted financial changes will not be accurate. In addition, the behavior costing model assumes a linear attitude-behavior relationship, but the actual relationship may well be curvilinear. Correlational methods are available to deal with curvilinear relations (for example, eta, the correlation ratio), but the point is that both the size and form of attitude-behavior relationships must be monitored over time with periodic corrections in the predicted savings based on the new relationships.

Special care must be taken not to over- or understate potential cost savings. Motivation and job satisfaction are likely to be improved by a combination of factors, such as job enrichment programs, participative management styles, or better employee selection procedures. Since the components of job attitudes (satisfaction, job involvement, intrinsic motivation, and so on) are rarely independent, to estimate separately the cost savings associated with each would overstate the resulting benefits. This suggests that monthly behavior measures should be related to the *set* of relevant attitude measures. This would probably result in more accurate estimates of the attitude-behavior relationships and the eventual financial benefits.

Financial benefits also might be overstated if substantial covariation exists among the rates or costs of absenteeism, turnover, and performance. It would seem appropriate, then, to remove statistically the effects of absenteeism and turnover from performance in estimating behavioral changes and financial benefits.

The costs of absenteeism, turnover, tardiness, and mistakes in job performance vary widely from one organization to another. Hence, comparisons across organizations may be less useful than intraorganizational comparisons of outcomes relative to baseline data.

A FINAL WORD

Clearly the time has arrived for behavioral scientists to speak the language of business. The methods described in this chapter provide a useful start in that direction, but the nonfinancial impact of changes in employee attitudes and motivation (for example, individual growth and well-being, organizational adaptability, and goodwill) cannot, and perhaps should not, be assigned an economic value. Management decisions made solely to optimize financial gains will miss completely the effects of organizational development or attitude change programs on nonfinancial results.

Nonetheless, while a number of problems are associated with relating attitudes to costs (see Exhibit 6.5), and refinements may be needed in the methods described here, the potential of cost-benefit comparisons of attitude-behavior relationships is enormous. The potential payoffs in improved personnel and financial planning provide ample justification for expending the necessary effort and resources to develop further methods for estimating the financial impact of employee attitudes.

EXHIBIT 6.5 Assumptions, advantages, and disadvantages of attitude-cost models

Model	*Assumptions*	*Advantages*	*Disadvantages*
Human Asset Valuation	Salary = value to organization; therefore attitudinal improvement enhances value to the organization.	a. Simple framework for measuring human assets b. Attitude Index may serve as a standard metric.	a. Effects of improved attitudes on job behavior are unknown b. No validation of predicted savings
Unit Cost	Changes in unit costs can be predicted from anticipated changes in attitudes. Therefore cost change = economic impact of attitudes	a. Reduces errors associated with equating to zero changes in the value of human organization from Time 1 to Time 2. b. Offers statistical method for relating attitudinal measures to financial results	a. Inclusion of fixed costs + inflationary trends in cost per unit yields irrelevant variance b. Ignores intervening processes between changes in attitudes and changes in unit cost c. Assumes constant attitude-behavior relationship over time

			d. Analysis is at work-group level, not at individual level
Behavior Costing	Attitudinal measures are indicators of subsequent employee behaviors—participation-membership and job performance	a. Relates attitudes to future costs b. Yields the financial measure most closely related to employee attitudes c. Analysis is at individual, not at work-group level	a. Difficult to validate cost savings since analyses are based on correlational data b. "Best" time lag for determining attitude-behavior relationships is unknown c. Instability in attitude-behavior relationships yields inaccurate financial changes

EXERCISES

1. You are given the following data relative to the five-member troubleshooting team of the Behrens Corporation:

Individual	Annual Salary	Job Grade	Tenure	Attitude Weight	Attitude Score
1. D. Hobbs	$34,000	32	10	8	1.15
2. P. Smith	18,000	24	6	5	1.04
3. T. Studley	30,000	37	14	10	1.28
4. B. Woo	28,000	30	10	7	1.20
5. W. Finkel	21,500	23	5	4	0.78

a. Use a human asset valuation approach to dollarize these attitudes, to compute the overall gain (or loss), and to compute the gain (or loss) per person.
b. What are two advantages and two drawbacks of this approach?

2. **a.** What is the purpose of each of the three components of the cost-benefit model of human resource development programs shown in Exhibit 6.1?
b. What are the three broad classes of costs (and savings) involved in human resource development programs? Give an example of each.

3. As a special project, top management wants to use behavior costing methodology as one input to its human resource planning model. Over a three-month period, you have found the correlation between job satisfaction and absenteeism to be -0.34 for a sample of clerical employees. Chronic absenteeism is a serious problem in this firm, and clerical employees average 2.2 days per month absent from work ($SD = 1.43$). Each such incident costs $158.26, of which $77.54 is a variable cost. If management were to institute a job enrichment program that would improve attitudes among the clerical employees by 0.45 standard deviation, what might be the potential savings per employee per month?

REFERENCES

AJZEN, I., and FISHBEIN, M. (1980). *Understanding attitudes and predicting social behavior.* Englewood Cliffs, NJ: Prentice-Hall.

CAMPBELL, J. P., and CAMPBELL, R. J. (Eds.). (1988). *Productivity in organizations.* San Francisco: Jossey-Bass.

CHAIKEN, S., and STANGOR, C. (1987). Attitudes and attitude change. *Annual Review of Psychology, 38,* 575–630.

FELDMAN, J. M., and LYNCH, J. G., JR. (1988). Self-generated validity and other effects of measurement on belief, attitude, intention, and behavior. *Journal of Applied Psychology, 73,* 421–435.

GOODMAN, P. S., DEVADAS, R., and GRIFFITH-HUGHSON, T. L. (1988). Groups and productivity: Analyzing the effectiveness of self-managing teams. In J. P. CAMPBELL and R. J. CAMPBELL (Eds.), *Productivity in organizations*. San Francisco: Jossey-Bass, pp. 295–327.

JONAH, B. A. (1984). Legislation and the prediction of reported seat belt use. *Journal of Applied Psychology, 69*, 401–407.

KATONA, G. (1975). *Psychological economics*. New York: Elsevier.

LAWLER, E. E. (1973) *Motivation in work organizations*. Monterey, CA: Brooks/Cole.

LAWLER, E. E., and RHODE, J. G. (1976). *Information and control in organizations*. Pacific Palisades, CA: Goodyear.

LIKERT, R. (1973). Human resource accounting: Building and assessing productive organizations. *Personnel, 50*, 8–24.

LIKERT, R., and BOWERS, D. G. (1973). Improving the accuracy of P/L reports by estimating the change in dollar value of the human organization. *Michigan Business Review, 25*, 15–24.

LOKEN, B. (1982). Heavy smokers', light smokers', and nonsmokers' beliefs about cigarette smoking. *Journal of Applied Psychology, 67*, 616–622.

MACY, B. A., and MIRVIS, P. H. (1976). A methodology for assessment of quality of work life and organizational effectiveness in behavioral-economic terms. *Administrative Science Quarterly, 21*, 212–226.

MARCH, J. O., and SIMON, H. A. (1958). *Organizations*. New York: Wiley.

MEYER, H. H., and RAICH, M. S. (1983). An objective evaluation of a behavior modeling training program. *Personnel Psychology, 36*, 755–761.

MIRVIS, P. H., and LAWLER, E. E., III. (1977). Measuring the financial impact of employee attitudes. *Journal of Applied Psychology, 62*, 1–8.

MIRVIS, P. H., and MACY, B. A. (1976). Accounting for the costs and benefits of human resource development programs: An interdisciplinary approach. *Accounting, Organizations, and Society, 1*, 79–93.

MOBLEY, W. H. (1982). *Employee turnover: Causes, consequences, and control*. Reading, MA: Addison-Wesley.

MYERS, M. S., and FLOWERS, V. S. (1974). A framework for measuring human assets. *California Management Review, 16* (4), 5–16.

ROTHENBERG, J. (1975). Cost–benefit analysis: A methodological exposition. In M. Guttentag and E. Struening (Eds.), *Handbook of evaluation research* (vol. 2). Beverly Hills, CA: Sage Publishing Co.

Survey Research Center. (1975). *Michigan organizational assessment package*. Ann Arbor, MI: Institute for Social Research.

TAYLOR, J., and BOWERS, D. (1972). *Survey of organizations*. Ann Arbor, MI: Institute for Social Research.

VROOM, V. H. (1964). *Work and motivation*. New York: Wiley.

ZALESNY, M. D. (1985). Comparison of economic and noneconomic factors in predicting faculty vote preference in a union representation election. *Journal of Applied Psychology, 70*, 243–256.

ZIMBARDO, P. G., EBBESEN, E. B., and MASLACH, C. (1990). *Influencing attitudes and changing behavior* (3rd ed.). New York: McGraw-Hill.

7

Labor Contract Costing

By far the largest costs incurred by U.S. corporations are labor costs. In capital-intensive organizations such as commercial airlines, labor costs account for about 36 percent of total expenses (Dubroff, 1986), but in labor-intensive organizations, such as the U.S. Postal Service, labor costs account for as much as 83 percent of total expenses (Karr, 1990). Given the magnitude of labor costs, their impact on profits is critical, and relatively small changes either in the size or in the compensation of the labor force can result in relatively large effects on profits. Hence it makes a difference—an important, practical difference—how management selects the best labor contract package to contribute to the achievement of organizational goals. Without a thorough knowledge of the effect of proposed labor expenditures on profits, cost control is impossible. In a collective bargaining situation, management must be able to know—or at least to estimate—the effect on profits of proposed changes in its labor contract before accepting or rejecting the changes.

Management's ability to control labor costs certainly is limited by its bargaining power relative to that of the unions. Nevertheless, management still can exert considerable influence on labor costs since the overall cost of labor depends not only on the size of the compensation package, but also on its component parts. For example, suppose a union is indifferent with respect to two alternative contract changes—the two have identical utility to union members. Yet the effect on profits of the two alternatives might be entirely different. To the extent that management is free to choose between the two alternatives, it has the opportunity to exercise important control over labor costs.

Evaluation of the costs of changes in labor contracts is particularly important when the potential costs of poor decisions are considered. Since many collective bargaining contracts are for three-year periods, mistakes made during negotiations are not easily rectified. Benefits granted for the duration of a contract may become permanent if a union can exact a high enough price when management wants to reduce or eliminate a benefit to which employees have become accustomed. If management overestimates the effect on profits of a wage package, it might take a costly (though unnecessary) strike rather than accede to union demands. Should management underestimate the effect on profits, the firm may find itself unable to compete successfully with other companies that did not sign a similar contract.

The task of evaluating the financial impact of contract proposals is formidable for three reasons, as Granof (1973) has pointed out. One, the financial burden of benefits (compensation in addition to direct payments) is difficult to estimate. Virtually all labor contracts contain provisions relating to benefits, and the number of workers receiving a variety of benefits is increasing rapidly. Two, contract clauses that do not involve compensation directly, such as those dealing with work schedules, job classifications, seniority rules, and training programs, are not easily quantified, yet, they have a considerable financial impact. Three, the relationships between labor costs and other aspects of a firm's operations often are elusive.

The U.S. Postal Service illustrates the difficulty of relating changes in operations to savings in labor costs. Despite an investment in automation of $11.7 billion from 1980 to 1989, postal productivity actually fell slightly during 1988 and 1989. Part of this drop was due to severe labor contract restrictions on work force reductions. Collective bargaining agreements ban layoffs, except of workers with less than six years on the job. Further, an employee cannot be laid off unless he or she is offered a job transfer first. Unfortunately, under the contracts, transferring a worker is even harder. In fact, junior workers with new skills are often the ones that supervisors want to keep. Due to situations such as these, the General Accounting Office concluded that the postal work force exceeded the service's estimates by 38,000 workers in fiscal 1989. The extra cost, some $1.34 billion, helps to explain why the postal service continues to lose money (Karr, 1990).

To be sure, changes in volume, product mix, and capital investment are likely to affect the amount of labor required. But changes in the amount of labor may in turn affect the firm's volume, product mix, and capital investment. Thus, Yamazaki, Japan's largest maker of machine tools, decided to invest $18 million in a new computer-controlled manufacturing plant that employs just 12 workers, instead of upgrading older plants (at far less cost) that would have required more than 200 skilled workers to produce the same number of precision components per month ("Look, No Hands," 1981).

Perhaps the most serious limitation is that firms tend to base their cost estimates on past experience rather than on future conditions (Mills, 1989). This is understandable, however, since historical data concerning labor costs, insurance premiums, labor mix, and the like are readily available, whereas data on future values of these variables are by necessity matters of conjecture. Despite these limitations, one of the most useful pieces of information management *and* the union can possess during the collective bargaining process is the effect of present demands on future operating costs. Such information not only aids each party during negotiations but also helps to prepare for future management of the work place. The process by which costs for a future contract may be computed is commonly referred to as "costing out." In the following sections we shall present a method by which either party may cost out demands. The method is adapted from a 1978 U.S. Department of Labor publication, *The Use of Economic Data in Collective Bargaining*, and from the June 1980 issue of *Midwest Monitor*. This method of costing out requires two basic pieces of information: the average compensation costs for the bargaining unit and the true value of increased demands made during negotiations.

AVERAGE COMPENSATION FOR THE BARGAINING UNIT

Average compensation, or weighted average compensation, represents the employer's average expense for each person on the payroll. When a settlement proposal is offered, this figure will help both parties in reaching a decision regarding the proposal. To compute average compensation costs, the following information is necessary:

- salary scales and benefit programs
- the distribution of employees in the unit according to pay steps, shifts, and length of service
- each employee's coverage status for each benefit offered

These figures may be chosen from a fixed point in time, preferably as close to the beginning of collective bargaining as possible. If the three figures above are known, almost all costs of compensation and the increases in compensation can be computed, except for overtime costs, which may vary from week to week.

The first step in computing compensation costs is to develop the *base* or existing compensation figure. This figure is essential in determining the percentage value of a requested increase in compensation. Thus, a $750 increase means different things to a unit whose base compensation is $30,000 (a 2.5 percent increase) and to a unit whose base compensation is $15,000 (a 5 percent increase).

To illustrate the process of computing a base compensation figure and of costing out a contract settlement, we will use as an example a bargaining unit of nurses in a city hospital. Although procedures for costing labor settlements differ slightly for public and for private sector organizations, the rapid proliferation of public sector unions makes such an example particularly appropriate. The unit has the characteristics shown in Exhibit 7.1. The information in Exhibit 7.1 allows a base compensation figure to be computed. Knowing the distribution of employees according to each classification and each of their salaries, we can compute the weighted salary for each classification. When this figure is divided by the total number of employees, the result is the weighted average annual base salary (see Exhibit 7.1). This method also will provide the average annual cost for longevity pay (additional pay given for length of service). The combined average salary cost and average annual cost of longevity pay for the nurses' bargaining unit is therefore $31,336.45 ($30,579 + $757.45) per year or $15.066 ($31,336.45/2,080) per hour. The hourly rate is needed to compute the cost of certain benefits—for example, overtime, shift differential, vacations, paid holidays, insurance, and pensions. Note that *both* salary and longevity pay are included in the weighted average hourly rate of pay. This is an important factor to consider when determining the effect of a salary increase on these benefits. Exhibits 7.2 through 7.5 show how the present cost of each of the above benefits is calculated.

The nine figures derived thus far may then be grouped together to provide a total figure for average annual compensation per employee:

base salary (Ex. 7.1)	$30,579.00
longevity pay (Ex. 7.1)	757.45
overtime (Ex. 7.2)	1,047.636
shift differential (Ex. 7.3)	2,229.06
vacations (Ex. 7.4)	1,369.19
holidays (Ex. 7.5)	1,205.28
hospitalization (Ex. 7.5)	1,128.48
clothing allowance (Ex. 7.5)	250.00
pension (Ex. 7.5)	2,769.09
total	$41,335.19

EXHIBIT 7.1 Nurses' bargaining unit

a. **Employment and Salaries**

Classification	*Number of Nurses*	*Salary*
Probationary		
Step 1	20	$24,000
Step 2	40	26,000
L.P.N.	125	28,000
R.N.	105	35,000
Head nurse	12	45,000
	302	

b. **Longevity Payments**

Longevity Step	*Number of Nurses*	*Longevity Pay*
Step 1	35 L.P.N.s + 30 R.N.s	$ 750
Step 2	58 L.P.N.s	1,500
Step 2	50 R.N.s	1,500
Step 2	12 head nurses	1,500

c. **Hours of Work**

The scheduled hours consist of five 8-hour shifts, or an average of 40 hours per week, and a total of 2,080 hours paid for per year.

d. **Overtime Premium**

All overtime hours are paid at the rate of time-and-one-half. The nurses' bargaining unit worked a total of 14,000 overtime hours during the preceding year.

e. **Shift Differential**

The shift differential is 10 percent for all hours between 4 P.M. and 8 A.M. However, 82 members of the unit work exclusively on the day shift, from 8 A.M. to 4 P.M. They are 4 head nurses, 35 R.N.s at longevity step 2, and 43 L.P.N.s at step 2.

f. **Vacations**

60 employees (probationers): 5 shifts
122 employees (longevity 0 or 1): 10 shifts
120 employees (all others): 15 shifts

g. **Holidays**

Each nurse is entitled to 10 paid holidays and receives 8 hours pay for each holiday.

h. **Clothing Allowance**

$250 per nurse per year.

(continues)

EXHIBIT 7.1 Nurses' bargaining unit (continued)

i. **Hospitalization**

Type of Coverage	*Number of Nurses*	*Employer's Monthly Payment*
Single coverage	45	$ 60.00
Family coverage	257	100.00

Average Annual Base Salary

(1) *Classification*	(2) *Number of Nurses*	(3) *Salary*	(4) *Weighted Salaries* (2) × (3)
Probationary			
Step 1	20	$24,000	$ 480,000
Step 2	40	26,000	1,040,000
L.P.N.	125	28,000	3,500,000
R.N.	105	35,000	3,675,000
Head nurse	12	45,000	540,000
			$9,235,000

average annual base salary = $9,235,000 ÷ 302
or $30,579 per year

j. **Pensions**

The employer contributes an amount equal to 8 percent of the payroll (including basic salaries, longevity, overtime, and shift differentials).

Longevity Pay

(1) *Longevity Step*	(2) *Number of Nurses*	(3) *Longevity Pay*	(4) *Total Longevity Pay* (2) × (3)
Step 1	65	$ 750	$ 48,750
Step 2	120	1,500	180,000
			$228,750

average annual longevity pay = $228,750 ÷ 302*
or $757.45 per year

*Since the unit is trying to determine its average base compensation—that is, all the salary and benefit items its members receive collectively—the total cost of longevity pay must be averaged over the entire unit of 302 nurses.

EXHIBIT 7.2 Overtime

Overtime work for the nurses' bargaining unit is paid at the rate of time-and-one-half. This means that part of the total overtime costs is an amount paid at straight-time rates and part is a premium payment.

	(1) *Annual Cost*	(2) *Number of Nurses*	(3) *Average Annual Cost* (1) ÷ (2)
Straight-time cost ($15.066 × 14,000 overtime hours)[a]	$210,924	302	$ 698.424
Half-time premium cost (½ × $210,924)	105,462	302	349.212
Total overtime cost	$316,386		$1,047.636

[a]Based on preceding year's total overtime hours.

The additional $10,756.19 each nurse receives in benefits ($41,335.19 − $30,579) represents 35.2 percent of base pay, slightly less than average in 1989 across all organizations ("Labor Letter," 1989).

Computing the Costs of Increases

Once the base compensation costs have been determined, increases in those costs can be computed. Assume that the nurses' bargaining unit negotiates a settlement that contains the following changes:

- a 5 percent increase in base salaries
- two additional vacation days for all employees at the second step of longevity
- an improvement in the benefits provided by the hospitalization program, which amounts to an additional $10.00 per month for family coverage and $5.00 for single coverage.

The objective in costing out this increase is to obtain the average cost of the increase per nurse per year. It is important to aggregate the costs of individual items in the contract so that the implications of the total "package" can be evaluated by both parties.

To compute the average annual increase, the base salary ($30,579) is multiplied by the percent increase (5 percent). This results in an increase

EXHIBIT 7.3 Shift differential

The nurses' bargaining unit receives a shift differential of 10 percent for all hours worked between 4 P.M. and 8 A.M. But 82 members of the unit who work exclusively on the day shift do not receive the differential. This leaves 220 nurses who do receive the differential.

(1) Classification	(2) No. on Shift Pay	(3) Salary	(4) 10% of (3)	(5) Total Cost (2) × (4)
Probationary				
Step 1	20	$24,000	$2,400	$ 48,000
Step 2	40	26,000	2,600	104,000
L.P.N.s				
Longevity 0	32	28,000	2,800	89,600
Longevity 1	35	28,750[a]	2,875	100,625
Longevity 2	15	29,500[a]	2,950	44,250
R.N.s				
Longevity 0	25	35,000	3,500	87,500
Longevity 1	30	35,750[a]	3,575	107,250
Longevity 2	15	36,500[a]	3,650	54,750
Head nurses	8	46,500[a]	4,650	37,200
	220			$673,175

average annual cost of shift differential = $673,175 ÷ 302[b] or $2,229.056 per year

[a]Base salary plus longevity pay ($750 for step 1 and $1,500 for step 2).

[b]Since the unit is trying to determine its average base compensation, that is, all the salary and benefit items its members receive collectively, the total cost of the shift differential must be averaged over the entire unit of 302.

of $1,528.95. There is no increase in longevity pay for this example. Had the longevity pay been tied to the base salary on a percentage basis there then would have been an increase in that amount also. As a result, the increase in the unit's average annual salary (base salary and longevity payments) is not 5 percent but 4.88 percent. This is determined by dividing the increase ($1,528.95) by the base salary plus longevity payments ($30,579 + $757.45 = $31,336.45).

Computing the cost of an increase is important because of the impact on the cost of benefits. This impact on benefits is often referred to as the *roll up*. As salary increases, so does the cost of benefits such as vacations,

EXHIBIT 7.4 Vacations

Vacation costs for the unit are influenced by the amount of vacations received by employees with different lengths of service and the pay scales of those employees.

(1) Classification	(2) Number of Nurses	(3) Hourly Rate[a]	(4) Hours of Vacation[b]	(5) Total Vacation Hours (2) × (4)	(6) Total Vacation Costs (3) × (5)
Probationary					
Step 1	20	$11.538	40	800	$ 9,230.40
Step 2	40	12.50	40	1,600	20,000.00
L.P.N.s					
Longevity 0	32	13.462	80	2,560	34,462.72
Longevity 1	35	13.822	80	2,800	38,701.60
Longevity 2	58	14.183	120	6,960	98,713.68
R.N.s					
Longevity 0	25	16.827	80	2,000	33,654.00
Longevity 1	30	17.188	80	2,400	41,251.20
Longevity 2	50	17.548	120	6,000	105,288.00
Head nurses	12	22.356	120	1,440	32,192.64
	302			26,560	$413,494.24

average annual vacation cost = $413,494.24 ÷ 302, or $1,369.19 per year

[a]Derived from annual salaries (including longevity pay), divided by 2,080 hours (40 hours × 52 weeks).

[b]Since each nurse works an 8-hour shift (excluding overtime), the hours of vacation are derived by multiplying the number of work shifts of vacation entitlement (see Exhibit 7.1) by 8 hours.

EXHIBIT 7.5 Paid holidays, hospitalization insurance, and other benefits

Paid Holidays

Unlike vacations, the number of holidays received by an employee is not typically tied to length of service. Where the level of benefits is uniform, as it is with paid holidays, the calculation to determine its average cost is less complex.

In the nurses' bargaining unit, each nurse receives 8 hours of pay for each of his or her 10 paid holidays, or a total of 80 hours of holiday pay.

average annual cost of paid holidays = $1,205.28 (80 hours × $15.066 average straight-time hourly rate derived from average salary cost plus average longevity cost)

Hospitalization Insurance

(1) Type of Coverage	(2) Number of Nurses	(3) Yearly Premium Cost to Employer	(4) Total Cost to Employer (2) × (3)
Single	45	$ 720	$ 32,400
Family	257	1,200	308,400
	302		$340,800

average annual cost of hospitalization insurance = $340,800 ÷ 302, or $1,128,477

Other Benefits

1. Pensions cost the employer 8 percent of payroll. The payroll amounts to $10,453,311 (salary cost of $9,235,000 [Exhibit 7.1], longevity cost of $228,750 [Exhibit 7.1], overtime cost of $316,386 [Exhibit 7.2], and shift differential cost of $673,175 [Exhibit 7.3]). Eight percent of this total is $836,264.88, which, when divided by 302, yields $2,769.09 as the average cost of pensions per nurse per year.
2. The yearly cost of the clothing allowance is $250 per nurse.

holidays, and overtime premiums. The *cost* of the benefits increases even if the *level* of benefits does not go up. In the example on longevity pay, the roll up did not come into play because the longevity pay was a fixed amount. Other types of benefits that are often exempt from the roll up are shift differentials, clothing allowances, and most group insurance plans.

Any of these examples might be affected by the roll up if their cost is tied to the base salary amount.

In our example, it has been determined already that no change in longevity pay will occur because it is a fixed dollar amount. The hours of work are not affected, nor is the clothing allowance. The remaining items in the budget will be affected to some degree. The next task is to identify exactly how they will be changed. In our example, the items whose cost will be changed as a result of the roll-up effect include overtime premiums, shift differentials, holidays, and pensions. These benefits are tied to the original average annual salary (base salary plus longevity). The 4.88 percent increase in the average annual salary will increase the *cost* of these benefits. The increased costs are shown in Exhibit 7.6.

Once the effect of roll up has been determined, the next step is to identify which items are changed by an *increase* in benefits. Items may be changed either by the roll-up effect or by an increase in benefits, or both. In the nurses' settlement, the hospitalization benefit costs are changed because of an increase in benefits. The cost is a fixed dollar amount and thus is not subject to an increase in benefits because of the roll up. Costing out this benefit for the new contract entails multiplying the cost of the new program by the number of employees receiving the benefits (see Exhibit 7.7).

Finally, one item is affected by both the roll up and an increase in benefits—the vacation program. All vacation days will be increased by the cost increase in base salaries plus an increase of two shifts (48 hours) for all employees at the second step of longevity. The first step in calculating the total additional cost of the new vacation program is to compute the

EXHIBIT 7.6 Roll-up costs of benefits in nurses' bargaining agreement

(1) Benefit	(2) Base Average Annual Cost[a]	(3) Roll-Up Factor	(4) Increased Cost (2) × (3)
Overtime (premium only)	$ 349.212	0.0488	$ 17.042
Shift differential	2,229.056	0.0488	108.778
Holidays	1,205.28	0.0488	58.818
Pensions	2,769.09	0.0488	135.132
			$319.77

[a]As derived in Exhibits 7.2, 7.3, and 7.5

EXHIBIT 7.7 Increased cost of hospitalization benefits in nurses' bargaining agreement

(1) *Type of Coverage*	(2) *Number Covered*	(3) *Annual Cost of Improvement*	(4) *Total New Cost* (2) × (3)
Single	45	$ 60	$ 2,700
Family	257	120	30,840
			$33,540

The unit's average hospitalization cost will be increased by $111.06 per year ($33,540 ÷ 302 employees).

cost of the two additional shifts prior to the 4.88 percent salary increase. These costs are shown in Exhibit 7.8. As the exhibit demonstrates, with no increase in salaries, the increase in vacation days would cost $31,492.57. The next step is to compute the total cost of the 4.88 percent increase. These figures are shown in Exhibit 7.9.

Exhibit 7.9 indicates two added costs to the vacation benefit: the $31,492.57 that represents the increase in benefits, and the $21,715.36 that is a result of the increase in wages. When the two are summed and divided by the number of nurses in the unit, the *total average cost* of the new vacation benefit is $176.19 ($53,207.93 ÷ 302 nurses). This calculation would have been different (and considerably easier) if the vacation improvement had been granted across the board, to everyone in the unit. If the entire bargaining unit were to receive an additional 16 hours of vacation, the total additional hours would then be 4,832 (16 × 302). These hours would then be multiplied by the unit's old straight-time rate (15.066) in order to arrive at the cost of the additional vacation improvement, which would have come to $72,798.91. In that case, the total cost of vacations (the across-the-board improvement plus the impact of the 4.88 percent average annual salary increase) would have been computed as follows:

roll up of old vacation costs ($413,494.24 × 0.0488)	$20,178.52
cost of vacation improvement	72,798.91
roll-up cost of improvement ($72,798.91 × 0.0488)	3,552.59
total incremental cost of vacations	$96,530.02

EXHIBIT 7.8 Incremental cost of vacations at present hourly rates

(1) Number of Nurses	(2) Hours of Increased Vacation	(3) Total Hours (1) × (2)	(4) Existing Hourly Rates[a]	(5) Cost of Improvement (3) × (4)
58 L.P.N.s	16	928	14.183	$13,161.82
50 R.N.s	16	800	17.548	14,038.40
12 head nurses	16	192	22.356	4,292.35
				$31,492.57

[a]See Exhibit 7.4 for derivation of hourly rates.

When spread over the entire bargaining unit, the increase in the average cost of vacations would have been $319.64 per nurse per year ($96,530.02 ÷ 302 nurses).

The method we have described above does not apply only to vacations. It applies to any situation where a salary-related benefit is to be improved equally for every member of the bargaining unit (such as an additional paid holiday).

The Total Increase in the Average Cost of Compensation

Summing the increases in each of the items that will change in the nurses' contract settlement yields the total increase in the bargaining unit's *average cost of compensation*. The items that we have considered include:

base salary (pp. 155–156)	$1,528.95
longevity pay	0.00
overtime	51.96[a]
shift differential (Exhibit 7.6)	108.78
vacations (p. 160)	176.19
holidays (Exhibit 7.6)	58.82
hospitalization (Exhibit 7.7)	111.06
clothing allowance	0.00
pensions (Exhibit 7.6)	135.13
total increase	$2,170.89

[a]The total increased cost of overtime includes the increased cost of straight-time earnings ($34.92), plus the increased cost of the premium ($17.04).

EXHIBIT 7.9 Incremental cost of vacations at increased hourly rates

(1) Classification	(2) Existing Vacation Costs[a]	(3) Increase in Cost[b]	(4) Adjusted Base Costs (2) + (3)	(5) Roll Up Factor	(6) Increased Cost from Roll Up (4) × (5)
Probationary					
Step 1	$ 9,230.40	———	$ 9,230.40	0.0488	$ 450.44
Step 2	20,000.00	———	20,000.00	0.0488	976.00
L.P.N.s					
Longevity 0	34,462.72	———	34,462.72	0.0488	1,681.78
Longevity 1	38,701.60	———	38,701.60	0.0488	1,888.64
Longevity 2	98,713.68	$13,161.82	111,875.50	0.0488	5,459.52
R.N.s					
Longevity 0	33,654.00	———	33,654.00	0.0488	1,642.32
Longevity 1	41,251.20	———	41,251.20	0.0488	2,013.06
Longevity 2	105,288.00	14,038.40	119,326.40	0.0488	5,823.13
Head nurses	32,192.64	4,292.35	36,484.99	0.0488	1,780.47
	$413,494.24	$31,492.57	$444,986.81	0.0488	$21,715.36

[a]The base or existing vacation costs are from Exhibit 7.4 and are derived from average annual salary (base salary plus longevity).

[b]From Exhibit 7.8

Remember that the nurses' average annual compensation (base pay plus benefits) was $41,335.19. The total dollar increase amounts to $2,170.89, or 5.25 percent. This is the amount by which the nurses' settlement increased the employer's average yearly cost per nurse.

Despite the apparent comprehensiveness of coverage of the items in the nurses' settlement, all of the possible items affected by roll up were not considered. In addition to overtime premiums, shift differentials, and pensions, other possible items include:

- *Social security and unemployment insurance contributions*: The employer's contribution to both of these programs is computed as a percentage of each employee's wage up to a fixed amount annually. To the extent that the annual earnings of some employees are less than the fixed amounts, an increase in wages will require an increase in social security and unemployment insurance contributions.
- *Life insurance*: Often the amount of insurance coverage for which the employer pays is a percentage of wages or a varying amount corresponding to graduated wages in a table. As employee earnings increase, so too will the amount and cost of coverage.
- *Disability insurance premiums*: To the extent that this benefit is a percentage of base pay, the employer's cost of providing it will also increase.

In costing out contract settlements, some analysts include the costs of holidays, vacations, rest periods, wash-up time, and paid absences in calculating roll up. Steckel (1980) has shown that including these items overstates the cost of roll up per se because a wage increase applies to the total 2,080 straight-time hours in a year (40 hours × 52 weeks). So, for example, a 50¢ per hour wage increase is not going to cost the company any more than the 50¢ per hour whether the employee works and is paid or does not work, but is paid for the time. In other words, there is a 50¢ per hour increase, and no more than that, whether the employee works 1,880 hours a year and has ten holidays and three weeks of vacation totalling 200 hours, or whether he or she works the full 2,080 hours in the year and has no established holidays and vacation. However, the company will pay more than the 50¢ per hour for the overtime premium, shift premium, and the other roll-up benefits we noted above, because they are based on a percentage of wages. When wages go up, they have a secondary impact on these benefits. To provide a more accurate picture of the cost of a labor settlement, a distinction should be made between hours paid for per year and hours worked per year (Hazelton, 1979). We'll continue with the nurses' bargaining unit example to show how this is done.

Computing the Hourly Cost of Compensation

In the case of the hourly computation, the goal is to obtain the cost per hour of *work*. Hence we must separate hours worked from hours paid. The difference between the two is leave time.

In the nurses' bargaining unit, for example, each nurse receives an annual salary that covers 2,080 regularly scheduled hours. In addition, each works an average of 46.36 hours of overtime per year. The sum of these two—regularly scheduled hours and overtime, or 2,126.36—equals the total hours paid.

However, hours paid is not the same as hours worked, because some of those hours are paid leave time. Nurses in the bargaining unit receive paid leave time in the form of vacations and holidays. The number of hours actually worked by each employee is 1,958 (2,126 hours paid, minus 168 hours of paid leave).

Each nurse receives 80 hours in paid holidays per year. The number of hours of vacation per year was derived as follows:

60 nurses (probationary) × 40 hours	2,400 hours
67 L.P.N.s × 80 hours	5,360 hours
58 L.P.N.s × 120 hours	6,960 hours
55 R.N.s × 80 hours	4,400 hours
50 R.N.s × 120 hours	6,000 hours
12 head nurses × 120 hours	1,440 hours
	26,560 hours

This averages out to 88 hours of vacation per nurse (26,560 ÷ 302) which, together with 80 holiday hours, totals 168 paid leave hours.

The paid leave hours are hours paid above and beyond hours worked. Thus, in order to obtain the hourly cost that they represent, the annual dollar cost of these benefits is divided by the annual hours *worked*.

So it is with all benefits, not only paid leave. In exchange for those benefits the employer receives hours of work (the straight-time hours and the overtime hours). Consequently, *the hourly cost of any benefit will be obtained by dividing the annual cost of the benefit by the annual number of hours worked.* In some instances that cost is converted into money that ends up in the employee's pocket, as is the case with benefits like shift differentials, overtime premiums, and clothing allowances. In other instances—such as hospitalization and pensions—the employee is provided with benefits in the form of insurance programs. And in the case of paid leave time, the return to the employee is in terms of fewer hours of work. Now we'll return to the problem of computing the hourly cost of compensation.

The average annual costs of the benefits of the nurses' bargaining unit were developed earlier in connection with the computations of the unit's average annual base compensation. In order to convert the costs of these benefits into an average hourly amount, they are divided by 1,958, the average hours worked during the year by each employee in the unit. As can be seen in Exhibit 7.10, the hourly cost of all benefits amounts to $4.749.

Total compensation includes base pay plus benefit costs. For the nurses in our example, base pay is $31,336.45 per year (average salary plus average longevity payments). On a straight-time hourly basis, this comes to $15.066 ($31,336.45 ÷ 2,080 hours). Even with the straight-time portion for the year's overtime included ($098.424), the average straight-time hourly rate of pay will remain at $15.066 ($32,034.874 ÷ 2,126.36 hours).

Now we'll recapitulate these salary and benefit cost data on an average annual compensation basis and on an average hourly compensation basis:

	Annually	*Hourly*
Straight-time earnings	$32,034.874 ÷ 2,126.36	$15.066
Benefits	9,300.31 ÷ 1,958	4.75
Total compensation	$41,335.19	$19.816

The $41,335.19 figure is identical to the figure developed earlier in the chapter to represent average annual compensation per employee, even though the method used to arrive at it is different. Essentially the same process is followed if the *increase* in compensation is to be measured on an hourly (instead of annual) basis.

The 5 percent pay increase that the nurses received would be worth 73.51¢ per hour ($30,579 × 0.05 = $1,528.95 ÷ 2,080 = $0.7351). The annual increase in the unit's cost of benefits per nurse—$607.02 for all items combined (overtime premium only, shift differential, vacation, holidays, hospitalization, and pensions)—works out to 31¢ per hour ($607.02 ÷ 1,958 hours).

Together these represent a gain in average compensation of $1.045 per hour, or 5.27 percent ($1.045 ÷ $19.816). This is 0.02 percent off the

EXHIBIT 7.10 Hourly cost of benefits

(1) Cost of Benefit	(2) Average Annual Cost	(3) Average Hours Worked	(4) Average Hourly Cost (2) ÷ (3)
Overtime premium[a]	$ 349.212	1,958	0.178
Shift differential	2,229.056	1,958	1.138
Vacations	1,369.19	1,958	0.699
Holidays	1,205.28	1,958	0.616
Hospitalization	1,128.477	1,958	0.576
Clothing allowance	250.00	1,958	0.128
Pensions	2,769.09	1,958	1.414
	$9,300.31		4.749

[a]Includes only the premium portion of the pay for overtime work.

amount of increase (5.25 percent) reflected by the annual data—a difference due to the rounding of decimals during computation.

Conclusion

If the data that were used for the nurses' bargaining unit in our discussion are available for an actual unit, almost all demands can be evaluated in terms of future costs. Costing out demands requires careful documentation and thorough record keeping. But in return, both of the parties will have the ability to see what effect the increases will have on the budget. Costing out prepares the parties for realistic negotiations; offers and demands are supported by the facts obtained through costing out. Finally, because costing out is a clearly defined method, it reduces the discrepancies and disagreements over budget items. Although costing out will not provide answers to every question that arises, it will provide important information for the parties' use during collective bargaining.

ROLE OF THE COMPUTER IN COLLECTIVE BARGAINING

Clearly, new approaches to the determination of the financial impact of proposed labor contracts are needed, and computers can help enormously in this effort. For example, cost-of-living adjustments (COLAs) present special analytical problems since the amount of increase to be granted over the life of a contract not only is variable, but also is beyond the control of management. Computer simulation would permit evaluation of financial impact on a "what if?" basis. That is, what if the maximum increase required by the proposed contract is the actual increase that must be granted? What if the price index reaches this level, or that one; what will it cost us?

Until recently few companies or unions used mathematical models or simulations during negotiations to test the effects of alternative "packages" of demands. The United Auto Workers union now uses a computer to examine quickly the effect of any given management proposal—for example, to alter the formula by which management adjusts workers' pay due to changes in the cost of living. Computers also can be of great help in *preparing* for negotiations: the International Brotherhood of Electrical Workers uses a computer to study about 100 items in each of its local contracts. Both the United Food and Commercial Workers union and the Service Employees union use computers to store their local contracts so that they can examine contract trends among the industries whose workers they represent ("Labor Letter," 1984).

Computer-based spreadsheet programs, such as Lotus® 1-2-3®, Quattro-Pro®, or Excel®, incorporate features that facilitate the modeling of current or proposed features of a labor contract. Indeed, the act of building a model on a spreadsheet defines all of the mathematical relationships in the model—sums, products, divisions, averages, and net present values. In this chapter, we have used many such operations to compute example values such as shift differentials, vacation costs, and pension costs.

Once such a model has been developed, the effects of changes in the model can be recalculated almost instantly and displayed in tabular or graphic form. This feature allows a researcher to ask an unlimited variety of "what if?" questions. To cost a labor contract, a researcher might examine the impact on total labor costs of changes in variables such as social security tax rates and wage bases, unemployment insurance rates, the impact of roll up on overtime costs and on the costs of other benefits that are tied to wage base rates, pension contributions, changes in the vesting schedule, changes in the premiums paid for health insurance, the effect over time of performance bonuses versus wage increases, the effect of proposed increases on wage differentials between supervisory and nonsupervisory employees, and the impact on labor costs of front-loaded versus back-loaded salary increases.

For example, a back-loaded wage increase over a three-year agreement of \$1.00, \$1.00, and \$1.50 (total = \$3.50) might cost the company less than a front-loaded increase of \$1.80, \$0.80, and \$0.60 (total = \$3.20).

EXHIBIT 7.11 Effect of front- versus back-loaded salary increases over a three-year collective bargaining contract

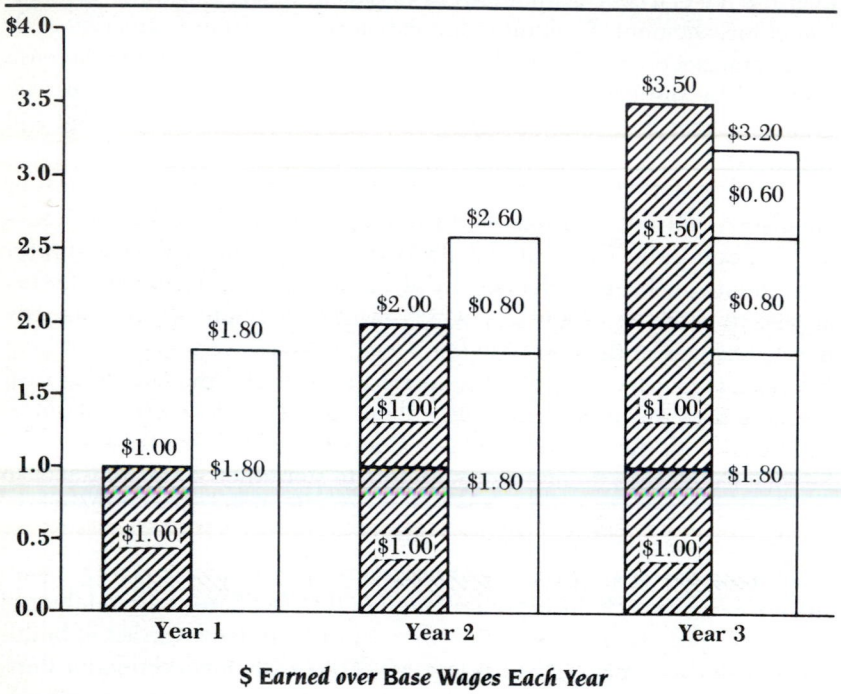

(continues)

Under the back-loaded arrangement, an employee will earn $1.00 more for three years, $1.00 more for two years, and $1.50 more for one year—a total of $6.50 more over the term of the contract. Under the front-loaded contract, an employee will earn $1.80 for three years, $0.80 for two years, and $0.60 for one year, for a total of $7.60. The conclusion: front-loading the increases yields a larger total increase over the life of the contract, but it has the effect of raising the base rate for subsequent negotiations. This might lead to uncompetitively higher total labor costs over, say, a ten-year horizon. Graphic displays, using bar charts, pie charts, or line graphs, can help all parties grasp more fully the impact of changes such as these, as Exhibit 7.11 illustrates.

The computer can also play a role with respect to process issues. For example, a personal computer program called "The Art of Negotiating" simulates the mechanics of negotiations. The program employs strict

EXHIBIT 7.11 Continued

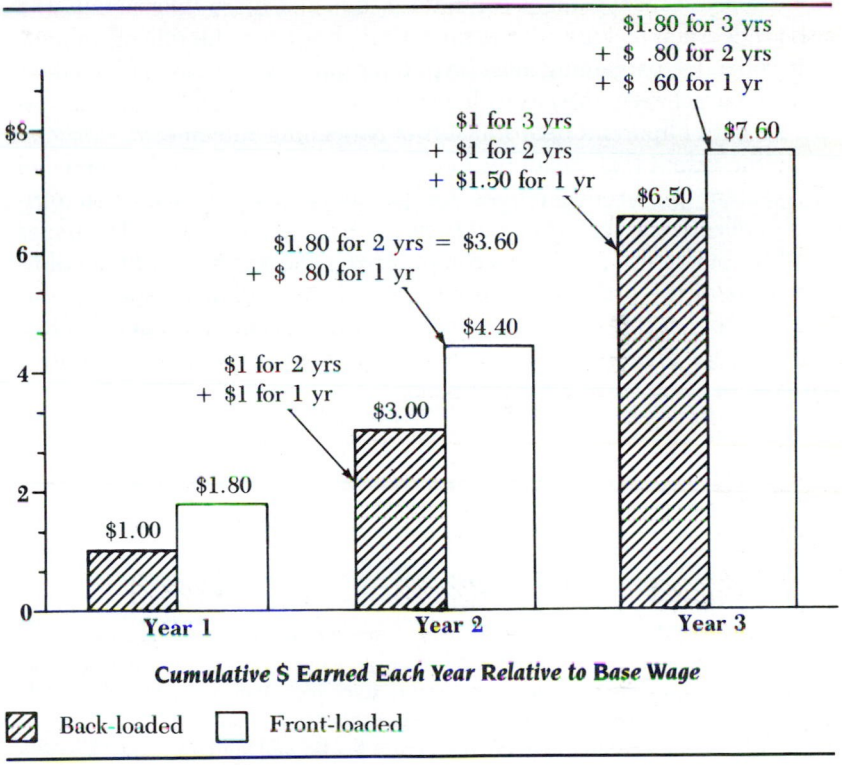

guidelines. For example, visual blocks (each of which must be supplied with information from the user) cover the eight stages of preparation for negotiations: subject matter, objectives, issues and positions, fact finding, needs and gambits, climates, strategies, and the agenda. The program provides the user with a number of options; for example, the user can revise previous entries or print out a cumulative summary of entered information. Can such a program be helpful? One reviewer summarized his experience as follows:

> I must admit that I approached "The Art of Negotiating" with considerable skepticism. Yet, upon using it, I found it to have the potential to be of help—if one happens to be the type of individual who is willing to spend the considerable time necessary to train oneself for negotiations rather than simply working with one's gut feelings (Sandberg-Diment, 1985, p. F13).

Computer models will probably be used more widely in the future as both labor and management continue to demand more information as a basis for decision making. At the same time, however, the role of computers in collective bargaining must be put in proper perspective, for content (actual contract elements) as well as process (interpersonal dynamics) issues are both important determinants of bargaining outcomes.

To the extent that computer models could track accurately union and management preference curves for particular settlements, then ultimately collective bargaining would cease to exist as we know it. The issues would become mere pawns in a computerized chess game, and the political aspects of the process would be scuttled. Since that prospect seems rather remote at this time, the most likely role of computers in collective bargaining for the foreseeable future will probably be to help the parties make decisions regarding content issues.

EXERCISES

1. a. Divide the class into two groups, with three or four students withdrawing to act as judges for the debate to follow. Half the class will prepare a debate, resolved that computer-based mathematical models that test the effects of alternative sets of demands should be used widely in preparation for collective bargaining. The other half prepares to argue that such computer-based models should not be used widely in preparation for collective bargaining.

b. Each team should appoint a discussion leader and spokesperson. Prepare arguments for about 20 minutes. During this time the judges should decide on the criteria they will use to evaluate the presentations.

c. The class should reassemble, and each side should present its arguments. Post arguments short-hand style on the chalkboard. Each group has 5 minutes to make its presentation. After the presentations each group has one minute for rebuttal. Judges act as timekeepers.

d. Judges then meet in front of the participants and decide on the winner. They should state clearly why they decided as they did.

2. a. Exhibit 7.12 provides information about a firefighters' bargaining unit. Using this information, compute the average annual compensation of each firefighter. Include the cost of the following items: base salary, longevity pay, overtime, shift differential, vacations, holidays, hospitalization, clothing allowance, and pensions.

b. Assume the bargaining unit negotiates a settlement that contains the following changes:

- a 5 percent increase in base salaries and longevity pay
- an additional vacation day for all employees in the bargaining unit

EXHIBIT 7.12 Firefighters' bargaining unit

a. **Employment and Salaries**

Classification	*Number of Firefighters*	*Salary*
Probationary		
Step 1	5	$27,000
Step 2	10	29,000
Private	65	31,000
Lieutenant	15	36,000
Captain	5	45,000
	100	

b. **Longevity Payments**

Longevity Step	*Number of Firefighters*	*Longevity Pay*
Step 1	20 Privates	$ 500
Step 2	10 Privates	1,000
Step 2	15 Lieutenants	1,000
Step 2	5 Captains	1,000

c. **Hours of Work**

The scheduled hours consist of one 24-hour shift every three days (one on, two off) or an average of 56 hours per week and a total of 2,912 hours per year.

d. **Overtime Premium**

All overtime hours are paid at the rate of time-and-one-half. The members of the bargaining unit worked a total of 5,000 overtime hours during the preceding year.

e. **Shift Differential**

The shift differential is 10 percent for all hours between 4 P.M. and 8 A.M. However, 10 members of the unit work exclusively on the day shift, from 8 A.M. to 4 P.M. They are 1 captain, 3 lieutenants, 3 privates at longevity step 2, and 3 privates at step 1.

(continues)

EXHIBIT 7.12 Continued

f. ***Vacations***

15 employees (probationers): 5 shifts
35 employees (privates): 10 shifts
50 employees (all others): 15 shifts

g. ***Holidays***

Each firefighter is entitled to 10 paid holidays and receives 8 hours pay for each holiday.

h. ***Clothing Allowance***

$250 per employee per year.

i. ***Hospitalization***

Type of Coverage	*Number of Fire-fighters*	*Employer's Monthly Payment*
Single coverage	15	$75.00
Family coverage	85	110.00

j. ***Pensions***

The employer contributes an amount equal to 8 percent of the payroll (including base salaries, longevity, overtime, and shift differentials).

- improvements in hospitalization insurance that amount to $11 a month for family coverage and $6 a month for single coverage

Cost out the average annual increases in the nine items noted in Exhibit 7.12.

c. Cost out the increases computed in part b on an average *hourly* basis.

REFERENCES

Costing out in the public sector. (1980, May/June). *Midwest Monitor*, pp. 1–7.

DUBROFF, H. (1986, May 12). Ill-feeling lingering at United. *Denver Post*, pp. 1B, 5B.

GRANOF, M. H. (1973). *How to cost your labor contract*. Washington, DC: Bureau of National Affairs.

HAZELTON, W. A. (1979, May). How to cost labor settlements. *Management Accounting*, 57, 19–23.

KARR, A. R. (1990, March 7). Letter bomb: Postal Service again asks for rate increase as automation lags. *Wall Street Journal*, pp. A1, A12.

Labor letter. (1984, November 20). *Wall Street Journal*, p. 1.

Labor letter. (1989, October 31). *Wall Street Journal*, p. A1.

Look, no hands. (1981, November 16). *Time*, p. 127.

MILLS, D. Q. (1989). *Labor-management relations* (4th ed.). New York: McGraw-Hill.

SANDBERG-DIMENT, E. (1985, April 21). How to hone negotiating skills. *New York Times*, p. F13.

STECKEL, R. G. (1980). The misuse of roll-up in costing contract settlements. *Personnel Administrator*, 25, (3), 33–34.

PART III

Personnel Programs: A Return-on-Investment Perspective

8

Utility: The Concept and Its Measurement

In the past, personnel programs often have been selected and implemented because they were fashionable (especially human relations programs) or commercially appealing, or because of the entertainment value they offered the target audience. But personnel costs continue to consume larger and larger portions of the total cost of doing business; for example, in 1990, U.S. Postal Service labor costs accounted for 83 percent of total expenses (Karr, 1990). As this trend continues HR executives may be under increased pressure to justify new or continuing programs. Such justification requires a consideration of the relative utilities to the organization of alternative strategies for reaching targeted objectives.

Utility analysis is the determination of institutional gain or loss (outcomes) anticipated from various courses of action. When faced with a choice among strategies, management should choose the strategy that maximizes the expected utility for the organization across all possible outcomes (Brealey and Myers, 1988). To make the choice, management must be able to estimate the utilities associated with various outcomes. Estimating utilities traditionally has been the Achilles heel of decision theory (Cronbach and Gleser, 1965), but a less accute problem in business settings. Although difficult to calculate, institutional gains and losses may be estimated by relatively objective behavioral or cost-accounting procedures, that is, in terms of dollars.

Our objective in this chapter is to introduce the concept of utility analysis, to describe three different models of utility analysis, and to describe situations in which each is most appropriate. Chapters 9, 10, and 11 will then build on these ideas to show how personnel programs can be evaluated from a return-on-investment perspective.

OVERVIEW

Utility analysis (or decision theory) is a tool that is particularly well suited to applications in business settings because it insists that costs and expected consequences of decisions always be taken into account. It stimulates the decision maker to formulate clearly what he or she is after, as well as to anticipate the consequences of alternative courses of action. Decision makers must state clearly their overall objectives and attempt to anticipate the consequences of each alternative before they make a decision.

It should serve as some comfort to know that all personnel decisions can be characterized identically. In the first place there is an individual about whom a decision is required. Based on certain information about the individual (for example, performance appraisals, assessment center ratings, a disciplinary report), decision makers may elect to pursue various alternative courses of action. The following is a simple example.

After conducting an extensive screening process, an organization has narrowed its list of candidates for vice president of finance to three candidates. Each candidate has particular strengths that are attractive to the company. Candidate *A* works for a large eastern conglomerate, candidate *B* is employed by an elite firm in the Midwest, and candidate *C* works for a small, innovative company on the West Coast. The candidates' financial requirements are all within $1,000 of each other, so the personnel cost to the company is an inconsequential measure of the comparative value of each candidate. The task for the organization, then, is to construct a payoff model and to determine payoff measures for each candidate. The organization must process the list of choices (candidates) according to well-defined criteria, and then select the alternative that best satisfies its objectives. The payoffs assigned to each possible outcome must therefore be assessed in value units consistent with these objectives. These value units may not be measurable in dollars. Assume that the organization selects technical knowledge, human relations skills, and administrative skills as valid measures of value payoff to associate with each candidate. On the basis of assessment results, the organization assigns a rating of zero to ten to measure the contribution for each component of payoff for each candidate. These ratings are shown in Exhibit 8.1.

To combine the components of payoff, the organization must determine the relative importance of these three components to payoff. Suppose the organization views technical knowledge as the most important component to this position, twice as important as either human relations or administrative skills. Thus, a weight of 2 is assigned to the scaled values

Exhibit 8.1 Payoff table for selection problem

	Candidate A	*Candidate B*	*Candidate C*
Technical knowledge	6	4	10
Human relations skills	6	9	5
Administrative skills	7	6	4

for technical skills, and weights of 1 to human relations skills and administrative skills. The following payoff measures may then be obtained:

$$\text{payoff, candidate } A = 6(2) + 6(1) + 7(1) = 25$$
$$\text{payoff, candidate } B = 4(2) + 9(1) + 6(1) = 23$$
$$\text{payoff, candidate } C = 10(2) + 5(1) + 4(1) = 29$$

On the basis of these results, candidate *C* should be selected.

Let us summarize our presentation thus far. In any given situation some strategies are better than others. Strategies are better or worse when evaluated against possible outcomes or consequences of decisions (payoffs). The first and most difficult step is to assign values to possible outcomes. Once this is accomplished, particular decisions or general strategies can then be compared, as Cronbach and Gleser (1965) noted:

> The unique feature of decision theory or utility theory is that it specifies evaluations by means of a payoff matrix or by conversion of the criterion to utility units. The values are thus plainly revealed and open to criticism. This is an asset rather than a defect of this system, as compared with systems where value judgments are imbedded and often pass unrecognized. (p. 121)

Utility theory provides a framework for making decisions by forcing the decision maker to define goals clearly, to enumerate the expected consequences or possible outcomes of his or her decision, and to attach differing utilities or values to each. Such an approach has merit since resulting decisions are likely to rest on a foundation of sound reasoning and conscious forethought.

UTILITY MODELS

In the context of personnel selection, three of the best known utility models are those of Taylor and Russell (1939); Naylor and Shine (1965); and Brogden (1946, 1949) and Cronbach and Gleser (1965). *The utility of a selection device is the degree to which its use improves the quality of the individuals selected beyond what would have occurred had that device not been used* (Blum and Naylor, 1968). Quality, in turn, may be defined in terms of (1) the proportion of individuals in the selected group who are considered successful, (2) the average standard score on some job performance criterion for the selected group, or (3) the dollar payoff to the organization resulting from the use of a particular selection procedure. The remainder of this chapter considers each of these utility models and its associated measure of quality in greater detail.

The Taylor-Russell Model

Taylor and Russell (1939) developed perhaps the most well-known utility model and pointed out that the overall utility of a selection device is a function of three parameters: the validity coefficient (the correlation between a predictor of job performance and a criterion measure of actual job performance), the selection ratio (the proportion of applicants selected), and the base rate (the proportion of applicants who would be successful without the selection procedure). This model demonstrates convincingly that even selection procedures with relatively low validities can increase substantially the percentage successful among those selected when the selection ratio is low. Let us consider the concepts of selection ratio (*SR*) and base rate (*BR*) in greater detail.

Whenever a quota exists on the total number of applicants that may be accepted, the selection ratio is a major concern. As the *SR* approaches 1.0 (all applicants must be selected), it becomes high or unfavorable from the organization's perspective. Conversely, as the *SR* approaches zero, it becomes low or favorable; the organization can afford to be selective. The wide-ranging effect that the *SR* may exert on a predictor with a given validity is illustrated in Exhibit 8.2. In each case, X_c represents a cutoff score on the predictor. As can be seen in Exhibit 8.2, even predictors with very low validities can be useful if the *SR* is low and if an organization needs to choose only the cream of the crop. Conversely, given high selection ratios, a predictor must possess very high validity in order to increase the percentage successful among those selected.

It might appear that given a particular validity, decreasing the *SR* (becoming more selective) always should be advocated. Unfortunately, the optimal strategy is not this simple (Sands, 1973). When the personnel manager must achieve a certain quota of satisfactory individuals, lowering the *SR* forces the recruiting and selection effort to be expanded. This strategy may not be cost-effective.

Utility, according to Taylor and Russell (1939), is also affected by the

EXHIBIT 8.2 Effect of varying selection ratios on a predictor with a given validity

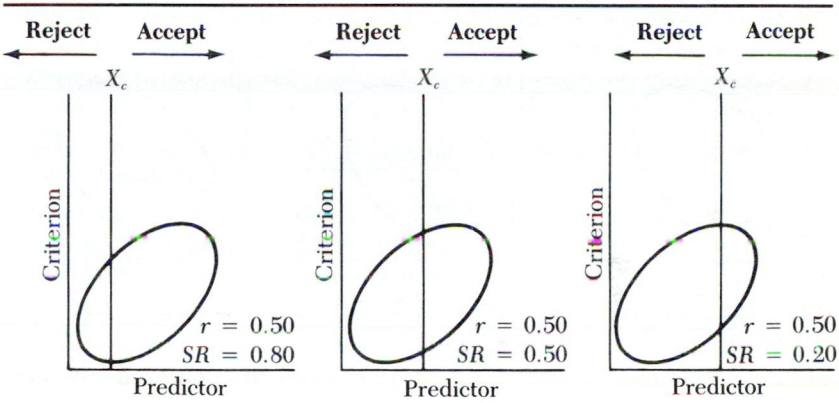

base rate (the proportion of applicants who would be successful without the selection measure). In order to be of any use in selection, the measure must demonstrate incremental validity by improving on the *BR*. That is, the selection measure must result in more correct decisions than could be made without using it. As Exhibit 8.3 demonstrates, the higher the *BR*, the more difficult it is for a selection measure to improve upon it.

In each case X_c represents the minimum criterion standard (criterion cutoff score) necessary for success. This value should not be altered arbitrarily. Rather it should be based upon the selection situation (the level of minimally acceptable criterion performance) and the applicant population (the proportion of the population that would exceed that level if hired; Boudreau, 1988). Exhibit 8.3 illustrates that with a *BR* of 0.80, it would be difficult for any selection measure to improve on the base rate. In fact, when the *BR* is 0.80 and half of the applicants are selected, a validity of 0.45 is required in order to produce an improvement of even 10 percent over base rate prediction. This is also true at very low *BR*s (as would be the case, for example, in the psychiatric screening of job applicants). Given a *BR* of 0.20 and *SR* of 0.50 and a validity of 0.45, the percentage successful among those selected is 0.30 — once again representing only a 10 percent improvement in correct decisions. Selection measures are most useful, however, when *BR*s are about 0.50 (Taylor and Russell, 1939). As the *BR* departs radically in either direction from this value, the benefit of an additional predictor becomes questionable, especially in view of the costs involved in gathering the additional information. The lesson is obvious: applications of selection measures to situations with

EXHIBIT 8.3 Effect of varying base rates on a predictor with a given validity

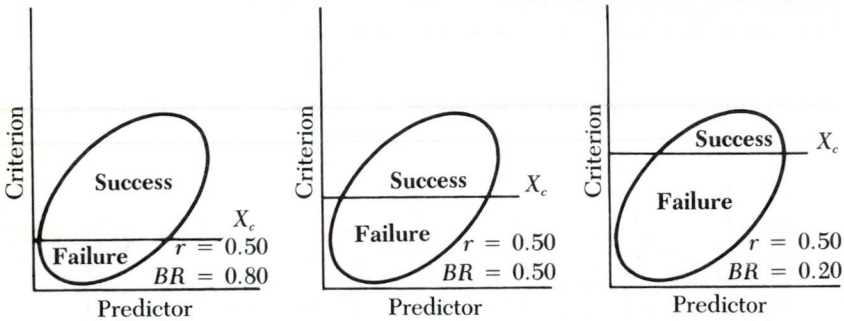

markedly different *SR*s or *BR*s can result in quite different predictive outcomes and cost-benefit ratios. When significant incremental validity cannot be demonstrated by adding a predictor, then the predictor should not be used, since it cannot improve on classification of persons by the base rate.

Taylor and Russell (1939) published a series of tables illustrating the interaction of the validity coefficient, the selection ratio, and the base rate on the success ratio (the proportion of selected applicants who subsequently are judged successful). The success ratio, then, serves as an operational measure of the value or utility of a selection device, when used in conjunction with methods presently used to select applicants.

The Taylor-Russell approach is presented graphically in Exhibit 8.4. In this figure, the criterion cutoff (set as described earlier) separates the present employee group into satisfactory and unsatisfactory workers. The predictor cutoff (set by the selection ratio) defines the relative proportion of workers who would be hired at a given level of selectivity. Areas *A* and *C* represent correct decisions. That is, if the selection measure were used to select applicants, those in area *A* would be hired and become satisfactory employees. Those in area *C* would be correctly rejected because they scored below the predictor cutoff and would have performed unsatisfactorily on the job. Areas *B* and *D* represent erroneous decisions. Those in area *B* would be hired because they scored above the predictor cutoff, but they would perform unsatisfactorily on the job. Those in area *D* would be rejected because they scored below the predictor cutoff, but they would have been successful if hired.

The following ratios were used by Taylor and Russell in developing their tables:

EXHIBIT 8.4 Effect of predictor and criterion cutoffs on a bivariate distribution of scores

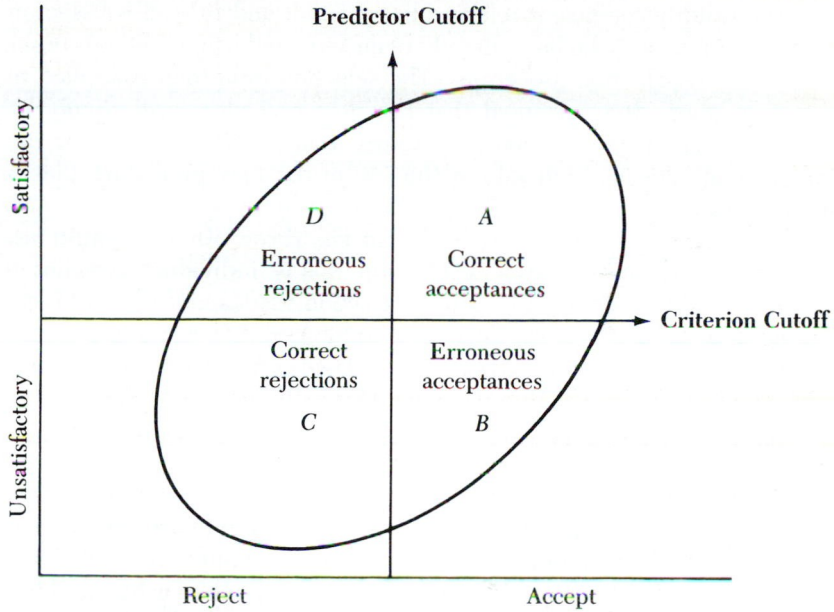

$$\text{base rate} = \frac{A + D}{A + B + C + D} \tag{1}$$

$$\text{selection ratio} = \frac{A + B}{A + B + C + D} \tag{2}$$

$$\text{success ratio} = \frac{A}{A + B} \tag{3}$$

By specifying the validity coefficient, the base rate, and the selection ratio, and making use of Pearson's "Tables for Finding the Volumes of the Normal Bivariate Surface" (1931), Taylor and Russell developed their tables (see Appendix A). The usefulness of a selection measure thus can be assessed in terms of the success ratio that will be obtained if the selection measure is used. The gain in utility to be expected from using the instrument (the expected increase in the percentage of successful workers) then can be derived by subtracting the base rate from the success ratio (equation 3 minus equation 1). For example, given an *SR* of 0.10, a validity of 0.30, and a *BR* of 0.50, the success ratio jumps to 0.71 — a 21 percent gain in utility over the base rate (to verify this figure, see Appendix A).

The validity coefficient referred to by Taylor and Russell is based on present employees who have already been screened using methods other than the new selection procedure. The selection ratio then is applied to this population. It is assumed that the new procedure will simply be added to a group of selection procedures used previously, and it is the incremental gain in validity from the use of the new procedure that is most relevant.

The Taylor-Russell approach also makes three other assumptions. First, it assumes fixed treatment selection (that is, individuals are chosen for one specified treatment or course of action that cannot be modified). For example, if a person is selected for Treatment A, a training program for slow learners, transfer to Treatment B, fast-track instruction, is impossible regardless of how well the person does in Treatment A. Second, the Taylor-Russell model does not take into account the percentage of rejected individuals who would have been successful if hired (erroneous rejections). Finally, the model classifies accepted individuals into successful and unsuccessful groups. All individuals within a group are regarded as making equal contributions. Because of these assumptions Taylor and Russell find different shapes for the validity–utility relationship at different selection ratios and nonlinear relationships given high validities and high base rates. However, the Taylor-Russell model is not used to choose optimal selection ratios (or cutoff scores), but rather only to evaluate those already selected.

Perhaps the major shortcoming of this utility model is that it allows the usefulness of a predictor to be reflected only in terms of the success ratio and nothing else. Criterion performance is described as a dichotomous classification — successful and unsuccessful — and as the tables in Appendix A demonstrate, when validity is fixed the success ratio increases as the selection ratio decreases. (Turn to Appendix A, choose any particular validity value, and note what happens to the success ratio as the selection ratio changes from 0.95 to 0.05.) Under these circumstances the success ratio tells us that more people are successful, but not *how much more* successful. While, in practice, situations may arise in which the average level of job performance would not be expected to change as a function of higher selection standards, for many jobs increased criterion mean performance would be expected to result from increased selectivity as long as the relationship between performance on the predictor and performance on the job can be described best by a straight line (is linear). If the predictor–criterion relationship is not linear, then the Taylor-Russell tables are inappropriate anyway, since they are based on the assumptions of bivariate normal,[1] linear, homoscedastic relationships between predictor and criterion.[2] In short, when it is reasonable to assume that the use of higher cutoff scores will lead to higher average job performance by those selected, the Taylor-Russell tables will underestimate the actual amount of gain to be expected.

The Naylor-Shine Model

In contrast to the Taylor-Russell utility model, the Naylor-Shine (1965) approach assumes a linear relationship between validity and utility. This relationship holds at all selection ratios. That is, given any arbitrarily defined cutoff on a selection measure, the higher the validity, the greater the increase in average criterion score for the selected group over that observed for the total group (mean criterion score of selectees minus mean criterion score of total group). Thus the Naylor-Shine index of utility (originally derived by Kelley [1923]) is defined in terms of the increase in average criterion score to be expected from the use of a selection measure with a given validity and selection ratio. Like Taylor and Russell, Naylor and Shine assume that the relationship between predictor and criterion is bivariate normal, linear, and homoscedastic, and that the validity coefficient used is based on the concurrent validity model.[3] Such a model is used in order to assess the gain in validity from the use of the new selection procedure *over and above* that which is presently available using current information. Unlike Taylor and Russell, however, Naylor and Shine do not require that employees be dichotomized into satisfactory and unsatisfactory groups by specifying an arbitrary cutoff on the criterion (job performance) dimension that represents minimally acceptable performance. Thus the Naylor-Shine utility model requires less information than the Taylor-Russell model. The basic equation underlying the Naylor-Shine model is

---

[1] *Bivariate normal* means that the two variables in question (in this case, predictor and criterion scores) are each normally distributed, that is, scores are dispersed in a bell-shaped fashion.

[2] *Homoscedastic* means that the variability in criterion scores is the same at high predictor scores as it is at low predictor scores.

[3] That is, the new selection procedure is administered to present employees who already have been screened using other methods. Then the correlation (validity coefficient) between scores on the new procedure and the employees' job performance scores is computed.

$$\bar{Z}_{yi} = r_{xy} \frac{\lambda_i}{\phi_i} \tag{4}$$

where $\bar{Z}_{yi}$ is the mean criterion score (in standard score units)[4] of all cases above the predictor cutoff; r_{xy} is the validity coefficient; λ_i is the ordinate of the normal distribution at the predictor cutoff, Z_{xi} (expressed in standard score units); ϕ_i is the selection ratio. Equation 4 applies whether r_{xy} is a zero order correlation coefficient or a multiple regression coefficient.[5]

Using Equation 4 as a basic building block, Naylor and Shine present a series of tables (see Appendix B) that specifies, for each selection ratio, the standard (predictor) score corresponding to that selection ratio, the ordinate of the normal curve at that point, and the quotient λ_i/ϕ_i. The table can be used to answer several important personnel questions. (1) Given a specified selection ratio, what will be the average performance level of those selected? (2) Given a desired selection ratio, what will $\bar{Z}_{yi}$ be? (3) Given a desired improvement in the average criterion score of those selected, what selection ratio and/or predictor cutoff value (in standard score units) should be used? Let us work through some examples, using the tables in Appendix B.

In each of the following examples assume that r_{xy}, the validity of our predictor, is positive and equal to 0.40.

1. Given the selection ratio $\phi_i = 0.50$, what will be the average performance level of those selected?
Solution: Enter the table at $\phi_i = 0.50$ and read $\lambda_i/\phi_i = 0.80$.

$$\bar{Z}_{yi} = r_{xy}\lambda_i/\phi_i = (0.40)(0.80) = 0.32$$

Thus, the mean criterion score of those selected, using a selection ratio of 0.50, is 0.32 Z-units (roughly one-third of a standard deviation) better than the unselected sample.

2. Given the desired cutoff score $Z_{xi} = -0.96$, what will $\bar{Z}_{yi}$ be?
Solution: Enter the table at $Z_{xi} = -0.96$ and read $\lambda_i/\phi_i = 0.30$.

$$\bar{Z}_{yi} = r_{xy}\lambda_i/\phi_i = (0.40)\,(0.30) = 0.12$$

Thus, using this cutoff score on our predictor results in an improvement of 0.12 Z-units in the average criterion score of those selected.

---

[4]To transform raw scores into standard scores, the following formula is used: $x - \bar{x}/SD$ where x is the raw score, $\bar{x}$ is the mean of the distribution of scores, and SD is the standard deviation of the distribution. Assuming the raw scores are distributed normally, about 99 percent of the standard scores will lie within the range -3 to $+3$. Standard scores (Z-scores) are expressed in standard deviation units.

[5]A zero order correlation coefficient is based on two variables. A multiple regression coefficient represents the correlation between a criterion and two or more predictors.

3. Given the desired improvement in the average criterion score of those selected $\bar{Z}_{yi} = 0.50$, what selection ratio and/or predictor cutoff value should be used?
Solution: Since $\bar{Z}_{yi} = r_{xy}\lambda_i/\phi_i$, then

$$\lambda_i/\phi_i = \bar{Z}_{yi}r_{xy} = 0.50/0.40 = 1.25$$

Enter the table at $\lambda_i/\phi_i = 1.25$ and read $\phi_i = 0.2578$ and $Z_{xi} = 0.65$. Thus, to achieve an average improvement of 0.50 (one half) standard deviation in job performance a selection ratio of 0.26 is necessary, and to achieve that particular ratio, one should employ a cutoff score on the predictor of 0.65 in Z-score (standard deviation) units.

In each of the following examples assume that r_{xy}, the validity of our predictor, is negative and equal to -0.40. The general rule for this case is to reverse the sign of r_{xy} and Z_{xi} everywhere in the calculations.

1. Given the selection ratio $\phi_i = 0.50$, what will be the average performance level of those selected?
Solution: Enter the table at $\phi_i = 0.50$ and read $\lambda_i/\phi_i = 0.80$. Taking the sign reversal on r_{xy} into account,

$$\bar{Z}_{yi} = (-r_{xy})\,\lambda_i/\phi_i = -(-0.40)\,(0.80) = 0.32$$

Thus, the mean criterion score of those selected, using a selection ratio of 0.50, is 0.32 Z-units better than the unselected sample.

2. Given the desired cutoff score $Z_{xi} = -0.96$, what will $\bar{Z}_{yi}$ be?
Solution: When r_{xy} is negative, ϕ_i is in the *left* tail of the score distribution instead of the right tail as it is when r_{xy} is positive. Thus, a cutoff score of -0.96 for the negative case is equivalent to a cutoff score of 0.96 with r_{xy} positive. We therefore reverse the sign of Z_{xi}, enter the table at $Z_{xi} = 0.96$, and read $\lambda_i/\phi_i = 1.49$. Taking the sign reversal on r_{xy} into account, we have

$$\bar{Z}_{yi} = (-r_{xy})\,\lambda_i/\phi_i = -(-0.40)\,(1.49) = 0.596$$

Thus, using a cutoff score of $Z_{xi} = -0.96$ on our predictor produces an improvement of about 0.60 Z-units in the average criterion score of selected personnel.

3. Given the desired improvement in the average criterion score of those selected $\bar{Z}_{yi} = 0.50$, what selection ratio and/or predictor cutoff value should be used?
Solution: Reversing the sign on r_{xy} gives

$$\bar{Z}_{yi} = (-r_{xy})\frac{\lambda_i}{\phi_i}$$

or

$$\frac{\lambda_i}{\phi_i} = \frac{\bar{Z}_{yi}}{(-r_{xy})}$$

Therefore,

$$\frac{\lambda_i}{\phi_i} = \frac{0.50}{-(-0.40)} = 1.25$$

Enter the table at $\lambda_i/\phi_i = 1.25$ and read $\phi_i = 0.2578$ and $Z_{xi} = -0.65$ (note that the sign on Z_{xi} has been reversed). Thus, to achieve the desired improvement in average criterion performance, a selection ratio of 0.26 is necessary, and to achieve that particular ratio, one should employ a cutoff score on the predictor of -0.65 in Z-score units.

The Naylor-Shine utility index appears more generally applicable than the Taylor-Russell index because in many if not most cases, given valid selection procedures, an organization could expect an increase in average criterion performance as it becomes more selective in deciding whom to accept. However, "average criterion performance" is expressed in terms of standard (Z) scores, which are more difficult to interpret than are outcomes more closely related to the specific nature of a business, such as dollar volume of sales, units produced or sold, or costs reduced. Moreover, as Boudreau (1988) has noted, with a standardized criterion scale one must ask questions such as, "Is it worth spending $10,000 to select fifty people per year, in order to obtain a criterion level 0.50 standard deviations (*SD*s) greater than what we would obtain without the predictor?" Some HR managers may not even be familiar with the concept of a standard deviation, and would find it difficult to attach a dollar value to a 0.50 *SD* increase in criterion performance.

Finally, neither the Taylor-Russell nor the Naylor-Shine model formally integrates the concept of cost of selection, or dollars gained or lost, into the utility index. Both simply imply that larger differences in the percentage of successful employees (Taylor-Russell) or larger increases in average criterion score (Naylor-Shine) will yield larger benefits to the employer in dollars saved.

The Brogden-Cronbach-Gleser Model

Brogden (1946) showed that when the predictor and criterion are continuous (i.e., they can assume an infinite number of values theoretically) and identical (not necessarily normal, but identical) in distribution form, the regression of the criterion on the predictor is linear, and the selection ratio is held constant, then the validity coefficient itself is a direct index of selective efficiency. If criterion performance is expressed in standard score units, then over all individuals r_{xy} represents the ratio of the average criterion score made by persons selected on the basis of their predictor scores ($\Sigma\bar{Z}_y$) to the average score made by selecting the same number of persons on the basis of their criterion scores ($\Sigma\bar{Z}_{y'}$). That is,

$$r_{xy} = \frac{\Sigma\bar{Z}_y}{\Sigma\bar{Z}_{y'}} \tag{5}$$

As an illustration, suppose a firm wants to hire 20 persons for a certain job and must choose the best 20 from 85 applicants. Ideally, the firm would hire all 85 for a period of time, collect criterion data, and retain the best 20, those obtaining the highest criterion scores. The average criterion score of the 20 so selected obviously would be the highest obtainable by any possible combination of 20 of the 85 original workers. Since such a procedure is usually out of the question, we administer a selection measure and select the 20 highest scorers. Equation 5 indicates that the validity coefficient may be interpreted as the ratio of the average criterion performance of the 20 persons selected on the basis of their predictor scores to the average performance of the 20 who would have been selected had the criterion itself been used as the basis for selection. Thus if persons could be selected on the basis of actual criterion behavior (or by means of a perfect selection device), and this would save an organization $100,000 per year over random selection, then a selection device with a validity of 0.50 could be expected to save $50,000 per year. Utility is therefore a direct linear function of validity, given the assumptions noted above.

Although Equation 5 does not include formally the cost of selection and was not advanced as an estimate of utility, in a later paper (1949) Brogden used the principles of linear regression to demonstrate the relationships of cost of selection, validity, and selection ratio to utility. The derivation is straightforward.

Let r_{xy} equal the correlation between a predictor (x) and job performance measured in dollars (y). The basic linear model is

$$y = \beta Z_x + \mu_y + e$$

where:

y = job performance measured in dollars

β = the linear regression weight on the predictor for forecasting job performance

Z_x = performance on the predictor in standard score form in the applicant group

μ_y = mean job performance in dollars of randomly selected employees

e = error of prediction

For those selected (s), the equation that gives the average job performance in this group is

$$E(y_s) = E(\beta Z_{x_s}) + E(\mu_y) + E(e)$$

where E = expected value. Since the expected value of e is zero, and β and μ are constants, the equation reduces to

$$\bar{Y}_s = \beta \bar{Z}_{x_s} + \mu_y$$

Remember that $\beta = r_{xy}(SD_y/SD_x)$, where SD_y is the standard deviation of dollar-valued job performance among randomly selected employees. Since $SD_x = 1.00$, $\beta = r_{xy}SD_y$. We therefore obtain

$$\bar{Y}_s = r_{xy}SD_y\bar{Z}_{x_s} + \mu_y$$

This equation tells us the *absolute* dollar value of average job performance in the selected group. What we really want, however, is an equation that gives the *increase* in dollar value of average performance that results from using the predictor. To get that equation, suppose that the new predictor was not used. Then $\bar{Y}_s = \mu_y$, for mean job performance in the selected group would be the same as mean performance in a group selected randomly from the applicant pool. Thus the increase due to use of a valid predictor is $r_{xy}SD_y\bar{Z}_{x_s}$. The equation we want is produced by transposing μ_y to give

$$\bar{Y}_s - \mu_y = r_{xy}SD_y\bar{Z}_{x_s}$$

The right side of the above equation represents the difference between mean productivity in the group selected using the new predictor and mean productivity in a group selected without using the new predictor, that is, a group selected randomly. The equation thus gives mean gain in productivity per selectee (marginal utility) resulting from the use of the new predictor, that is,

$$\Delta\bar{U}/\text{selectee} = r_{xy}SD_y\bar{Z}_{x_s} \tag{6}$$

where $\bar{U}$ is utility and $\Delta\bar{U}$ is marginal utility.

Equation 6 states that the average productivity gain in dollars per person hired is the product of the validity coefficient, the standard deviation of job performance in dollars, and the average standard score on the predictor of those hired. The value $r_{xy}\bar{Z}_{x_s}$ is the mean standard score on the dollar criterion of those selected, $\bar{Z}_{y}$.

Assuming predictor scores are distributed normally and the predictor-criterion relationship is linear, then $\bar{Z}_{x_s}$ for the selected group may be computed by the formula λ/ϕ, where λ is the height of the normal curve at the point of cut, and ϕ is the percentage in the selected group (the selection ratio). $\bar{Z}_{y_s}$ (the average standard criterion score for the selected group) is then obtained as the product $r\,\lambda/\phi$. This is the same formula (Equation 4) used by Naylor and Shine to derive the values in their tables.

The total utility of the new predictor depends on the number of persons hired. The total utility (total productivity) gain is simply the mean gain per selectee times the number of people selected, N_s. That is, the total productivity gain is

$$\Delta U = N_s r_{xy} SD_y \lambda/\phi \tag{7}$$

Suppose the average marginal utility is \$5,000. If 10 people were hired, the actual utility would be \$50,000. If 100 people were hired, then the utility would be \$500,000. Obviously, the total dollar value of the new predictor is greater for large employers than for small employers. However, this fact can be misleading. On a percentage basis it is average gain in utility that counts, and that is what counts to each individual employer.

The cost of selection is another factor that must be considered in estimating the savings expected from a selection program. Since the expected saving per individual selected is $r_{xy}SD_y\lambda/\phi$, the saving with allowance for the cost of testing can be determined by subtracting c/ϕ from the above value, where c is the cost of testing a single individual. Cost of testing is divided by ϕ, so that c/ϕ represents the total cost of the testing required to fill one vacancy. For example, if the per applicant cost of testing is \$25, and one of every four applicants is selected ($SR = 0.25$), then the cost to fill one vacancy is \$25/0.25 = \$100. The expected saving per selectee corrected for the cost of testing is therefore

$$\Delta U = r_{xy} SD_y \lambda/\phi - c/\phi \tag{8}$$

and the total gain is

$$\Delta U = N_s r_{xy} SD_y \lambda/\phi - N_s c/\phi \tag{9}$$

The effect of the cost of testing can be evaluated, as Brogden (1949) has shown, by computing the ratio, per applicant cost of testing/

(validity × SD_y). This value represents the ratio of the cost of testing to the expected gain in dollar value of production with an increase in applicant test score of one standard deviation unit. Thus, if the cost of evaluating an applicant for an executive position is $300, the validity of the selection procedure is 0.35, and the criterion standard deviation is $15,000, then the ratio is about 0.06. If this ratio can be held below 0.05, then Taylor and Russell's conclusions are substantially correct. In practice, this will almost always be the case, since the benefits of improved selection will accrue for more than one time period (in fact, over the entire tenure of the group selected). Thus, SD_y will be large, relative to the one-time cost of testing, and testing costs are unlikely to reduce utility significantly except at very low selection ratios.

Cronbach and Gleser (1965) elaborated and refined Brogden's (1949) derivations with respect to utility in fixed treatment selection and, in addition, thoroughly explored the application of utility theory to selection with adaptive treatment, two-stage and multistage selection, placement decisions, and classification decisions. With respect to utility in fixed treatment selection, Cronbach and Gleser adopt Taylor and Russell's interpretation of the validity coefficient for utility calculations, that is, concurrent validity. The validity coefficient based on present employees presupposes a population that has been screened using information other than the new selection measure. It is to this population that the selection ratio will be applied.

Cronbach and Gleser argue, as did Taylor and Russell and Naylor and Shine, that selection procedures should be judged on the basis of their contribution over and above the best strategy available that makes use of prior information. Thus, any new procedure must demonstrate incremental utility before it is put to use. However, suppose an organization wishes to replace its old selection procedures with new ones. Under these circumstances, as Boudreau (1988) has noted, the appropriate population for deriving a validity coefficient, SD_y, and selection ratio, should be the *unscreened* population. In short, selection procedures should be evaluated in light of the conditions under which they actually will be applied. With respect to fixed treatment selection Cronbach and Gleser make the following assumptions:

1. Decisions are made regarding an indefinitely large population. This "a priori population" consists of all applicants after screening by any procedure which is presently in use and will continue to be used.
2. Regarding any person, i, there are two possible alternative decisions: accept (t_a) and reject (t_b).

3. Each person has a test score, y_i, which has zero mean and unit standard deviation. [Test scores are assumed to be distributed normally.]
4. For every person there is a payoff e_{it_a} that results when a person is accepted. This payoff has a linear regression on test score. The test will be scored so that r_{ye} is positive.
5. When a person is rejected, the payoff e_{it_b} results. This payoff is unrelated to test score, and may be set equal to zero.
6. The average cost of testing a person on test y is c_y, where $c_y > 0$.
7. The strategy will be to accept high scorers in preference to others. A cutoff y' will be located on the y continuum so that any desired proportion $\phi(y')$ of the group falls above y'. Above that point the probability of acceptance is 1.00; below it, 0.00. Cochran (1951) shows that such a strategy is optimal for selection with fixed quota.[6]

The assumption of a normal distribution of test scores (assumption 3 above) implies that the expected payoffs from randomly selected persons also are normally distributed. As both Brogden (1949) and Cronbach and Gleser have noted, this assumption may not always be met, nor would it be desirable that it always be met. Standards set by management often place a lower limit on production (which produces a positively skewed payoff distribution) and voluntary restrictions on output by a work group skew the curve negatively. In the extreme, complete task standardization eliminates variability entirely among those who remain on the job. However, with highly skewed distributions, as long as linear regression is present, payoffs resulting from cutoff points on the tail of the distribution skew could be relatively greater than those obtained at the same percentile point of cut with a normally distributed variable. This implies a comparison of relative payoffs at different selection ratios.

When the assumptions noted earlier are met, however, Cronbach and Gleser demonstrate that the net gain in utility from testing N persons in fixed treatment selection is

$$\Delta U = NSD_e r_{ye} \lambda(y') - Nc_y \tag{10}$$

where c_y is the cost of testing one person; r_{ye} is the correlation of the selection procedure with the dollar-scale-evaluated criterion in the a priori population; SD_e is the standard deviation of this criterion; y' is the

[6]Cronbach, L. J., and Gleser, G. C. (1965). *Psychological tests and personnel decisions* (2nd ed.) (p. 307). Urbana, IL: University of Illinois Press.

cutoff score on the selection procedure; and $\lambda(y')$ is the ordinate of the normal curve at that point. In this expression, $SD_e r_{ye}$ is the slope of the payoff function relating expected payoff to score. An increase in validity leads to an increase in slope, but as Equation 10 demonstrates, slope also depends on the dispersion of criterion scores. For any one treatment SD_e is constant and indicates both the magnitude and practical significance of individual differences in payoff. Thus a selection procedure with $r_{xy} = 0.25$ and $SD_e = \$10{,}000$ for one selection decision is just as useful as a procedure with $r_{xy} = 0.50$ and $SD_e = \$5{,}000$ for some other decision (holding other parameters constant). Even procedures with low validity can be useful when SD_e is large.

If Equation 10 is expressed as the net gain in utility per person accepted in fixed treatment selection, it is identical to Brogden's (1949) formula (Equation 8). Therefore,

$$\Delta U = SD_e r_{ye} \frac{\lambda(y')}{\phi(y')} - \frac{c_y}{\phi(y')} \tag{11}$$

where all terms are as defined above. In short, both Brogden (1946, 1949) and Cronbach and Gleser arrived at the same conclusions regarding the effects of r, SD_e, the cost of selection, and the selection ratio on utility in fixed treatment selection. Utility properly is regarded as a linear function of validity and, if cost is zero, is proportional to validity. Contrary to the Taylor-Russell results, the linear relation holds at all selection ratios. Exhibit 8.5 presents a summary of the three approaches discussed so far.

APPROPRIATE APPLICATIONS OF EACH MODEL

Only by understanding thoroughly the theory, assumptions, and data requirements of the various utility models can the models be used properly. Yet their proper (and more widespread) use is essential in order to satisfy the demand for accountability in personnel programs.

Taylor-Russell

The Taylor-Russell (1939) model is most appropriate under the following circumstances: (1) differences in ability beyond the minimum necessary to perform the job do not yield differences in benefit (for example, in various types of clerical or technician's jobs). (2) Individuals are placed into two (or more) groups based on their scores on a test battery, interest

EXHIBIT 8.5 Summary of the utility indexes, data requirements, and assumptions of the Taylor-Russell, Naylor-Shine, and Brogden-Cronbach-Gleser utility models

Models	*Utility Index*	*Data Requirements*	*Distinctive Assumptions*
Taylor-Russell (1939)	Increase in percentage successful in selected group	Validity, base rate, selection ratio	All selectees classified as either successful or unsuccessful. Equal criterion performance by all members of each group; cost of selection = $0.
Naylor-Shine (1965)	Increase in mean criterion score of selected group	Validity, selection ratio	Validity linearly related to utility; cost of selection = $0.
Brogden-Cronbach-Gleser (1965)	Increase in dollar payoff of selected group	Validity, selection ratio, criterion standard deviation in dollars	Validity linearly related to utility; cost of selection ≠ $0; criterion performance evaluated in dollars.

Note: All three models assume a validity coefficient based on present employees (concurrent validity).

Source: Cascio, W.F. (1980). Responding to the demand for accountability: A critical analysis of three utility models. *Organizational Behavior and Human Performance*, *25*, 42.

inventory, or other procedure. All individuals remain within the organization, but they are treated differently. By assigning particular values to "hits" and "misses" for each possible assignment, cutoff scores can be adjusted to maximize expected utility. (3) Differences in output are believed to occur, but are presently unmeasurable (for example, in nursing care, teaching performance, or credit counseling). In these instances, estimating utility according to the magnitude of the increase in the success ratio makes good sense. It makes even better sense, however, to attach cost estimates to expected payoffs. Thus, Sands (1973) developed the cost of attaining personnel requirements (CAPER) model on the basis of the Taylor-Russell approach. CAPER is a decision-oriented system whose objective is to determine an optimal recruiting-selection strategy for minimizing the total cost of recruiting, inducting, selecting, and training a sufficient number of persons to meet a quota of satisfactory employees. The two major advantages to such an approach are: (1) results can be communicated and understood easily by operating managers (that is, they are given in numbers of persons and dollar costs), and (2) by broadening the perspective of personnel selection from selection per se to all phases of the personnel system (from initial recruiting through the completion of training), the likelihood of over- or under-optimization of one component of the system at the expense of all others is minimized. Nevertheless, CAPER, like the Taylor-Russell model, can be justified only under the conditions noted above. Its lack of general applicability is its major drawback.

Naylor-Shine

The Naylor-Shine model is most appropriate when differences in criterion performance cannot be expressed in dollar terms, but when the function relating payoff (performance under some treatment) to predictor score can be assumed to be linear. Consider the following examples:

1. In classification and placement decisions (for example, in the military or in large organizations) all selected individuals are assigned to available treatments (jobs, training programs) so that individual and institutional outcomes are maximized. In classification, for example, the decision maker has a number of available jobs on the one hand and a number of people on the other. The objective is to make the most effective matching of people and jobs (Ghiselli, 1956). Thus criterion performance must be forecast for each individual for each job,

for example, by using least-squares estimates.[7] If the predicted criterion scores for each job (units produced, dollar value of sales, and so on) are expressed in standard score units, then the expected increase in mean criterion performance as a function of variation in the selection ratio can be assessed by means of the Naylor-Shine model.

2. In the prediction of labor turnover, expressed as a percentage, based on scores from a predictor that demonstrates some validity, if percentages are expressed as standard scores, then the expected decrease in the percentage of turnover can be assessed as a function of variation in the selection ratio (the predictor cutoff score). If appropriate costing procedures are used to calculate actual turnover costs (see Chapter 2), expected savings resulting from reduced turnover then can be estimated.

3. In the selection of students based on predicted academic performance in college or graduate school, or in training programs where the cost per trainee is high (e.g., police academy training), if academic performance is expressed in standard score units, institutions might profitably examine variations in expected criterion performance as a function of variations in predictor scores by means of the Naylor-Shine utility model.

Brogden-Cronbach-Gleser

The Brogden-Cronbach-Gleser continuous variable utility model is the most versatile utility model available, and it is receiving increasing attention by researchers and practitioners alike. It is most appropriate in situations where criterion performance can be expressed in dollars and where linear regression of the criterion on the predictor can be assumed. In short, this model provides a direct estimate of the monetary value of a selection program by making use of the "dollar criterion" (Brogden and Taylor, 1950). Consider the following examples:

1. Roche (1965) used cost accounting procedures to estimate the payoff from a program designed to select radial drill operators in a man-

[7] In attempting to forecast job performance on the basis of a composite of predictor scores, a mathematical formula (regression equation) must be developed. Although many such equations are possible, statisticians generally agree that the best (most accurate) equation is that for which the sum of the squared deviations between actual and predicted job performance scores is a minimum. Thus the term *least-squares*.

ufacturing operation. Although the cost-accounting methods were relatively straightforward, many subjective estimates and arbitrary allocations entered into the estimated profit accruing to the firm as a result of the radial drill operator's work. Such elements as the cost of materials used in producing the company's products, the cost of direct labor hours consumed in the manufacture of a product, and the cost of capital investment, jigs, fixtures, power, perishable tools, and floor space all had to be expressed in dollars. The determination of the standard deviation of criterion outcomes expressed in dollars is clearly a complex undertaking, as a later study of route salesmen for a soft drink company also demonstrates (Greer and Cascio, 1987). However, joint efforts by personnel psychologists and cost accountants may make such a problem more tractable. Chapter 9 is devoted exclusively to this topic.

2. In a service organization, Schmidt and Hoffman (1973) applied the Brogden-Cronbach-Gleser model to a weighted application blank developed to predict turnover among nurse's aides. Using cost-accounting methods, the dollar cost of turnover was estimated. When actual dollar savings over a two-year period were compared to estimated dollar savings at two selection ratios using the Brogden-Cronbach-Gleser model, the differences were no greater than 7 percent.

3. Two other studies investigated the utility of an assessment center in selection by means of the Brogden-Cronbach-Gleser utility model (Cascio and Silbey, 1979; Cascio and Ramos, 1986). In the latter study, the payoff associated with first-level management assessment, given that 1,116 managers were selected and that their average tenure at first level was 4.4 years, was over $13 million. This represents about $12,000 in improved job performance per manager over 4.4 years, or about $2,700 per year.

In summary, as personnel costs and the costs of personnel programs continue to escalate, demands for accountability also are likely to escalate. Utility-based decision systems can meet this challenge, but their proper application requires careful attention to the assumptions and data requirements of each model. "Garbage in–garbage out" is as true in this context as it is in the context of an information system.

EXERCISES

1. Use the Taylor-Russell tables (Appendix A) to solve these problems:

Validity	SR	BR	*Success Ratio*
0.25	0.20	0.30	_____
0.55	0.70	0.80	_____
0.20	0.70	0.80	_____
0.10	0.50	0.50	_____
0.55	0.50	0.50	_____

2. Use the Naylor-Shine tables (Appendix B) to solve these problems:

r_{xy}	ϕ_i	Z_{xi}	$\bar{Z}_{yi}$
0.35	0.7019		_____
0.22		−0.30	_____
0.47	_____	_____	0.65
−0.47	_____	_____	0.65

3. Using the Brogden-Cronbach-Gleser continuous variable utility model, what is the net gain over random selection (ΔU) overall, and per selectee, given the following information?

- quota for selection: 20
- SR: 0.20
- SD_e (standard deviation of job performance expressed in dollars): \$10,000
- r_{ye}: 0.25
- $\lambda(y')$: 0.28
- c_y: \$25

Hint: To find N, the number recruited, divide the quota for selection by the SR.

4. As in question 3, find the net gain in utility (ΔU) over random selection overall and per selectee, given the following information:

- quota: 125
- SR: 0.50
- SD_e: \$7,500
- r_{ye}: 0.35
- $\lambda(y')$: 0.3988
- c_y: \$400

5. Given the following information on two selection procedures, and using the Brogden-Cronbach-Gleser model, what is the relative *difference* in payoff (overall and per selectee) between the two procedures? For both procedures, quota = 50, SR = 0.50, $\lambda(y')$ = 0.3989, and SD_e = \$15,000.

r_{y_1}: 0.20 c_1: \$100

r_{y_2}: 0.40 c_2: \$500

6. You are a management consultant whose task is to do a utility analysis using the following information regarding secretaries at Inko, Inc. The validity of the Secretarial Aptitude Test (SAT) is 0.40, applicants must score 70 or better (Z_x of 0.5) to be hired, and only about half of those who apply actually are hired. Of those hired, about half are considered satisfactory by their bosses. How selective should Inko be to upgrade the average criterion score of those selected by $\bar{Z}_y = 0.5$? What utility model did you use to solve the problem? Why?

REFERENCES

BLUM, M. L., and NAYLOR, J. C. (1968). *Industrial psychology: Its theoretical and social foundations* (rev. ed.). New York: Harper & Row.

BOUDREAU, J. W. (1988, December). *Utility analysis for decisions in human resource management*. Working Paper 88–21, Center for Advanced Human Resource Studies, New York State School of Industrial and Labor Relations. Ithaca, NY: Cornell University.

BREALEY, R., and MYERS, S. (1988). *Principles of corporate finance* (3rd ed.). New York: McGraw-Hill.

BROGDEN, H. E. (1946). On the interpretation of the correlation coefficient as a measure of predictive efficiency. *Journal of Educational Psychology, 37*, 64–76.

BROGDEN, H. E. (1949). When testing pays off. *Personnel Psychology, 2*, 171–185.

BROGDEN, H. E., and TAYLOR, E. K. (1950). The dollar criterion — Applying the cost accounting concept to criterion construction. *Personnel Psychology, 3*, 133–154.

CASCIO, W. F., and RAMOS, R. A. (1986). Development and application of a new method for assessing job performance in behavioral/economic terms. *Journal of Applied Psychology, 71*, 20–28.

CASCIO, W. F., and SILBEY, V. (1979). Utility of the assessment center as a selection device, *Journal of Applied Psychology, 64*, 107–118.

COCHRAN, W. G. (1951). Improvement by means of selection. In J. Neyman (Ed.), *Second Berkeley symposium on mathematical statistics and probability*. Berkeley: University of California Press.

CRONBACH, L. J., and GLESER, G. C. (1965). *Psychological tests and personnel decisions* (2nd ed.). Urbana, IL: University of Illinois Press.

GHISELLI, E. E. (1956). The placement of workers: Concepts and problems. *Personnel Psychology, 9*, 1–16.

GREER, O. L., and CASCIO, W. F. (1987). Is cost accounting the answer? Comparison of two behaviorally-based methods for estimating the standard deviation of job performance in dollars with a cost-accounting–based approach. *Journal of Applied Psychology, 72*, 588–595.

KARR, A. R. (1990, March 7). Letter bomb: Postal Service again asks for rate increase as automation lags. *Wall Street Journal*, pp. A1, A12.

KELLEY, T. L. (1923). *Statistical method.* New York: Macmillan.

NAYLOR, J. C., and SHINE, L. C. (1965). A table for determining the increase in mean criterion score obtained by using a selection device. *Journal of Industrial Psychology, 3*, 33–42.

PEARSON, K. (1931). *Tables for statisticians and biometricians: Vol. 2.* London: Biometric Laboratory, University College, pp. 78–109.

ROCHE, W. J., JR. (1961). The Cronbach-Gleser utility function in fixed-treatment employee selection. *Dissertation Abstracts International, 22*, 4413. (University Microfilms No. 62–1570). Portions reproduced in L. J. Cronbach and G. C. Gleser (Eds.), *Psychological tests and personnel decisions* (2nd ed.). Urbana, IL: University of Illinois Press.

SANDS, W. A. (1973). A method for evaluating alternative recruiting-selection strategies: The CAPER model. *Journal of Applied Psychology, 57*, 222–227.

SCHMIDT, F. L., and HOFFMAN, B. (1973). An empirical comparison of three methods of assessing the utility of a selection device. *Journal of Industrial and Organizational Psychology, 1*, 1–11.

TAYLOR, H. C., and RUSSELL, J. T. (1939). The relationship of validity coefficients to the practical effectiveness of tests in selection. *Journal of Applied Psychology, 23*, 565–578.

9

Estimating the Economic Value of Job Performance

As Equation 6 in Chapter 8 showed, the function of the parameter SD_y (the dollar value of a one-standard-deviation difference in criterion level) is to translate the incremental gain that results from the use of a more valid selection procedure into economic terms. If the SD_y parameter was not included in the general utility equation, then the effect of a change in criterion performance could be expressed only in terms of standard Z-score units. However, when the product, $r_{xy}\bar{Z}_{x_s}$ is multiplied by the dollar value SD_y, the result is an expression of gain that decision makers understand and are familiar with — dollars.

While most parameters of the general utility equation can be obtained from records such as the number of people tested, the cost of testing, and the selection ratio, SD_y cannot. Traditionally, as now, SD_y has been the most difficult parameter of the general utility equation to obtain (Cronbach and Gleser, 1965, p. 121; Raju, Burke, and Normand, 1990). In the past, it has been assumed that SD_y could be estimated only by using complicated cost-accounting methods that are both costly and time-consuming. In general, these procedures involve first costing out the dollar value of the job behaviors of each employee (Brogden and Taylor, 1950) and then computing the standard deviation of these values. Several newer approaches require only estimates from knowledgeable persons. In this chapter, we shall examine briefly the cost-accounting approach to estimating SD_y, and then we shall examine the newer estimation procedures in greater detail.

COST-ACCOUNTING APPROACH

In the simplest terms, the objective of a business is to make money. Consequently, monetary gain is the appropriate measure of the degree to which on-the-job activity of the individual contributes to or detracts from this overall objective. Brogden and Taylor (1950) summarize this idea as follows:

> Only after we have succeeded in evaluating on-the-job performance in these terms can we be sure that our criterion measures conform to the objectives of the organization. . . . Unless criterion elements are of such a nature that they can be expressed in dollar units, their use as criterion measures cannot be justified and do [*sic*] not satisfy the requirement of logical face validity. (pp. 139–140)

In using cost accounting to develop a dollar criterion, a number of elements must be considered. Brogden and Taylor list the following as examples:

1. Average value of production or service units.
2. Quality of objects produced or services accomplished.
3. Overhead — including rent, light, heat, cost depreciation, or rental of machines and equipment.
4. Errors, accidents, spoilage, wastage, damage to machines or equipment due to unusual wear and tear, etc.
5. Such factors as appearance, friendliness, poise, and general social effectiveness in public relations. (Here, some approximate value would have to be assigned by an individual or individuals having the required responsibility and background.)
6. The cost of spent time of other personnel. This would include not only the time of the supervisory personnel but also that of other workers. (p. 146)

Roche (1961) attempted to apply these ideas to 291 beginning level radial drill operators (RDO-1s) working in a large midwestern industrial plant that employs about 25,000 persons. The company's job description for an RDO-1 is:

> Sets up and operates a radial drill, performing drill, ream, line ream, tap (stud, pipe, and standard), countersink, chamfer, bore, counterbore, spotface, backface, and hollow mill operations. Involves various types of parts such as castings, forgings, bar stock, structural steel and welded fabrications. Grinds drills when necessary.

Work assignments to the RDO-1s are made by the planning department according to machine number, not according to specific operators. Consequently, the RDO-1s have no control over the type of parts on which they perform machining operations. Typically, any single worker will work on a variety of parts, and the mix differs from worker to worker.

It was assumed that the dollar profit that accrues to the company as a result of an individual's work provides the best estimate of his or her worth to the company. The following cost-accounting procedures were used to develop this dollar criterion. As described by Roche (1961), the method is one of "standard costing," which is an effective tool for volume production accounting. It also permits the application of the "principle of exception," whereby attention is directed chiefly to variations from standard cost that indicate trends in volume output. Standard cost for the company's products is determined by procuring costs on three basic factors: material used to produce products; direct labor hours used to alter the size, shape, quality, or consistency of material; and facility usage required to perform direct labor. Standard cost must remain stable or fixed for a specific period in order to attain its objective. Usually, all standards remain frozen for a period of five years, or until a general cost revision is officially authorized.

The company uses "lifo" (last in–first out) inventory accounting,[1] so that latest costs are used first to allocate costs in a manner closely related to price levels prevailing at the time of sale. The seven major cost elements in the accounting are:

- material, unformed steel
- material, grey iron castings
- material, forgings, stampings, and so on
- material, purchased finished
- direct labor
- general burden
- machine burden

Prime product costs are built up from costs of piece-parts or units into costs for assemblies, then costs for groups, arrangements, and finally for

[1] Using lifo, the earliest-acquired stock is assumed to be still on hand; the last-acquired stock is assumed to have been used immediately. Lifo releases the most recent (or last) inventory costs as cost of goods used or sold. It attempts to match the most current cost of obtaining inventory against sales for a period (Horngren, 1987).

the general arrangements or complete model. The total cost figure has four basic components: variable, fixed, office, and parts warehousing. Variable or out-of-pocket cost includes only those costs that fluctuate with production output: it includes actual cost of material, plus material-handling burden; direct labor cost plus an allocation to cover indirect labor, supplies, and so on; and facility usage, which generally reflects normal maintenance, power consumption, perishable tool usage, and facility supplies. These variable costs are most useful in determining costs where facility usage is not affected; however, fixed costs are used where facility usage is affected. Fixed costs are based on a given percentage of the production capacity of the plant. In determining them, allocations are made to cover portions of material-handling burden, plant labor and burden (such as overtime premium, special indirect labor, and management salaries), and plant facility usage (such as building and machinery depreciation, repairs and maintenance, tool design). Office and parts warehousing costs are figured as a percentage allocation.

The income from the RDO-1's work is determined readily, since the parts manufactured are sold to dealers and a price for each part has been established. Subtracting the cost at standard production from the price yields a profit figure.

Measuring Each Individual's Productivity

A productivity measure called the *performance ratio* was developed to express the payoff for each individual. Since the length of time it takes a competent operator to complete a machining operation on a particular piece-part was established by standard time study procedures, the number of piece-parts per hour that an operator should be able to process was known. A performance ratio for any period of work could then be computed by dividing actual production per hour by the standard hourly production for the piece-part on which an RDO-1 was then working. For example, if the standard production for a piece-part is ten pieces per hour and an operator produces seven pieces in an hour, his or her performance ratio for that one hour's work is 0.70. This index makes it possible to determine the operator's performance ratio over a month or more during which he or she has worked on a number of different piece-parts, each of which has a different production standard. Only rarely does an operator turn out more than standard production over an extended period of time. At the time of the study, operators had varying lengths of time of company service, ranging from a few months to over ten years. A rigid attempt to control the experience factor would have seriously reduced the size of the group. Management personnel stated that most individuals with no previous machine operator experience could reach their typical level of RDO-1 performance within a few weeks. In Roche's (1961) study, therefore, performance ratios for each operator were obtained monthly for a six-month period, and the mean was taken as the operator's typical performance. These results are shown in Exhibit 9.1. An analysis of variance indicated that the mean performance ratios over the six-month period did not differ significantly from each other. Thus, it was concluded that the group's performance was stable over the period of study, and the mean performance for each of the operators was used as his or her typical performance.

The Burden Adjustment

If an operator produces at less than standard, the actual burden per hour for this inefficiency is greater than the standard burden per hour determined for his or her operation. An operator producing at 80 percent of standard actually takes one and one-quarter hours to produce an hour's work. In order to take into account this additional burden, each below-standard performance ratio was corrected. It was assumed that the amount of burden in excess of the standard burden reduced in a proportional amount an operator's contribution. The formula used for such corrections was $2 - 1/PR$, where PR is performance ratio. Thus, when a person is working at 80 percent of standard, the burden is 1.25 hours instead of 1.00 hour, and the corrected performance ratio is 0.75.

Determination of Payoff

The procedures for determining each operator's payoff (y) were as follows:

1. Computation of each operator's typical performance ratio. This figure was his or her mean performance ratio for the six-month period of the study.
2. Adjustment of the typical performance ratio for below-standard production (the burden adjustment).
3. Computation of the average profit at standard production, attributable to the radical drill operation.

   a. Tabulation of the standard production rate for each type of piece-part machined by radial drill operators. These data were provided by the time study division.

EXHIBIT 9.1 Monthly performance ratios for RDO-1s as a group

Month	*Mean*	SD
First	79.92	17.84
Second	81.21	17.88
Third	79.70	16.71
Fourth	83.16	16.87
Fifth	79.23	20.25
Sixth	80.69	17.72

Source: Roche, W. J., Jr. (1965). A dollar criterion in fixed treatment employee selection. In L. J. Cronbach and G. C. Gleser (Eds.), *Psychological tests and personnel decisions* (p. 262). Urbana, IL: University of Illinois Press.

b. Profit for each type of piece-part attributable to the radial drill operation.

c. Profit per hour for each piece-part attributable to the radial drill operation at standard production. These figures were determined by multiplying the profit per piece by the standard production rate for the piece.

d. Average hourly profit attributable to the radial drill operation at standard production. This was determined by weighting the profit per hour for each piece-part (step 3c) by the number of such parts in the work flow.

4. Determination of y, the profit for each radial drill operator at his or her corrected performance ratio and the standard hourly profit.

5. Computation of SD_y. This is merely the standard deviation of the y values computed in step 4.

In actually computing the payoff values, Roche (1961) reported that the 291 radial drill operators worked on approximately 2,500 different piece-parts. Because determining the profit attributable to the radial drill operation for every piece-part would require an enormous amount of clerical labor, a random sample of 275 parts (about 10 percent of the total) was drawn and the necessary computations were performed for these. Averaged over the sample of parts, the profit per hour attributable to the radial drill operation was $5.512; the standard deviation was $3.947.[2] This is not

[2]These figures are in 1961 dollars. Assuming a 6 percent inflation rate, the comparable figures in 1990 dollars are $29.87 and $21.39, respectively.

directly a part of company earnings. Out of this line in the balance sheet must come various costs of doing business, such as interest on loans and bonds and taxes.

The y value for each operator was the hourly profit at standard production attributable to RDO-1 multiplied by his or her corrected performance ratio. The standard deviation of this distribution (SD_y) was $0.585.[3]

Despite the complexity and apparent objectivity of the cost-accounting approach, Roche (1961) admitted that "many estimates and arbitrary allocations entered into the cost accounting" (Cronbach and Gleser, 1965, p. 263). The development of an estimate of SD_y clearly required a prodigious effort in the Roche study. (The actual utility estimates will be described in the next chapter.) This is probably a major reason why more such studies were not undertaken for over fifteen years following its publication. A subsequent attempt to use cost-accounting methodology to develop an objective estimate of SD_y for the job of route salesperson for a soft drink bottling company resulted in the same conclusion made by Roche (Greer and Cascio, 1987). Their method involved estimating the "contribution margin" (revenue less variable costs) associated with selling cases of different sizes and types, multiplying that value by the number of cases each salesperson sold, and then multiplying that value by the percentage of sales attributable to the salesperson's effort on each route. This produced an estimate of each salesperson's contribution margin, and the standard deviation of these values represented SD_y.

Cost-accounting systems focus on determining the costs and benefits of units of product, not units of performance. Hence, many estimates are needed, and the presumed objectivity and reliability of the cost-accounting data may become suspect. Paradoxically, therefore, if personnel researchers can establish the validity of their methods, behavioral approaches may be more valid, reliable, and credible with practitioners than are cost-accounting approaches. Beginning in the late 1970s, several new approaches for estimating the economic value of job performance were developed. All require considerably less effort than the cost-accounting method, and comparative research has made possible some general conclusions about the relative merits of these methods. First we will consider the methods themselves; then we will consider the findings of comparative research.

[3] $3.17 in 1990 dollars.

The 40 Percent Rule

When time or resources do not permit a more detailed estimation of SD_y, Schmidt and Hunter (1983) recommend that 40 percent of average salary be used. Further, since wages and salaries average 57 percent of the value of goods and services in the U.S. economy, this SD_y figure is 22.8 percent (0.40×0.57) or roughly 20 percent of mean output. If we substitute 40 percent of salary for SD_y, then utility can be expressed in terms of dollars. If instead we substitute 20 percent for SD_y (this value is known as SD_p), then utility may be expressed in terms of the *percentage increase* in output.

In a later study, Hunter et al. (1990) tested the hypothesis that SD_p increases as the complexity (that is, information processing requirements) of jobs increases. Results of sixty-eight studies that measured work output on the job, and seventeen work sample studies revealed that as jobs increase in complexity from routine clerical or blue collar work to medium complexity (for example, first-line supervisors, skilled crafts, technicians) to high complexity (managerial/professional, complex technical jobs), SD_p increased from 15 percent to 25 percent to 46 percent, respectively. For life insurance sales jobs, SD_p is very large (97 percent), and it is about 39 percent for other sales jobs. These results suggest that there are sizable differences in performance across individuals and that potentially large gains in productivity may be realized when valid personnel selection procedures are used to identify the best talent available.

The substitution of SD_p for SD_y is provocative because it suggests that in situations where job complexity can be estimated, SD_p also can be estimated, thereby removing a barrier to more widespread application of utility analysis methods. On the other hand, Boudreau (1988) has noted that SD_p allows one to estimate only the percentage increase that is likely to result from HRM programs. Determining whether such increases offset dollar costs, or whether to invest resources in different jobs requires assumptions or estimates of the dollar value of this percentage. For this reason, other behaviorally based methods for estimating the variability of job performance in dollars have been developed. We will consider several of them in the sections that follow.

GLOBAL ESTIMATION OF THE DOLLAR VALUE OF JOB PERFORMANCE

Fortunately, estimates of utility need not be accurate down to the last dollar. Utility estimates typically are used to make decisions about selection procedures, and for this purpose only errors large enough to lead to incorrect decisions are of any consequence. Further, when cost-accounting procedures are used, errors may be as frequent or more frequent and may become a more severe problem as one moves up the corporate ladder. What objective cost-accounting techniques, for example, can be used to assess the dollar value of an executive's impact on the morale of his or her subordinates? It is precisely the jobs with the largest SD_y values, that is, the jobs for which ΔU/selectee is potentially greatest, that are handled least well by cost-accounting methods. Rational estimates, to one degree or another, are virtually unavoidable at the higher job levels.

One procedure for obtaining rational estimates of SD_y has been developed by Schmidt, Hunter, McKenzie, and Muldrow (1979). This method was used in a pilot study by sixty-two experienced supervisors of budget analysts to estimate SD_y for that occupation. Supervisors were used as judges because they have the best opportunities to observe actual performance and output differences among employees on a day-to-day basis. The method is based on the following reasoning: If job performance in dollar terms is normally distributed, then the difference between the value to the organization of the products and services produced by an employee at the eighty-fifth percentile in performance and that of an employee at the fiftieth percentile in performance is equal to SD_y. Budget analyst supervisors were asked to estimate both these values; the final estimate was the average difference across the sixty-two supervisors. Such a global estimation procedure (in which a total figure is derived directly instead of summing individual cost elements) has at least two advantages. First, the mental standard to be used by the supervisor-judges is the estimated cost to the organization of having an outside consulting firm provide the same products or services. In many occupations, this is a relatively concrete standard. Second, the idiosyncratic tendencies, biases, and random errors of individual experts can be controlled by averaging across a large number of judges. Unless the group has an upward or downward bias as a whole, such an average should be fairly accurate. In the budget analyst example, the standard error of the mean was $1,120. This means that the interval $9,480 to $13,175 should contain 90 percent of such estimates. Thus to be extremely conservative one could employ the lower bound of this interval in calculations.

Methods similar to this global estimation procedure have been used successfully by the Decision Analysis Group of the Stanford Research Institute to scale otherwise unmeasurable but critical variables. Resulting measures have been used in the application of the principles of decision theory to high-level policy decision making in such areas as nuclear power plant construction, corporate risk policies, investment and expansion programs, and hurricane seeding (Howard, 1966; Howard, Matheson, and North, 1972; Matheson, 1969). All indications are that the response to the work of this group has been positive; these methods have been judged by high-level decision makers to contribute valuably to improvement of socially and economically important decisions.

We'll now describe in detail how the global estimation procedure has been used to estimate SD_y. The application to be described was reported by Schmidt et al. (1979) using supervisors of computer programmers in ten federal agencies. To test the hypothesis that dollar outcomes are normally distributed, the supervisors were asked to estimate values for the fifteenth percentile (low-performing programmers), the fiftieth percentile (average programmers), and the eighty-fifth percentile (superior programmers). The resulting data thus provide two estimates of SD_y. If the distribution is approximately normal, these two estimates will not differ substantially in value.

> The instructions to the supervisors were as follows: The dollar utility estimates we are asking you to make are critical in estimating the relative dollar value to the government of different selection methods. In answering these questions, you will have to make some very *difficult judgments*. We realize they are difficult and that they are judgments or estimates. You will have to ponder for some time before giving each estimate, and there is probably no way you can be absolutely certain your estimate is accurate when you do reach a decision. But keep in mind three things:
>
> (1) The alternative to estimates of this kind is application of cost accounting procedures to the evaluation of job performance. Such applications are usually prohibitively expensive. And in the end, they produce only imperfect estimates, like this estimation procedure.
>
> (2) Your estimates will be averaged in with those of other supervisors of computer programmers. Thus errors produced by too high and too low estimates will tend to be averaged out, providing more accurate final estimates.
>
> (3) The decisions that must be made about selection methods do not require that all estimates be accurate down to the last dollar. Substantially accurate estimates will lead to the same decisions as perfectly accurate estimates.
>
> Based on your experience with agency programmers, we would like for you to estimate the yearly value to your agency of the products and services produced by the average GS 9–11 computer programmer. Consider the quality and quantity of output typical of the *average programmer* and the value of this output. In placing an overall dollar value on

this output, it may help to consider what the cost would be of having an outside firm provide these products and services.

Based on my experience, I estimate the value to my agency of the average GS 9–11 computer programmer at _____dollars per year.

We would now like for you to consider the *"superior" programmer*. Let us define a superior performer as a programmer who is at the 85th percentile. That is, his or her performance is better than that of 85% of his or her fellow GS 9–11 programmers, and only 15% turn in better performances. Consider the quality and quantity of the output typical of the superior programmer. Then estimate the value of these products and services. In placing an overall dollar value on this output, it may again help to consider what the cost would be of having an outside firm provide these products and services.

Based on my experience, I estimate the value to my agency of a superior GS 9–11 computer programmer to be _____dollars per year.

Finally, we would like you to consider the *"low-performing" computer programmer*. Let us define a low-performing programmer as one who is at the 15th percentile. That is, 85% of all GS 9–11 computer programmers turn in performances better than the low-performing programmer, and only 15% turn in worse performances. Consider the quality and quantity of the output typical of the low-performing programmer. Then estimate the value of these products and services. In placing an overall dollar value on this output, it may again help to consider what the cost would be of having an outside firm provide these products and services.

Based on my experience, I estimate the value to my agency of the low-performing GS 9–11 computer programmer at _____dollars per year. (Schmidt et al., 1979, p. 621, used by permission)

The wording of this questionnaire was developed carefully and pretested on a small sample of programmer supervisors and personnel psychologists. None of the programmer supervisors who returned questionnaires in the study reported any difficulty in understanding the questionnaire or in making the estimates. Participation in the study was completely voluntary. Of 147 questionnaires distributed, 105 were returned (all in usable form), for a return rate of 71.4 percent.

Results

The two estimates of SD_y were similar. The mean estimated difference in dollar value of yearly job performance between programmers at the eighty-fifth and fiftieth percentiles in job performance was \$10,871 (SE = \$1,673). The difference between the fiftieth and fifteenth percentiles was \$9,955 (SE = \$1,035). The difference of \$916 was roughly 8 percent of each of the estimates and was not statistically significant. Thus, the hypothesis that computer programmer productivity in dollars is normally distributed could not be rejected. The distribution was at least approximately normal. The average of these two estimates, \$10,413, was the SD_y figure used in the utility calculations to be described in Chapter 10. This figure must be considered an underestimate, since it applies to incumbents rather than to the applicant pool.

Although this global estimation procedure is easy to use and provides fairly reliable estimates across supervisors, it has three drawbacks: (1) the dollar-valued job performance outcomes are often not normally distributed (Burke and Frederick, 1984; Rich and Boudreau, 1987); (2) the procedure lacks face validity (that is, it does not appear to measure what it purports to measure) since the components of each supervisor's estimates are unknown and unverifiable; and (3) subjects often find the task of estimating the dollar value of various percentiles in the distribution of job performance to be rather difficult. Moreover, the variation among each rater's SD_y estimates is usually as large or larger than the mean SD_y estimate. In fact, DeSimone et al. (1986) found both the level of agreement among raters and the stability over time of their SD_y estimates to be low.

To improve consensus among raters, two strategies have been used: (1) provide an anchor for the fiftieth percentile (Bobko et al., 1983; Burke and Frederick, 1984, 1986); (2) have groups of raters provide consensus judgments of different percentiles. Despite these problems, several studies have reported close correspondence between estimated and actual standard deviations when sales dollars (Bobko et al., 1983) or cost-accounting estimates (Greer and Cascio, 1987) were used. An alternative procedure that makes no assumption regarding the underlying normality of the performance distribution, and that does identify the components of each supervisor's estimate, is described next.

THE CASCIO-RAMOS ESTIMATE OF PERFORMANCE IN DOLLARS (CREPID)

The Cascio-Ramos estimate of performance in dollars (CREPID) was developed under the auspices of the American Telephone and Telegraph Company, and was tested on 602 first-level managers in a Bell operating company (Cascio and Ramos, 1986). The rationale underlying CREPID is as follows. Assuming an organization's compensation program reflects current market rates for jobs, then the economic value of each employee's labor is reflected best in his or her annual wage or salary. CREPID breaks down each employee's job into its principal activities, assigns a proportional amount of the annual salary to each principal activity, and then requires supervisors to rate each employee's job performance on each principal activity. The resulting ratings then are translated into estimates of dollar value for each principal activity. The sum of the dollar values assigned to each principal activity equals the economic value of each employee's job performance to the company. Let us explain each of these steps in greater detail.

1. *Identify principal activities.* In order to assign a dollar value to each employee's job performance, first we must identify what tasks each employee performs. In many job analysis systems, principal activities (or critical work behaviors) are identified expressly. In others they can be derived, under the assumption that to be considered "principal" an activity should comprise at least 10 percent of total work time. As an illustration, consider Exhibit 9.2, a portion of a hypothetical job description for an accounting supervisor. As Exhibit 9.2 indicates, this job involves eight principal activities.

2. *Rate each principal activity in terms of time/frequency and importance.* It has long been recognized that rating job activities simply in terms of the time or frequency with which each is performed is an incomplete indication of the overall weight to be assigned to each activity. For example, a nurse may spend most of the work week performing the routine tasks of patient care. However, suppose the nurse must respond to one medical emergency per week that requires, on an average, one hour of his or her time. To be sure, the time/frequency of this activity is short, but its importance is critical. Ratings of time/frequency and importance should be expressed on a scale that has a zero point so that in theory complete absence of a property can be indicated. Sample rating scales for principal activities are shown in Exhibit 9.3.

Research results using job analysis ratings derived from CREPID have shown two things. First, only the time/frequency and importance of each principal activity need to be rated in order to derive and assign an overall weight to each principal activity (Cascio and Ramos, 1986). Second, for rating time/frequency and importance, simple 0–7 point Likert-type rating scales provide results that are almost identical to those derived from more complicated scales (Weekley, Frank, O'Connor, and Peters, 1985).

EXHIBIT 9.2 Portion of a job description for an accounting supervisor

Function

Under general supervision of the Manager-Accounting (Accounts analysis and Bills and Vouchers) Supervises the Accounts Payable System of the Central Region.

Know How

This position is responsible, through subordinates, for the processing, payment, and journalization of suppliers' bills (all bills except those handled by intercompany settlement) and employees' expense vouchers through input to the accounts payable system. Bills and vouchers are received along with authorization forms from company employees initiating the expense. The following steps then take place:

- Receive summaries and log into accounts payable system by office, summary, and total dollars for control purposes.
- Edit for correctness, for example proper authorization or coding.
- Enter bill and voucher information into accounts payable system for check issuance and subsequently into mechanized system for journalization.
- Return erroneous bills and vouchers to employee originating for correction and then correct the initial cumulative total in accounts payable system.
- Update the master file of suppliers contained in system.

Incumbent is directly responsible for the manual processing, payment, and journalization of special bills that cannot be processed via computer (for example, relocation expenses, tuition aid, employee refunds and commissions) and various special reports. Also responsible for the issuance of Forms 1099—U.S. Information Return-to-suppliers and the Internal Revenue Service.

Incumbent must have a thorough knowledge of accounting principles, of the accounts payable data entry system, and of the bill payment process. Also needed is a familiarity with disbursement accounting practices and other guides and reference manuals. Incumbent must have analytical and investigative ability, communicative skills, mathematical aptitude, and supervisory skills.

Subordinates consist of eleven Senior Clerks.

Principal Activities

1. Performs normal supervisory functions.
2. Receives questions on billing problems from suppliers. Investigates and furnishes answers, expedites late checks.

(continues)

EXHIBIT 9.2 continued

3. Adjudicates bills and vouchers for legitimacy of purpose or amount when clerks cannot make determination. Contacts originators at all levels of management when necessary.
4. Verifies and signs reports sent to Corporate Books and other departments.
5. Performs immediate action in the event of computer problems, notifies programmer if necessary.
6. Interprets procedural changes, trains subordinates or arranges for formal training.
7. Coordinates the review of bills and vouchers by internal and external auditors or state authorities.
8. Ensures implementation of proper security precautions.

Problem Solving

The incumbent's major problems involve questions from subordinates and other departments regarding correct chargeable account, if expenditure is reimbursable, etc.; investigating and answering suppliers' inquiries regarding late or improper payment of bills; maintaining work production with a consistently changing force; contending with computer breakdowns.

Accountability

Incumbent in this position is accountable for receiving, logging, totaling, editing, payment, and journalization of all company vouchers and bills (except those handled through inter-company settlements) for the Central Region. Incumbent is also accountable for acting as the information center where suppliers and other departments can call to have their questions answered regarding bill payments and voucher processing information. Subordinates' salaries approximately $XXX,000 annually.

Bills processed = $XX,000 per month
Totaling = $XX.X million

3. *Multiply the numerical ratings for time/frequency and importance for each principal activity.* The purpose of this step is to develop an overall relative weight to assign each principal activity. The ratings are multiplied together so that if a zero rating is assigned to any category, the relative weight of that principal activity is zero. Thus, if an activity never is done, or if it is totally unimportant, then the relative weight for that activity should be zero. The following illustration presents hypothetical ratings of the eight principal activities identified for the accounting supervisor's job shown in Exhibit 9.2.

EXHIBIT 9.3 CREPID rating scales for principal activities

1. *Time/frequency*: Please rate each principal activity on the 0–7 scale shown below. Stepping back and looking at the whole job, say, over a one-year period, how would you allocate the principal activities in terms of the time/frequency with which each is done?

0	1	2	3	4	5	6	7
very rarely		sometimes			often		very often

2. *Importance*: Please rate each principal activity on a 0–7 scale that reflects, in your opinion, how important that principal activity is to overall job performance. Use the scale below as a guide to help you rate.

0	1	2	3	4	5	6	7
of no importance		moderately important			very important		of greatest importance

Principal Activity	*Time/ Frequency*	×	*Importance*	=	*Total*	*Relative Weight* (%)
1	4.0		4		16.0	16.8
2	5.0		7		35.0	36.8
3	1.0		5		5.0	5.3
4	0.5		3		1.5	1.6
5	2.0		7		14.0	14.7
6	1.0		4		4.0	4.2
7	0.5		3		1.5	1.6
8	3.0		6		18.0	19.0
					95.0	100.0%

After all the multiplication is done, the overall ratings assigned each principal activity are totaled (95 in the preceding example). The overall rating for each principal activity then is divided by the grand total to derive the relative weight for the activity (for example, 16 ÷ 95 = 0.168 or 16.8 percent). Knowing each principal activity's relative weight allows us to allocate proportional shares of the employee's overall salary to each principal activity. This is done in step 4.

4. *Assign dollar values to each principal activity.* Take an average (or weighted average) annual rate of pay for all participants in the study (employees in a particular job class) and allocate it across principal activities according to the relative weights obtained in step 3.

To illustrate, suppose the annual salary of each accounting supervisor is $35,000.

Principal Activity	Relative Weight (%)	Dollar Value
1	16.8	$ 5,880
2	36.8	12,880
3	5.3	1,855
4	1.6	560
5	14.7	5,145
6	4.2	1,470
7	1.6	560
8	19.0	6,650
		$35,000

5. *Rate performance on each principal activity on a zero to two hundred scale.* Now that we know what each employee does, the relative weight of each principal activity, and the dollar value of each principal activity, the next task is to determine *how well* the employee does each principal activity. The higher the rating on each principal activity, the greater the economic value of that activity to the organization. CREPID uses a modified magnitude estimation scale (Stevens, 1971) to obtain information on performance. In order to use this procedure, a value (say 100) is assigned to a referent concept (for example, the average employee, one at the fiftieth percentile on job performance), and then all comparisons are made relative to this value. Discussions with operating managers indicated that, given current selection procedures, it is highly unlikely that even the very best employee is more than twice as effective as the average employee. Thus a continuous 0–200 scale was used to rate each employee on each principal activity. The actual form used is shown in Exhibit 9.4. Managers reported that they found this format helpful and easy to use.

6. *Multiply the point rating (expressed as a decimal number) assigned to each principal activity by the activity's dollar value.* To illustrate, suppose the following point totals are assigned to accounting supervisor C. P. Ayh:

Principal Activity	Points Assigned	×	Dollar Value of Activity	=	Net Dollar Value
1	1.35		5,880		7,938.00
2	1.00		12,880		12,880.00
3	1.25		1,855		2,318.75

Principal Activity	Points Assigned	×	Dollar Value of Activity	=	Net Dollar Value
4	2.00		560		1,120.00
5	1.00		5,145		5,145.00
6	0.50		1,470		735.00
7	0.75		560		420.00
8	1.50		6,650		9,975.00

7. *Compute the overall economic value of each employee's job performance by adding the results of step 6.* In our example, the overall economic value of Mr. Ayh's job performance is $40,531.75, or $5,531.75 more than he is being paid.

8. *Over all employees in the study, compute the mean and standard*

EXHIBIT 9.4 Performance appraisal form used with CREPID

In this last part of the exercise we would like you to rate the job performance of your subordinate, _____, relative to the principal activities identified in Part I. Use the rating scale below for each of the principal activities listed in the job analysis to rate your subordinate.

0	50	100	150	200
	better than 25% of employees I've seen do this activity	better than 50%	better than 75%	better than 99%

In your opinion, based on the principal activities described in the job analysis and relative to others you have seen do these activities, how does the job performance of _____ compare? (Use any number of the 0–200 scale shown above.)

Principal Activity	***Points Assigned***
1	_____
2	_____
3	_____
4	_____
5	_____
6	_____
7	_____
8	_____

deviation of dollar-valued job performance. When CREPID was tested on 602 first-level managers at a Bell operating company, the mean of dollar-valued job performance was only $988 (3.4 percent) more than the average actual salary of all employees in the study. However, the standard deviation (SD_y) was over $10,000, which was more than three and a half times larger than the standard deviation of the actual distribution of salaries. Such high variability suggests that supervisors recognized significant differences in performance throughout the rating process. As we shall see in Chapter 10, this is precisely the type of situation in which valid selection procedures have the greatest payoff — when individual differences in job performance are high, and therefore the cost of error is substantial.

It is important to point out that CREPID requires only two sets of ratings from a supervisor: (1) a rating of each principal activity in terms of time/frequency and importance (this is the job analysis phase), and (2) a rating of a specific subordinate's performance on each principal activity (this is the performance appraisal phase). The actual identification of principal activities (step 1), multiplication of the numerical ratings assigned during the job analysis phase (step 3), the assignment of dollar values to each principal activity (step 4), and the determination of the overall economic value of job performance (steps 6, 7, and 8) is done by personnel specialists who use a simple, computerized scoring program. A summary of the entire CREPID procedure is presented in Exhibit 9.5.

Edwards, Frederick, and Burke (1988) modified the basic CREPID procedure by substituting archival data for either performance ratings or job analysis ratings, or for both. They found that when they substituted *either* archival performance ratings or archival job analysis ratings, results were similar to those produced using the original procedure. However, SD_y was much smaller when archival data were used for *both* performance ratings and job analysis.

As Boudreau (1988) has noted, CREPID has the advantage of assigning each employee a specific value that can be explicitly analyzed for appropriateness and that may also provide a more understandable or credible estimate for decision makers. However, CREPID assumes that average wage equals the economic value of a worker's performance. This assumption is used in national income accounting to generate the GNP and labor cost figures for jobs where output is not readily measurable (for example, government services). That is, the same value is assigned to both output and wages. Because, as Boudreau (1988) pointed out, this assumption does not hold in pay systems that are based on rank, tenure, or hourly pay rates, CREPID should not be used in these situations.

EXHIBIT 9.5 Summary of the Cascio-Ramos procedure for determining the economic value of management performance

1. Identify principal activities.
2. Rate each principal activity in terms of time/frequency and importance.
3. Multiply the numerical ratings for time/frequency and importance for each principal activity.
4. Assign dollar values to each principal activity. Take an average rate of pay of participants in the study and allocate it across principal activities according to the results obtained in step 3.
5. Rate each principal activity on a 0–200 point scale.
6. Multiply (for each principal activity) its dollar value by the point rating assigned (expressed as a decimal number).
7. Compute the overall economic value of job performance by adding together results of step 6.
8. Over all employees in the study, compute the mean and standard deviation of dollar-valued job performance.

SYSTEM EFFECTIVENESS TECHNIQUE

This method was developed by Eaton, Wing, and Mitchell (1985) specifically for use in situations where individual salary is only a small percentage of the value of performance to the organization or of the equipment operated (e.g., an army tank commander or a fighter pilot). It evaluates changes in the performance levels of system units that lead to improved overall performance.

With this approach, Eaton et al. distinguish $SD\$$, the standard deviation of performance in dollars, from SD_y, the standard deviation of output units of performance (e.g., number of hits per firing from an army tank commander). They have shown that

$$SD\$ = C_u(SD_y/Y1) \tag{1}$$

where C_u is the cost of the unit in the system — it includes equipment, support, and personnel, rather than salary alone. $Y1$ is the mean performance of units at the initial performance level.

Equation 1 indicates that $SD\$$ equals the cost per unit times the ratio of the SD_y of performance to the initial mean level of performance, $Y1$. However, estimates from Equation 1 are appropriate *only when the performance of the unit in the system is largely a function of the performance of the individual in the job under investigation.* Examples of performance scales that might fit this method are probability of hits per firing (army tank commander), number of convictions per year (detective), or other frequency-type variables.

To assess $SD\$$ using the system effectiveness technique, Eaton et al. collected data on U.S. Army tank commanders. They obtained these data from technical reports of previous research and from an approximation of tank costs. Previous research indicated that meaningful values for the ratio $SD_y/Y1$ range from 0.2 to 0.5. Tank costs, consisting of purchase costs, maintenance, and personnel, were estimated between \$300,000 and \$500,000 per year. For purposes of Equation 1, C_u was estimated at \$300,000 per year, and $SD_y/Y1$ was estimated at 0.2. This yielded

$$SD\$ = \$300{,}000 \times 0.2 = \$60{,}000$$

An alternative method, also developed by Eaton et al. for similar kinds of situations, is the superior equivalents technique. It is somewhat like the global estimation procedure, but with one important difference. Instead of using estimates of the dollar value of performance at the eighty-fifth percentile, the technique uses estimates of how many superior (eighty-fifth percentile) performers would be needed to produce the output of a fixed number of average (fiftieth percentile) performers. This estimate, combined with an estimate of the dollar value of average performance, provides an estimate of SD_y, and is the basis for the title "superior equivalents technique."

SUPERIOR EQUIVALENTS TECHNIQUE

The basic concept of this method is that of estimating the standard deviation of performance in performance units, and then converting this estimate to dollar units. Accordingly, the first step is to estimate the *number* ($N85$) of eighty-fifth percentile employees required to equal the performance of some fixed number ($N50$) of average performers. Where the *value* of average performance ($V50$) is known, or can be estimated, SD_y may be estimated by using the ratio $N50 \div N85$ times $V50$ to obtain $V85$, and then subtracting $V50$. This reduces to

$$SD_y = V85 - V50 \tag{2}$$

but,

$$V85 = (V50 \times N50) \div N85 \tag{3}$$

Hence,

$$SD_y = V50\,[(N50 \div N85) - 1] \tag{4}$$

A questionnaire was developed to obtain an estimate of the number of tanks with superior tank commanders needed to equal the performance of a standard company of 17 tanks with average commanders. A fill-in-the-blanks format was used, as shown in the following excerpt.

> For the purpose of this questionnaire an "average" tank commander is an NCO or commissioned officer whose performance is better than about half his fellow TCs. A "superior" tank commander is one whose performance is better than 85% of his fellow tank commanders.
>
> The first question deals with relative value. For example, if a "superior" clerk types 10 letters a day and an "average" clerk types 5 letters a day then, all else being equal, 5 "superior" clerks have the same value in an office as 10 "average" clerks.
>
> In the same way, we want to know your estimate or opinion of the relative value of "average" vs. "superior" tank commanders in combat.
>
> 1. I estimate that, all else being equal, _____tanks with "superior" tank commanders would be about equal in combat to 17 tanks with "average" tank commanders.

Questionnaire data were gathered from 100 tank commanders enrolled in advanced training at a U.S. Army post. *N*50 was set at 17 as a fixed number of tanks with average commanders, because a tank company has 17 tanks. Assuming that organizations pay average employees their approximate worth, the equivalent civilian salary for a tank commander was set at $30,000.

Results

The median response given for the number of superior TCs judged equivalent to 17 average TCs was 9, and the mode was 10. The response "9" was used as most representative of central tendency. Making use of Equation 3, *V*85 was calculated as follows:

$$(\$30{,}000 \times 17) \div 9 = \$56{,}666$$

In terms of Equation 4,

$$SD_y = \$30{,}000\,[(17 \div 9) - 1] = \$26{,}666$$

This is considerably less that the *SD*$ value ($60,000) that resulted from the system effectiveness technique. SD_y also was estimated using the global estimation procedure. However, there was minimal agreement either within or between groups for estimates of superior performance, and the distributions were skewed positively. Distributions of average performance also were skewed positively. For these reasons, results of the global estimation procedure were not used in the calculation of overall utility. Such extreme response variability illustrates the difficulty of making these kinds of judgments when the cost of contracting work is unknown, equipment is expensive, or other financially intangible factors exist. Such is frequently the case for public employees, particularly when private industry counterparts do not exist. Under these circumstances, the system effectiveness technique or the superior equivalents technique may apply.

Eaton et al. point out that one possible problem with both of these techniques is that the *quality* of performance in some situations may not translate easily into a unidimensional, quantitative scale. For example, a police department may decide that the conviction of one murderer is equivalent to the conviction of five burglars. Whether managers do in fact develop informal algorithms to compare the performance of different individuals, perhaps on different factors, is an empirical question. Certainly the terms or dimensions that are most meaningful and useful will vary across jobs. Having examined five different methods for estimating the economic value of job performance, at this point, the reader might naturally ask whether any one method is superior to the others. Our final section addresses that question.

COMPARATIVE RESEARCH

After reviewing thirty-four studies that included over 100 estimates of SD_y, Boudreau (1988) concluded that differences among alternative methods for estimating SD_y are often less than 50 percent (and may be less than $5,000 in many cases). Still, small differences can become magnified when multiplied by the number of persons selected, the validity, and the selection ratio. Without any meaningful external criterion against which to compare SD_y estimates, one is left with little basis for choosing one method over another.

Yet let us not lose sight of our overall objective — to improve HRM decision making. To be useful, utility analyses should reflect the context in which decisions are made. For example, is the task to choose among alternative selection procedures? Or is it to decide whether to fund a selection program or to buy new equipment? All utility analyses are plagued by uncertainty and risk. By taking uncertainty into account through sensitivity or break-even analysis, *any* of the SD_y estimation methods may be (and often is) acceptable because none yield a result so discrepant as to change the decision in question. The next chapter examines the actual outcomes of utility analyses, and the role of economic factors, employee flows, and break-even analysis in interpreting such results.

EXERCISES

1. Divide into four- to six-person teams and do either a or b depending on feasibility.

a. Choose a production job at a fast food restaurant and, using the standard costing approach described by Roche (1961), estimate the mean and standard deviation of dollar-valued job performance.

b. The Tiny Company manufactures components for word processors. Most of the work is done at the 2,000-employee Tiny plant in the Midwest. Your task is to estimate the mean and standard deviation of dollar-valued job performance for Assembler-1s (about 200 employees). You are free to make any assumptions you like about the Tiny Assembler-1s, but be prepared to defend your assumptions. List and describe all of the factors (along with how you would measure each one) your team would consider in using standard costing to estimate SD_y.

2. Using the instructions provided for the Schmidt et al. (1979) global estimation procedure, each class member should attempt to estimate the mean, standard deviation, standard error of the mean $SD/\sqrt{N}$, and 90 percent confidence interval for the mean value of a stockbroker working for a major brokerage firm in New York.[4] Each class member should make three estimates of the dollar value to the firm: (a) the value of a stockbroker at the fiftieth percentile in merit, (b) at the eighty-fifth percentile in merit, and (c) at the fifteenth percentile in merit. For purposes of this exercise, accuracy of your estimates is less important than your understanding of the process and mechanics of the estimation procedure.

3. Jim Hill is manager of subscriber accounts for the Prosper Company. The results of a job analysis indicate that Jim's job includes four principal activities. A summary of Jim's superior's ratings of the activities and Jim's performance of each of them is shown in the table that follows.

---

[4] A 90 percent confidence interval for the mean may be calculated by the following formula: $\bar{X} \pm 1.64\ SD/\sqrt{N}$. The interpretation of the result is: If we were to repeat the above procedure often, each time selecting a different sample from the same population, then, on the average, 90 out of every 100 intervals similarly obtained would contain the true value of the population mean.

Principal Activity	Time/ Frequency	Importance	Performance Rating (points)
1	4.5	3	1.00
2	3.0	5	2.00
3	6.0	2	0.50
4	1.0	7	1.00

Assuming Jim is paid $30,000 per year, use CREPID to estimate the overall economic value of his job performance.

4. Assume that an average SWAT team member is paid $28,000 per year. Complete the following questionnaire. Then use the results to estimate SD_y by means of the superior equivalents technique.

> For purposes of this questionnaire, a "superior" SWAT team member is one whose performance is better than about 85 percent of his fellow SWAT team members. Please complete the following item:
>
> I estimate that, all else being equal, _____"superior" SWAT team members would be about equal to 20 "average" SWAT team members.

REFERENCES

BOBKO, P., KARREN, R., and PARKINGTON, J. J. (1983). The estimation of standard deviations in utility analyses: An empirical test. *Journal of Applied Psychology, 68*, 170–176.

BOUDREAU, J. W. (1988, December). *Utility analysis for decisions in human resource management.* Working Paper 88–21, Center for Advanced Human Resource Studies, New York State School of Industrial and Labor Relations, Ithaca, NY: Cornell University.

BROGDEN, H. E., and TAYLOR, E. K. (1950). The dollar criterion—Applying the cost accounting concept to criterion construction. *Personnel Psychology, 3*, 133–154.

BURKE, M. J., and FREDERICK, J. T. (1984). Two modified procedures for estimating standard deviations in utility analyses. *Journal of Applied Psychology, 69*, 482–489.

BURKE, M. J., and FREDERICK, J. T. (1986). A comparison of economic utility estimates for alternative rational SD_y estimation procedures. *Journal of Applied Psychology, 71*, 334–339.

CASCIO, W. F., and RAMOS, R. A. (1986). Development and application of a new method for assessing job performance in behavioral/economic terms. *Journal of Applied Psychology, 71*, 20–28.

CRONBACH, L. J., and GLESER, G. C. (Eds.). (1965). *Psychological tests and personnel decisions* (2nd ed.). Urbana: University of Illinois Press.

DESIMONE, R. L., ALEXANDER, R. A., and CRONSHAW, S. F. (1986). Accuracy and reliability of SD_y estimates in utility analysis. *Journal of Occupational Psychology*, 59, 93–102.

EATON, N. K., WING, H., and MITCHELL, K. J. (1985). Alternate methods of estimating the dollar value of performance. *Personnel Psychology*, 38, 27–40.

EDWARDS, J. E., FREDERICK, J. T., and BURKE, M. J. (1988). Efficacy of modified CREPID SD_y's on the basis of archival organizational data. *Journal of Applied Psychology*, 73, 529–535.

GREER, O. L., and CASCIO, W. F. (1987). Is cost accounting the answer? Comparison of two behaviorally based methods for estimating the standard deviation of job performance in dollars with a cost-accounting-based approach. *Journal of Applied Psychology*, 72, 588–595.

HORNGREN, C. T. (1987). *Cost accounting: A managerial emphasis* (6th ed.). Englewood Cliffs, NJ: Prentice-Hall.

HOWARD, R. A. (Ed.). (1966). *Proceedings of the fourth international conference on operations research*. New York: Wiley.

HOWARD, R. A., MATHESON, J. E., and NORTH, D. W. (1972). The decision to seed hurricanes. *Science, 176*, 1191–1202.

HUNTER, J. E., SCHMIDT, F. L., and JUDIESCH, M. K. (1990). Individual differences in output variability as a function of job complexity. *Journal of Applied Psychology*, 75, 28–42.

MATHESON, J. E. (1969). Decision analysis practice: Examples and insights. *Proceedings of the fifth international conference on operations research*. London: Tavistock.

RAJU, N. S., BURKE, M. J., and NORMAND, J. (1990). A new approach for utility analysis. *Journal of Applied Psychology*, 75, 3–12.

RICH, J. R., and BOUDREAU, J. W. (1987). The effects of variability and risk on selection utility analysis: An empirical simulation and comparison. *Personnel Psychology, 40*, 55–84.

ROCHE, W. J., JR. (1961). The Cronbach-Gleser utility function in fixed-treatment employee selection. *Dissertation Abstracts International*, 22, 4413. (University Microfilms No. 62–1570). Portions reproduced in L. J. Cronbach and G. C. Gleser (Eds.), *Psychological tests and personnel decisions* (2nd ed.). Urbana: University of Illinois Press.

SCHMIDT, F. L., and HUNTER, J. E. (1983). Individual differences in productivity: An empirical test of estimates derived from studies of selection procedure utility. *Journal of Applied Psychology, 68*, 407–414.

SCHMIDT, F. L., HUNTER, J. E., MCKENZIE, R. C., and MULDROW, T. W. (1979). Impact of valid selection procedures on work-force productivity. *Journal of Applied Psychology, 64*, 609–626.

STEVENS, S. S. (1971). Issues in psychophysical measurement. *Psychological Review, 78*, 426–450.

WEEKLEY, J. A., FRANK, B., O'CONNOR, E. J., and PETERS, L. H. (1985). A comparison of three methods of estimating the standard deviation of performance in dollars. *Journal of Applied Psychology, 70*, 122–126.

10

Valid Selection Procedures Can Pay Off

In Chapters 8 and 9, we introduced the concept of utility analysis, described the assumptions and data requirements of alternative utility models, and presented methods for estimating the economic value of each employee's job performance. Our objective in this chapter is to tie these ideas together to demonstrate how they can and have been applied in work settings. We will show how valid selection (or promotion) procedures can save organizations nationwide millions of dollars annually. The gains that can be realized have not yet been recognized because utility analysis has not been used widely. However, as the pressure increases on human resource executives to justify new or continuing personnel programs in the face of budgetary constraints and escalating labor costs, one might expect that those programs that can be justified economically will be most likely to be retained. As examples of the savings to be expected from valid selection procedures, we will present results from three studies previously mentioned: the Roche (1961) study of radial drill operators; the Schmidt, Hunter, McKenzie, and Muldrow (1979) study of computer programmers in ten federal agencies; and the Cascio and Silbey (1979) study of the assessment center in a sales organization. In addition, we shall discuss three new developments: (1) the impact of variable costs, taxes, and discounting on utility estimates, (2) the impact of employee flows on utility estimates, and (3) the use of break-even analysis as an aid in decision making.

THE UTILITY OF A SELECTION TEST FOR RADIAL DRILL OPERATORS

As we noted in Chapter 9, the average payoff of a radial drill operator (RDO-1) was calculated as the hourly profit at standard production ($5.51 in 1961 dollars) multiplied by his or her corrected performance ratio (the burden adjustment). The standard deviation of this distribution (SD_y) was $0.585 in 1961 dollars.[1]

Calculation of Savings

Determination of the Validity of Test Performance (r_{ye})

Validities were determined by computing the Pearson product-moment correlations between payoff-values and scores on the following predictors: the Personnel Test (Wonderlic, Form F), the Test of Mechanical Comprehension (Bennett, Form AA), the Cornell Word Form, and the Cornell Selectee Index. These tests comprised the basic battery used in the selection of factory employees by the company. Among the test-payoff correlations, only the correlation with the Test of Mechanical Comprehension was significant ($r = 0.313$). Thus, utility was computed only for this variable.

Determination of the Ordinate Corresponding to the Selection Ratio Used $\lambda(y')$

To determine the cutoff point at and above which selection is made, company records were checked for the ten years preceding the study. During this time the company's average selection ratio for factory employees was 0.33. The ordinate therefore was set at the point corresponding to this selection ratio. (To verify this, consult a table of areas of the normal curve, find 0.33 under "area in the smaller portion," and read the ordinate corresponding to this area.) In other words, it was assumed that RDO-1s are taken at random from the highest third of the test-score distribution of applicants. Assuming a normal distribution, $\lambda(y')$ is therefore 0.366.

[1]Assuming a 6 percent inflation rate, the comparable figures in 1990 dollars are $29.87 and $3.17, respectively.

Determination of the Cost of Testing (c_y)

Only the actual cost of the tests used in the employment battery was considered in the determination of c_y, since some of the pertinent cost elements were already included in the burden factor (for example, salaries of management personnel, rental of office space, heat, light, and taxes). The cost of each test was taken from the most recent publisher's catalogue. Since the element SD_{ey} is expressed in dollars per hour, the cost of testing had to be expressed in comparable units. Cost of testing must be distributed over the period of time that an employee can be expected to work as a radial drill operator. For purposes of the study an employee was assumed to work in this classification for one year, or 2,080 hours. (This estimate is very conservative, since company records indicate that most RDO-1 employees remain in that job for more than one year.) In determining c_y, the cost of those not selected also must be included in the cost of those selected. The cost of testing per employee selected, in dollars per hour, is derived by multiplying the cost of one battery of tests by 3 (three persons are tested for each one hired), and dividing by 2,080 (hours per year). The total cost of the test battery per applicant in 1961 was \$0.117. The cost of testing per employee selected is therefore $(0.117 \times 3) \div 2{,}080$ or approximately \$0.0002 per hour.

Computation of ΔU

For the Mechanical Comprehension Test (the only significant predictor), the gain in utility per person selected (ΔU) was computed by substituting into Equation 11 from Chapter 8:

$$\Delta U = SD_e r_{ye} \frac{\lambda(y')}{\phi(y')} - \frac{c_y}{\phi(y')}$$

where ΔU is the net gain in utility; SD_e is the standard deviation of the payoff; r_{ye} is the correlation of the predictor with the evaluated payoff; $\lambda(y')$ is the ordinate of the normal curve at the cutting score on the test; $\phi(y')$ is the area (upper tail) corresponding to the cutting score; and c_y is the cost of testing. The actual values included were

$$\Delta U = (\$0.585)\,(0.313)\frac{(0.336)}{(0.326)} - \frac{(\$0.0002)}{(0.326)} = \$0.205$$

Therefore, when the company selects a radial drill operator on the basis of the test score rather than by a random process, the company can expect an average gain of 20 cents per hour ($1.11 per hour in 1990 dollars) for the duration of his or her employment. This represents a potential gain in profit per hour of 3.7 percent at standard production (0.203 ÷ $5.51). Hence, for each RDO-1 who remains in that classification for three years (6,240 hours), the company would realize an average gain in profit of $6,761 (in 1990 dollars) by selecting RDO-1s on the basis of test scores rather than randomly. If only half of the 291 RDO-1s employed by the company remained RDO-1s for three years, the company still would save almost a million dollars ($983,726).

Discussion

Roche's (1961) study is important for three reasons. First, it demonstrates that the economic value of job performance (the dollar criterion) *can* be developed and then applied in the Brogden-Cronbach-Gleser utility model. Second, the results also demonstrate that a test of relatively low validity has appreciable practical value, as had been argued on theoretical grounds. In this case, selection with the aid of a test having a validity of 0.313 made possible an increase in earnings (before taxes and fixed charges) of 3 or 4 percent on the operation in question. Benefits of this magnitude are by no means unimportant to management. Finally, and perhaps most importantly, Roche (1961) showed that the dollar criterion can be determined even where employees in a job classification are working on different tasks, where the tasks assigned a particular employee vary from week to week, and where the tasks vary in profitability.

On the other hand, a number of questions were raised about the accuracy of the cost-accounting procedures themselves. Consider the cost of testing. The analysis took into account only the cost of the tests themselves. Factors classified by the cost accountants as overhead, such as salaries of management personnel, cost of utilities, and rent, were included in the determination of payoff rather than in c_y. The employment division of the company offered the figure of $105 ($569 in 1990 dollars) as a conservative estimate of the cost of placing a factory employee on the job. This figure includes the cost of recruiting, interviewing, and physical examination. It can be argued that a c_y that includes only the cost of tests is sufficient, because most other employment procedure costs would be constant values if tests were not used. These other costs need not be added to the determination of c_y. In fact, an organization will incur fixed utility costs, overhead costs, and so forth just to stay in business. Such costs are irrelevant to the determination of utility because costs or benefits that do not change as a result of a program have no role in defining the utility of that program. Ordinarily personnel programs do not affect fixed costs. Boudreau (1983a) pointed out that while fixed costs lower the *average* profit obtained from all workers, the *variability* of fixed costs is zero. Hence, SD_y is the same whether it reflects fixed costs or not. This implies that Roche (1961) probably *underestimated* selection utility by allocating profit (revenue minus fixed *and* variable costs) to workers according to the speed of their production.

Secondly, Roche (1961) based his calculations on an assumed joint normal distribution of test and payoff, but as Cronbach (1965) later commented, using the *actual* joint distribution would have been preferable. If data are available for the total applicant population, complete information on skewness and curvature is taken into account. Roche's payoffs have a marked skew, since few workers performed far above standard. If the available data come only from workers screened by a test or by on-the-job observations, extrapolation to the total applicant population is required; even so, comparing the actual mean payoff in the selected population with that estimated for the unselected population might be better. This estimate would depend on the regression line but would not entail an assumption of normality.

In summary, the dollar payoff resulting from an employee's work is clearly an elusive concept. As the costs of selection errors continue to grow, the economic implications of alternative selection procedures must be examined more closely. We cannot ignore the problem of cost–benefit analysis of personnel programs. Rather we must deal directly with this issue, using the most current techniques research makes available. In our next section, we will consider a more recent approach to the analysis of the utility of a selection program.

THE UTILITY OF A SELECTION TEST FOR COMPUTER PROGRAMMERS

The purpose of the Schmidt et al. (1979) study of computer programmers in the federal government was to examine the productivity (economic utility) implications of a valid selection procedure (the Programmer Aptitude Test), as we pointed out in Chapter 9. A global estimation procedure was used to estimate the standard deviation of job performance in dollars (SD_y). The average SD_y estimated was $10,413 per year. The Programmer Aptitude Test (PAT) was selected for consideration because previous research had demonstrated that the total PAT score validity is high for predicting performance of computer programmers (the estimated true validity is 0.76) and that this validity is essentially constant across situations (organizations). Thus it is possible to estimate PAT payoffs in the federal government as well as in the economy as a whole. The estimated cost of the PAT per examinee is $10. The study focused on the selection of federal government computer programmers at the GS-5 through GS-9 levels, GS-5 being the lowest level in this occupational series. Beyond GS-9, it is unlikely that an aptitude test like the PAT would be used in selection: applicants for higher level programmer positions are required to have considerable expertise in programming and are selected on the basis of achievement and experience rather than directly on aptitude. The majority of programmers hired at the GS-9 level are promoted to GS-11 after one year. Similarly, all but a minority hired at the GS-5 level advance to GS-7 in one year and to GS-9 the following year. Therefore, the SD_y estimates were obtained for the GS-9 through GS-11 levels. The average yearly selection rate of GS-5 through GS-9 programmers is 618, and their average tenure is 9.69 years. Estimating on the basis of 1970 U.S. census data, 10,210 computer programmers could be hired each year in the U.S. economy using the PAT. In view of the current rapid expansion of this occupation, this number is probably a substantial underestimate.

Since determining the prevailing selection ratio (*SR*) for computer programmers either in the general economy or in the federal government was not possible, utilities were calculated for *SR*s of 0.05 and intervals of 0.10 from 0.10 to 0.80. The gains in utility or productivity are those that result when a valid procedure is introduced where previously no procedure or a totally invalid procedure has been used. The assumption that the true validity of the previous procedure is essentially zero may be valid in some cases, but in other situations the PAT would, if introduced, replace a procedure with lower but nonzero true validity. Hence, utilities were calculated assuming previous procedure true validities of 0.20, 0.30, 0.40, and 0.50, as well as zero.

To estimate the impact of the PAT on productivity, utilities that would result from one year's use of the PAT for selection of new programmers in the federal government and the economy as a whole were computed for each of the combinations of *SR* and previous procedure validity just given. When the previous procedure was assumed to have zero validity, its associated testing cost also was assumed to be zero; that is, it was assumed that no procedure was used and that otherwise prescreened applicants were hired randomly. When the previous procedure was assumed to have a nonzero validity, its associated cost was assumed to be the same as that of the PAT, that is, $10 per applicant. As already mentioned, average tenure for government programmers was found to be 9.69 years; in the absence of other information, this tenure figure also was assumed for the private sector. The average gain in utility per selectee per year was multiplied by 9.69 to give a total average gain in utility per selectee. Cost of testing was charged only to the first year. The Brogden-Cronbach-Gleser general utility equation then was modified in order to obtain the equation actually used in computing the utilities:

$$\Delta U = tN_s(r_1 - r_2)SD_y \lambda/\phi - N_s(c_1 - c_2)/\phi \qquad (1)$$

where ΔU is the gain in productivity in dollars from using the new selection procedure for one year; t is the tenure in years of the average selectee (here 9.69); N_s is the number selected in a given year (this figure was 618 for the federal government and 10,210 for the U.S. economy); r_1 is the validity of the new procedure, here the PAT ($r_1 = 0.76$); r_2 is the validity of the previous procedure (r_2 ranges from 0 to 0.50); c_1 is the cost per applicant of the new procedure, here $10; and c_2 is the cost per applicant of the previous procedure, here zero or $10. The terms SD_e, ϕ, and λ are as defined previously. The figure SD_y was the average of the two estimates obtained by using the global estimation procedure. Note that although this equation gives the productivity gain that results from substituting for one year the new (more valid) selection procedure for the previous procedure, not all these gains are realized the first year. They are spread out over the tenure of the new employees.

Results

Exhibit 10.1 shows the estimated gains in productivity in millions of dollars that would result from one year's use of the PAT to select computer programmers in the federal government for different combinations of *SR* and previous procedure validity. As expected, these gains increase as *SR* decreases and as the validity of the previous procedure decreases. When *SR* is 0.05 and the previous procedure has no validity, use of the PAT for one year produces an aggregate productivity gain of $97.2 million. At the other extreme, if *SR* is 0.80 and the procedure the PAT replaces has a validity of 0.50, the estimated gain is only $5.6 million.

To illustrate how entries for Exhibit 10.1 were derived, assume that the $SR = 0.20$ and the previous procedure has a validity of 0.30. All other terms are as defined previously.

EXHIBIT 10.1 Estimated productivity increase from one year's use of the programmer aptitude test to select computer programmers in the federal government (in millions of dollars)

Selection Ratio	True Validity of Previous Procedure				
	0.00	0.20	0.30	0.40	0.50
0.05	97.2	71.7	58.9	46.1	33.3
0.10	82.8	60.1	50.1	39.2	28.3
0.20	66.0	48.6	40.0	31.3	22.6
0.30	54.7	40.3	33.1	25.9	18.7
0.40	45.6	34.6	27.6	21.6	15.6
0.50	37.6	27.7	22.8	17.8	12.9
0.60	30.4	22.4	18.4	14.4	10.4
0.70	23.4	17.2	14.1	11.1	8.0
0.80	16.5	12.2	10.0	7.8	5.6

Source: Schmidt, F. L., Hunter, J. E., McKenzie, R. C., and Muldrow, T. W. (1979). Impact of valid selection procedures on work-force productivity. *Journal of Applied Psychology, 64*, 622.

$$\Delta U = 9.69(618)(0.76 - 0.30)(10{,}413)(0.2789 \div 0.20) - 618(10 - 10)/0.20$$
$$\Delta U = 9.69(618)(0.46)(10{,}413)(1.3945) - 0$$
$$\Delta U = 40{,}000{,}412$$

To be sure, the figures in Exhibit 10.1 are larger than most of us would have expected; however, these figures are for total utility. The gain per selectee for any cell in the table can be obtained by dividing the cell entry by 618, the assumed yearly number of selectees. When this is done for our example (40,000,412 ÷ 618), the gain per selectee is $64,725.59. This figure is still quite high, but remember that the gains shown in Exhibit 10.1 are produced by one year's use of the PAT. As we pointed out earlier, not all of these gains are realized during the first year. They are spread out over the tenure of the new employees. Gains per year per selectee for any cell in Exhibit 10.1 can be obtained by dividing the cell entry first by 618 and then by 9.69, the average tenure of computer programmers. In our example, this produces a per year gain of $6,679.63 per selectee, or to carry it even further, a $3.21 gain per hour per year per selectee (assuming 2,080 hours per work year). As might be expected, estimated productivity gains resulting from use of the PAT in the economy as a whole are even greater, exceeding $1 billion in several cells.

In addition to the assumptions of linearity of the predictor–criterion relationship and normality of dollar outcomes of job performance, the productivity gains in Exhibit 10.1 are based on two more assumptions. The first is that selection proceeds from top-scoring applicants down until the *SR* has been reached. That is, these analyses assume that selection procedures are used optimally. Because of the linearity of the relation between test score and job performance, any other use of a valid test would result in lower mean productivity levels among selectees. For example, if a cutoff score were set at a point lower than that corresponding to the *SR* and if applicants scoring above this minimum score then were selected randomly (or selected using other nonvalid procedures or considerations), productivity gains, while still substantial, would be considerably lower than those shown in Exhibit 10.1.

Thus Schmidt, Mack, and Hunter (1984) examined the impact on the productivity of forest rangers of three modes of test use: (1) top-down selection, (2) minimum required test scores equal to the mean, and (3) a minimum score set at one *SD* below the mean. Top-down selection produces an increase in productivity of about 13 percent (which translates into millions of dollars saved). Under standard 2, the dollar value of output gains was only 45 percent as large as the dollar value for top-down selection, and the percentage in output was only 5.9. Under standard 3, the dollar value of output gains was only 16 percent of the top-down figure, and the percentage increase in output was only 2.1. Conclusion: Employers who use standard 3 do so at substantial economic cost.

Both Hunter and Hunter (1984) and Hartigan and Wigdor (1989) found that hiring in a top-down fashion *within* minority and nonminority groups produced about 90 percent of the gains that would be realized by strict top-down hiring. A third strategy, using a low cutting score, would decrease utility by 83 percent.

The second assumption is that all applicants who are offered jobs accept and are hired. This is probably not realistic because, in practice, lower-scoring candidates must be accepted in place of higher-scoring candidates who decline initial offers. Hence, the average ability of those *actually* selected almost always will be lower than the average ability of those who receive the initial offers.

The same effect may be observed in a tight labor market, where the supply of available workers is low relative to the aggregate demand for them. Under these circumstances unemployment is low, and, as Becker (1989) has shown, firms may be forced to lower their minimum hiring requirements in order to fill vacancies. Lower hiring requirements mean higher selection ratios.

In summary, rejection of job offers or a reduction in minimum hiring requirements produce identical effects. They increase *SR*s and thus lower the productivity gains from selection. For example, if an *SR* of 0.20 would yield the needed number of new employees given no rejections by applicants and if half of all job offers are rejected, the *SR* must be increased to 0.40 to yield the desired number of selectees. If the validity of the previous procedure were zero, Exhibit 10.1 shows that rejection by applicants would reduce productivity gains from $66.0 to $45.6 million, a reduction of $20.4 million. If the validity of the previous procedure were not zero, job rejection by applicants would reduce both its utility and utility of the new test. However, since the utility function is multiplicative, the utility of the more valid procedure would be reduced by a greater amount. Therefore, the utility advantage of the more valid procedure over the less valid procedure would be reduced. For example, Exhibit 10.1 shows that if the validity of the previous procedure were 0.30, the productivity advantage of the more valid test would be $40 million if the needed workers could be hired using a selection ratio of 0.20. But if half of the applicants rejected job offers, we would have to use an *SR* of 0.40, and the advantage of the more valid test would drop by almost 45 percent to $27.6 million. Murphy (1986) presented formulas for calculating the average ability of those actually selected when the proportion of initial offers accepted is less than 100 percent. He showed that under realistic circumstances, utility formulas currently used could overestimate gains by 30 to 80 percent. To some extent, these utility losses caused by job offer rejection can be offset by additional recruiting efforts that increase the size of the applicant pool and, therefore, restore use of smaller *SR*s.

Thus far, we have been proceeding on the assumption that a new, more valid selection procedure simply is substituted for an older, less valid one. But, often, work force productivity will be optimized by combining an existing procedure and a new procedure to obtain validity higher than either procedure can provide individually. This possibility should be investigated whenever utility analysis is done.

Finally, Schmidt et al. caution that productivity gains in individual jobs from improved selection cannot be extrapolated directly to productivity gains in the composite of all jobs making up the national economy. To illustrate, if the potential gain economywide in the computer programmer occupation is $10.78 billion and if there is a total of *N* jobs in the economy (that is, programmers and all other jobs), the gain to be expected from use of improved selection procedures in all *N* jobs will not be as great in general as *N* times $10.78 billion. Since the total talent pool is not unlimited, gains due to selection in one job are offset partially by losses in other jobs. The size of the net gain for the economy depends on such factors as the number of jobs, the correlation between jobs of predicted success composites, and differences between jobs in SD_e. Nevertheless, potential net gains for the economy as a whole are large.

A later study examined similar productivity gains for most white collar jobs in the federal government (Schmidt, Hunter, Outerbridge, and Trattner, 1986). The researchers found that the job performance of test-selected employees averaged about one-half a standard deviation (roughly 17 percent) higher than that of non–test-selected employees. Results also indicated that use of valid measures of cognitive skills in place of less valid selection methods for selection of a one-year cohort in the federal government would lead to increases in output worth almost $600 million per year for every year the new hires remain on the job. This gain corresponds to a 9.7 percent gain in output among new hires. If total output is to be held constant rather than increased, the use of more valid selection methods would allow a yearly decrease in the number of new hires of just over 20,000 (a 9 percent decrease), resulting in payroll cost savings of $272 million for every year the new employees remain on the job. Finally, the number of new hires in the bottom 10 percent of job performance would decrease from 10 to 3.86 percent.

Evidence presented in these studies leads to the inescapable conclusion that how people are selected makes an important, practical difference. The implications of valid selection procedures for work force productivity are clearly much greater than most of us might have suspected.

Impact of Economic Considerations on Utility Estimates

Boudreau (1983a) pointed out that utility analyses computed according to Equation 10 in Chapter 8 (page 193) or Equation 1 in this chapter will misrepresent the benefits accrued by an organization as a result of increases in productivity under any or all of three conditions. First, where variable costs rise or fall with productivity (e.g., incentive- or commission-based pay, benefits, variable raw materials costs, variable production overhead), then a portion (V) of the gain in product sales value will go to pay such costs (or will be reflected in additional cost savings).

Second, for organizations that face tax liabilities, a portion (TAX) of the organization's profits (sales value less variable costs) must be allocated to pay taxes. Third, where costs and benefits accrue over time, the value of future costs and benefits must be discounted to reflect the opportunity costs of returns foregone. That is, future monetary values cannot be equated with present monetary values because benefits received in the present or costs delayed into the future would be invested to earn returns. Thus, \$1.00 received today at a 10 percent annual return would be worth \$1.21 in two years. Conversely, a future benefit worth \$1.21 in two years has a "present value" of \$1.00 (\$1.21 ÷ 1.10^2). Boudreau (1983b) derived the following utility formula to take these three economic factors into account:

$$\Delta U = (N)\left\{\sum_{t=1}^{T}[1/(1+i)^t]\right\}(SD_{sv})(1+V) \times (1-TAX)(r_{x,sv})(\bar{Z}_x) - C(1-TAX) \tag{2}$$

where ΔU is the change in overall worth or utility after variable costs, taxes, and discounting; N is the number of employees selected; t is the time period in which an increase in productivity occurs; T is the total number of periods (e.g., years) that benefits continue to accrue to an organization; i is the discount rate; SD_{sv} is the standard deviation of the sales value of productivity among the applicant or employee population (similar to SD_y in previous utility models); V is the proportion of sales value represented by variable costs; TAX is the organization's applicable tax rate $r_{x,sv}$ is the validity coefficient between predictor (x) and sales value (similar to $r_{x,y}$ in previous utility models); and C is the total selection cost for all applicants.

These economic considerations suggest large potential reductions in published utility estimates. For example, Schmidt et al. (1979) computed an SD_y value of \$10,413 in their utility analysis of the Programmer Aptitude Test (PAT). This value does not account for variable costs or taxes. While this may have been appropriate for the federal government jobs studied since the federal government is not taxed, it would not be appropriate for private sector organizations that face variable costs and taxes.

Assuming the net effect of positively and negatively correlated variable costs is $V = -0.05$, and assuming a marginal tax rate (the tax rate applicable to changes in reported profits generated by a decision) of 45 percent, Boudreau (1983a) showed that the after-cost, after-tax, one-year SD_y value is

$$(SD_y) \times (1+V) \times (1-TAX) \times (\$10{,}413) \times (1-0.05) \times (1-0.45) = \$5{,}441$$

This is 52 percent of the reported value. In addition, assume a discount rate of 10 percent. If the average tenure of computer programmers in the federal government was just two years, the appropriate discount factor (DF) adjustment would be

$$DF = \sum_{t=1}^{T} [1/(1 + i)^t] \\ = 1/(1 + 0.10)^1 + 1/(1 + 0.10)^2 = 1.74 \quad (3)$$

Over 10 years, $DF = 6.14$, but the average tenure of computer programmers in the federal government was computed to be 9.69 years (Schmidt et al., 1979). Hence, the appropriate adjustment needed to discount the computed utility values is 6.14 ÷ 9.69, or 0.634.

When all three of these factors — variable costs, taxes, and discounting — are considered, the utility values per selectee reported by Schmidt et al. and shown in Exhibit 10.1 range from $2,987 ($5.6 million ÷ 618 = $9,061 per selectee × 0.634 × 0.52) to $51,853 ($97.2 million ÷ 618 = $157,282 per selectee × 0.634 × 0.52).

These values still are substantial, but they are 67 percent lower than the values reported. Thus, $97,200,000 ÷ 618 = $157,282; $51,853 ÷ $157,282 = 33 percent.

Effects of Employee Flows on Utility Estimates

Failure to consider the combined effects of variable costs, taxes, and discounting may produce utility estimates that are *overstated* considerably. On the other hand, failure to consider the effect of employee flows may produce utility estimates that are *understated* considerably. That is, most utility analyses assume that a selection program is applied to one group of applicants. Hence they express the utility of adding one treated cohort to the existing work force. In practice, however, valid selection programs tend to be reapplied year after year, as employees flow into and out of the work force. Thus, selection programs are applied to entering employee cohorts of size N and the program's benefits are reflected in that cohort for T periods. Often a program's effects on subsequent cohorts will occur in addition to its lasting effects on previously treated cohorts. Boudreau (1983b) called these *additive cohort effects*. He then proposed that the terms N and T be altered in Equation 2 to account for the effect of employee flows. The derivation is as follows.

Employee flows generally affect utility through the period-to-period changes in the number of treated employees in the work force. The number of treated employees in the work force k periods in the future (N_k) may be expressed as

$$N_k = \sum_{t=1}^{k} (N_{a_t} - N_{s_t}) \quad (4)$$

where N_{a_t} is the number of treated employees added to the work force in period t, and N_{s_t} is the number of treated employees subtracted from the work force in period t. For example, suppose that at the end of the fourth year that a new selection procedure is applied ($k = 4$) and the following results are observed from the inception of the program ($t = 1$) to year 4 ($t = 4$):

$$N_4 = (100 - 0) + (100 - 10) + (100 - 15) + (100 - 20)$$
$$N_4 = 355$$

Thus, the term N_k reflects both the number of employees treated in previous periods and their expected tenure. The formula for the utility (ΔU_k) occurring in the kth future period that includes the economic considerations of Equation 2 may be written:

$$\begin{aligned}\Delta U_k = {} & [\sum_{t=1}^{k} (N_{a_t} - N_{s_t})]\{[1/(1 + i)^k](r_{x,sv}) \\ & \times (\bar{Z}_x)(SD_{sv})(1 + V)(1 - TAX)\} \\ & - C_k(1 - TAX)[1/(1 + i)^{(k-1)}]\end{aligned} \tag{5}$$

Note that for the sake of simplicity, the utility parameters $r_{x,sv}$ V, SD_{sv}, and TAX are assumed to be constant over time. This assumption is not critical to this utility model, and the factors may vary. Note also that the cost of treating the N_{ak} employees added in period k (C_k) is now allowed to vary over time. However, C_k is not simply a constant multiplied by N_{ak}. Some programs (e.g., assessment centers) have high initial startup costs of development, but these costs do not vary with the number treated in future periods. Also, the discount factor for costs $[1/(1 + i)^{(k-1)}]$ reflects the exponent $k - 1$, assuming that such costs are incurred one period prior to receiving benefits. Where costs are incurred in the same period as benefits are received, k is the proper exponent (Boudreau, 1983b).

To continue with our previous example, assume the following values in order to compute the dollar gain in productivity to an organization during the fourth year of a new selection program: $N_k = 355$; the discount rate is 10 percent; the validity of the procedure is 0.40; the selection ratio is 0.50 (and therefore the average score of those selected is $0.3989 \div 0.50 = 0.80$); SD_y is \$5,000; variable costs $= -0.05$; taxes $= 0.45$; and C_k, the cost of treating the 100 employees added in year 4, is $100 \times \$10 = \$1{,}000$.

$$\begin{aligned}\Delta U_4 = {} & 355 \times [(1/1.10^1 + 1/1.10^2 + 1/1.10^3 + 1/1.10^4) \\ & \times 0.40 \times 0.80 \times \$5{,}000 \times 0.95 \times 0.55] - \$1{,}000 \\ & \times 0.55\,(1/1.10^1 + 1/1.10^2 + 1/1.10^3)\end{aligned}$$

$$\begin{aligned}\Delta U_4 &= 355 \times [(3.17) \times \$836] - \$550\ (2.49)\\ &= \$940{,}793 - \$1{,}370\\ &= \$939{,}423\end{aligned}$$

To express the utility of a program's effects over F periods, the one-period utility estimates (ΔU_k) are summed. Thus, the complete utility model reflecting employee flow through the work force for a program affecting productivity in F future periods may be written:

$$\begin{aligned}\Delta U = \sum_{k=1}^{F}[\sum_{t=1}^{k}(N_{a_t} - N_{s_t})]\{[1/(1+i)^k](r_{x,sv})\\ \times (\bar{Z}_x)(SD_{sv})(1+V)(1-TAX)\}\\ - \sum_{k=1}^{F}\{C_k(1-TAX)[1/(1+i)^{(k-1)}]\}\end{aligned} \tag{6}$$

The duration parameter F in Equation 6 is not simply a function of employee tenure, but also depends on how long a program is applied. For example, Boudreau (1983b) assumed that the PAT evaluated by Schmidt et al. is applied for 15 years, or 5 years after the first cohort separates. If 618 programmers are added each year, then for the first 10 future periods N_k will increase by 618 in each period. That is:

$$N_{10} = \sum_{t=1}^{10}(618 - 0)$$

By year 10, therefore, 6,180 programmers selected by the PAT have been added to the work force, and none have left. Beginning in future period 11, however, one PAT-selected cohort leaves in each period ($N_{s_t} = 618$). However, by continuing to apply the PAT to select 618 new replacements, the employee inflow is maintained (i.e., $N_{a_t} = 618$). Thus, in future periods 11 through 15, N_{a_t} and N_{s_t} offset each other and N_k remains unchanged. Beginning in future period 16, the PAT no longer is used (C_k and N_{a_t} become zero, assuming the organization returns to random selection). However, the treated portion of the work force does not disappear immediately. Earlier-selected cohorts continue to separate (i.e., $N_{s_t} = 618$), and N_k falls by 618 each period until the last treated cohort (selected in future period 15) separates in future period 25. N_k for each of the 25 periods is shown in Exhibit 10.2.

In Exhibit 10.2, $F = 25$ periods. Assuming, as we did in our earlier example, that $V = -0.05$, $TAX = 0.45$, and the discount rate is 10 percent, Boudreau (1983b) showed that the total expected utility of the 15-year selection program (the sum of the 25 one-period utility estimates,

EXHIBIT 10.2 Hypothetical employee flows resulting from the PAT

Period (k)	N_k
1	618
2	1,236
3	1,854
4	2,472
5	3,090
6	3,708
7	4,326
8	4,944
9	5,562
10	6,180
11	6,180
12	6,180
13	6,180
14	6,180
15	6,180
16	5,562
17	4,944
18	4,326
19	3,708
20	3,090
21	2,472
22	1,854
23	1,236
24	618
25	0

Source: Boudreau, J. W. (1983). Effects of employee flows on utility analysis of human resource productivity improvement programs. *Journal of Applied Psychology*, *68*, 396–406. Reprinted by permission.

ΔU_k in equation 5) is \$105.01 million. This is considerably higher than the Schmidt et al. estimate of \$37.6 million, even after reflecting variable costs, taxes, and discounting. Perhaps the most important lesson to learn from these results is that one-cohort utility models often will *understate* actual utility because they reflect only the first part of a larger series of outcomes (Boudreau, 1983b).

After working through all of this, you may be tempted to conclude that the actual dollar payoff from valid selection programs is two or three times higher than one-cohort models predict. Be careful! All existing utility models contain parameters that must be estimated, and in most cases we simply have no way to measure the accuracy of our estimates. Beyond that, as we noted earlier, utility values often are based on the assumption that variable costs, SD_y, and the selection ratio are constant over time. This may be unrealistic. Equation 6 does permit these parameters to vary, but until our measurement systems begin to assess multiperiod variations in these parameters, we will not know just how unrealistic these assumptions are. Research in utility analysis has produced some exciting new developments, but we still have a long way to go in refining our measurements of the parameters of the model.

THE UTILITY OF AN ASSESSMENT CENTER AS A SELECTION DEVICE

Ever since pioneering studies by Bray (1964) at American Telephone and Telegraph in the 1950s, the assessment center approach to personnel selection has been an extremely popular technique. The attractiveness of the method is not surprising, for it is rooted firmly in sound psychometric principles. By using multiple assessment techniques, by standardizing methods of making inferences from such techniques, and by pooling the judgments of multiple assessors in rating each candidate's behavior, the likelihood of successfully predicting performance is enhanced considerably. Reviews of the predictive validity of assessment center ratings and subsequent job performance consistently have been positive (Gaugler et al., 1987; Howard and Bray, 1989; Hunter and Hunter 1984). Assessment centers do predict performance, and they do it well, with predictive validities in the 0.50s and 0.60s not uncommon.

In short, the assessment center has easily met the psychometric requirements of the classical validity approach to selection. Emphasis has been placed on measurement and prediction, and the primary objective has been to maximize the correlation (simple or multiple) between predicted and actual criterion scores.

Regardless of how many validity studies are conducted, however, the overall worth of the assessment center as a selection device in a particular organization or across organizations cannot be established definitively in the absence of utility analyses. The objective of the study by Cascio and Silbey (1979) is to use examples to make the utility model a more meaningful tool for those who must interpret the data from the assessment center method. The utility analysis was accomplished by means of the Brogden-Cronbach-Gleser continuous variable utility model.

Six parameters were varied systematically: the validity and cost of the assessment center, the validity of the ordinary selection procedure, the selection ratio, the standard deviation of job performance in dollars, and the number of assessment centers. Then the payoff of the assessment center was compared to an ordinary selection procedure and to random selection. By expressly including the estimated costs of recruiting, inducting, selecting, and training a sufficient number of persons to meet a quota of personnel, this model enables decision makers to evaluate the costs of alternative selection strategies in terms of their systemwide implications.

Input and Cost Assumptions

The utility model was applied to the selection and placement of second-level managers in a hypothetical firm. Since both costs and benefits can be expected to vary considerably from firm to firm, a representative range of values was used to calculate the outcomes. Each parameter's impact was determined by holding all other parameters constant while one parameter was varied.[2] It was assumed that selection for promotion ranged from first- to second-level management; that promotion from within was company policy; and that there was a fixed quota of fifty managers. The original study included descriptions and computations of recruitment, induction, and training costs. For purposes of comparing the payoff of the interview to that of the assessment center, at any given selection ratio, these costs were equal. While they did serve to illustrate the total cost of the selection system, Boudreau (1984) noted that they did not vary with the decision, and therefore were not relevant to that decision. Hence, this example will include only the costs that were incurred or avoided depending on the selection option chosen.

When the selection ratio was allowed to vary, model values ranged from 0.1 to 0.9 in steps of 0.1. When other parameters were varied, the selection ratio was set at 0.5. This value was chosen because in a typical assessment center only about half of those assessed are rated acceptable. The cost of selection was different for the ordinary procedure and for the assessment center. The overall cost of the ordinary selection procedure (a series of three interviews with third-level managers, spread over a two-day period) was estimated at $290 per candidate.

The validity of the ordinary selection procedure was another param-

[2]This procedure, known as sensitivity analysis, is not the only way to investigate the expected variability of utility estimates. For more on this, see Alexander and Barrick, 1987; Boudreau, 1988; or Rich and Boudreau, 1987.

eter varied in the model. When the validity of ordinary selection was varied, it ranged from 0.05 to 0.95 in steps of 0.05. A validity of 0.25 for the ordinary selection procedure (i.e., multiple interviews) was assumed when other parameters were varied. This value is considerably higher than that reported in a meta-analysis of the predictive validity of the interview ($r = 0.14$) by Hunter and Hunter (1984).

Assessment center costs fell into three categories: costs of establishing the assessment center, costs of the assessors, and costs of the candidates (assessees). The costs of establishing the assessment center were estimated at $3,200; each of six assessors was estimated to cost $361 during the three days over which each assessment center was conducted (for a total of $2,166); and total candidate costs were estimated at $198 per candidate. (In a later study Cascio and Ramos [1986] computed the per-person cost of the assessment center to be $688.) Note also that although assessment centers have high start-up costs, use of employee flow analysis allows those costs to be reflected at the beginning of a program, and lower costs to be reflected later on. This provides a truer picture of the payoff of the program over time.

The total cost per candidate of the assessment center could not be calculated beforehand, since that cost was determined by the number of assessment centers to be conducted. Instead, costs per candidate were calculated by spreading the costs of the assessment center procedure (start-up of $3,200, assessor costs of $2,166 × the number of assessment centers, and candidate costs of $198 × the number of candidates) over all of the candidates in a particular run of the utility model

Regardless of which other parameters were being varied, the validity of the assessment center always varied from 0.05 to 0.95. However, for comparisons, a validity of 0.35 was used. Actually, this figure is slightly conservative. A meta-analysis of fifty studies of the assessment center, containing 107 validity coefficients, revealed a corrected average $r = .37$ (Gaugler et al., 1987). The rationale underlying each of the input and cost assumptions described previously is developed more fully by Cascio and Silbey (1979).

For benefit calculations, the mean and standard deviation of the job performance distribution were determined by the global estimation procedure (Schmidt et al., 1979) outlined in Chapter 9. Average yearly dollar values for the second-level managers were about $30,000, with a standard deviation of approximately $9,500 in this firm.

This figure provides an estimate of each second-level manager's yearly value of sales to the company. For purposes of the model, we assumed that all second-level managers made approximately equal contributions to the firm. Admittedly, this is a questionable assumption, and for this reason a range of standard deviations of job performance was examined. The SD_e values varied from \$1,000 to \$20,000 in the first year in steps of \$1,000. These SD_e values center about the \$9,500 value that was used as a constant when other parameters were varied.

Remember that this figure is pertinent for one year only. Assuming that the average tenure of second-level managers is five years and that the average stability of performance is 0.7 from year to year, then the standard deviation of job performance (SD_e) for a five-year period can be calculated using the formula for the standard deviation of a sum (Guilford and Fruchter, 1978):

$$\begin{aligned}[SD_{(e_1+e_2+\ldots+e_n)}]^2 = {} & S_1^2 + S_2^2 + \ldots + S_n^2 + 2r_{12}SD_1SD_2 \\ & + 2r_{13}SD_1SD_3 + \ldots + 2r_{1n}SD_1SD_n \\ & + \ldots + 2r_{(n-1)n}SD_{(n-1)}SD_n\end{aligned} \tag{7}$$

Taking the square root of both sides and substituting in our assumed values

$$SD_e = \sqrt{5(9{,}500^2) + 0.7(2)(10)(9{,}500)(9{,}500)}$$
$$SD_e = \$41{,}409.54$$

where the term (2) × (10) in Equation 7 refers to 2 times the number of pairs of correlation coefficients (10) in the formula.

Results

The impact of each parameter was evaluated in terms of assessment center payoff per selectee. Payoff refers to the dollar amount of incremental gain (or loss if negative) accruing to a firm that uses the assessment center instead of the ordinary selection procedure.

Neither variations in the number of assessment centers nor variations in the cost of the assessment center exerted any significant effects on payoffs. However, variations in the selection ratio and in the standard deviation of job performance clearly did have a major impact on payoffs. For example, consider Exhibit 10.3, which shows the effect of changes in the standard deviation of job performance on the assessment center payoff per selectee. The lines from top to bottom represent five-year standard deviations of \$87,178, \$65,389, \$43,589, \$21,794, and \$4,359. These values correspond to first-year standard deviations of \$20,000, \$15,000, \$10,000, \$5,000, and \$1,000.

EXHIBIT 10.3 Effect of variations in the standard deviation of job performance (σ_e) and assessment center validity on assessment center payoff

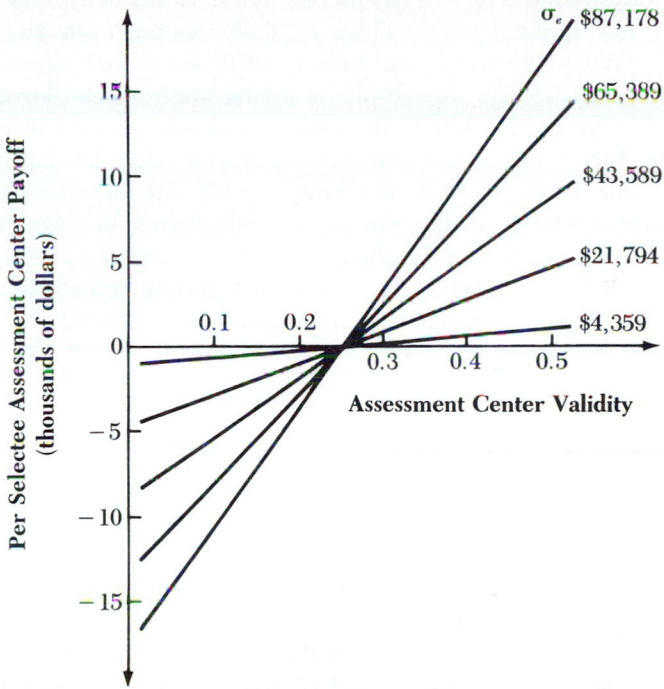

Source: Cascio, W. F., and Silbey, V. (1979). Utility of the assessment center as a selection device. *Journal of Applied Psychology, 64*, 113.

All lines radiate from a point located at an assessment center validity of 0.25 and an assessment center payoff per selectee of $226.56. At this point, the validity of the assessment center is equal to the validity of the ordinary selection procedure used in the utility analysis (0.25), and the assessment center payoff is equal to the difference in cost between the assessment center and the ordinary selection procedure.

As can be seen from Exhibit 10.3, the larger the standard deviation of job performance, the larger the payoff of the assessment center, assuming, of course, that assessment center validity exceeds the validity of the ordinary selection procedure.

Variations in the validity of the ordinary selection procedure and the validity of the assessment center also had a major impact on payoffs. Since the impact on payoff of increasing the ordinary selection procedure's validity is equivalent to lowering the assessment center's validity, the discussion of these changes can be combined. Ordinary selection procedure validities varied from 0.05 to 0.95 and resulted in assessment center payoffs at an assessment center validity of 0.35 ranging from $9,684 to −$20,048. (When the Cascio and Silbey [1979] results are adjusted for inflation from 1979–1986, the results of a later study of mid-level sales managers [Burke and Frederick, 1986] are remarkably similar.) To put the magnitude of these changes in perspective, consider that the slope of the regression line relating payoff to validity (33,036.53) indicates that for every change of 0.01 in validity, the payoff would change by $330.37. The only difference is that when the change means an increase in validity for the ordinary selection procedure, then the assessment center payoff decreases; and when the change means an increase in assessment center validity, then the assessment center payoff increases.

CONCLUSION

One of the most significant impacts on assessment center payoff appears to come from the size of the standard deviation of job performance. In this respect the assessment center can make a major contribution to a selection program — when individual differences in job performance are large and significant — yet the classical validity approach to selection ignores this fact. In fact, even when the standard deviation of the distribution of job performance is as low as $5,000 in the first year, assessment centers with validities of only 0.1 still show positive gains in utility over random selection. However, since the ordinary selection procedure is cheaper, it demonstrates positive utility over random selection at even lower criterion standard deviations. This study also demonstrated what Brogden pointed out in 1949: Since gains in utility depend on the product $r_{ye}SD_e$ and since a large SD_e indicates that individual differences in job performance have large practical importance, predictors with low validity still may yield considerable benefit if SD_e is large. Conversely, procedures with high validity may be less useful if individual differences in payoff are small. These results demonstrate that validities must be considered not in isolation but in comparison to other parameters.

The cost of the assessment center played a relatively minor role in determining payoffs. At first glance, this may seem surprising, but when one stops to consider that for many jobs the standard deviation of job performance outcomes can be as high as $15,000 to $20,000 in the first year (and $65,000 to $87,000 over five years), the increased cost of a more valid selection procedure may be a small price to pay for the long-term payoff that the procedure may provide.

Certainly the same criticisms leveled at the Schmidt et al. (1979) study apply to this study; namely, that failure to consider the combined effects of variable costs, discounting, and taxes produced an overestimate of the net payoff of the assessment center. This overestimate may have been as high as 73 percent (Boudreau, 1983a). However, let us consider the decision to be made, whether to adopt an assessment center or multiple interviews to select second-level managers, from a different perspective.

Break-Even Analysis

Instead of estimating the *level* of expected utility for each expected alternative (assessment center or interview), suppose decision makers focus instead on the *break-even values* that are critical to making the decision. In other words, what is the smallest value of any given parameter that will permit a choice of one selection technique over another or over random selection?

To illustrate this approach, we will use the same parameter estimates as did Cascio and Silbey (1979): N is 50, T is 5 (but since year-to-year performance correlates 0.70, this has the effect of multiplying the yearly SD_y estimates by 4.36 rather than by 5); SR is 0.50 (and therefore the average score of selectees is 0.80); validity of assessment is 0.35; validity of the interview is 0.25; the direct cost per applicant assessed is \$403.28; and the direct cost per applicant interviewed is \$290. Substituting these values into the general utility equation (Equation 10 in Chapter 8 on page 193) produces two utility formulas. For the assessment center, utility may be expressed as:

$$\Delta U_{ac} = 50 \times 4.36 \times 0.35 \times 0.80 \times SD_y - 100 \times \$403.28 \quad (8)$$
$$\Delta U_{ac} = 61.04 \times SD_y - \$40{,}328$$

For the interview, these values are:

$$\Delta U_{int} = 50 \times 4.36 \times 0.25 \times 0.80 \times SD_y - 100 \times \$290 \quad (9)$$
$$\Delta U_{int} = 43.6 \times SD_y - \$29{,}000$$

As Boudreau (1984) has noted, the determination of critical SD_y values requires answers to only three questions: (1) Above what value of SD_y does the interview break even? (2) Above what value of SD_y does the assessment center break even? (3) Above what value of SD_y does one option dominate the other?

The minimum value of SD_y that will justify the use of either alternative is computed by setting $\Delta U = \$0.00$. For the assessment center, it is $\$40,328 \div 61.04 = \$661$. For the interview, it is $\$29,000 \div 43.6 = \$665$. These values of SD_y guarantee that the costs of the assessment center or the interview will be matched by equivalent benefits — no more, no less. Thus the term "break-even" analysis.

Both options produce equal payoff ($\Delta U_{ac} - \Delta U_{int} = \$0.00$) when SD_y is \$650. As might be expected, this payoff is slightly negative, as can be seen from Exhibit 10.4. The decision rule in this case is: if SD_y is less than \$661, do not use the assessment center or the interview; if SD_y is \$662 or more, use the assessment center since it yields a higher payoff than the interview (i.e., it "dominates" the interview) at all values of SD_y greater than \$661.[3]

Cascio and Silbey reported a mean SD_y value of \$9,500 using the global estimation procedure. At this SD_y value, the assessment center was the preferred option. However, the break-even analysis shows that *any* SD_y value above \$661 would have produced the same decision.

At a broader level, Boudreau (1988) computed break-even values for 42 studies that estimated SD_y. Without exception, the break-even values fell at or below 60 percent of the estimated value of SD_y. In many cases, the break-even value was less than 1 percent of the estimated value of SD_y. However, as Weekley et al. (1985) noted, even though the break-even value might be low when deciding whether or not to implement an HRM program, comparing HRM programs to other organizational investments might produce decision situations where differences in SD_y estimates do affect the ultimate decision. (For more on research needs in the estimation of SD_y, see Bobko et al. [1987])

Break-even analysis seems to provide two important advantages: (1) it allows practicing managers to appreciate how little variability in job performance is necessary before valid selection procedures begin to pay positive dividends, and (2) even if decision makers cannot agree on an exact point estimate of SD_y, they can probably agree that it is higher than the break-even value. Despite these positive features, we insert a cautionary note: The overall validity of break-even analysis hinges on the as-

[3] Boudreau (1984) used the identical parameters from Cascio and Silbey for illustrative purposes, but a mathematical error in the computation of the total cost of the assessment center led him to an erroneous conclusion regarding the decision rule to be used in this case. However, this error does not affect Boudreau's conclusion that even very low SD_y estimates that may be subject to disagreement among experts often are sufficient to justify investing in improved selection.

EXHIBIT 10.4 Break-even analysis: The effect of variations in SD_y on the relative payoffs of the assessment center and the interview[a]

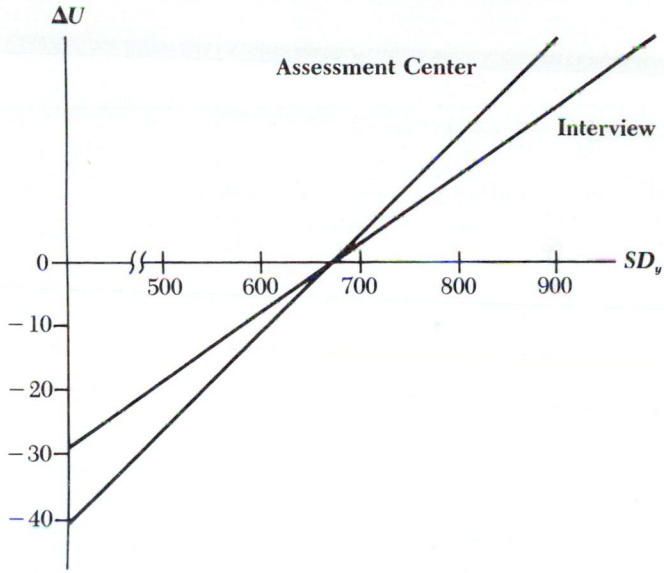

[a]Data for this example were drawn from Cascio and Silbey (1979).

sumption that performance is related linearly to payoff, that the relationship between performance and payoff is described best by a straight line. In many if not most cases, this assumption is tenable. However, to the extent that this assumption is untenable, then an alternative procedure such as Monte Carlo simulation (Rich and Boudreau, 1987) should be used to assess the extent of variability of utility values, and thus to provide a sound basis for decision making.

This completes our three-chapter look at utility analysis. Although the theory itself is fairly well developed, many more practical applications are needed to enhance our understanding of the actual gains to be derived from valid selection procedures. The term *selection procedures* is intentionally broad. Just like the legal definition of a test, a selection procedure refers to any basis for an employment decision. This may include, for example, a written test, an assessment center, a drug test, or an interview. As long as results from the procedure can be quantified and correlated with dollar-valued job performance, the general utility equation can be used. Indeed, even when the general utility equation cannot be used, the model on which it is based should still guide decision making. In this sense, utility analysis is more than an equation or series of equations: it is a stimulating way of thinking.

EXERCISES

1. You are given the following information regarding the CAP test for clerical personnel (clerk-2s) at the Berol Corporation:

- average tenure as a clerk-2: 7.26 years
- number selected per year: 120
- validity of the CAP test: 0.61
- validity of previously used test: 0.18
- cost per applicant of CAP: $8
- cost per applicant of old test: $5
- SR: 0.50
- ordinate at SR: 0.399
- SD_e in first year: $3,000

Use Equation 1 to determine (a) the total utility of the CAP test, (b) utility per selectee, and (c) per year gain in utility per selectee.

2. Referring to Exercise 1, suppose that after consulting with the chief financial officer at Berol, you are given the following additional information: variable costs are −0.08; taxes are 40 percent; and the discount rate is 8 percent. Use Equation 2 in this chapter to recompute (a) the total utility of the CAP test, (b) the utility per selectee, and (c) the utility per selectee in the first year.

3. The Top Dollar Co. is trying to decide whether to use an assessment center to select middle managers for its consumer products operations. The following information has been determined: variable costs are −0.10; corporate taxes are 44 percent; the discount rate is 9 percent; the ordinary selection procedure costs $500 per candidate; the assessment center costs $2,000 per candidate; the standard deviation of job performance is $25,000; the validity of the ordinary procedure is 0.20; the validity of the assessment center is 0.50; the selection ratio is 0.20; the ordinate at that selection ratio is 0.2789; and the average tenure as a middle manager is 3 years. The program is designed to last 6 years, with 20 managers added each year. Beginning in year 4, however, one cohort separates each year until all hires from the program leave.

Use Equation 6 in this chapter to determine if Top Dollar Co. should adopt the assessment center to select middle managers. What payoffs can be expected (a) in total, (b) per selectee, and (c) per selectee in the first year?

REFERENCES

ALEXANDER, R. A., and BARRICK M. R. (1987). Estimating the standard error of projected dollar gains in utility analysis. *Journal of Applied Psychology, 72,* 475–479.

BECKER, B. E. (1989). The influence of labor markets on human resources utility estimates. *Personnel Psychology, 42,* 531–546.

BOBKO, P., KARREN, R., and KERKAR, S. P. (1987). Systematic research needs for estimating supervisory-based estimates of SD_y in utility analysis. *Organizational Behavior and Human Decision Processes, 40,* 69–95.

BOUDREAU, J. W. (1983). Economic considerations in estimating the utility of human resource productivity improvement programs. *Personnel Psychology, 36,* 551–576. (a)

BOUDREAU, J. W. (1983). Effects of employee flows on utility analysis of human resource productivity improvement programs. *Journal of Applied Psychology, 68,* 396–406. (b)

BOUDREAU, J. W. (1984). Decision theory contributions to HRM research and practice. *Industrial Relations, 23,* 198–217.

BOUDREAU, J. W. (1988, December). *Utility analysis for decisions in human resource management.* Working Paper 88–21, Center for Advanced Human Resource Studies, New York State School of Industrial and Labor Relations. Ithaca, NY: Cornell University.

BRAY, D. W. (1964). The management progress study. *American Psychologist, 19,* 419–420.

BROGDEN, H. E. (1949). When testing pays off. *Personnel Psychology, 2,* 171–185.

BURKE, M. J., and FREDERICK, J. T. (1986). A comparison of economic utility estimates for alternative rational SD_y estimation procedures. *Journal of Applied Psychology, 71,* 334–339.

CASCIO, W. F., and RAMOS, R. A. (1986). Development and application of a new method for assessing job performance in behavioral/economic terms. *Journal of Applied Psychology, 71,* 20–28.

CASCIO, W. F., and SILBEY, V. (1979). Utility of the assessment center as a selection device. *Journal of Applied Psychology, 64,* 107–118.

CRONBACH, L. J. (1965). Comments on "A dollar criterion in fixed-treatment employee selection" in L. J. Cronbach and G. C. Gleser (Eds.), *Psychological tests and personnel decisions* (2nd ed.). Urbana: University of Illinois Press.

GAUGLER, B. B., ROSENTHAL, D. B., THORNTON, G. C. III, and BENTSON, C. (1987). Meta-analysis of assessment center validity. *Journal of Applied Psychology, 72,* 493–511.

GUILFORD, J. P., and FRUCHTER, B. (1978). *Fundamental statistics in psychology and education* (6th ed.). New York: McGraw-Hill.

HARTIGAN, J. A., and WIGDOR, A. K. (Eds.). (1989). *Fairness in employment testing*. Washington, D.C.: National Academy Press.

HOWARD, A., and BRAY, D. W. (1989). *Managerial lives in transition*. NY: Guilford.

HUNTER, J. E., and HUNTER, R. F. (1984). Validity and utility of alternative predictors of job performance. *Psychological Bulletin*, *97*, 72–98.

MURPHY, K. R. (1986). When your top choice turns you down: Effects of rejected offers on the utility of selection tests. *Psychological Bulletin*, *99*, 133–138.

RICH, J. R., and BOUDREAU, J. W. (1987). The effects of variability and risk on selection utility analysis: An empirical simulation and comparison. *Personnel Psychology*, *40*, 55–84.

ROCHE, W. J., JR. (1961). The Cronbach-Gleser utility function in fixed-treatment employee selection. *Dissertation Abstracts International*, *22*, 4413. (University Microfilms No. 62–1570). Portions reproduced in L. J. Cronbach and G. C. Gleser (Eds.), *Psychological tests and personnel decisions* (2nd ed.). Urbana: University of Illinois Press.

SCHMIDT, F. L., HUNTER, J. E., MCKENZIE, R. C., and MULDROW, T. W. (1979). Impact of valid selection procedures on work-force productivity. *Journal of Applied Psychology*, *64*, 609–626.

SCHMIDT, F. L., HUNTER, J. E., OUTERBRIDGE, A. N., and TRATTNER, M. H. (1986). The economic impact of job selection methods on size, productivity, and payroll costs of the federal work force: An empirically-based demonstration. *Personnel Psychology*, *39*, 1–30.

SCHMIDT, F. L., MACK, M. J., and HUNTER, J. E. (1984). Selection utility in the occupation of U.S. park ranger for three modes of test use. *Journal of Applied Psychology*, *69*, 490–497.

WEEKLEY, J. A., O'CONNOR, E. J., FRANK, B., and PETERS, L. W. (1985). A comparison of three methods of estimating the standard deviation of performance in dollars. *Journal of Applied Psychology*, *70*, 122–126.

11

Estimating the Costs and Benefits of Human Resource Development Programs

Organizations in the United States spend billions each year on employee training (Offerman and Gowing, 1990). These outlays reflect (1) the aggregate cost of keeping abreast of technological and social changes, (2) the extent of managerial commitment to achieving a competent, productive work force, and (3) the broad array of opportunities available for individuals to improve their productive and social skills. Indeed, the large amount of money spent on training in both public and private organizations is likely to *increase* in the coming years for at least three reasons: (1) demographic projections suggest that large numbers of skilled people will be needed for entry-level jobs while the available pool of young workers will be comprised of large numbers of unskilled and undereducated individuals; (2) the increasing sophistication of technological systems will require greater emphasis on training workers to use the new technology; and (3) the increase in service jobs, the inclusion of more women, minorities, and older workers in the work force, and increasingly complex national and international competition among all sizes and types of firms will make training in interpersonal skills a high priority in the development of managers (Goldstein and Gilliam, 1990).

Mills (1975) coined the term *human resource development* (HRD) to represent the wide range of behavioral science and management technologies intended to improve both the operating effectiveness of a firm and the quality of working life experienced by its employees. The technologies range from basic skills training to job enrichment and training in interpersonal skills, team building, and decision making (see Latham, 1988 for a thorough review). Unfortunately, while billions may be spent providing training and development programs, little is spent assessing the social and financial outcomes of these activities. As a result, little comparative evidence exists by which to generalize or to evaluate the impact of the various technologies. Decision makers thus remain unguided by systematic evaluations of past experiments and uninformed about the costs and benefits of alternative HRD programs when considering training efforts in their own organizations. "Billions for training, but not one cent for evaluation" is an exaggerated, but not altogether untrue, characterization of present training practice in many organizations.

Our intent in this chapter is not to present true experimental or quasi-experimental designs for evaluating HRD programs (see Arvey and Cole, 1989; Cascio, 1991; also Cook and Campbell, 1979). Rather, it is to illustrate how the economic consequences of HRD programs can be expressed. To do so, we present three very different examples of efforts to assess the financial impact of specific programs. Let us begin by considering how to determine the true cost of off-site meetings.

EXAMPLE 1: DETERMINING OFF-SITE MEETING COSTS

Off-site meetings, those conducted away from organizational property, are becoming increasingly popular for a variety of purposes: for conducting HRD programs, for communicating information, for strategic planning, and for decision making. In many cases, however, the true dollar costs of an off-site meeting remain unknown as long as attendee costs are not included in the final tally along with the direct and obvious expenses. The method described here enables planners to compute actual off-site meeting costs and in addition offers two advantages: the identification and the evaluation of the dollars invested in each type of activity included in the program.

The method for costing off-site meetings was developed by McKeon (1981). We make the following assumptions about a hypothetical firm, Valco Ltd. The firm has 500 employees, including 100 first-line supervisors and management personnel. A total of ten days of off-site meetings per year (either training sessions or various types of meetings for managers) are held under the general planning and direction of Valco's training department (one manager and one secretary). Outside speakers and consultants are engaged to develop and conduct the meetings. On the average, twenty managers attend each meeting, and the typical meeting lasts two full days. Costs shown in Exhibit 11.1 are based on these figures.

These estimates are broad averages intended only to create a model for purposes of comparison. Note that no attempt is made to place a dollar value on the loss of productive time from the job, although such costs are realistic and also could be figured into the calculations. As with the illustrations in other chapters, we have attempted to make the numbers as realistic as possible, but primary concern should be with the methodology rather than with the numbers.

As can be seen in Exhibit 11.1, the per day, per person cost of Valco's meeting comes to $636. Actually, this figure probably distorts the true costs of the meeting since no distinction is made between recurring and nonrecurring costs (Mathieu and Leonard, 1987).

During the development of a program, organizations absorb nonrecurring costs such as equipment purchases and trainers' salaries. Recurring costs absorbed each time a program is presented include session expenses, such as facilities and trainers' salaries, and costs that correspond to the number of participants in a program, such as training materials and trainees' salaries.

Separating costs allows each set of costs to be incorporated into utility calculations for the time period in which each expense is incurred. Thus, the high initial expenses associated with a program may indicate that costs exceed benefits for some period of time or over a certain number of groups of trainees. However, at some point an organization may begin to derive program benefits that signal the beginning of a payback period. Separating costs helps decision makers to clarify information about the utility of personnel programs and return-on-investment (Mathieu and Leonard, 1987).

The influence of the environment in training is the chief reason cited for selecting an outside facility for a meeting. Not only can a professionally designed and operated meeting facility make a meeting more productive, it also can make that meeting more enjoyable. The task for decision makers is to consider whether facility costs as a percentage of the total—that is, the total of the true meeting costs identified—will or will not be offset by a corresponding increase in learning effectiveness. In the example shown in Exhibit 11.1, the cost per person, per day was $636. If an additional $30, $40, or even $50 was added per day to hold the meeting in a superior facility, the extra cost would be 5 to 8 percent. However, if learn-

EXHIBIT 11.1 Cost breakdown for an off-site management meeting

Cost Elements	*Subtotal Costs*	*Total Costs*	*Cost per Participant per Day*
A. Development of programs (figured on an annual basis)			
1. Training department overhead			
2. Training staff salaries			
3. Use of outside consultants			
4. Equipment and materials for meeting (films, supplies, workbooks)		$155,000	$155[a]
B. Participant cost (figured on an annual basis)			
1. Salaries and benefits of participants (figured for average participant)	$31,000		
2. Capital investment in participants (based on an average of various industries from *Fortune* magazine)	$38,800	$ 69,800	$295.76[b]
C. Delivery of one meeting for 20 persons			
1. Facility costs			
a. Sleeping rooms	$ 1,551		
b. Three meals daily	$ 1,241		
c. Coffee breaks	$ 93		
d. Misc. tips, telephone	$ 310		
e. Reception	$ 310	$ 3,505	$ 87.63[c]

2. Meeting charges		
a. Room rental		
b. A/V rental		
c. Secretarial services		
3. Transportation to the meeting	$ 3,878	$ 96.95[d]

Summary: Total per Participant per Day Cost

A.	Development of programs	$155
B.	Participant cost	296
C.	Delivery of one meeting (hotel and transportation)	185
		Total $636

Note: Meeting duration: two full days. Number of attendees: 20 people. These costs do not reflect a figure for the productive time lost of the people in the program. If that cost were added—and it would be realistic to do so—the above cost would increase dramatically. All costs are expressed in terms of 1990 dollars, assuming an average 5 percent inflation rate from 1981 to 1990.

[a]To determine per day cost, divide $155,000 by number of meeting days held per year (10). Then divide answer ($15,500) by total number of management people (100) attending all programs = $155 per day of a meeting.

[b]To determine per day cost, divide total of $69,800 by 236 (average number of working days in a year) = $295.76 per day of work year.

[c]To determine per day, per person cost, divide group total ($3,505) by number of participants (20) and then divide resulting figure ($175.25) by number of meeting days (2) = $87.63 per day.

[d]To determine per day, per person cost, divide group total ($3,878) by number of participants (20) and then divide resulting figure ($193.90) by number of meeting days (2) = $96.95 per day.

Source: Adapted from McKeon, W. J. (1981, May). How to determine off-site meeting costs. *Training and Development Journal*, 117.

ing effectiveness were increased by a factor of greater than 10 percent—and over 20 percent is a realistic possibility—the desirability of the trade-off is obvious. In short, only by considering all of the factors that have an impact on learning effectiveness—program planning and administration, trainer, program delivery, and learning environment—can we derive the greatest return, in time and dollars spent, on this substantial investment in people.

EXAMPLE 2: THE VALUE OF STRUCTURED VERSUS UNSTRUCTURED TRAINING IN BASIC SKILLS

In broad terms, industrial training may be characterized as structured or unstructured. The term *structure* implies a systematically developed educational program designed to train a new worker in a logical progression from no job competency to a specified mastery of the job. The trainee is the focal point of the training effect. Unstructured training, on the other hand, implies on-the-job training of a new worker, without a specific program, by an experienced worker who continues to perform his or her regular duties. Ongoing production output is the focal point of the worker-trainer instead of the training experience of the trainee, and mastery is not defined.

Structured job skills training is widely *assumed* to be more effective than unstructured training, although little controlled research has been done. To some extent this is understandable since the variables in ongoing plant operations are so complex. Controlling them in a simulation is, in itself, very difficult. Nevertheless, failure to conduct controlled studies is perhaps the most serious shortcoming of industrial training programs, many of which are, in fact, extremely well done, for there is no empirical linkage of the results of training to improved productivity. In the absence of such a connection, training activities often are the first to go when profits tumble. This need not always be the case, as a fourteen-month study in a university industrial manufacturing laboratory indicates (Cullen, Sawzin, Sisson, and Swanson, 1976). The origins of the study and its financial support came from the Johns-Manville Corporation.

The Experiment

The purpose of the study was to conduct an experimental comparison of the structured versus unstructured training of semiskilled production workers. The job studied was the Rainville plastics extruder. This job was selected because it was representative of Johns-Manville (J-M) operations and because of its general difficulty of operation. The job involves processing raw materials into quality plastic pipe from a plastic extrusion machine.

There were six major steps in the development of the extruder operator structured-training program:

1. job and task analysis
2. general training-design decisions
3. specific training-design decisions
4. production of the training program
5. pilot test
6. training-program revision

Subjects responded to recruitment methods either by telephoning about the position or by applying in person. As part of the selection procedure, subjects were asked to complete an application form and the Bennett Mechanical Comprehension Test. Forty subjects were selected, matched on characteristics such as age, education, community background, and test scores (to help ensure pre-experimental equivalence), and then assigned randomly to the structured and unstructured groups (twenty in each group). Measures of product quantity and quality, worker competence, cost-benefit, and worker attitudes were as follows.

Measures of Quantity and Quality

Quantity was measured by count and weight. The quality of pipe production was based on visual and dimensional criteria. To aid visual judgments, samples of defective pipe were used as standards. The dimensional criteria of pipe roundness and concentricity required the development and validation of a mechanical test device.

Worker Competence

Worker competence was defined as the ability to start up production, to develop quality pipe, and to recover from two production problems (remotely manipulated machine variables) without a loss of production rate. A concealed closed-circuit television system was set up to monitor the extruder operator's work area and was broadcast to the project office some 100 feet away. In addition, all production rates and observation logs were time-referenced systematically.

Cost-Benefit

Inputs to a cost-benefit model for the two industrial training methods were handled in a very practical manner: actual expenditures were used. Simply stated, the hourly rate of the research assistant performing as the industrial trainer was used, as were all the project costs, even to the point of costing out the paper on which the job analysis was written.

Worker Attitudes

A worker attitude inventory was developed to assess the attitudes of trainees toward their training and job. Content validity was established through the development of questions about attitudes toward the job, the training, the trainer, and the equipment.

Subjects in both groups were trained individually since most new workers at a J-M plant enter singly, to replace workers who have left, and not in groups. Methods for collecting and recording data depended on the type of data needed. The times a trainee reported for work and ended work, the hours a subject was a trainee, and the hours a subject was a worker-trainer were recorded in a log.

To compare the material efficiency of one group to another, data were collected on production rates, production weight, and material waste (scrap). Production rate was recorded as the number of acceptable pieces of pipe extruded per hour of work. At the end of each hour the researcher collected and counted the production, and recorded the production count and weight in the log.

At the end of each hour the researcher collected, weighed, and recorded the plastic determined as scrap. Scrap was defined as plastic extruded not as pipe and pipe not meeting the dimensional and visual standards. Comparisons were made between production weight and scrap weight per training group.

The subjects recorded their attitudes on a questionnaire at the end of the employment period.

Study Results

Time to Achieve Competence

Mean training time for individuals in the unstructured group was 16.3 hours, compared to an average 4.6 hours for those in the structured group. This difference is statistically significant ($p < 0.005$) and indicates a 72 percent savings in training time using the structured method.

Level of Job Competence

Subjects in the structured training group achieved significantly higher ($p < 0.01$) job competence after four hours of training. Though statistically significant differences were not found at eight- and twelve-hour intervals, there were still substantial differences in training times. Certainly statistical power would have been greater with a larger sample size.[1]

Costs of Training

The $56.25 ($127 in 1990 dollars) average cost to train a group of twenty extruder operators by the structured method was not significantly different ($p > 0.05$) from the $57.25 ($129 in 1990 dollars) average to train an identical-size group by the unstructured method. Such a conclusion is probably an artifact of group size in this study. Normally a firm would use an industrial training program to train considerably more than twenty workers. As the number of trainees increases under a structured-training program, the average cost per trainee is reduced because the cost to develop a structured program is fixed while the number of trainees increases. In an unstructured approach, however, the entire cost varies directly with the number of trainees. Exhibit 11.2 illustrates this break-even concept. For the extruder operator experiment, break-even was about eighteen people.

Production Losses

As might be expected, training under both the structured and unstructured methods resulted in reductions from standard minimum-production rates. The average 2.91 pounds of production loss resulting from structured training was significantly less ($p < 0.01$) than the average 9.35 pounds of production loss resulting from the unstructured training. This represents approximately a 70 percent difference in production losses between unstructured and structured training. Such a comparison can be useful in projecting the potential returns for very specific training programs.

Resolution of Production Problems

The 80 percent rate of success in production troubleshooting by the structured program trainees was significantly higher ($p < 0.025$) than the 33

[1]Statistical power is the probability of detecting a significant effect, given that it is indeed present.

EXHIBIT 11.2 Cost comparisons between the unstructured and structured training of 1–20 semiskilled workers

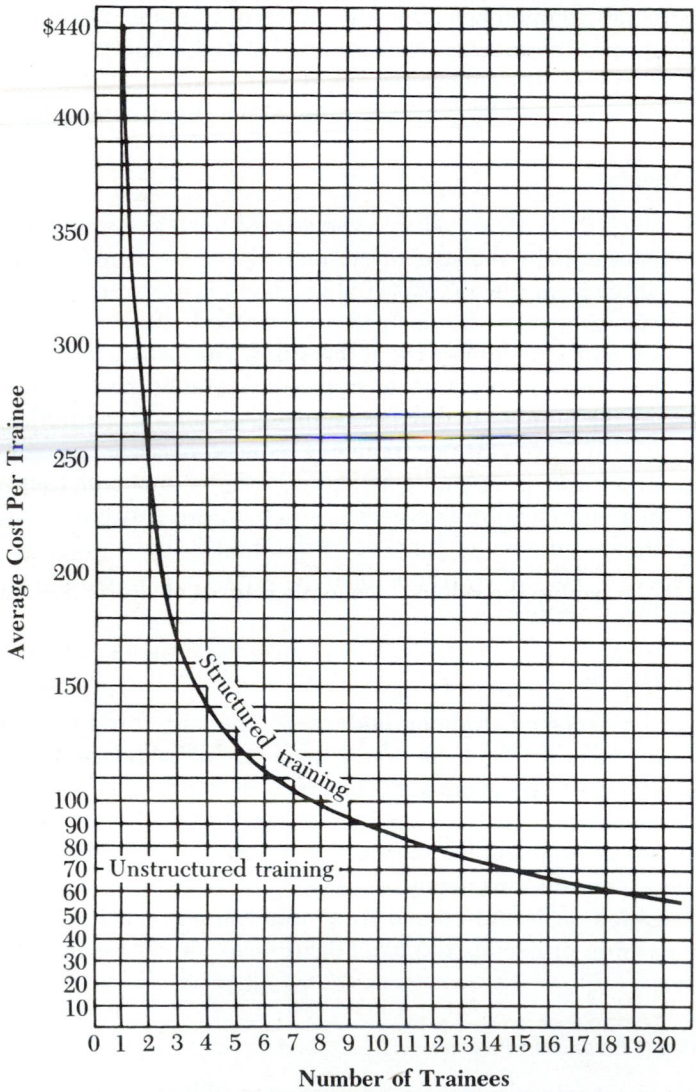

Source: Cullen, J. G., Sawzin, S. A., Sisson, G. R., and Swanson, R. A. (1976). Training: What's it worth? *Training and Development Journal, 30,* 17.

percent rate of success by unstructured program trainees. This represents a 130 percent increase in solved production problems when structured training is used. Industrial situations characterized by expensive production downtime or difficult start-up procedures would make the reported differences of even greater concern.

Job Attitudes

Trainees in the structured and unstructured groups displayed no significant difference ($p > 0.8$) in their attitudes toward the pipe-extrusion job.

The Economics of Training: A Cost-Benefit Model

To estimate accurately the resources that should be allocated to industrial training, management must know the expected gains of that training. Controversy over training often is fueled by inadequate knowledge of its economic returns. At face value, training costs appear to be an economic burden that reduces company profits. However, since some form of training is necessary to maintain worker productivity, a cost-benefit model is needed to determine the relative economic returns of alternative training strategies.

At the most basic level, the lesson from the comparison of structured to unstructured training is that money spent for structured training will be returned many times over. A company can therefore view training as an investment to further its objectives. It can consider the gains or losses derived from training as returns, and comparing returns to investment results in the subsequent cost-benefits or cost-effectiveness of the training.

A cost-benefit model developed by Cullen et al. (1978) for assessing the outcomes of industrial training programs is presented in Exhibit 11.3. To illustrate how the model works, we'll use as an example the comparison of structured versus unstructured training for plastic extruder operators that we just described.

Training Costs

For the cost-benefit model, the costs for training are classified either as fixed or variable. Fixed costs are costs that do not vary with numbers of

EXHIBIT 11.3 Industrial training cost–benefit model

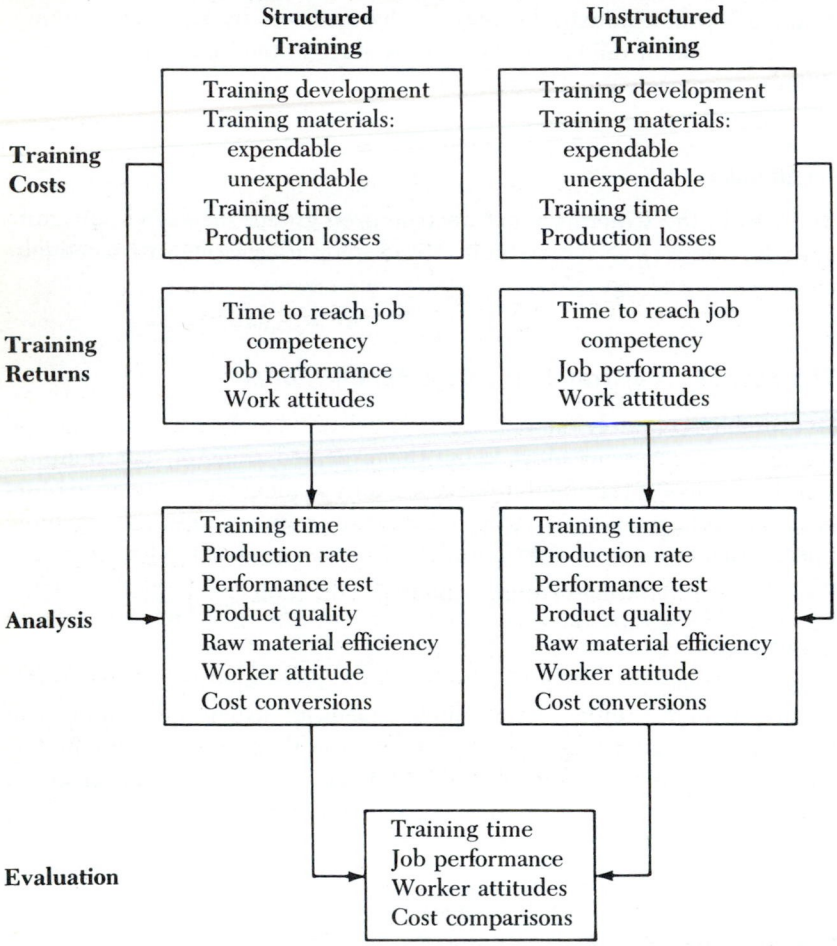

Source: Cullen, J. G., Sawzin, S. A., Sisson, G. R., and Swanson, R. A. (1978). Cost-effectiveness: A model for assessing the training investment. *Training and Development Journal, 32,* 27.

trainees, training time, or training program development. Variable costs are costs that change as the number of trainees, training time, and training program development vary. For example, if regular production equipment (which is a fixed cost for production) is used for training, the losses in production are considered a variable cost.

Training costs in the top left box of Exhibit 11.3 include the following elements:

1. training development:
   a. analysis time: total staff hours to analyze the job
   b. design time: total staff hours to design the training program
   c. material costs: all material costs incurred from onset through completion of one training program, including supplies to facilitate training-program development (secretarial, graphics work, travel, duplicating, display boards, training aids, and so on)
2. training materials (expendable): cost of reproducing copies of developed training program
3. training materials (unexpendable):
   a. instructional hardware: shelf items purchased for the training program (such as production machine to be used just for training, videocassette recorder, or tape recorder)
   b. instructional software: shelf items of instructional content purchased for the training program (such as manufacturer's operating manual, videotapes, or transparencies)
4. training time:
   a. trainee time: total hours, and resulting salary, incurred for trainee to reach competency:
   b. trainer time: total hours, and resulting salary, incurred for trainee to reach competency
5. production losses resulting from training:
   a. production rate losses
   b. material losses

Training Returns

The resulting return of the training program, either structured or unstructured, is a competent production worker. To evaluate a competent production worker, one must specify the competencies required in each situation. The sum of the components then determines the total evaluation. For the plastic extruder operator training program, production task performance included the following components:

1. Trainee can successfully perform job start-up.
2. Trainee can maintain set standard of plastic tubing.

3. Trainee can successfully perform in production malfunction performance tests.
4. Trainee can successfully perform job shutdown.

Analyses of Training Returns

Measurements of actual task performance, for purposes of assessing training returns, included:

1. measurement of task performance:
   a. time: to reach competency, to deal successfully with deliberately induced machine malfunctions, to follow start-up procedures
   b. production rate: number of three-foot lengths of acceptable pipe per hour of production
   c. performance test: reaction to induction of machine malfunctions via performance test (downtime, loss of tubing, time of malfunction injection versus time to respond to malfunction, time to correct malfunction)
   d. product quality: measured by visual and dimensional criteria (comparison to samples of defective and nondefective pipe)
   e. raw material usage: weight of raw material supplied to the machine versus weight of scrap and amount of acceptable product produced (weight of raw material supplied, scrap, and hour bundles of acceptable tubing)
2. measurement of trainee attitudes toward training and the job: measured by the worker attitude inventory described earlier in the chapter
3. monetary value of returns:
   a. convert trainee performance data to a monetary value
   b. total returns of structured training program and unstructured training program

Evaluation

Evaluation comprises the final phase of assessing costs and benefits. As Exhibit 11.3 demonstrates, the structured and unstructured training methods should be compared on all the points just mentioned. Each variable under training costs and training returns should be quantified. For those that are expressed in nonmonetary indexes (for example, time), monetary equivalents should be calculated whenever possible. As we have shown in Chapter 6, the financial impact of employee attitudes also can be estimated. These figures then can be used for the analysis and evaluation stage.

The general approach to cost-benefit comparison of alternative training strategies is to analyze the training variables, to convert them to monetary equivalents, and then to compare costs. If desired, individual variables such as "time taken to reach competency" also can be compared and reported as separate indexes of effectiveness.

The cost-benefit model we have just described has been used successfully in several industrial training situations. Granted, some types of HRD programs (such as programs to change attitudes or improve decision-making skills) may find the components of the model to be inappropriate. The general model or approach to cost-benefit analysis still should guide evaluation in these circumstances. While evaluation isn't always easy, failure to establish empirically the links between HRD and improvements in productivity will ensure that training will continue to be viewed as a cost rather than as an investment in many organizations.

EXAMPLE 3: ESTIMATING THE COSTS AND BENEFITS OF PROPOSED OR ONGOING HRD PROGRAMS

As is true of all functional areas of business that have to operate within budgetary limits, the key question personnel decision makers must answer is, How can we best allocate our scarce resources toward the most cost-effective undertakings? Faced with a bewildering array of alternatives, decision makers must select the programs that will improve productivity and profits. They then must allocate staff resources only to those programs. Utility analysis, a powerful tool used to evaluate selection programs, also can be used to evaluate proposed or ongoing HRD programs. The only difference between the basic equation for calculating selection utility (Equation 10 in Chapter 8 on page 193) and that for calculating utility from HRD programs is that the term d_t is substituted for the product $r_{xy} \times \bar{Z}_x$ (that is, the validity coefficient times the average standard score on the predictor achieved by selectees (Schmidt, Hunter, and Pearlman, 1982). The resulting utility formula is therefore

$$\Delta U = (N)(T)(d_t)(SD_y) - C \tag{1}$$

where ΔU is the gain to the firm in dollars resulting from the program; N is the number of employees trained; T is the expected duration of benefits in the trained group; d_t is the true difference in job performance between the trained and untrained groups in standard deviation units; SD_y is the standard deviation of dollar-valued job performance among untrained employees; and C is the total cost of training N employees.

The parameter d_t is the *effect size*. Like r, it describes the degree of departure from the null hypothesis. In the case of HRD programs, the null hypothesis is that training had no effect—that is, after training the job performance of the trained group is no different from that of the untrained group.

To illustrate this idea graphically, we'll plot the (hypothetical) distribution of job performance outcomes of the trained and untrained groups on the same baseline (expressed in Z-units, with a mean of zero and a standard deviation of 1.0) like in Exhibit 11.4. In Exhibit 11.4, d represents the size of the effect of the training program—the degree of departure from the null hypothesis. How is d computed? It is simply the difference between the mean job performance of the trained and untrained groups in standard (Z) score units. Thus:

$$d = \bar{X}_t - \bar{X}_u / SD_y \tag{2}$$

where d is the effect size; $\bar{X}_t$ is the average job performance score of the trained group; $\bar{X}_u$ is the average job performance score of the untrained group; and SD_y is the standard deviation of the job performance scores of the total group, trained and untrained. If the *SD*s of the two groups are unequal, then the *SD* of the untrained group should be used, since it is more representative of the incumbent employee population.

Hypothetically, suppose that we are evaluating the impact of a training program for quality control inspectors. Job performance is evaluated in terms of a work sample, that is, the number of defects identified in a standard sample of products with a known number (e.g., 10) of defects. Suppose the average job performance score of employees in the trained group is 7, for those in the untrained group it is 6.5, and the standard deviation of the job performance scores is 1.0. The effect size is therefore

$$d = 7 - 6.5/1 = 0.5\ SD$$

In other words, the performance of the trained group is half a standard deviation (roughly 17 percent) better than that of the untrained group. Since a perfectly reliable, objective measure of job performance was used in this case, the estimate of d need not be corrected for unreliability. In many if not most cases, managers will be using criteria that are less than perfectly reliable, such as supervisory ratings of the job performance of subordinates. In such cases, d must be corrected statistically for unrelia-

EXHIBIT 11.4. Standard score distributions of job performance outcomes of trained and untrained groups

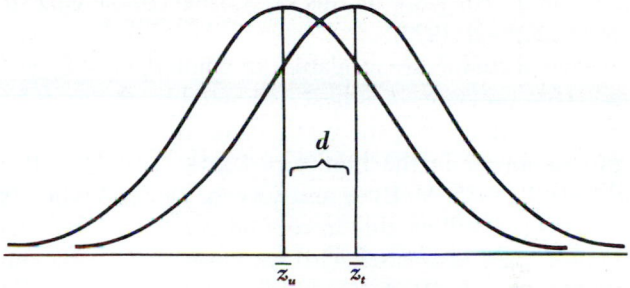

Note: $\bar{Z}_u$ is the average job performance score of the untrained group; $\bar{Z}_t$ is the average job performance score of the trained group; and d is the effect size.

bility or measurement error in the criterion. Failure to do so would produce a biased (conservative) estimate of d.

If supervisory ratings are used as job performance criteria, then reliability probably will be estimated in terms of the extent of interrater agreement. A quantitative review of the literature indicates that the mean correlation between the true score evaluations of two raters is 0.60 (King, Hunter, and Schmidt, 1980). This figure provides a conservative estimate of interrater reliability. Regardless of how the reliability of job performance measures is estimated, the formula for computing the true difference in job performance between the trained and untrained groups is

$$d_t = d/\sqrt{r_{yy}} \tag{3}$$

alternatively,

$$d_t = (\bar{X}_t - \bar{X}_u)/(SD_y)(\sqrt{r_{yy}}) \tag{4}$$

where all terms are as defined above, and $\sqrt{r_{yy}}$ is the square root of the reliability of the job performance measure.

Issues in Estimating d_t

If an organization already has conducted a training program and possesses the necessary data, then it can compute d_t on the basis of an empirical study. Pre- and post-measures of job performance in the trained and untrained groups should be collected systematically, with special care taken to prevent the ratings or other measures of job performance from being influenced by knowledge of who has or has not been trained. These are the same kinds of problems that bedevil all HRD evaluation research, not just research on d_t. For more on this see Cascio (1991), Goldstein (1986), or Cook and Campbell (1979).

When several studies are available, or when d_t must be estimated for a proposed HRD program, d_t is best estimated by the cumulated results of all available studies, using the methods of meta-analysis. Such studies have begun to appear in the literature (Burke and Day, 1986; Guzzo, Jette, and Katzell, 1985; McEvoy and Cascio, 1985). As these studies accumulate, managers will be able to rely on cumulative knowledge of the expected effect sizes associated with proposed HRD programs. Such a "menu" of effect sizes for HRD programs will allow personnel professionals to compute the expected utilities of proposed HRD programs before the decision is made to allocate resources to such programs.

Sometimes, the results of evaluation research are presented in terms of statistics such as r, t, or F. Each of these can be transformed into d by means of the following formulas (Schmidt et al., 1982). When two groups are compared (and therefore $df = 1$),

$$t = \sqrt{F} \tag{5}$$

The t-statistic then can be converted into the point-biserial correlation (r_{pb}) between the dichotomous variable (training versus no training) and rated performance by the following formula:

$$r_{pb} = t/\sqrt{t^2 + (N_t - 2)} \tag{6}$$

where N_t is the total number of persons in the study, the sum of the trained and untrained groups. To transform r_{pb} into d, use the following formula:

$$d = \frac{1}{\sqrt{pq}}\sqrt{\frac{N_t - 2}{N_t}} \times \frac{r}{\sqrt{1 - r^2}} \tag{7}$$

where p and q are the proportions of the total group in the trained and untrained groups, respectively. Let us illustrate the use of these formulas through an example. Suppose 100 employees are trained and 100 serve in a control group. Results of training are expressed as $F = 6.0$, using supervisors' ratings as criteria ($r_{yy} = 0.60$). Using Equation 5,

$$t = 2.45$$

Using Equation 6,

$$r_{pb} = 2.45/\sqrt{6.0 + (200 - 2)}$$
$$r_{pb} = 0.17$$

Using Equation 7,

$$d = 1/0.5\ (0.9950)(0.17/0.985)$$
$$d = 0.34$$

Therefore, d_t is $0.34/\sqrt{0.60} = 0.44$

Break-Even Analysis Applied to Proposed HRD Programs

Having determined an expected value of d_t, we can use Equation 1 to compute a break-even value of SD_y, that is, the value at which benefits equal costs and $\Delta U = \$0.00$. For example, suppose 300 employees are trained, the duration of the training effect is expected to be 2 years, $d_t = 0.55$, and the per person cost of training is \$800. Setting $\Delta U = \$0.00$ yields:

$$\$0.00 = 2(300)(0.55)(SD_y) - 300\ (\$800)$$
$$SD_y = \$727$$

Even if d_t is as low as 0.10, SD_y is still only \$4,000, well below the observed values of SD_y (e.g., \$10,000 to \$15,000) typically reported in the literature. To the extent that precise estimates of d_t and SD_y are unavailable, break-even analysis still allows a decision maker to use the general utility model to assess the impact of a proposed HRD program. If estimates of d_t and SD_y are available, then utility can be computed, and the *expected* payoff from the program can be compared with the break-even values for d_t or SD_y. The comparison of "expected case" and "worst case" scenarios thus provides a more complete set of information for purposes of decision making.

Duration of the Effects of an HRD Program

A key parameter in Equation 1 is T, the duration of the effect of a training or HRD program. In most cases, this parameter is difficult to estimate. One approach that has proven useful is the Delphi method, often used in long-range forecasting. With this method, a group of subject matter experts is asked to provide judgments about the duration of the training effect. Each expert responds individually and anonymously to a neutral third party (called an intermediary). The intermediary's task is to collect and summarize the experts' opinions and redistribute that information back to the experts for another round of judgment. The cycle continues until the experts reach a consensus, often after three or four rounds of judgments.

Economic Considerations and Employee Flows Applied to Proposed or Ongoing HRD Programs

Boudreau (1983) pointed out that since training activities lead to "diminishing returns" over time (that is, training effects dissipate over time), a utility model that incorporates employee flows should be used to assess the net payoff of the program over time. Beyond that, variable costs, taxes, and discounting must be considered in order to assess correctly the true impact of a proposed or ongoing HRD program. Since we considered these issues in Chapter 10, here we need only present the summary model that incorporates all of these factors. Then we will present a worked example to demonstrate how the utility analysis proceeds. The model is shown in Equation 8.

$$\begin{aligned}\Delta U = \sum_{k=1}^{F}[\sum_{t=1}^{k}(N_{a_t} - N_{s_t}]\{[1/(1+i)^k] \\ \times (d_t)(SD_{st})(1+V)(1-TAX)\} \\ - \sum_{k=1}^{F}[C_k(1-TAX)[1/(1+i)^{(k-1)}]\}\end{aligned} \tag{8}$$

For purposes of illustration let us adopt the d_t value we computed earlier, 0.44. Assume that 100 employees are trained each year for five years, and that for each cohort, the training effect dissipates gradually at the rate of 25 percent per year. No employees separate during this period (and therefore $N_{st} = 0$). This information allows us to compute a weighted average d_t value for the trained group each year, as a new cohort of trainees is added. Exhibit 11.5 shows the weighted average d_t values.

In order to use Equation 8, assume that $SD_y = \$10{,}000$, variable costs $(V) = -0.10$, the tax rate is 45 percent, and the discount rate is 8 percent. Since costs ($500 per person) are incurred in the same period that benefits are received, we will use k as the exponent in the cost term in Equation 8. The total payoff of the HRD program is the sum of the utilities of each of the five periods:

- $\Delta U_1 = 100(0.926)(0.44)(\$10{,}000)(0.90)(0.55) - \$50{,}000(0.55)(0.926)$
- $\Delta U_1 = \$176{,}218$
- $\Delta U_2 = 200(0.857)(0.385)(\$10{,}000)(0.90)(0.55) - \$50{,}000(0.55)(0.857)$
- $\Delta U_2 = \$303{,}078$
- $\Delta U_3 = 300(0.794)(0.33)(\$10{,}000)(0.90)(0.55) - \$50{,}000(0.55)(0.794)$
- $\Delta U_3 = \$367{,}265$
- $\Delta U_4 = 400(0.735)(0.275)(\$10{,}000)(0.90)(0.55) - \$50{,}000(0.55)(0.735)$

EXHIBIT 11.5 The diminishing returns of an HRD program over five years

Year	N_k	*Weighted Average*
1	100	100(0.44)/100
2	200	100(0.44) + 100(0.44 − 25%)/200
3	300	100(0.44) + 100(0.44 − 25%) + 100(0.44 − 50%)/300
4	400	100(0.44) + 100(0.44 − 25%) + 100(0.44 − 50%) + 100(0.44 − 75%)/400
5	500	100(0.44) + 100(0.44 − 25%) + 100(0.44 − 50%) + 100(0.44 − 75%) + 100(0.44 − 100%)/500

Year	d_t
1	0.44
2	0.385
3	0.33
4	0.275
5	0.22

- $\Delta U_4 = \$379,995$
- $\Delta U_5 = 500(0.681)(0.22)(\$10,000)(0.90)(0.55) - \$50,000(0.55)(0.681)$
- $\Delta U_5 = \$352,077$

The sum of these one-period utility estimates is $1,578,633. This is the total expected payoff of the HRD program over the five-year period.

The utility analysis techniques discussed thus far are illustrated nicely in a study of the utility of a supervisory skills training program applied in a large commercial bank (Mathieu and Leonard, 1987). The study incorporates the following features:

1. Training costs were tabulated using cost accounting techniques.
2. The Schmidt-Hunter global estimation procedure was used to estimate SD_y.
3. Pre- and post-training ratings of the job performance of (non-randomly assigned) experimental and control group subjects were compared in order to determine d_t.
4. Utility analysis results that included adjustments for economic factors (discounting, variable costs, and taxes) were compared to utility results that did not include such adjustments.

5. Break-even analysis was used to assess the minimum change in SD_y required to recoup the costs invested in the program.
6. The effect on estimated payoffs of employee flows, decay in training effects, and employee turnover were considered explicitly.

Results showed that the training program paid off handsomely over time, even under highly conservative assumptions. Training sixty-five bank managers in supervisory skills produced an estimated net payoff (after adjustment for the economic factors noted earlier) of $34,627 in year 1, and $148,465 by year 5. Not surprisingly, differences between adjusted and unadjusted estimates of payoff tended to become greater the further in time they were projected. In general, however, utility figures adjusted for economic factors were 60 percent to 80 percent smaller than unadjusted figures.

When break-even analysis was used, even assuming a 25 percent yearly reduction in the strength of the training effect, break-even values of SD_y were still less than 50 percent of the values used in the utility analysis. Finally, in terms of employee flows, the economic impact of training additional groups was also considerable. For example, the estimate for the tenth year of the utility of training 225 employees in the first five years was over $364,300 even after adjustment for economic factors. Data like these are useful to decision makers, whether their focus is on the broad allocation of organizational resources across functional lines or on the choice of specific personnel programs from a larger menu of possible programs.

One of the important lessons to be learned from the material presented in this chapter is that methods are available *now* for estimating the costs and benefits of HRD programs, proposed, ongoing, or completed. Instead of depending on the power of persuasion to convince decision makers of the value of HRD programs, human resource professionals can, by the use of cost-benefit models, join with the other functional areas of business in justifying the allocation of scarce organizational resources on the basis of evidence, rather than on that of beliefs.

EXERCISES

1. Pilgrim Industries, a 2,000-employee firm with 400 management personnel, holds 40 days of off-site meetings per year. Outside consultants develop and conduct the meetings, and on the average 20 managers attend each meeting. The

typical meeting lasts two full days. Last year, total program development costs consumed $250,000. The average attendee's salary (plus benefits) was $30,000, and Pilgrim's capital investment in each attendee was, on the average, an additional $30,000. To deliver each two-day meeting for 20 people, sleeping accommodations, food, telephone, and a cocktail reception cost $3,000. In addition, transportation, secretarial services, room, and audiovisual equipment rental totaled another $4,000. Determine the total per day, per person cost of one off-site meeting.

2. Soclear, Inc., a janitorial service firm, wants to conduct a controlled study of structured versus unstructured training for window washers of office buildings. How would you design the structured and unstructured training programs? In order to use the cost-benefit model shown in Exhibit 11.3, what criteria of job performance might you use? How will data be collected and recorded? How can cost comparisons be made?

3. Jane Burns, a personnel analyst for Standard City, USA, knows that SD_y for fire fighters in her city is $11,000. The fire department has asked the city to provide training in team building for 500 of its employees, at a cost of $1,000 per employee. The effects of this organization development effort are expected to last for two years. Using Equation 1, compute the break-even value for d_t necessary for the city to recoup the costs of the program.

4. Suppose, in exercise 3, that you have just read a meta-analysis of team building studies and know that the cumulated estimate of d_t is 0.45. Compute an expected utility for the program, and compare it to the break-even value you identified earlier. How might this affect the chances that the project will be funded?

5. With regard to exercise 4, suppose that the discount rate is 10 percent, and variable costs are −0.10. The city is not taxed. How do these factors affect the estimate of expected utility that you developed in exercise 4?

REFERENCES

ARVEY, R. D., and COLE, D. A. (1989). Evaluating change due to training. In I. L. Goldstein and Associates, *Training and development in organizations*. San Francisco: Jossey-Bass, 1989, pp. 89–117.

BOUDREAU, J. W. (1983). Effects of employee flows on utility analysis of human resource productivity improvement programs. *Journal of Applied Psychology*, *68*, 396–406.

BURKE, M. J., and DAY, R. R. (1986). A cumulative study of the effectiveness of managerial training. *Journal of Applied Psychology*, *71*, 232–246.

CASCIO, W. F. (1991). *Applied psychology in personnel management* (4th ed.). Englewood Cliffs, NJ: Prentice-Hall.

COOK, T. D., and CAMPBELL, D. T. (1979). *Quasi-experimentation: Design and analysis issues for field settings*. Chicago: Rand-McNally.

CULLEN, J. G., SAWZIN, S. A., SISSON, G. R., and SWANSON, R. A. (1976). Training: What's it worth? *Training and Development Journal, 30* (8), 12–20.

CULLEN, J. G., SAWZIN, S. A., SISSON, G. R., and SWANSON, R. A. (1978). Cost effectiveness: A model for assessing the training investment. *Training and Development Journal, 32* (1), 24–29.

GOLDSTEIN, I. L. (1986). *Training: Program design and evaluation* (2nd ed.). Monterey, CA: Brooks/Cole.

GOLDSTEIN, I. L., and GILLIAM, P. (1990). Training system issues in the year 2000. *American Psychologist, 45*, 134–143.

GUZZO, R. A., JETTE, R. D., and KATZELL, R. A. (1985). The effects of psychologically based intervention programs on worker productivity: A meta-analysis. *Personnel Psychology, 38*, 275–291.

KING, L. M., HUNTER, J. E., and SCHMIDT, F. L. (1980). Halo in a multidimensional, force-choice evaluation scale. *Journal of Applied Psychology, 65*, 507–516.

LATHAM, G. P. (1988). Human resource training and development. *Annual Review of Psychology, 39*, 545–582.

MATHIEU, J. E., and LEONARD, R. L., JR. (1987). Applying utility concepts to a training program in supervisory skills: A time-based approach. *Academy of Management Journal, 30*, 316–335.

MCEVOY, G. M., and CASCIO, W. F. (1985). Strategies for reducing employee turnover: A meta-analysis. *Journal of Applied Psychology, 70*, 342–353.

MCKEON, W. J. (1981, May). How to determine off-site meeting costs. *Training and Development Journal, 35*, 116–122.

MILLS, T. (1975, March–April). Human resources—Why the new concern? *Harvard Business Review*, 120–134.

OFFERMAN, L. R., and GOWING, M. K. (1990). Organizations of the future: Changes and challenges. *American Psychologist, 45*, 95–108.

SCHMIDT, F. L., HUNTER, J. E., and PEARLMAN, K. (1982). Assessing the economic impact of personnel programs on workforce productivity. *Personnel Psychology, 35*, 333–347.

12

Integrating Alternative Measures of Behavioral and Performance Outcomes

The preceding eleven chapters all have shared a common objective: to quantify in financial terms the outcomes associated with a set of common topics in human resource management. Traditionally, and more often, such outcomes have been expressed only in terms of behavior or performance. Topics presented in chapters 1 through 7 have focused on reducing controllable costs. Topics presented in chapters 8 through 11 have focused on improving productivity. Both reduction of costs and improvement of productivity enhance corporate profits—an important objective in almost all for-profit enterprises.

An integration of these approaches is needed so that HR professionals can develop a financial reporting system for HR activities most directly related to the strategic thrust of the business or business unit that they serve. Hence, an important underlying assumption is that any attempt to assess the outcomes associated with activities of the HR function must focus on outcomes that are regarded as most salient to the various constituencies that the HR function serves. The objective of Chapter 12 is to develop a broad set of guidelines for determining which outcomes to consider.

We will begin by showing the relationship between effective HRM and profits, and why the assessment of HR activities must take into account specific types of outcomes (quantitative *and* qualitative), the management level at which those outcomes are most important, and the strategic nature of HRM activities. We discuss strategic HRM in some detail, focusing on the role of HR professionals as "strategic partners" along with line managers. We emphasize the important linkage between HR strategy and general business (competitive) strategy, and show how the HR function is inextricably linked to the achievement of the competitive strategic goals of the broader organization or organizational units.

Our scope is limited to the topics addressed in this book. We make no attempt to identify the myriad potential measures of HR quality or quantity of HR services that are available. For an excellent treatment of those issues, see Tsui and Gomez-Mejia (1988).

LINKING EFFECTIVE HUMAN RESOURCE MANAGEMENT TO PROFITS

The HR function derives power from its ability to help line managers to solve business-related problems. Unfortunately the perception in some companies is that the HR function is exclusively a cost center, that it makes no contribution to profits. To change this perception, HR professionals must be able to answer the question "How much more product can be sold because of your services?" While many HR contributions are not related directly to the bottom line, HR activities are related to the purposes of the organization. Some possible HR department responses to questions from senior management in six key areas (Bellman, 1986) include:

- "Here's what we did for you and here's what it cost, and here's what you would have done without us and what it would have cost you" (for example, in recruiting).
- "Here's how much money we saved you in our benefits package by changing insurers."
- "Here's an idea that workers developed in a training program we lead. It's now working and saving you $50,000 per year."
- "If you had not asked us to do this executive search, you would have had to hire an outside consultant at a cost of $30,000. We did it for $5,000."
- "You used to have an unhappy person doing this job for $40,000 per year. As a result of our job redesign efforts, you now have a motivated person doing the same work for $20,000."

- "In working with the union on a new contract, we found a way to reduce grievances by 30 percent, saving the company 6,429 hours per year in management time."

To be most useful, however, responses should be tailored to address three key considerations: types of outcomes, level of analysis, and the focus of HR activities.

Types of Outcomes

Outcomes may be expressed in quantitative terms (as in the preceding responses) or in qualitative terms (such as indicators of overall morale, individual job satisfaction, or reactions to a training program). Alone, each type of outcome is incomplete, for both quantitative and qualitative outcomes are important to describe the rich results of HR programs. Although we have emphasized quantitative outcomes, qualitative measures are no less useful or important.

Level of Analysis

As Tsui and Gomez-Mejia (1988) have noted, most attempts to evaluate the HR function have not distinguished HR activities performed at the corporate level from those performed at the management level or at the operating level. At the corporate level, HR decisions involve the design of policies that meet the organization's strategic challenges such as business objectives, corporate values or culture, technology, structure, and responses to constraints posed by the external environment.

At the management level, key HR decisions involve the design of systems or programs that are consistent with policy guidelines and that will facilitate the cost-effective achievement of business goals. The objective at this level is management control, and it is accomplished by assessing the cost-effectiveness of HR programs.

At the operating level, managers implement HR policies and programs and make decisions that affect the attraction, retention, and motivation of employees. This level includes the hands-on HR practices of line managers (for example, in reducing absenteeism or controllable turnover) and the day-to-day services provided by the HR function (for example, recruiting, staffing, training) that directly affect HR outcomes.

Focus of HR Activities

Such activities may be tactical or strategic. Tactical decisions, which are short-range in nature, may involve the deployment of staff for a temporary project, to conduct a recruitment program, or to conduct or respond to an investigation by an agency of the federal government. Since tactical issues demand attention from HR professionals in the short run, it is easy to avoid consideration of issues such as the long-term fit of HR activities and programs with the strategic objectives of the larger organization.

Unless HR professionals can look at both short-term and long-term issues, they will not be able to meet a fundamental challenge: to discard "low-payoff" activities, while focusing on those that will yield the highest payoffs. This kind of thinking is strategic, and long-range in nature. It is known as *strategic human resource management*, and we will examine it more fully in the following sections.

STRATEGIC HUMAN RESOURCE MANAGEMENT

Strategic HRM consists of three major tasks (Dyer and Holder, 1988). The first arises during the formulation of general business strategies. The task is to ensure that HR issues and the implications of various alternatives or proposals are considered fully. The next task is to establish HR goals or action plans—HR strategies—to support the general business strategies. The final task is to work with line managers as principal clients to ensure that action plans are implemented. These three tasks parallel the three levels of analysis of HR activities described earlier: those that take place at the corporate level, at the management level, and at the operating level.

Traditionally, the relationship between general business strategy and HR strategy (if any) consisted of a one-way flow of information. General business strategies were developed and almost as an afterthought, the HR implications of those strategies were examined (for example, the number of fully competent workers available to staff a new plant, or the amount of training and development necessary to implement new technology).

The new role conceptualized for HR professionals is that of "strategic partners," along with line managers, in the overall operation of an organization (Dyer and Holder, 1988). The new role requires a two-way flow of information. HR strategy is an integral component of general business strategy; each provides useful planning information for the other during the formulation of general business strategy. The goal of HR executives is to exercise leadership in all matters concerning HR strategy and policy. They constantly search for ways in which their organizations might achieve or enhance a competitive advantage through more effective management of people (Schuler and Jackson, 1987). They question the wisdom of business strategies that might appear risky because of potential HR problems. When the strategic direction of a business changes, they take the lead in evaluating the continued relevance of broad HR strategies and in making any necessary changes (Dyer and Holder, 1988).

When strategy is an integral part of the HR function, success is not defined in terms of measures that show how busy the HR department has been (for example, numbers of employees recruited, tested, or trained; numbers of claims processed). Rather, success is defined in terms of the nature of the contribution toward achievement of HR goals, and, in the longer run, in terms of the nature of the contribution to the success of the organization's business strategies (Dyer and Holder, 1988).

What are the implications of strategic HRM? It is necessary to understand HR and general business strategy before any assessment of behavioral or performance outcomes becomes relevant. The following example illustrates strategic HRM as we have discussed it thus far.

Employee Involvement at Ford Motor Company

In November of 1979, Philip Caldwell, then president of Ford Motor Company, articulated top management policy on employee involvement with a Policy Letter on Employee Involvement. The policy applied to all employees in the company and it provided guidelines to managers about how to operate. The essence of the policy is captured in the first paragraph: "It is the policy of the Company to encourage and enable all employees to become involved in and contribute to the success of the Company. A work climate should be created and maintained in which employees at all levels can achieve individual goals and work satisfaction by directing their talents and energies toward clearly defined Company goals" (Banas, 1988, p. 390).

With this statement of policy as a guide, HR professionals focused their efforts on activities that would contribute to enhanced involvement of employees at all levels of the company. The policy letter set the parameters under which such a joint labor–management initiative would be carried out, but it was the responsibility of the local parties to determine what would be done, how it would be done, when it would be done, and at what rate. HR professionals developed "Employee Involvement Guidelines" as a framework for carrying out these responsibilities. In developing these guidelines, they assumed the role of "strategic partners." They were actively involved in the initial formulation of employee involvement as a business strategy, in establishing action plans (HR strategies) to support the general business strategy, and in working closely with line managers and employees to ensure that established action plans were actually implemented (Banas, 1988).

The guidelines included eight elements, or steps, that were considered essential to successfully involving employees in each location or part of the business. Implementation of the guidelines consumed the time of many HR professionals over the next several years. Briefly (see Banas, 1988 for a more thorough discussion), the guidelines include:

1. gaining rank-and-file and management support at the local level
2. guidance of a joint labor–management steering committee
3. collecting information about work relationships and the work environment to determine the readiness of the organization for employee involvement
4. selection of a pilot site by the steering committee
5. preparation of the local organization for the introduction of employee involvement
6. initiation of the pilot project (design, training, facilitation of meetings, feedback to the steering committee on progress and problems)
7. evaluation and fine tuning
8. expansion to other work groups

This enormous effort involved thousands of workers and managers in a common cause. To be successful, it required considerable learning and training by managers and workers. Here is a sample of the many types of education and training opportunities that were made available:

- The Joint UAW–Ford Employee Involvement Process Workshop (designed for employee involvement coordinators and facilitators)
- Employee Involvement Creative Problem-Solving Workshop (designed for labor and management employees)
- Instructional Skills Workshop (designed for coordinators, facilitators, and problem-solving group leaders)
- Consulting Skills Workshop (designed for trainers, coordinators and facilitators)
- Participative Management—Employee Involvement Workshop (designed for managers and supervisors)

Traditional measures of the effectiveness of an HR department would emphasize the number of workshops conducted or the number of employees who were trained, along with the reactions of trainers and trainees to these workshops. Such measures focus more on process than substance, more on tactics than strategy. From a strategic perspective, the important consideration is the extent to which the activities of HR professionals have contributed to the achievement of Ford's overall company objectives. By most accounts they have done so admirably. Why? Because in the course of the next decade both line managers and rank-and-file employees were able to achieve the strategic objectives set forth in Caldwell's 1979 Policy Letter on Employee Involvement. Furthermore, the employee involvement strategy proved to be quite profitable.

Results of Employee Involvement

The 1982 negotiating process between the UAW and Ford, as well as the resulting agreement, were hailed by the news media as a major breakthrough in labor relations. Both union and company representatives expressed the belief that their participation in employee involvement (following the implementation strategy developed by HR professionals) had provided firsthand experience on how to build trust, open communications, and relate to each other more effectively. As a result, because of a history of successful local experiences, when they came to the bargaining table they came ready to resolve problems. Ford and the UAW reached a new agreement after only thirteen days of actual bargaining.

Throughout the 1980s, Ford's "Quality Is Job One" advertisements and commercials featured team members demonstrating the contributions of employee involvement to product quality, thereby providing recognition for the employees, the union, and the company. According to company indices, since the inception of the employee involvement process, product quality has improved more than 50 percent for cars and 47 percent for trucks. Beyond that, it is generally agreed that Ford has the best quality of the three principal U.S. automobile manufacturers (Banas, 1988). High quality, in turn, has led to high profits for the company, and both employees and managers have shared in those benefits. For example, in its 1987 profit-sharing plan, Ford disbursed checks to each of its 156,500 eligible U.S. salaried and hourly workers that equaled 11 percent of paychecks—an average of $3,700 per employee (Schroeder, 1988). Certainly employee involvement, subsequent improvements in quality, and profit-sharing have contributed to the 40 percent improvement in Ford's break-even point for its North American automotive operations.

In its quest for improved performance and to compete more effectively in the marketplace, Ford adopted a broad competitive strategy that has been termed "quality enhancement." Other organizations have adopted different strategies to achieve the same objectives. In the following section we examine three competitive strategies.

ALTERNATIVE COMPETITIVE STRATEGIES

The means that firms use to compete for business in the marketplace and to gain competitive advantage are known as *competitive strategies* (Porter, 1985). Competitive strategies can differ in a number of ways, including the extent to which firms emphasize innovation, quality enhancement, or cost reduction (Schuler and Jackson, 1987). Moreover, there is growing recognition that the different types of strategies require different types of HR practices (Jackson and Schuler, 1990).

As in the Ford Motor Company example, the role of the HR department as a strategic partner makes good business sense to the extent that HR professionals convey an important message to top management in everything they say and do: *human resources represent a competitive advantage that can increase profits when managed wisely.* Wise HRM, in turn, requires a careful alignment between competitive strategy and HR strategy.

Because different types of HR practices are important in different organizations or units of organizations, the assessment of outcomes associated with HR activities should focus on activities associated with the HR practices that are most crucial to the implementation of the competitive strategy chosen. Later, we will attempt to map the HR topics discussed in this book to alternative competitive strategies. First, however, let us describe each strategy.

Innovation strategy is used to develop products or services that differ from those of competitors; its primary objective is to offer something new and different. Enhancing product or service quality is the major objective of the *quality-enhancement strategy*. Finally, the objective of a *cost-reduction strategy* is to gain competitive advantage by being the lowest-cost producer of goods or provider of services. As noted by Schuler and Jackson (1987), innovation strategy emphasizes managing people so that they work *differently*, quality-enhancement strategy emphasizes managing people so that they work *smarter*, and cost-reduction strategy emphasizes managing people so that they work *harder*.

While it is convenient to think of these three competitive strategies as pure types applied to entire organizations, business units, or even functional specialties, reality is more complex. Various combinations of the three strategies can be observed in practice.

Consider an initial statement of employee involvement strategy at the Ford Motor Company. According to Banas (1988), in October 1978 Philip Caldwell, then president of Ford, made the following statement at a meeting of the top executives of the company: "Our strategy for the years ahead will come to nothing unless we ask for greater participation of our work force. Without motivated and concerned workers, we're not going to lower our costs as much as we need to—and we aren't going to get the product quality we need" (p. 391). Elements of cost-reduction as well as quality-enhancement strategies are evident in Caldwell's statement.

Role Behaviors Appropriate to Each Competitive Strategy

Innovation Strategy

The implications of pursuing a competitive strategy of innovation for managing people may include selecting highly skilled individuals, giving employees more discretion, using minimal controls, making a greater investment in human resources, providing more resources for experimentation, allowing and even rewarding occasional failure, and appraising performance for its long-run implications. Successful innovative firms such as Hewlett-Packard, 3M, Raytheon, and PepsiCo illustrate this strategy (Schuler and Jackson, 1987).

Because the innovation process depends heavily on individual expertise and creativity, employee turnover can have disastrous consequences (Kanter, 1985). Also, firms pursuing an innovation strategy are more likely to emphasize long-term needs in their training programs for managers and to offer training to more employees throughout the organization (Jackson, Schuler, and Rivero, 1989). Desired role behaviors of employees suggest that any assessment of contributions of the HR function should focus attention primarily on the utility of selection and training programs and also on reducing controllable turnover, especially among high performers who are not easy to replace. Because innovation strategy requires a long-term orientation that focuses on the personal and professional development of employees, HR activities that involve employee assistance programs (EAPs), wellness programs, or smoking cessation programs could help achieve success.

Quality-Enhancement Strategy

The profile of behaviors appropriate for a quality-enhancement strategy includes (Schuler and Jackson, 1987): relatively repetitive and predictable behaviors; a longer-term focus; a modest amount of cooperative, interdependent behavior; a high concern for quality with a modest concern for quantity of output; a high concern for how goods or services are made or delivered; low risk-taking activity; and commitment to the goals of the organization. To be sure, many of these behaviors can be found in Ford's quality-enhancement strategy discussed earlier.

Because quality enhancement typically involves greater employee commitment and fuller use of employees' abilities, fewer employees are needed to produce the same level of output. This phenomenon has been observed at such firms as L. L. Bean, Corning Glass, Honda, and Toyota.

It is well known that productivity gains resulting from improved selection or training can be expressed in various ways: in dollars, in increases in output, in decreases in hiring needs, or in savings in payroll costs (see Cascio, 1989). Since fewer workers *may* be needed after the implementation of valid selection programs, the change in staffing requirements may be useful for assessing behavioral and performance outcomes associated with the implementation of a quality-enhancement strategy.

Since reliable and predictable behavior is important to the implementation of this strategy, another objective is to minimize absenteeism, tardiness, and turnover. Cost savings associated with any HR programs designed to control these undesirable behaviors should therefore be documented carefully. Moreover, a long-term commitment to the goals of the organization and flexibility to change on the part of employees are strengthened by constant informal and formal training programs. Another way to signal concern for the long-term welfare of employees is by actively promoting EAPs, wellness programs, and smoking cessation programs.

Finally, commitment to the goals of the organization can be assessed through the measurement of employee attitudes over multiple time periods. As we have seen, methods are also available to assess the financial consequences associated with improvements (or decrements) in these attitudes.

In summary, assessment of behavioral and performance outcomes, in the context of a quality-enhancement strategy, should focus on the utility of selection and training programs, on the financial gains associated with promoting positive changes in employees' attitudes and in their lifestyles, and on the cost savings associated with decreasing absenteeism and turnover.

Cost-Reduction Strategy

Firms pursuing a cost-reduction strategy are characterized by tight fiscal and management controls, minimization of overhead, and pursuit of economies of scale. The primary objective is to increase productivity, that is, the unit cost of output per person. Strategies for reducing costs include reducing the number of employees; reducing wage levels; using part-time workers, subcontractors, or automation; changing work rules, and permitting flexibility in job assignments (Schuler and Jackson, 1987).

The profile of role behaviors in the context of a cost-reduction strategy includes relatively repetitive and predictable behaviors, a relatively short-term focus, primarily autonomous or individual activity, a modest concern for quality coupled with a high concern for quantity of output (goods or services), emphasis on results, low risk-taking, and stability. In addition, there is minimal use of training and development.

An example of one approach to cost-reduction is the collective bargaining agreement reached between the Great Atlantic and Pacific Tea Company (A&P) and the United Food and Commercial Workers (UFCW) union. After four years of losses and an eight-year decrease in the number of company stores from 3,500 to about 1,000, both the company and the union recognized that they had two choices: either reduce costs and be competitive, or go out of business. To survive, the company and the union agreed to an experimental arrangement at sixty stores in the Philadelphia area. Workers took a 25 percent pay cut in exchange for the opportunity to earn more. That is, if a store's employees could keep labor costs at 10 percent of sales—by working more efficiently or by boosting store traffic—they would receive a cash bonus equal to 1 percent of the store's sales. They would receive a 0.5 percent bonus at 11 percent of sales or 1.5 percent at 9.5 percent of sales. It was a gamble in the low-margin supermarket business, but it worked (McComas, 1986). Two years later, operating profits had increased by 81 percent, and A&P's stock price had doubled. As noted earlier, cost-reduction strategies can be implemented over a relatively short term. Strategies that focus on innovation or quality-enhancement typically take much longer.

The profile of role behaviors for employees and managers under a cost-reduction strategy suggests that an assessment of the contributions of the HR function should emphasize the control of labor costs associated with collective bargaining agreements, dysfunctional turnover, and unscheduled employee absenteeism. Low-cost options associated with the control of health care costs and fire and life insurance premiums (for example, smoking bans) also should be implemented and assessed.

CONCLUSION

Exhibits 12.1 and 12.2 summarize the ideas discussed thus far. In using these exhibits, we add these cautions.

1. Our treatment is limited to the topics discussed in this book. In practice, a broader mix of qualitative and quantitative measures should be used to assess the contribution of the HR function to the achievement of strategic business goals.

2. The range of competitive strategies (and HR strategies to support them) should not be limited to the three that we have discussed: innovation, quality-enhancement, and cost-reduction. In practice, others are likely to be found, along with hybrid versions of these three. Nevertheless, meaningful contributions from the HR function are most likely to occur when a careful "mapping" of HR strategies onto long-term business strategies has been done.

3. The mapping of outcomes onto strategies, as shown in Exhibit 12.2, should be regarded only as a rough taxonomy. As research evidence accumulates, a more comprehensive classification scheme can be developed; this remains an important challenge in HRM research.

EXHIBIT 12.1 Primary and secondary objectives of topics examined in Chapters 2–11

	Objectives[a]	
Topic	*Reduce Costs*	*Increase Productivity*
Turnover (Ch. 2)	1	2
Absenteeism (Ch. 3)	1	2
Smoking (Ch. 4)	1	2
EAPs/Wellness programs (Ch. 5)	1	2
Attitudes (Ch. 6)	1	2
Labor contracts (Ch. 7)	1	2
Utility (selection) (Chs. 8–10)	2	1
Utility (training) (Ch. 11)	2	1

[a]1 = primary objective; 2 = secondary objective

EXHIBIT 12.2 Relationship between competitive strategy and measures of outcomes that are most appropriate under each strategy

	Measures of Outcomes	
Competitive Strategy	*Primary*	*Secondary*
Innovation	Increase productivity	Reduce costs
Quality-enhancement	Increase productivity	Reduce costs
Cost-reduction	Reduce costs	Increase productivity

Note: The mix of HR strategies designed to increase productivity and to decrease costs is likely to be somewhat different under an innovation strategy as opposed to a quality-enhancement strategy (see text for a fuller discussion).

EXERCISES

1. As senior vice-president for human resources, you have received the following memo from top management: "Please join the Top Executive Group for three days of strategic planning beginning one month from today. As you know, the major item under consideration is our possible involvement in the development of the Eastern European market for our products." In order to assume the role of "strategic partner" what specific issues will you raise? Further, assuming that the company does decide to exploit this new market, outline a set of strategic HR initiatives that will guide your activities as the company's strategy unfolds over time.

2. Your company has embarked on an aggressive strategy of innovation across all of its product and service lines. What specific HR activities will you recommend that the company adopt over short- as well as long-range horizons?

3. You have read about the employee involvement strategy used at the Ford Motor Company as part of its long-term quality-enhancement strategy. The strategy was clearly successful throughout the 1980s. What specific HR initiatives might you recommend to top management in order to maintain the success of this strategy through the 1990s? How might the implementation guidelines developed in the early 1980s be revised?

4. You work for an airline that is caught up in the consolidation of that industry. Unless you can control costs in the short run, the long-run viability of the airline may be in jeopardy. What specific HR strategies would you recommend in order to achieve this objective?

REFERENCES

BANAS, P. A. (1988). Employee involvement: A sustained labor/management initiative at the Ford Motor Company. In J. P. Campbell and R. J. Campbell

(Eds.), *Productivity in organizations*. San Francisco: Jossey-Bass, pp. 388–416.

BELLMAN, G. M. (1986). Doing more with less. *Personnel Administrator, 31*, 46–52.

CASCIO, W. F. (1989). Using utility analysis to assess training outcomes. In I. L. Goldstein (Ed.), *Training and development in organizations*. San Francisco: Jossey-Bass, pp. 63–88.

DYER, L., and HOLDER, G. W. (1988). A strategic perspective of human resource management. In L. Dyer and G. W. Holder (Eds.), *Human resource management: Evolving Roles and Responsibilities*. Washington, D.C.: Bureau of National Affairs, pp. 1-1–1-46.

JACKSON, S. E., and SCHULER, R. S. (1990). Human resource planning. *American Psychologist, 45*, 223–239.

JACKSON, S. E., SCHULER, R. S., and RIVERO, J. C. (1989). Organizational characteristics as predictors of personnel practices. *Personnel Psychology, 42*, 727–736.

KANTER, R. M. (1985, Winter). Supporting innovation and venture development in established companies. *Journal of Business Venturing, 1*, 47–60.

MCCOMAS, M. (1986, December 22). How A&P fattens profits by sharing them. *Business Week*, p. 44.

PORTER, M. E. (1985). *Competitive advantage*. New York: Free Press.

SCHROEDER, M. (1988, November 7). Watching the bottom line instead of the clock. *Business Week*, pp. 134, 136.

SCHULER, R. S., and JACKSON, S. E. (1987). Linking competitive strategies with human resource management practices. *Academy of Management Executive, 1* (3), 207–219.

TSUI, A. S., and GOMEZ-MEJIA, L. R. (1988). Evaluating human resource effectiveness. In L. Dyer and G. W. Holder (Eds.), *Human resource management: Evolving Roles and Responsibilities*. Washington, D.C.: Bureau of National Affairs, pp. 1-187–1-227.

Appendix A
The Taylor-Russell Tables

These are tables of the proportion of employees who will be satisfactory among those selected (success ratio) for given values of the proportion of present employees considered satisfactory (base rate), the selection ratio, and *r*.

Proportion of employees considered satisfactory = 0.05

	Selection Ratio										
r	0.05	0.10	0.20	0.30	0.40	0.50	0.60	0.70	0.80	0.90	0.95
0.00	0.05	0.05	0.05	0.05	0.05	0.05	0.05	0.05	0.05	0.05	0.05
0.05	0.06	0.06	0.06	0.06	0.06	0.05	0.05	0.05	0.05	0.05	0.05
0.10	0.07	0.07	0.07	0.06	0.06	0.06	0.06	0.05	0.05	0.05	0.05
0.15	0.09	0.08	0.07	0.07	0.07	0.06	0.06	0.06	0.05	0.05	0.05
0.20	0.11	0.09	0.08	0.08	0.07	0.07	0.06	0.06	0.06	0.05	0.05
0.25	0.12	0.11	0.09	0.08	0.08	0.07	0.07	0.06	0.06	0.05	0.05
0.30	0.14	0.12	0.10	0.09	0.08	0.07	0.07	0.06	0.06	0.05	0.05
0.35	0.17	0.14	0.11	0.10	0.09	0.08	0.07	0.06	0.06	0.05	0.05
0.40	0.19	0.16	0.12	0.10	0.09	0.08	0.07	0.07	0.06	0.05	0.05
0.45	0.22	0.17	0.13	0.11	0.10	0.08	0.08	0.07	0.06	0.06	0.05
0.50	0.24	0.19	0.15	0.12	0.10	0.09	0.08	0.07	0.06	0.06	0.05
0.55	0.28	0.22	0.16	0.13	0.11	0.09	0.08	0.07	0.06	0.06	0.05
0.60	0.31	0.24	0.17	0.13	0.11	0.09	0.08	0.07	0.06	0.06	0.05
0.65	0.35	0.26	0.18	0.14	0.11	0.10	0.08	0.07	0.06	0.06	0.05
0.70	0.39	0.29	0.20	0.15	0.12	0.10	0.08	0.07	0.06	0.06	0.05

Proportion of employees considered satisfactory = 0.05 (cont.)

	Selection Ratio										
r	0.05	0.10	0.20	0.30	0.40	0.50	0.60	0.70	0.80	0.90	0.95
0.75	0.44	0.32	0.21	0.15	0.12	0.10	0.08	0.07	0.06	0.06	0.05
0.80	0.50	0.35	0.22	0.16	0.12	0.10	0.08	0.07	0.06	0.06	0.05
0.85	0.56	0.39	0.23	0.16	0.12	0.10	0.08	0.07	0.06	0.06	0.05
0.90	0.64	0.43	0.24	0.17	0.13	0.10	0.08	0.07	0.06	0.06	0.05
0.95	0.73	0.47	0.25	0.17	0.13	0.10	0.08	0.07	0.06	0.06	0.05
1.00	1.00	0.50	0.25	0.17	0.13	0.10	0.08	0.07	0.06	0.06	0.05

Proportion of employees considered satisfactory = 0.10

	Selection Ratio										
r	0.05	0.10	0.20	0.30	0.40	0.50	0.60	0.70	0.80	0.90	0.95
0.00	0.10	0.10	0.10	0.10	0.10	0.10	0.10	0.10	0.10	0.10	0.10
0.05	0.12	0.12	0.11	0.11	0.11	0.11	0.11	0.10	0.10	0.10	0.10
0.10	0.14	0.13	0.13	0.12	0.12	0.11	0.11	0.11	0.11	0.10	0.10
0.15	0.16	0.15	0.14	0.13	0.13	0.12	0.12	0.11	0.11	0.10	0.10
0.20	0.19	0.17	0.15	0.14	0.14	0.13	0.12	0.12	0.11	0.11	0.10
0.25	0.22	0.19	0.17	0.16	0.14	0.13	0.13	0.12	0.11	0.11	0.10
0.30	0.25	0.22	0.19	0.17	0.15	0.14	0.13	0.12	0.12	0.11	0.10
0.35	0.28	0.24	0.20	0.18	0.16	0.15	0.14	0.13	0.12	0.11	0.10
0.40	0.31	0.27	0.22	0.19	0.17	0.16	0.14	0.13	0.12	0.11	0.10
0.45	0.35	0.29	0.24	0.20	0.18	0.16	0.15	0.13	0.12	0.11	0.10
0.50	0.39	0.32	0.26	0.22	0.19	0.17	0.15	0.13	0.12	0.11	0.11
0.55	0.43	0.36	0.28	0.23	0.20	0.17	0.15	0.14	0.12	0.11	0.11
0.60	0.48	0.39	0.30	0.25	0.21	0.18	0.16	0.14	0.12	0.11	0.11
0.65	0.53	0.43	0.32	0.26	0.22	0.18	0.16	0.14	0.12	0.11	0.11
0.70	0.58	0.47	0.35	0.27	0.22	0.19	0.16	0.14	0.12	0.11	0.11
0.75	0.64	0.51	0.37	0.29	0.23	0.19	0.16	0.14	0.12	0.11	0.11
0.80	0.71	0.56	0.40	0.30	0.24	0.20	0.17	0.14	0.12	0.11	0.11
0.85	0.78	0.62	0.43	0.31	0.25	0.20	0.17	0.14	0.12	0.11	0.11
0.90	0.86	0.69	0.46	0.33	0.25	0.20	0.17	0.14	0.12	0.11	0.11
0.95	0.95	0.78	0.49	0.33	0.25	0.20	0.17	0.14	0.12	0.11	0.11
1.00	1.00	1.00	0.50	0.33	0.25	0.20	0.17	0.14	0.13	0.11	0.11

Proportion of employees considered satisfactory = 0.20

	Selection Ratio										
r	0.05	0.10	0.20	0.30	0.40	0.50	0.60	0.70	0.80	0.90	0.95
0.00	0.20	0.20	0.20	0.20	0.20	0.20	0.20	0.20	0.20	0.20	0.20
0.05	0.23	0.23	0.22	0.22	0.21	0.21	0.21	0.21	0.20	0.20	0.20
0.10	0.26	0.25	0.24	0.23	0.23	0.22	0.22	0.21	0.21	0.21	0.20
0.15	0.30	0.28	0.26	0.25	0.24	0.23	0.23	0.22	0.21	0.21	0.20
0.20	0.33	0.31	0.28	0.27	0.26	0.25	0.24	0.23	0.22	0.21	0.21
0.25	0.37	0.34	0.31	0.29	0.27	0.26	0.24	0.23	0.22	0.21	0.21
0.30	0.41	0.37	0.33	0.30	0.28	0.27	0.25	0.24	0.23	0.21	0.21
0.35	0.45	0.41	0.36	0.32	0.30	0.28	0.26	0.24	0.23	0.22	0.21
0.40	0.49	0.44	0.38	0.34	0.31	0.29	0.27	0.25	0.23	0.22	0.21
0.45	0.54	0.48	0.41	0.36	0.33	0.30	0.28	0.26	0.24	0.22	0.21
0.50	0.59	0.52	0.44	0.38	0.35	0.31	0.29	0.26	0.24	0.22	0.21
0.55	0.63	0.56	0.47	0.41	0.36	0.32	0.29	0.27	0.24	0.22	0.21
0.60	0.68	0.60	0.50	0.43	0.38	0.34	0.30	0.27	0.24	0.22	0.21
0.65	0.73	0.64	0.53	0.45	0.39	0.35	0.31	0.27	0.25	0.22	0.21
0.70	0.79	0.69	0.56	0.48	0.41	0.36	0.31	0.28	0.25	0.22	0.21
0.75	0.84	0.74	0.60	0.50	0.43	0.37	0.32	0.28	0.25	0.22	0.21
0.80	0.89	0.79	0.64	0.53	0.45	0.38	0.33	0.28	0.25	0.22	0.21
0.85	0.94	0.85	0.69	0.56	0.47	0.39	0.33	0.28	0.25	0.22	0.21
0.90	0.98	0.91	0.75	0.60	0.48	0.40	0.33	0.29	0.25	0.22	0.21
0.95	1.00	0.97	0.82	0.64	0.50	0.40	0.33	0.29	0.25	0.22	0.21
1.00	1.00	1.00	1.00	0.67	0.50	0.40	0.33	0.29	0.25	0.22	0.21

Proportion of employees considered satisfactory = 0.30

	Selection Ratio										
r	0.05	0.10	0.20	0.30	0.40	0.50	0.60	0.70	0.80	0.90	0.95
0.00	0.30	0.30	0.30	0.30	0.30	0.30	0.30	0.30	0.30	0.30	0.30
0.05	0.34	0.33	0.33	0.32	0.32	0.31	0.31	0.31	0.31	0.30	0.30
0.10	0.38	0.36	0.35	0.34	0.33	0.33	0.32	0.32	0.31	0.31	0.30
0.15	0.42	0.40	0.38	0.36	0.35	0.34	0.33	0.33	0.32	0.31	0.31
0.20	0.46	0.43	0.40	0.38	0.37	0.36	0.34	0.33	0.32	0.31	0.31
0.25	0.50	0.47	0.43	0.41	0.39	0.37	0.36	0.34	0.33	0.32	0.31
0.30	0.54	0.50	0.46	0.43	0.40	0.38	0.37	0.35	0.33	0.32	0.31
0.35	0.58	0.54	0.49	0.45	0.42	0.40	0.38	0.36	0.34	0.32	0.31
0.40	0.63	0.58	0.51	0.47	0.44	0.41	0.39	0.37	0.34	0.32	0.31
0.45	0.67	0.61	0.55	0.50	0.46	0.43	0.40	0.37	0.35	0.32	0.31

Proportion of employees considered satisfactory = 0.30 (cont.)

	Selection Ratio										
r	0.05	0.10	0.20	0.30	0.40	0.50	0.60	0.70	0.80	0.90	0.95
0.50	0.72	0.65	0.58	0.52	0.48	0.44	0.41	0.38	0.35	0.33	0.31
0.55	0.76	0.69	0.61	0.55	0.50	0.46	0.42	0.39	0.36	0.33	0.31
0.60	0.81	0.74	0.64	0.58	0.52	0.47	0.43	0.40	0.36	0.33	0.31
0.65	0.85	0.78	0.68	0.60	0.54	0.49	0.44	0.40	0.37	0.33	0.32
0.70	0.89	0.82	0.72	0.63	0.57	0.51	0.46	0.41	0.37	0.33	0.32
0.75	0.93	0.86	0.76	0.67	0.59	0.52	0.47	0.42	0.37	0.33	0.32
0.80	0.96	0.90	0.80	0.70	0.62	0.54	0.48	0.42	0.37	0.33	0.32
0.85	0.99	0.94	0.85	0.74	0.65	0.56	0.49	0.43	0.37	0.33	0.32
0.90	1.00	0.98	0.90	0.79	0.68	0.58	0.49	0.43	0.37	0.33	0.32
0.95	1.00	1.00	0.96	0.85	0.72	0.60	0.50	0.43	0.37	0.33	0.32
1.00	1.00	1.00	1.00	1.00	0.75	0.60	0.50	0.43	0.38	0.33	0.32

Proportion of employees considered satisfactory = 0.40

	Selection Ratio										
r	0.05	0.10	0.20	0.30	0.40	0.50	0.60	0.70	0.80	0.90	0.95
0.00	0.40	0.40	0.40	0.40	0.40	0.40	0.40	0.40	0.40	0.40	0.40
0.05	0.44	0.43	0.43	0.42	0.42	0.42	0.41	0.41	0.41	0.40	0.40
0.10	0.48	0.47	0.46	0.45	0.44	0.43	0.42	0.42	0.41	0.41	0.40
0.15	0.52	0.50	0.48	0.47	0.46	0.45	0.44	0.43	0.42	0.41	0.41
0.20	0.57	0.54	0.51	0.49	0.48	0.46	0.45	0.44	0.43	0.41	0.41
0.25	0.61	0.58	0.54	0.51	0.49	0.48	0.46	0.45	0.43	0.42	0.41
0.30	0.65	0.61	0.57	0.54	0.51	0.49	0.47	0.46	0.44	0.42	0.41
0.35	0.69	0.65	0.60	0.56	0.53	0.51	0.49	0.47	0.45	0.42	0.41
0.40	0.73	0.69	0.63	0.59	0.56	0.53	0.50	0.48	0.45	0.43	0.41
0.45	0.77	0.72	0.66	0.61	0.58	0.54	0.51	0.49	0.46	0.43	0.42
0.50	0.81	0.76	0.69	0.64	0.60	0.56	0.53	0.49	0.46	0.43	0.42
0.55	0.85	0.79	0.72	0.67	0.62	0.58	0.54	0.50	0.47	0.44	0.42
0.60	0.89	0.83	0.75	0.69	0.64	0.60	0.55	0.51	0.48	0.44	0.42
0.65	0.92	0.87	0.79	0.72	0.67	0.62	0.57	0.52	0.48	0.44	0.42
0.70	0.95	0.90	0.82	0.76	0.69	0.64	0.58	0.53	0.49	0.44	0.42
0.75	0.97	0.93	0.86	0.79	0.72	0.66	0.60	0.54	0.49	0.44	0.42
0.80	0.99	0.96	0.89	0.82	0.75	0.68	0.61	0.55	0.49	0.44	0.42
0.85	1.00	0.98	0.93	0.86	0.79	0.71	0.63	0.56	0.50	0.44	0.42
0.90	1.00	1.00	0.97	0.91	0.82	0.74	0.65	0.57	0.50	0.44	0.42
0.95	1.00	1.00	0.99	0.96	0.87	0.77	0.66	0.57	0.50	0.44	0.42
1.00	1.00	1.00	1.00	1.00	1.00	0.80	0.67	0.57	0.50	0.44	0.42

Proportion of employees considered satisfactory = 0.50

	Selection Ratio										
r	0.05	0.10	0.20	0.30	0.40	0.50	0.60	0.70	0.80	0.90	0.95
0.00	0.50	0.50	0.50	0.50	0.50	0.50	0.50	0.50	0.50	0.50	0.50
0.05	0.54	0.54	0.53	0.52	0.52	0.52	0.51	0.51	0.51	0.50	0.50
0.10	0.58	0.57	0.56	0.55	0.54	0.53	0.53	0.52	0.51	0.51	0.50
0.15	0.63	0.61	0.58	0.57	0.56	0.55	0.54	0.53	0.52	0.51	0.51
0.20	0.67	0.64	0.61	0.59	0.58	0.56	0.55	0.54	0.53	0.52	0.51
0.25	0.70	0.67	0.64	0.62	0.60	0.58	0.56	0.55	0.54	0.52	0.51
0.30	0.74	0.71	0.67	0.64	0.62	0.60	0.58	0.56	0.54	0.52	0.51
0.35	0.78	0.74	0.70	0.66	0.64	0.61	0.59	0.57	0.55	0.53	0.51
0.40	0.82	0.78	0.73	0.69	0.66	0.63	0.61	0.58	0.56	0.53	0.52
0.45	0.85	0.81	0.75	0.71	0.68	0.65	0.62	0.59	0.56	0.53	0.52
0.50	0.88	0.84	0.78	0.74	0.70	0.67	0.63	0.60	0.57	0.54	0.52
0.55	0.91	0.87	0.81	0.76	0.72	0.69	0.65	0.61	0.58	0.54	0.52
0.60	0.94	0.90	0.84	0.79	0.75	0.70	0.66	0.62	0.59	0.54	0.52
0.65	0.96	0.92	0.87	0.82	0.77	0.73	0.68	0.64	0.59	0.55	0.52
0.70	0.98	0.95	0.90	0.85	0.80	0.75	0.70	0.65	0.60	0.55	0.53
0.75	0.99	0.97	0.92	0.87	0.82	0.77	0.72	0.66	0.61	0.55	0.53
0.80	1.00	0.99	0.95	0.90	0.85	0.80	0.73	0.67	0.61	0.55	0.53
0.85	1.00	0.99	0.97	0.94	0.88	0.82	0.76	0.69	0.62	0.55	0.53
0.90	1.00	1.00	0.99	0.97	0.92	0.86	0.78	0.70	0.62	0.56	0.53
0.95	1.00	1.00	1.00	0.99	0.96	0.90	0.81	0.71	0.63	0.56	0.53
1.00	1.00	1.00	1.00	1.00	1.00	1.00	0.83	0.71	0.63	0.56	0.53

Proportion of employees considered satisfactory = 0.60

	Selection Ratio										
r	0.05	0.10	0.20	0.30	0.40	0.50	0.60	0.70	0.80	0.90	0.95
0.00	0.60	0.60	0.60	0.60	0.60	0.60	0.60	0.60	0.60	0.60	0.60
0.05	0.64	0.63	0.63	0.62	0.62	0.62	0.61	0.61	0.61	0.60	0.60
0.10	0.68	0.67	0.65	0.64	0.64	0.63	0.63	0.62	0.61	0.61	0.60
0.15	0.71	0.70	0.68	0.67	0.66	0.65	0.64	0.63	0.62	0.61	0.61
0.20	0.75	0.73	0.71	0.69	0.67	0.66	0.65	0.64	0.63	0.62	0.61
0.25	0.78	0.76	0.73	0.71	0.69	0.68	0.66	0.65	0.63	0.62	0.61
0.30	0.82	0.79	0.76	0.73	0.71	0.69	0.68	0.66	0.64	0.62	0.61
0.35	0.85	0.82	0.78	0.75	0.73	0.71	0.69	0.67	0.65	0.63	0.62
0.40	0.88	0.85	0.81	0.78	0.75	0.73	0.70	0.68	0.66	0.63	0.62
0.45	0.90	0.87	0.83	0.80	0.77	0.74	0.72	0.69	0.66	0.64	0.62

Proportion of employees considered satisfactory = 0.60

	Selection Ratio (*cont.*)										
r	0.05	0.10	0.20	0.30	0.40	0.50	0.60	0.70	0.80	0.90	0.95
0.50	0.93	0.90	0.86	0.82	0.79	0.76	0.73	0.70	0.67	0.64	0.62
0.55	0.95	0.92	0.88	0.84	0.81	0.78	0.75	0.71	0.68	0.64	0.62
0.60	0.96	0.94	0.90	0.87	0.83	0.80	0.76	0.73	0.69	0.65	0.63
0.65	0.98	0.96	0.92	0.89	0.85	0.82	0.78	0.74	0.70	0.65	0.63
0.70	0.99	0.97	0.94	0.91	0.87	0.84	0.80	0.75	0.71	0.66	0.63
0.75	0.99	0.99	0.96	0.93	0.90	0.86	0.81	0.77	0.71	0.66	0.63
0.80	1.00	0.99	0.98	0.95	0.92	0.88	0.83	0.78	0.72	0.66	0.63
0.85	1.00	1.00	0.99	0.97	0.95	0.91	0.86	0.80	0.73	0.66	0.63
0.90	1.00	1.00	1.00	0.99	0.97	0.94	0.88	0.82	0.74	0.67	0.63
0.95	1.00	1.00	1.00	1.00	0.99	0.97	0.92	0.84	0.75	0.67	0.63
1.00	1.00	1.00	1.00	1.00	1.00	1.00	1.00	0.86	0.75	0.67	0.63

Proportion of employees considered satisfactory = 0.70

	Selection Ratio										
r	0.05	0.10	0.20	0.30	0.40	0.50	0.60	0.70	0.80	0.90	0.95
0.00	0.70	0.70	0.70	0.70	0.70	0.70	0.70	0.70	0.70	0.70	0.70
0.05	0.73	0.73	0.72	0.72	0.72	0.71	0.71	0.71	0.71	0.70	0.70
0.10	0.77	0.76	0.75	0.74	0.73	0.73	0.72	0.72	0.71	0.71	0.70
0.15	0.80	0.79	0.77	0.76	0.75	0.74	0.73	0.73	0.72	0.71	0.71
0.20	0.83	0.81	0.79	0.78	0.77	0.76	0.75	0.74	0.73	0.71	0.71
0.25	0.86	0.84	0.81	0.80	0.78	0.77	0.76	0.75	0.73	0.72	0.71
0.30	0.88	0.86	0.84	0.82	0.80	0.78	0.77	0.75	0.74	0.72	0.71
0.35	0.91	0.89	0.86	0.83	0.82	0.80	0.78	0.76	0.75	0.73	0.71
0.40	0.93	0.91	0.88	0.85	0.83	0.81	0.79	0.77	0.75	0.73	0.72
0.45	0.94	0.93	0.90	0.87	0.85	0.83	0.81	0.78	0.76	0.73	0.72
0.50	0.96	0.94	0.91	0.89	0.87	0.84	0.82	0.80	0.77	0.74	0.72
0.55	0.97	0.96	0.93	0.91	0.88	0.86	0.83	0.81	0.78	0.74	0.72
0.60	0.98	0.97	0.95	0.92	0.90	0.87	0.85	0.82	0.79	0.75	0.73
0.65	0.99	0.98	0.96	0.94	0.92	0.89	0.86	0.83	0.80	0.75	0.73
0.70	1.00	0.99	0.97	0.96	0.93	0.91	0.88	0.84	0.80	0.76	0.73
0.75	1.00	1.00	0.98	0.97	0.95	0.92	0.89	0.86	0.81	0.76	0.73
0.80	1.00	1.00	0.99	0.98	0.97	0.94	0.91	0.87	0.82	0.77	0.73
0.85	1.00	1.00	1.00	0.99	0.98	0.96	0.93	0.89	0.84	0.77	0.74
0.90	1.00	1.00	1.00	1.00	0.99	0.98	0.95	0.91	0.85	0.78	0.74
0.95	1.00	1.00	1.00	1.00	1.00	0.99	0.98	0.94	0.86	0.78	0.74
1.00	1.00	1.00	1.00	1.00	1.00	1.00	1.00	1.00	0.88	0.78	0.74

Proportion of employees considered satisfactory = 0.80

	Selection Ratio										
r	0.05	0.10	0.20	0.30	0.40	0.50	0.60	0.70	0.80	0.90	0.95
0.00	0.80	0.80	0.80	0.80	0.80	0.80	0.80	0.80	0.80	0.80	0.80
0.05	0.83	0.82	0.82	0.82	0.81	0.81	0.81	0.81	0.81	0.80	0.80
0.10	0.85	0.85	0.84	0.83	0.83	0.82	0.82	0.81	0.81	0.81	0.80
0.15	0.88	0.87	0.86	0.85	0.84	0.83	0.83	0.82	0.82	0.81	0.81
0.20	0.90	0.89	0.87	0.86	0.85	0.84	0.84	0.83	0.82	0.81	0.81
0.25	0.92	0.91	0.89	0.88	0.87	0.86	0.85	0.84	0.83	0.82	0.81
0.30	0.94	0.92	0.90	0.89	0.88	0.87	0.86	0.84	0.83	0.82	0.81
0.35	0.95	0.94	0.92	0.90	0.89	0.89	0.87	0.85	0.84	0.82	0.81
0.40	0.96	0.95	0.93	0.92	0.90	0.89	0.88	0.86	0.85	0.83	0.82
0.45	0.97	0.96	0.95	0.93	0.92	0.90	0.89	0.87	0.85	0.83	0.82
0.50	0.98	0.97	0.96	0.94	0.93	0.91	0.90	0.88	0.86	0.84	0.82
0.55	0.99	0.98	0.97	0.95	0.94	0.92	0.91	0.89	0.87	0.84	0.82
0.60	0.99	0.99	0.98	0.96	0.95	0.94	0.92	0.90	0.87	0.84	0.83
0.65	1.00	0.99	0.98	0.97	0.96	0.95	0.93	0.91	0.88	0.85	0.83
0.70	1.00	1.00	0.99	0.98	0.97	0.96	0.94	0.92	0.89	0.85	0.83
0.75	1.00	1.00	1.00	0.99	0.98	0.97	0.95	0.93	0.90	0.86	0.83
0.80	1.00	1.00	1.00	1.00	0.99	0.98	0.96	0.94	0.91	0.87	0.84
0.85	1.00	1.00	1.00	1.00	1.00	0.99	0.98	0.96	0.92	0.87	0.84
0.90	1.00	1.00	1.00	1.00	1.00	1.00	0.99	0.97	0.94	0.88	0.84
0.95	1.00	1.00	1.00	1.00	1.00	1.00	1.00	0.99	0.96	0.89	0.84
1.00	1.00	1.00	1.00	1.00	1.00	1.00	1.00	1.00	1.00	0.89	0.84

Proportion of employees considered satisfactory = 0.90

	Selection Ratio										
r	0.05	0.10	0.20	0.30	0.40	0.50	0.60	0.70	0.80	0.90	0.95
0.00	0.90	0.90	0.90	0.90	0.90	0.90	0.90	0.90	0.90	0.90	0.90
0.05	0.92	0.91	0.91	0.91	0.91	0.91	0.91	0.90	0.90	0.90	0.90
0.10	0.93	0.93	0.92	0.92	0.92	0.91	0.91	0.91	0.91	0.90	0.90
0.15	0.95	0.94	0.93	0.93	0.92	0.92	0.92	0.91	0.91	0.91	0.90
0.20	0.96	0.95	0.94	0.94	0.93	0.93	0.92	0.92	0.91	0.91	0.90
0.25	0.97	0.96	0.95	0.95	0.94	0.93	0.93	0.92	0.92	0.91	0.91
0.30	0.98	0.97	0.96	0.95	0.94	0.94	0.94	0.93	0.92	0.91	0.91
0.35	0.98	0.98	0.97	0.96	0.95	0.95	0.94	0.93	0.93	0.92	0.91
0.40	0.99	0.98	0.98	0.97	0.96	0.95	0.95	0.94	0.93	0.92	0.91
0.45	0.99	0.99	0.98	0.98	0.97	0.96	0.95	0.94	0.93	0.92	0.91

Proportion of employees considered satisfactory = 0.90 (cont.)

	Selection Ratio										
r	0.05	0.10	0.20	0.30	0.40	0.50	0.60	0.70	0.80	0.90	0.95
0.50	1.00	0.99	0.99	0.98	0.97	0.97	0.96	0.95	0.94	0.92	0.92
0.55	1.00	1.00	0.99	0.99	0.98	0.97	0.97	0.96	0.94	0.93	0.92
0.60	1.00	1.00	0.99	0.99	0.99	0.98	0.97	0.96	0.95	0.93	0.92
0.65	1.00	1.00	1.00	0.99	0.99	0.98	0.98	0.97	0.96	0.94	0.92
0.70	1.00	1.00	1.00	1.00	0.99	0.99	0.98	0.97	0.96	0.94	0.93
0.75	1.00	1.00	1.00	1.00	1.00	0.99	0.99	0.98	0.97	0.95	0.93
0.80	1.00	1.00	1.00	1.00	1.00	1.00	0.99	0.99	0.97	0.95	0.93
0.85	1.00	1.00	1.00	1.00	1.00	1.00	1.00	0.99	0.98	0.96	0.94
0.90	1.00	1.00	1.00	1.00	1.00	1.00	1.00	1.00	0.99	0.97	0.94
0.95	1.00	1.00	1.00	1.00	1.00	1.00	1.00	1.00	1.00	0.98	0.94
1.00	1.00	1.00	1.00	1.00	1.00	1.00	1.00	1.00	1.00	1.00	0.95

Source: Taylor, H. C., and Russell, J. T. (1939). The relationship of validity coefficients to the practical effectiveness of tests in selection: Discussion and tables. *Journal of Applied Psychology, 23*, 565–578.

Appendix B
The Naylor-Shine Table for Determining the Increase in Mean Criterion Score Obtained by Using a Selection Device

USING THE TABLE

The following definitions are used in the table:

r_{xy} = validity coefficient

Z_{xi} = cutoff point (score) on the predictor in standard score units

ϕ_i = selection ratio

$\bar{Z}_{yi}$ = mean criterion score (in standard score units) of all cases above cutoff

λ_i = ordinate of normal distribution at Z_{xi}

and the table is based upon the following equation:

$$\bar{Z}_{yi} = r_{xy} \frac{\lambda_i}{\phi_i}$$

Note: The use of the table may differ slightly in the case where r_{xy} is really a multiple regression coefficient. The major difference occurs in the Z_{xi} column. With a single predictor there is no difficulty in expressing a cutoff score in terms of a particular value of X, the predictor variable (thus we use Z_{xi}). However, in the case of multiple predictors, it is no longer feasible to do so, since there are several X variables. The easiest procedure, therefore, is to reduce conceptually the multivariate case to the bivariate case by treating the multiple correlation coefficient as the correlation coefficient between the observed criterion scores (Z_y) and the predicted criterion scores (Z'_y). Thus it becomes possible to talk about cutoff values for the multiple predictor case, but these cutoff scores are expressed in terms of Z'_{yi} values, rather than Z_{xi} values. The only difficulty this creates is that $s^2_{z'y} \neq 1$, but will always be equal to R^2_{xy}, the squared multiple correlation coefficient. Thus, in order to use the tables when r_{xy} is actually a multiple correlation coefficient, it is necessary to transform Z'_{yi} values by

$$Z_{xi} = \frac{Z'_{yi}}{R_{xy}}$$

A table for computing the mean criterion score (Z_{yi}) for the group falling above some cutoff score (Z_{xi})[1]

ϕ_i	Z_{xi}	λ_i	λ_i/ϕ_i	ϕ_i	Z_{xi}	λ_i	λ_i/ϕ_i	ϕ_i	Z_{xi}	λ_i	λ_i/ϕ_i
0.9987	−3.00	0.0044	0.00	0.9974	−2.79	0.0081	0.01	0.9951	−2.58	0.0143	0.01
0.9986	−2.99	0.0046	0.00	0.9973	−2.78	0.0084	0.01	0.9949	−2.57	0.0147	0.01
0.9986	−2.98	0.0047	0.00	0.9972	−2.77	0.0086	0.01	0.9948	−2.56	0.0151	0.02
0.9985	−2.97	0.0048	0.00	0.9971	−2.76	0.0088	0.01	0.9946	−2.55	0.0154	0.02
0.9985	−2.96	0.0050	0.01	0.9970	−2.75	0.0091	0.01	0.9945	−2.54	0.0158	0.02
0.9984	−2.95	0.0051	0.01	0.9969	−2.74	0.0093	0.01	0.9943	−2.53	0.0163	0.02
0.9984	−2.94	0.0053	0.01	0.9968	−2.73	0.0096	0.01	0.9941	−2.52	0.0167	0.02
0.9983	−2.93	0.0055	0.01	0.9967	−2.72	0.0099	0.01	0.9940	−2.51	0.0171	0.02
0.9982	−2.92	0.0056	0.01	0.9966	−2.71	0.0101	0.01	0.9938	−2.50	0.0175	0.02
0.9982	−2.91	0.0058	0.01	0.9965	−2.70	0.0104	0.01	0.9936	−2.49	0.0180	0.02
0.9981	−2.90	0.0060	0.01	0.9964	−2.69	0.0107	0.01	0.9934	−2.48	0.0184	0.02
0.9981	−2.89	0.0061	0.01	0.9963	−2.68	0.0110	0.01	0.9932	−2.47	0.0189	0.02
0.9980	−2.88	0.0063	0.01	0.9962	−2.67	0.0113	0.01	0.9931	−2.46	0.0194	0.02
0.9979	−2.87	0.0065	0.01	0.9961	−2.66	0.0116	0.01	0.9929	−2.45	0.0198	0.02
0.9979	−2.86	0.0067	0.01	0.9960	−2.65	0.0119	0.01	0.9927	−2.44	0.0203	0.02
0.9978	−2.85	0.0069	0.01	0.9959	−2.64	0.0122	0.01	0.9925	−2.43	0.0208	0.02
0.9977	−2.84	0.0071	0.01	0.9957	−2.63	0.0126	0.01	0.9922	−2.42	0.0213	0.02
0.9977	−2.83	0.0073	0.01	0.9956	−2.62	0.0129	0.01	0.9920	−2.41	0.0219	0.02
0.9976	−2.82	0.0075	0.01	0.9955	−2.61	0.0132	0.01	0.9918	−2.40	0.0224	0.02
0.9975	−2.81	0.0077	0.01	0.9953	−2.60	0.0136	0.01	0.9916	−2.39	0.0229	0.02
0.9974	−2.80	0.0079	0.01	0.9952	−2.59	0.0139	0.01	0.9913	−2.38	0.0235	0.02

[1] ϕ_i = proportion above cutoff (selection ratio)
Z_{xi} = predictor cutoff value in standard score form
λ_i = normal curve ordinate at Z_{xi}

A table for computing the mean criterion score (Z_{yi}) for the group falling above some cutoff score (Z_{xi})[1] (cont'd.)

ϕ_i	Z_{xi}	λ_i	λ_i/ϕ_i	ϕ_i	Z_{xi}	λ_i	λ_i/ϕ_i	ϕ_i	Z_{xi}	λ_i	λ_i/ϕ_i
0.9911	−2.37	0.0241	0.02	0.9834	−2.13	0.0413	0.04	0.9706	−1.89	0.0669	0.07
0.9909	−2.36	0.0246	0.02	0.9830	−2.12	0.0422	0.04	0.9699	−1.88	0.0681	0.07
0.9906	−2.35	0.0252	0.03	0.9826	−2.11	0.0431	0.04	0.9693	−1.87	0.0694	0.07
0.9904	−2.34	0.0258	0.03	0.9821	−2.10	0.0440	0.04	0.9686	−1.86	0.0707	0.07
0.9901	−2.33	0.0264	0.03	0.9817	−2.09	0.0449	0.05	0.9678	−1.85	0.0721	0.07
0.9898	−2.32	0.0270	0.03	0.9812	−2.08	0.0459	0.05	0.9671	−1.84	0.0734	0.08
0.9896	−2.31	0.0277	0.03	0.9808	−2.07	0.0468	0.05	0.9664	−1.83	0.0748	0.08
0.9893	−2.30	0.0283	0.03	0.9803	−2.06	0.0478	0.05	0.9656	−1.82	0.0761	0.08
0.9890	−2.29	0.0290	0.03	0.9798	−2.05	0.0488	0.05	0.9649	−1.81	0.0775	0.08
0.9887	−2.28	0.0297	0.03	0.9793	−2.04	0.0498	0.05	0.9641	−1.80	0.0790	0.08
0.9884	−2.27	0.0303	0.03	0.9788	−2.03	0.0508	0.05	0.9633	−1.79	0.0804	0.08
0.9881	−2.26	0.0310	0.03	0.9783	−2.02	0.0519	0.05	0.9625	−1.78	0.0818	0.08
0.9878	−2.25	0.0317	0.03	0.9778	−2.01	0.0529	0.05	0.9616	−1.77	0.0833	0.09
0.9875	−2.24	0.0325	0.03	0.9772	−2.00	0.0540	0.06	0.9608	−1.76	0.0848	0.09
0.9871	−2.23	0.0332	0.03	0.9767	−1.99	0.0551	0.06	0.9599	−1.75	0.0863	0.09
0.9868	−2.22	0.0339	0.03	0.9761	−1.98	0.0562	0.06	0.9591	−1.74	0.0878	0.09
0.9864	−2.21	0.0347	0.04	0.9756	−1.97	0.0573	0.06	0.9582	−1.73	0.0893	0.09
0.9861	−2.20	0.0355	0.04	0.9750	−1.96	0.0584	0.06	0.9573	−1.72	0.0909	0.09
0.9857	−2.19	0.0363	0.04	0.9744	−1.95	0.0596	0.06	0.9564	−1.71	0.0925	0.10
0.9854	−2.18	0.0371	0.04	0.9738	−1.94	0.0608	0.06	0.9554	−1.70	0.0940	0.10
0.9850	−2.17	0.0379	0.04	0.9732	−1.93	0.0620	0.06	0.9545	−1.69	0.0957	0.10
0.9846	−2.16	0.0387	0.04	0.9726	−1.92	0.0632	0.06	0.9535	−1.68	0.0973	0.10
0.9842	−2.15	0.0396	0.04	0.9719	−1.91	0.0644	0.07	0.9525	−1.67	0.0989	0.10
0.9838	−2.14	0.0404	0.04	0.9713	−1.90	0.0656	0.07	0.9515	−1.66	0.1006	0.11

0.9505	−1.65	0.1023	0.11	0.9192	−1.40	0.1497	0.16	0.8749	−1.15	0.2059	0.24
0.9495	−1.64	0.1040	0.11	0.9177	−1.39	0.1518	0.17	0.8729	−1.14	0.2083	0.24
0.9484	−1.63	0.1057	0.11	0.9162	−1.38	0.1539	0.17	0.8708	−1.13	0.2107	0.24
0.9474	−1.62	0.1074	0.11	0.9147	−1.37	0.1561	0.17	0.8686	−1.12	0.2131	0.25
0.9463	−1.61	0.1092	0.12	0.9131	−1.36	0.1582	0.17	0.8665	−1.11	0.2155	0.25
0.9452	−1.60	0.1109	0.12	0.9115	−1.35	0.1604	0.18	0.8643	−1.10	0.2179	0.25
0.9441	−1.59	0.1127	0.12	0.9099	−1.34	0.1626	0.18	0.8621	−1.09	0.2203	0.26
0.9429	−1.58	0.1145	0.12	0.9082	−1.33	0.1647	0.18	0.8599	−1.08	0.2227	0.26
0.9418	−1.57	0.1163	0.12	0.9066	−1.32	0.1669	0.18	0.8577	−1.07	0.2251	0.26
0.9406	−1.56	0.1182	0.13	0.9049	−1.31	0.1691	0.19	0.8554	−1.06	0.2275	0.27
0.9394	−1.55	0.1200	0.13	0.9032	−1.30	0.1714	0.19	0.8531	−1.05	0.2299	0.27
0.9382	−1.54	0.1219	0.13	0.9015	−1.29	0.1736	0.19	0.8508	−1.04	0.2323	0.27
0.9370	−1.53	0.1238	0.13	0.8997	−1.28	0.1758	0.20	0.8485	−1.03	0.2347	0.28
0.9357	−1.52	0.1257	0.13	0.8980	−1.27	0.1781	0.20	0.8461	−1.02	0.2371	0.28
0.9345	−1.51	0.1276	0.14	0.8962	−1.26	0.1804	0.20	0.8438	−1.01	0.2396	0.28
0.9332	−1.50	0.1295	0.14	0.8944	−1.25	0.1826	0.20	0.8413	−1.00	0.2420	0.29
0.9319	−1.49	0.1315	0.14	0.8925	−1.24	0.1849	0.21	0.8389	−0.99	0.2444	0.29
0.9306	−1.48	0.1334	0.14	0.8907	−1.23	0.1872	0.21	0.8365	−0.98	0.2468	0.30
0.9292	−1.47	0.1354	0.15	0.8888	−1.22	0.1895	0.21	0.8340	−0.97	0.2492	0.30
0.9279	−1.46	0.1374	0.15	0.8869	−1.21	0.1919	0.22	0.8315	−0.96	0.2516	0.30
0.9265	−1.45	0.1394	0.15	0.8849	−1.20	0.1942	0.22	0.8289	−0.95	0.2541	0.31
0.9251	−1.44	0.1415	0.15	0.8830	−1.19	0.1965	0.22	0.8264	−0.94	0.2565	0.31
0.9236	−1.43	0.1435	0.16	0.8810	−1.18	0.1989	0.23	0.8238	−0.93	0.2589	0.31
0.9222	−1.42	0.1456	0.16	0.8790	−1.17	0.2012	0.23	0.8212	−0.92	0.2613	0.32
0.9207	−1.41	0.1476	0.16	0.8770	−1.16	0.2036	0.23	0.8186	−0.91	0.2637	0.32

[1] ϕ_i = proportion above cutoff (selection ratio)
Z_{xi} = predictor cutoff value in standard score form
λ_i = normal curve ordinate at Z_{xi}

A table for computing the mean criterion score (Z_{yi}) for the group falling above some cutoff score (Z_{xi})[1] (cont'd.)

ϕ_i	Z_{xi}	λ_i	λ_i/ϕ_i	ϕ_i	Z_{xi}	λ_i	λ_i/ϕ_i	ϕ_i	Z_{xi}	λ_i	λ_i/ϕ_i
0.8159	−0.90	0.2661	0.33	0.7454	−0.66	0.3209	0.43	0.6628	−0.42	0.3653	0.55
0.8133	−0.89	0.2685	0.33	0.7422	−0.65	0.3230	0.44	0.6591	−0.41	0.3668	0.56
0.8106	−0.88	0.2709	0.33	0.7389	−0.64	0.3251	0.44	0.6554	−0.40	0.3683	0.56
0.8078	−0.87	0.2732	0.34	0.7357	−0.63	0.3271	0.44	0.6517	−0.39	0.3697	0.57
0.8051	−0.86	0.2756	0.34	0.7324	−0.62	0.3292	0.45	0.6480	−0.38	0.3712	0.57
0.8023	−0.85	0.2780	0.35	0.7291	−0.61	0.3312	0.45	0.6443	−0.37	0.3725	0.58
0.7995	−0.84	0.2803	0.35	0.7257	−0.60	0.3332	0.46	0.6406	−0.36	0.3739	0.58
0.7967	−0.83	0.2827	0.35	0.7224	−0.59	0.3352	0.46	0.6368	−0.35	0.3752	0.59
0.7939	−0.82	0.2850	0.36	0.7190	−0.58	0.3372	0.47	0.6331	−0.34	0.3765	0.59
0.7910	−0.81	0.2874	0.36	0.7157	−0.57	0.3391	0.47	0.6293	−0.33	0.3778	0.60
0.7881	−0.80	0.2897	0.37	0.7123	−0.56	0.3410	0.48	0.6255	−0.32	0.3790	0.61
0.7852	−0.79	0.2920	0.37	0.7088	−0.55	0.3429	0.48	0.6217	−0.31	0.3802	0.61
0.7823	−0.78	0.2943	0.38	0.7054	−0.54	0.3448	0.49	0.6179	−0.30	0.3814	0.62
0.7794	−0.77	0.2966	0.38	0.7019	−0.53	0.3467	0.49	0.6141	−0.29	0.3825	0.62
0.7764	−0.76	0.2989	0.38	0.6985	−0.52	0.3485	0.50	0.6103	−0.28	0.3836	0.63
0.7734	−0.75	0.3011	0.39	0.6950	−0.51	0.3503	0.50	0.6064	−0.27	0.3847	0.64
0.7704	−0.74	0.3034	0.39	0.6915	−0.50	0.3521	0.51	0.6026	−0.26	0.3857	0.64
0.7673	−0.73	0.3056	0.40	0.6879	−0.49	0.3538	0.51	0.5987	−0.25	0.3867	0.65
0.7642	−0.72	0.3079	0.40	0.6844	−0.48	0.3555	0.52	0.5948	−0.24	0.3876	0.65
0.7611	−0.71	0.3101	0.41	0.6808	−0.47	0.3572	0.52	0.5910	−0.23	0.3885	0.66
0.7580	−0.70	0.3123	0.41	0.6772	−0.46	0.3589	0.53	0.5871	−0.22	0.3894	0.66
0.7549	−0.69	0.3144	0.42	0.6736	−0.45	0.3605	0.54	0.5832	−0.21	0.3902	0.67
0.7517	−0.68	0.3166	0.42	0.6700	−0.44	0.3621	0.54	0.5793	−0.20	0.3910	0.67
0.7486	−0.67	0.3187	0.43	0.6664	−0.43	0.3637	0.55	0.5753	−0.19	0.3918	0.68
0.5714	−0.18	0.3925	0.69	0.4721	0.07	0.3980	0.84	0.3745	0.32	0.3790	1.01

0.5675	−0.17	0.3932	0.69	0.4681	0.08	0.3977	0.85	0.3707	0.33	0.3778	1.02
0.5636	−0.16	0.3939	0.70	0.4641	0.09	0.3973	0.86	0.3669	0.34	0.3765	1.03
0.5596	−0.15	0.3945	0.70	0.4602	0.10	0.3970	0.86	0.3632	0.35	0.3752	1.03
0.5557	−0.14	0.3951	0.71	0.4562	0.11	0.3965	0.87	0.3594	0.36	0.3739	1.04
0.5517	−0.13	0.3956	0.72	0.4522	0.12	0.3961	0.88	0.3557	0.37	0.3725	1.05
0.5478	−0.12	0.3961	0.72	0.4483	0.13	0.3956	0.88	0.3520	0.38	0.3712	1.05
0.5438	−0.11	0.3965	0.73	0.4443	0.14	0.3951	0.89	0.3483	0.39	0.3697	1.06
0.5398	−0.10	0.3970	0.74	0.4404	0.15	0.3945	0.90	0.3446	0.40	0.3683	1.07
0.5359	−0.09	0.3973	0.74	0.4364	0.16	0.3939	0.90	0.3409	0.41	0.3668	1.08
0.5319	−0.08	0.3977	0.75	0.4325	0.17	0.3932	0.91	0.3372	0.42	0.3653	1.08
0.5279	−0.07	0.3980	0.75	0.4286	0.18	0.3925	0.92	0.3336	0.43	0.3637	1.09
0.5239	−0.06	0.3982	0.76	0.4247	0.19	0.3918	0.92	0.3300	0.44	0.3621	1.10
0.5199	−0.05	0.3984	0.77	0.4207	0.20	0.3910	0.93	0.3264	0.45	0.3605	1.10
0.5160	−0.04	0.3986	0.77	0.4168	0.21	0.3902	0.94	0.3228	0.46	0.3589	1.11
0.5120	−0.03	0.3988	0.78	0.4129	0.22	0.3894	0.94	0.3192	0.47	0.3572	1.12
0.5080	−0.02	0.3989	0.79	0.4090	0.23	0.3885	0.95	0.3156	0.48	0.3555	1.13
0.5040	−0.01	0.3989	0.79	0.4052	0.24	0.3876	0.96	0.3121	0.49	0.3538	1.13
0.5000	0.00	0.3989	0.80	0.4013	0.25	0.3867	0.96	0.3085	0.50	0.3521	1.14
0.4960	0.01	0.3989	0.80	0.3974	0.26	0.3857	0.97	0.3050	0.51	0.3503	1.15
0.4920	0.02	0.3989	0.81	0.3936	0.27	0.3847	0.98	0.3015	0.52	0.3485	1.16
0.4880	0.03	0.3988	0.82	0.3897	0.28	0.3836	0.98	0.2981	0.53	0.3467	1.16
0.4840	0.04	0.3986	0.82	0.3859	0.29	0.3825	0.99	0.2946	0.54	0.3448	1.17
0.4801	0.05	0.3984	0.83	0.3821	0.30	0.3814	1.00	0.2912	0.55	0.3429	1.18
0.4761	0.06	0.3982	0.84	0.3783	0.31	0.3802	1.01	0.2877	0.56	0.3410	1.19

[1]ϕ_i = proportion above cutoff (selection ratio)
Z_{xi} = predictor cutoff value in standard score form
λ_i = normal curve ordinate at Z_{xi}

A table for computing the mean criterion score (Z_{yi}) for the group falling above some cutoff score (Z_{xi})[1] (cont'd.)

ϕ_i	Z_{xi}	λ_i	λ_i/ϕ_i	ϕ_i	Z_{xi}	λ_i	λ_i/ϕ_i	ϕ_i	Z_{xi}	λ_i	λ_i/ϕ_i
0.2843	0.57	0.3391	1.19	0.2090	0.81	0.2874	1.38	0.1469	1.05	0.2299	1.57
0.2810	0.58	0.3372	1.20	0.2061	0.82	0.2850	1.38	0.1446	1.06	0.2275	1.57
0.2776	0.59	0.3352	1.21	0.2033	0.83	0.2827	1.39	0.1423	1.07	0.2251	1.58
0.2743	0.60	0.3332	1.21	0.2005	0.84	0.2803	1.40	0.1401	1.08	0.2227	1.59
0.2709	0.61	0.3212	1.22	0.1977	0.85	0.2780	1.41	0.1379	1.09	0.2203	1.60
0.2676	0.62	0.3292	1.23	0.1949	0.86	0.2756	1.41	0.1357	1.10	0.2179	1.61
0.2643	0.63	0.3271	1.24	0.1922	0.87	0.2732	1.42	0.1335	1.11	0.2155	1.61
0.2611	0.64	0.3251	1.25	0.1894	0.88	0.2709	1.43	0.1314	1.12	0.2131	1.62
0.2578	0.65	0.3230	1.25	0.1867	0.89	0.2685	1.44	0.1292	1.13	0.2107	1.63
0.2546	0.66	0.3209	1.26	0.1841	0.90	0.2661	1.45	0.1271	1.14	0.2083	1.64
0.2514	0.67	0.3187	1.27	0.1814	0.91	0.2637	1.45	0.1251	1.15	0.2059	1.65
0.2483	0.68	0.3166	1.28	0.1788	0.92	0.2613	1.46	0.1230	1.16	0.2036	1.66
0.2451	0.69	0.3144	1.28	0.1762	0.93	0.2589	1.47	0.1210	1.17	0.2012	1.66
0.2420	0.70	0.3123	1.29	0.1736	0.94	0.2565	1.48	0.1190	1.18	0.1989	1.67
0.2389	0.71	0.3101	1.30	0.1711	0.95	0.2541	1.49	0.1170	1.19	0.1965	1.68
0.2358	0.72	0.3079	1.31	0.1685	0.96	0.2516	1.49	0.1151	1.20	0.1942	1.69
0.2327	0.73	0.3056	1.31	0.1660	0.97	0.2492	1.50	0.1131	1.21	0.1919	1.70
0.2296	0.74	0.3034	1.32	0.1635	0.98	0.2468	1.51	0.1112	1.22	0.1895	1.70
0.2266	0.75	0.3011	1.33	0.1611	0.99	0.2444	1.52	0.1093	1.23	0.1872	1.71
0.2236	0.76	0.2989	1.34	0.1587	1.00	0.2420	1.52	0.1075	1.24	0.1849	1.72
0.2206	0.77	0.2966	1.34	0.1562	1.01	0.2396	1.53	0.1056	1.25	0.1826	1.73
0.2177	0.78	0.2943	1.35	0.1539	1.02	0.2371	1.54	0.1038	1.26	0.1804	1.74
0.2148	0.79	0.2920	1.36	0.1515	1.03	0.2347	1.55	0.1020	1.27	0.1781	1.75
0.2119	0.80	0.2897	1.37	0.1492	1.04	0.2323	1.56	0.1003	1.28	0.1758	1.75
0.0985	1.29	0.1736	1.76	0.0618	1.54	0.1219	1.97	0.0367	1.79	0.0804	2.19

0.0968	1.30	0.1714	1.77	0.0606	1.55	0.1200	1.98	0.0359	1.80	0.0790	2.20
0.0951	1.31	0.1691	1.78	0.0594	1.56	0.1182	1.99	0.0351	1.81	0.0775	2.21
0.0934	1.32	0.1669	1.79	0.0582	1.57	0.1163	2.00	0.0344	1.82	0.0761	2.21
0.0918	1.33	0.1647	1.79	0.0571	1.58	0.1145	2.01	0.0336	1.83	0.0748	2.23
0.0901	1.34	0.1626	1.80	0.0559	1.59	0.1127	2.02	0.0329	1.84	0.0734	2.23
0.0885	1.35	0.1604	1.81	0.0548	1.60	0.1109	2.02	0.0322	1.85	0.0721	2.24
0.0869	1.36	0.1582	1.82	0.0537	1.61	0.1092	2.03	0.0314	1.86	0.0707	2.25
0.0853	1.37	0.1561	1.83	0.0526	1.62	0.1074	2.04	0.0307	1.87	0.0694	2.26
0.0838	1.38	0.1539	1.84	0.0516	1.63	0.1057	2.05	0.0301	1.88	0.0681	2.26
0.0823	1.39	0.1518	1.84	0.0505	1.64	0.1040	2.06	0.0294	1.89	0.0669	2.28
0.0808	1.40	0.1497	1.85	0.0495	1.65	0.1023	2.07	0.0287	1.90	0.0656	2.29
0.0793	1.41	0.1476	1.86	0.0485	1.66	0.1006	2.07	0.0281	1.91	0.0644	2.29
0.0778	1.42	0.1456	1.87	0.0475	1.67	0.0989	2.08	0.0274	1.92	0.0632	2.31
0.0764	1.43	0.1435	1.88	0.0465	1.68	0.0973	2.09	0.0268	1.93	0.0620	2.31
0.0749	1.44	0.1415	1.89	0.0455	1.69	0.0957	2.10	0.0262	1.94	0.0608	2.32
0.0735	1.45	0.1394	1.90	0.0446	1.70	0.0940	2.11	0.0256	1.95	0.0596	2.33
0.0721	1.46	0.1374	1.91	0.0436	1.71	0.0925	2.12	0.0250	1.96	0.0584	2.34
0.0708	1.47	0.1354	1.91	0.0427	1.72	0.0909	2.13	0.0244	1.97	0.0573	2.35
0.0694	1.48	0.1334	1.92	0.0418	1.73	0.0893	2.14	0.0239	1.98	0.0562	2.35
0.0681	1.49	0.1315	1.93	0.0409	1.74	0.0878	2.15	0.0233	1.99	0.0551	2.36
0.0668	1.50	0.1295	1.94	0.0401	1.75	0.0863	2.15	0.0228	2.00	0.0540	2.37
0.0655	1.51	0.1276	1.95	0.0392	1.76	0.0848	2.16	0.0222	2.01	0.0529	2.38
0.0643	1.52	0.1257	1.95	0.0384	1.77	0.0833	2.17	0.0217	2.02	0.0519	2.39
0.0630	1.53	0.1238	1.97	0.0375	1.78	0.0818	2.18	0.0212	2.03	0.0508	2.40

[1]ϕ_i = proportion above cutoff (selection ratio)

Z_{xi} = predictor cutoff value in standard score form

λ_i = normal curve ordinate at Z_{xi}

A table for computing the mean criterion score (Z_{yi}) for the group falling above some cutoff score (Z_{xi})[1] (cont'd.)

ϕ_i	Z_{xi}	λ_i	λ_i/ϕ_i	ϕ_i	Z_{xi}	λ_i	λ_i/ϕ_i	ϕ_i	Z_{xi}	λ_i	λ_i/ϕ_i
0.0207	2.04	0.0498	2.41	0.0113	2.28	0.0297	2.63	0.0059	2.52	0.0167	2.84
0.0202	2.05	0.0488	2.42	0.0110	2.29	0.0290	2.64	0.0057	2.53	0.0163	2.85
0.0197	2.06	0.0478	2.43	0.0107	2.30	0.0283	2.64	0.0055	2.54	0.0158	2.86
0.0192	2.07	0.0468	2.44	0.0104	2.31	0.0277	2.65	0.0054	2.55	0.0154	2.87
0.0188	2.08	0.0459	2.44	0.0102	2.32	0.0270	2.66	0.0052	2.56	0.0151	2.88
0.0183	2.09	0.0449	2.45	0.0099	2.33	0.0264	2.67	0.0051	2.57	0.0147	2.89
0.0179	2.10	0.0440	2.46	0.0096	2.34	0.0258	2.68	0.0049	2.58	0.0143	2.90
0.0174	2.11	0.0431	2.48	0.0094	2.35	0.0252	2.68	0.0048	2.59	0.0139	2.90
0.0170	2.12	0.0422	2.48	0.0091	2.36	0.0246	2.69	0.0047	2.60	0.0136	2.91
0.0166	2.13	0.0413	2.49	0.0089	2.37	0.0241	2.71	0.0045	2.61	0.0132	2.92
0.0162	2.14	0.0404	2.49	0.0087	2.38	0.0235	2.71	0.0044	2.62	0.0129	2.93
0.0158	2.15	0.0396	2.51	0.0084	2.39	0.0229	2.72	0.0043	2.63	0.0126	2.94
0.0154	2.16	0.0387	2.51	0.0082	2.40	0.0224	2.73	0.0041	2.64	0.0122	2.95
0.0150	2.17	0.0379	2.53	0.0080	2.41	0.0219	2.74	0.0040	2.65	0.0119	2.96
0.0146	2.18	0.0371	2.54	0.0078	2.42	0.0213	2.74	0.0039	2.66	0.0116	2.97
0.0143	2.19	0.0363	2.54	0.0075	2.43	0.0208	2.76	0.0038	2.67	0.0113	2.98
0.0139	2.20	0.0355	2.55	0.0073	2.44	0.0203	2.76	0.0037	2.68	0.0110	2.99
0.0136	2.21	0.0347	2.55	0.0071	2.45	0.0198	2.77	0.0036	2.69	0.0107	3.00
0.0132	2.22	0.0339	2.57	0.0069	2.46	0.0194	2.79	0.0035	2.70	0.0104	3.01
0.0129	2.23	0.0332	2.57	0.0068	2.47	0.0189	2.80	0.0034	2.71	0.0101	3.01
0.0125	2.24	0.0325	2.60	0.0066	2.48	0.0184	2.80	0.0033	2.72	0.0099	3.02
0.0122	2.25	0.0317	2.60	0.0064	2.49	0.0180	2.82	0.0032	2.73	0.0096	3.03
0.0119	2.26	0.0310	2.61	0.0062	2.50	0.0175	2.82	0.0031	2.74	0.0093	3.04
0.0116	2.27	0.0303	2.61	0.0060	2.51	0.0171	2.83	0.0030	2.75	0.0091	3.05

0.0029	2.76	0.0088	3.06	0.0022	2.85	0.0069	3.14	0.0016	2.94	0.0053	3.23
0.0028	2.77	0.0086	3.07	0.0021	2.86	0.0067	3.15	0.0016	2.95	0.0051	3.24
0.0027	2.78	0.0084	3.08	0.0021	2.87	0.0065	3.16	0.0015	2.96	0.0050	3.25
0.0026	2.79	0.0081	3.09	0.0020	2.88	0.0063	3.17	0.0015	2.97	0.0048	3.26
0.0026	2.80	0.0079	3.10	0.0019	2.89	0.0061	3.18	0.0014	2.98	0.0047	3.26
0.0025	2.81	0.0077	3.11	0.0019	2.90	0.0060	3.19	0.0014	2.99	0.0046	3.27
0.0024	2.82	0.0075	3.12	0.0018	2.91	0.0058	3.20	0.0013	3.00	0.0044	3.28
0.0023	2.83	0.0073	3.13	0.0018	2.92	0.0056	3.21				
0.0023	2.84	0.0071	3.13	0.0017	2.93	0.0055	3.22				

[1]ϕ_i = proportion above cutoff (selection ratio)
Z_{xi} = predictor cutoff value in standard score form
λ_i = normal curve ordinate at Z_{xi}

Source: Naylor, J. C., and Shine, L. C. (1965). A table for determining the increase in mean criterion score obtained by using a selection device. *Journal of Industrial Psychology*, *3*, 33–42. Used by permission.

Index

Aberth, J., 117, 119, 127
Absenteeism
  aggregate cost of, 58
  costing of, 60–69
  definition, 59, 75
  due to smoking, 84, 85
  incremental, 84
  management of, 71–77
  no-fault, 73–76
Absenteeism costs, interpretation of, 69–71
Absenteeism rate, computation of, 60
Additive cohort effects, 241
Adolph Coors Company, 115, 123
Affirmative action, 11, 12
AFL-CIO, 48, 94
Ajzen, I., 30, 146
Alcohol abuse, firm-level cost of, 106–108
Alexander, R. A., 227, 246, 255
Allan, W., 71, 79
Ameiss, R. P., 12
American Airlines, 48
American Cancer Society, 117, 118
American Heart Association, 117
American Lung Association, 90, 92, 97
American Telephone and Telegraph Company, 111, 245
Andrews, C., 114, 116, 118, 129
A priori population, 192
Arvey, R. D., 258, 279
Ashbach, N. W., 19, 57
Asher, J. J., 47, 56
Assessment center, utility of, 198, 245–251
At-risk employees, 116
Attitude–cost models (table), 144–145
Attitudes
  behavior costing of, 134–145
  definition, 130
  elements of, 130
  financial impact of changes in, 130–145
  human asset valuation of, 134, 135, 144
  relation to behavior, 130, 131
  unit cost valuation, 135, 136, 144

Background investigations, cost of, 29
Baker, G. M. N., 3–5
Banas, P. A., 285–287, 289, 294
Barrick, M. R., 246, 255
Bartol, K. M., 42, 43, 57
Base compensation, cost of, 152–158
Base rate, 180–184
Becker, B. E., 237, 255
Becker, G. S., 39, 56
Bednarek, R. J., 108, 128
Behavior costing
  of attitudes, 136–143, 145
  general approach, 7–9
  objective of, 21
Bellman, G. M., 282, 294
Benefits
  effect of roll-up costs, 156–163

hourly cost of, 164–166
as a percentage of payroll, 65
Benefits administration, 9, 10
Bensinger, A., 109, 127
Bentson, C., 255
Berger, F., 6, 15
Berkelman, R., 129
Berol Corporation, 117
Bivariate normal relationships, 185
Blue Cross and Blue Shield of Indiana, 124
Blum, M. L., 180
Bobko, P., 213, 226, 252, 255
Boeing Company, 93
Boudreau, J. W., 181, 188, 192, 200, 209, 213, 220, 224, 226, 233, 239–244, 246, 251–253, 255, 276, 279
Bowers, D. G., 135, 142, 147
Bray, D. W., 245, 255
Break-even analysis, 251–254
use in HRD programs, 275, 278
Brealey, R., 177, 200
Bridging pay, 13
Brogden, H. E., 1, 7, 15, 179, 188, 189, 192, 194, 197, 200, 202, 203, 226, 250, 255
Brogden-Cronbach-Gleser model, 188–195, 197, 198, 232, 235, 245
Brummet, R. L., 3, 15
Burden adjustment, 205, 206
Burke, M. J., 202, 213, 220, 226, 227, 250, 255, 274, 279
Bycio, P., 59, 79
Byram, G., 111, 129

Caldwell, P., 285, 287, 289
Calkins, D., 82, 86, 87, 97
Campbell, D. T., 258, 274, 280
Campbell, J. P., 131, 146
Campbell, R. J., 131, 146
Cascio, W. F., 29, 41, 46, 47, 52, 57, 125, 129, 195, 198, 200, 201, 208, 213, 214, 227, 229, 245, 247, 249–253, 255, 258, 274, 279, 280, 290, 294
Cascio-Ramos estimate of performance in dollars (CREPID), 213–221
Caspersen, C. J., 129
Chaiken, S., 131, 146
Chandler, W. U., 82, 97
Cherskov, M., 103, 127
Chrysler Corporation, 114
Cochran, W. G., 193, 200
Coefficient
multiple regression, 186
zero-order correlation, 186
Coff, R., 4, 15
Cole, D. A., 258, 279
Collective bargaining
computer and, 166–170
contracts, financial implications of, 150, 151
give-back strategy, 76
Compa-ratio, 38, 39
Compensation
hourly cost of, 164–166
policies, 9
total, 165
as turnover reduction strategy, 49
Competitive strategy, 288–293
Computers, role in collective bargaining, 166–170
Consolidated annual leave, 77
Continuous variable, 188
Contribution margin, 208
Control Data Corporation, 122
Cook, T. D., 258, 274, 280
Corey, P., 129
Corning Glass Works, 19, 290
Correlation coefficient, zero-order, 186
Cost accounting, use in estimating SD_y, 197, 198, 202–208, 210
Cost–benefit analysis, 120
model of training, 267–271
Cost–effectiveness analysis, 119
Costing out, 151
Cost of attaining personnel requirements (CAPER), model, 196
Cost-of-living adjustments, 166, 167
Cost of selection, use in utility analysis, 188, 189, 191, 192, 250
Cost of testing, 191, 192, 231
Cost-reduction strategy, 288, 291–293
Costs
direct, 117
fixed, 7, 33, 205, 233, 267, 268
indirect, 72, 73, 117
opportunity, 39, 47, 70, 71, 133

Costs (*cont.*)
outlay, 7
replacement 19, 22, 29–35
separation, 23–29
time, 7
variable, 7, 133, 136, 138, 205, 233, 239–241, 267, 268
Cox, M. H., 124, 125, 127
Cronbach, L. J., 1, 177, 179, 192–194, 200, 202, 208, 227, 233, 255
Cronshaw, S. F., 227
Crump, C. E., 115, 116, 121, 123–125, 128
Cullen, J. G., 262, 266–268, 280
Cunningham, J. B., 50, 56
Cut-off scores, 181–184, 196, 237

Dalton, D. R., 41, 56
Day, R. R., 274, 279
Delphi method, 275
Depreciation, 90
DeSimone, R. L., 213, 227
Devadas, R., 147
Dickman, F., 105, 127
Difference in performance (DP), 38–41
DiGiuseppe, R., 128
DiMattia, D. J., 128
Discipline without punishment, 71, 72
Discounting, effect on utility, 239–241, 276, 277
Discount rate, 240, 241, 276
Dollar criterion, 7, 197, 202, 203
Driessnack, C. H., 9, 11, 12
Drug tests, costs of, 32
Dubroff, H., 149, 173
DuPont, 119
Dyer, L., 2, 15, 284, 285, 294

Eaton, N. K., 221, 222, 224, 227
Ebbesen, E. B., 148
Eberle, T., 50, 56
Economic factors, effect on HRD programs, 276–278
Edwards, J. E., 220, 227
Effect size, 272–275
Effect size, relation to other statistics, 274, 275
Eicher, D., 74, 79
Electronic Data Systems Corporation, 48
Emener, W. G., 105, 127
Employee assistance programs
absenteeism, savings from, 110
accidents, savings from, 111
attributes and costs, 105
definition, 104
difficulties in evaluating, 106, 107
future of, 125, 126
insurance benefits savings, 112, 113
prevalence of, 105
productivity losses from troubled employees, 106–108
substance abuse treatment, 109, 110
supervisors' time, savings in, 110, 111
training and replacement cost savings, 111, 112
turnover, savings from, 108, 109
unemployment compensation, savings from, 109
Employee flows
effect on HRD programs, 276, 277
effect on utility, 241–245
Employee involvement, 285–288
Equal Employment Opportunity Commission (EEOC), 11
Erfurt, J., 128
Erroneous acceptance and rejections, 183, 184
Eta, the correlation ratio, 142
Evaluation, ex-ante versus ex-post, 106
Everly, G. S., Jr., 129
Exit interviews, costing of, 23, 24, 26

Fair Labor Standards Act, 26
Farkas, G. M., 103, 105, 127
Farm Credit Services Bank, 90
Featherston, H. J., 108, 128
Feaver, T., 95, 97
Feldman, J. M., 131, 146
Ferguson, D. H., 6, 15
Filipowicz, C., 104, 128
Findlay, S., 82, 97
Firm-specific human capital, 39
Fishbein, M., 130, 146
Fitz-Enz, J., 2, 8, 15
Fixed costs. *See* Costs, fixed
Fixed treatment selection, 184
Flamholtz, E., 3, 4, 15

Fletcher, M., 117, 119, 128
Flowers, V. S., 134, 135, 147
Foote, A., 112, 128
Ford Motor Company, 95, 285–289
Forty percent rule, 209
Foulkes, F. K., 2
Frank, B., 214, 228
F-ratio, relation to effect size, 274
Frederick, J. T., 213, 220, 226, 250, 255
Freudenheim, M., 104, 128
Fritz, W. S., 114, 128
Front-loading, 167–169
Fruchter, B., 248, 256

Gaeta, E., 111, 128
Garber, S., 59, 79
Gaugler, B. B., 245, 247
Gazzardo, T., 128
Gebhardt, D. L., 115, 116, 121, 123–125, 128
General Accounting Office, 150
General Motors Corp., 58, 59, 71, 103, 114
Gertz, L., 129
Gettings, L., 117, 122, 128
Geyelin, M., 86, 94, 97
Ghiselli, E. E., 196, 200
Gilliam, P., 257, 280
Give-back bargaining strategy, 76
Gleser, G. C., 1, 177, 179, 192–194, 200, 202, 208, 227
Global estimation of SD_y, 209–213, 277
Goldstein, I. L., 257, 274, 280
Gomez-Mejia, L. R., 283, 294
Goodman, P. S., 59, 79, 130, 147
Goodyear Tire & Rubber Company, 94
Gorman, C., 81, 97
Gowing, M. K., 257, 280
Graf, T., 92, 97
Granof, M. H., 150, 173
Great Atlantic and Pacific Tea Company, 291
Greer, O. L., 198, 201, 208, 213, 227
Grey, L., 128
Griffith-Hughson, T. L., 147
Guilford, J. P., 248, 256
Guion, R. M., 59, 79
Guzzo, R. A., 274, 280

Hackett, R. D., 59, 79
Hackman, J. R., 50–52, 56
Haight, G. T., 129
Hartigan, J. A., 237, 256
Hazelton, W. A., 164, 173
Health care, aggregate cost of, 114, 122
Health Research Institute, 116, 118, 119
Hekimian, J. S., 5, 15
Henderson, R. I., 38, 57
Hermanson, R. H., 5, 15
Herzlinger, R. E., 82, 86, 87, 97
Hewlett-Packard Corporation, 289
Hirschey, M., 39, 57
Historical costs, 3
Hoffman, B., 198, 201
Holder, G. W., 2, 15, 284, 285, 294
Homoscedastic relationships, 185
Honda USA, 71, 290
Horngren, C. T., 204, 227
Hours paid versus hours worked, 64, 163–166
Howard, A., 245, 256
Howard, J. S., 115, 117, 128
Howard, R. A., 211, 227
Human asset valuation of attitudes, 134, 135
Human capital theory, 39, 40
Human resource accounting, 2–7
  asset models, 3–7
  expense models, 6–13
Human resource development (HRD)
  aggregate costs of, 257
  definition, 257, 258
Human resource development (HRD) programs
  break-even analysis and, 275, 278
  cost–benefit model of, 267–271
  duration of effects, 275
  economic considerations and employee flows in, 276–278
  off-site meeting costs, 258–262
  structured versus unstructured, 262–271
Human resource management, definition, 1
  focus of activities, 283, 284
  level of analysis of activities, 283
  link to profits, 282–284
  strategic, 284–288

Hunter, J. E., 209, 210, 227–229, 236, 237, 239, 245, 256, 271, 273, 277, 280
Hunter, R. F., 237, 245, 256

Increases in pay, cost of, 155–164
Indirect costs, 72, 73
Innovation strategy, 288, 289, 293
International Brotherhood of Electrical Workers, 167
Interrater reliability, 273
Interviews
  employment, cost of, 29, 30, 32
  exit, cost of, 3, 24, 26
Inwald, R. E., 47, 57

Jackson, S. E., 284, 288, 291, 294
Jacobs, S. L., 29, 56
James, F. B., 123, 128
Janson, R., 50, 51, 56
Jette, R. D., 274, 280
Job complexity, effect on SD_y, 209
Job enrichment, 50–52
Job offers, rejection of, effect on utility, 237, 238
Job performance tests, 47, 48
Job satisfaction, definition, 130
Johns-Manville Corp., 262, 263
Johnson, S., 123, 128
Johnson & Johnson, 123
Jonah, B. A., 131, 147
Jones, C. H., 5, 15
Judiesch, M. K., 227

Kanter, R. M., 289, 294
Karr, A. R., 149, 150, 173, 177, 201
Karren, R., 226, 255
Katona, G., 142, 147
Katzell, R. A., 274, 280
Kelley, T. L., 185, 201
Kendrick, J. S., 129
Kerkar, S. P., 255
Kimberly-Clark Corporation, 118
King, L. M., 273, 280
Kittrell, A., 116, 118, 128
Klarreich, S. H., 106, 110, 128
Krackardt, D. M., 41, 56
Kristein, M. M., 88, 93, 97
Kuzmits, F. E., 58, 60, 70, 73–75

Labor contracts, costing of, 149–170
  effect of front- versus back-loading, 167–169
Labor costs, 149, 150, 177
Lagged effects, 119
Last in–first out inventory accounting (lifo), 204
Latham, G. P., 258, 280
Lawler, E. E., III, 6, 134, 136, 137, 140, 142, 147
Leary, W. E., 82, 97
Least squares estimates, 197
Leib, J., 105, 128
Leonard, R. L., Jr., 259, 277, 280
Lev, B., 4, 16
Likert R., 16, 134, 135, 139, 147
Linear relationships
  definition, 185
  effect on break-even analysis, 253
  effect on utility analyses, 237
L. L. Bean, Inc., 290
Lockheed Corp., 48
Loken, B., 31, 147
Luce, B. R., 87, 93, 97
Lynn, R., 128

McComas, M., 291, 294
McEvoy, G. M., 41, 46, 52, 57, 125, 129, 274, 280
McFadden, R. D., 83, 98
McGill, M. C., 82, 98
Mack, M. J., 237, 256
McKenzie, R. C., 210, 228, 229, 236
McKeon, W. J., 258, 261, 280
Macy, B. A., 6, 7, 16, 22, 57, 131–133, 138, 147
Maddox, E. N., 117, 122, 128
Mainstream smoke, 94
Malcolm, A. H., 95, 98
March, J. O., 137, 147
Margolick, D., 94, 98
Martin, D. C., 42, 43, 57
Masi, D., 103, 107, 108, 129
Maslach, C., 148
Matheson, J. E., 211, 227
Mathieu, J. E., 259, 277, 280
Maurer, S. D., 4, 16
Medical examinations, preemployment, 31, 33
Merck & Company, 19

Merle Norman Cosmetics, 91
Metcalfe, L. L., 116, 129
Meyer, H. H., 142, 147
Mihalik, M., 84, 98
Miller, B. W., 89, 91, 98
Mills, D. Q., 151
Mills, T., 257, 280
Minnesota Mining & Manufacturing Company, 289
Mirvis, P. H., 6, 7, 16, 22, 57, 131–134, 136, 138, 140–142, 147
Mitchell, K. J., 221, 227
Mobley, W. H., 130, 139, 147
Monte Carlo simulation, use in utility analysis, 253
Motorola, Inc., 111
Moving costs, 31, 32
Muldrow, T. W., 210, 228, 229, 236
Murphy, K. R., 238, 256
Myers, M. S., 134, 135, 147
Myers, S., 177, 200

Naylor, J. C., 179, 180, 185, 186, 188, 192, 195–197, 200, 201, 304
Naylor-Shine model, 185–188, 195–197
  tables, 303–312
Nichter, R., 93, 98
No-fault absenteeism, 73–76
Normand, J., 202, 227
North, D. W., 211, 227
No work, no pay, 71

O'Connor, E. J., 214, 228
Offerman, L. R., 257, 280
Off-site meeting costs, 258–262
Oldham, G. R., 50, 51, 56
Opportunity costs, 7, 39, 70, 71, 133
Opportunity savings, 133
Ordinate, of normal curve, 186, 230
Outcomes, quantitative versus qualitative, 283
Outerbridge, A. N., 239, 256
Outplacement, 12, 13

Pacific Mutual Life Insurance Company, 122
Pacific Northwest Bell, 95
Pappas, J. L., 39, 57
Parker, D. L., 106, 107, 129
Parkington, J. J., 226
Passive smoking, 91, 92
Pay increases, cost of, 155–164
Payoffs
  definition, 179
  normality of, 193, 211–213
Pearlman, K., 271, 280
Pearson, J. M., 109, 129
Pearson, K., 183, 201, 230
Pennzoil Corporation, 118
PepsiCo, 289
Performance ratio, 205–207
Performance replaceability strategy matrix, 41–43
Performance tests, 47, 48
Personnel decisions, characteristics of, 178
Personnel tax management, 10
Peters, L. H., 214, 228
Phillips, N. F., 47, 56
Pilkington, C. F., 109, 127
Point-biserial correlation, relation to effect size, 274
Porter, M. E., 288, 294
Positive incentives, as absence control, 72, 73
Prehire payback agreements, 48, 49
Present value of future earnings, 4, 5
Prudential Insurance Company, 124
Psychological tests and turnover reduction, 46, 47
Purdy, K., 50, 51, 56
Pyle, W., 3, 5, 15

Quality, definition in utility analysis, 180
Quality-enhancement strategy, 287, 288, 290, 293
Quayle, D., 103, 129

Radar Electric Company, 91
Raich, M. S., 142, 147
Raju, N. S., 202, 227
Ramos, R. A., 198, 200, 213, 214, 227, 247, 255
Raytheon Corporation, 289
Realistic job preview, 44–46
Recruiting, 10, 11
Red Cross, 117
Referral methods, effect on utility, 237
Reliability, correction for, 273

Renner, J. F., 122, 129
Replacement costs, 3, 4, 19, 23, 29–35
Return-on-investment (ROI) analysis, 120, 121
R. G. Barry Corporation, 2, 3
Rhode, J. G., 141, 147
Rich, J. R., 213, 227, 246, 253, 256
Rivero, J. C., 289, 294
Roche, W. J., Jr., 197, 203–208, 227, 229, 232, 233, 256
Roll-up costs, effect on benefits, 156–163
Rosenthal, D. B., 255
Rosse, J. G., 72, 80
Rothenberg, J., 133, 147
Rule, C., 86
Russell, C., 92, 98
Russell, J. T., 179–185, 188, 192, 194–196, 201

St. Benedict's Hospital, 108, 109
Sandberg-Diment, E., 169, 173
Sands, W. A., 180, 196, 201
Savings, fixed, variable and opportunity, 133
Sawzin, S. A., 262, 266, 268, 280
Scarpello, V., 4, 6, 16
Schlotzhauer, D. L., 72, 80
Schmidt, F. L., 198, 201, 209–212, 227–229, 233, 236–241, 243, 244, 247, 251, 256, 271, 273, 274, 277, 280
Schroeder, M., 287, 294
Schuler, R. S., 284, 288–291,294
Schwartz, A., 4, 16
Schweitzer, S. O., 87, 93, 97
Sciacca, J. P., 116, 129
Sciarrino, J. A., 47, 56
SD_y
  effect on utility, 190, 191, 202, 250
  estimation of
    break-even analysis, 251–254, 275, 278
    cost-accounting method, 197, 198, 202–208, 210
    CREPID method, 213–221
    forty percent rule, 209
    global estimation model, 209–213, 233, 277
    over multiple years, 248
    superior equivalents technique, 222–224
    system effectiveness technique, 221, 222
Searfoss, D. G., 4, 15
Selection procedure, definition, 253
Selection ratio, 180–189, 234–236
Sensitivity analysis, 246
Separation costs, 23–29
Separation pay, 23, 25, 26. *See also* Severance pay
Service Employees Union, 167
Severance pay, 26
Sheet Metal Workers Union, 49
Shephard, R. J., 127
Shine, L. C., 179, 185, 186, 188, 192, 195–197
Shultz, J. M., 129
Sick leave, management of, 71–77
Sidestream smoke, 94
Silbey, V., 198, 200, 229, 245, 247, 249–253, 255
Simon, H. A., 137, 147
Sisson, G. R., 262, 266, 268, 280
Skewness, positive versus negative, 193, 233
Smith, H. L., 23, 57
Smith, K. J., 119, 120, 129
Smoking
  absenteeism and, 83–85
  aggregate cost of, 82, 83, 93, 94
  consequences of, 81, 82, 92
  incidence of, 81, 82
  insurance costs and, 88
  involuntary, 91, 92
  legality of bans, 94, 95
  maintenance and, 90, 91
  medical care, morbidity, premature mortality, 85–88
  on-the-job time lost, 88–90
  ordinances prohibiting, 83
  property damage and, 90, 91
Social security tax, 26, 27
Solomon, J., 19, 57, 59, 80
Solomon, L., 85, 87, 89, 98
Southern New England Telephone Company (SNET), 44
Sperling, D., 105, 109, 129
Standard costing, 204
Standard deviation of a sum, 248

Standard (Z-) scores, 186
Stanford Research Institute, 210
Stangor, C., 131, 146
Starr, A., 111, 129
State Mutual Life Assurance Company of America, 88
Statistical power, definition, 265
Steckel, R. G., 163, 173
Steffy, B. D., 4, 16
Stellman, S. D., 92, 93, 99
Stevens, S. S., 218, 228
Strategic HRM, 284–288
Strategic partner role for HRM, 284–286, 288
Strauchy, P., 128
Structured versus unstructured training, 262–271
Substance abuse
  cost of, 103
  treatment of, 109, 110
Success ratio, 182–184
Sunbeam Corporation, 118
Sunnen Products Company, 71
Superior equivalents technique, 222–224
Swanson, R. A., 262, 266, 268, 280
Sweet, D. H., 12, 16
System effectiveness technique, 221, 222

Tactical versus strategic HRM, 283, 284
Taxes, effect on utility, 239–241, 276, 277
Taylor, E. K., 7, 15, 197, 202, 203, 226
Taylor, H. C., 179–185, 188, 192, 194–196, 201
Taylor, J., 142, 147
Taylor-Russell model, 180–185, 194–196
  tables, 295–302
Terborg, J. R., 114, 116, 117, 120, 129
Tests
  costs of, 30, 32
  effect of use on job performance, 239
  performance, 47, 48
Theeke, H. A., 4, 6, 16
Thompson, P. D., 129
Thornton, G. C., III, 255
Tobacco Institute, 83
Todor, W. D., 41, 56
Top-down hiring, effect on utility, 237
Toufexis, A., 81, 98
Toyota Motor Company, 290
Training
  costs of, 35–38, 257
  development and, 10, 11. *See also* Human resource development
  trends in, 257
Trattner, M. H., 239, 256
Travel costs, 31, 32
Travelers Insurance Company, 50–52
Tsay, J. J., 3, 6, 16
t-statistic, relation to effect size, 274
Tsui, A. S., 283, 294
Turnover
  benefits of, 22
  computation of rates, 19
  control of, 12, 13
  costing of, 19–40
  definition, 22
  functional versus dysfunctional, 41, 42
  management of, 41–52
  among new college hires, 12
  in public accounting firms, new hires, 112
  rates (table), 20, 21
  replacement costs, 29–35
  separation costs, 19, 23–29
  training costs, 19, 35–38

Unemployment tax, 10, 23, 25–28
Union Bank, 59
Unit cost valuation of attitudes, 135, 136, 144
United Auto Workers, 71, 167, 286, 287
United Food and Commerical Workers, 167, 291
United Technologies Corporation, 109
U.S. Department of Health and Human Services, 84, 86, 96, 98
U.S. Department of Labor, 151
U.S. Postal Service, 149, 150
U.S. Public Health Service, 84, 96, 98
Utility
  assessment center, 198, 245–251
  base rate and, 181, 182
  discounting and, 239–241, 276, 277

Utility (*cont.*)
employee flows and, 241–245, 276, 277
incremental, 192
labor markets and, 237
marginal, 190, 191
payroll savings and, 239
percentage increase in output and, 209, 239
reduced hiring needs and, 239
rejected job offers and, 237, 238
relation to validity, 189, 194
selection ratio and, 180, 181
taxes and, 239–241
of valid selection tests, 230–239
variable costs and, 239–241
Utility analysis
cost of selection, 188, 189, 191, 192, 250
definition, 177, 179, 180
fixed treatment selection and, 193
of HRD programs, 271–278
models, 179–198. *See also model names*
Monte Carlo simulation, use in, 253
normal distribution for payoffs and, 193, 211–213
overview, 178, 179
quality defined, 180
SD_y, effect of, 190, 191, 202, 250

Validity
concurrent, 185
content, 264
face, 213
incremental, 181
relation to utility, 184, 185, 189, 232, 238, 250
Validity coefficient, use in utility analysis, 180, 184, 185, 189, 232, 238
Variable costs, effect on utility, 239–241. *See also* Costs, variable
Vertical loading, definition, 51
Vroom, V. H., 133, 147

Wagel, W. H., 2, 16
Wagner, W. G., 108, 129
Wald, M. L., 86, 94, 98
Wanous, J. P., 44–46, 57
Ward, J. C., 48, 49, 57
Warner, K. E., 115, 129
Watkins, W. E., 23, 57
Weekley, J. A., 214, 228, 252, 256
Weighted application blank, utility of, 198
Weighted average pay rate, formula, 23, 64
Weiss, W. L., 84, 87–93, 98
Wellness
definition, 113, 114
distinguished from fitness, 116
Wellness programs
absenteeism and turnover savings, 124, 125
cost of, 117, 118
evaluation, difficulties of, 118–121
data needed, 121–123
future of, 125, 126
health care cost savings, 122–124
incentives for participation, 117
levels and types, 115, 116
participation rates, 116
prevalence of, 113
rationale for, 114, 115
theory of, 113
Wessel, D., 32, 57
Wikstrom, W. S., 66, 80
Williams, D. E., Jr., 12
Wing, H., 221, 227
Woodruff, R. C., Jr., 3, 16
Work sample tests, 47, 48
Wynder, E. L., 92, 93, 99

Yamazaki Corporation, 150

Zalesny, M. D., 130, 148
Zimbardo, P. G., 130, 148
Zippo, M., 49, 57
Z-scores, 186